821.1 Sti
Stillinger.
The song of Troilus.

The Lorette Wilmot Library
Nazareth College of Rochester

The Song of Troilus

University of Pennsylvania Press
MIDDLE AGES SERIES
Edited by
Edward Peters
Henry Charles Lea Professor
of Medieval History
University of Pennsylvania

A listing of the available books
in the series appears at the
back of this volume

The Song of Troilus

Lyric Authority in the Medieval Book

Thomas C. Stillinger

upp

University of Pennsylvania Press
Philadelphia

DISCARDED

LORETTE WILMOT LIBRARY
NAZARETH COLLEGE

Copyright © 1992 by the University of Pennsylvania Press
All rights reserved
Printed in the United States of America

Library of Congress Cataloging-in-Publication Data
Stillinger, Thomas C.
The song of Troilus : lyric authority in the medieval book / Thomas C. Stillinger.
p. cm. — (Middle Ages series)
Based on the author's Ph.D. thesis, Cornell University.
Includes bibliographical references and index.
ISBN 0-8122-3144-9
1. Chaucer, Geoffrey, d. 1400. Troilus and Cressida. 2. Troilus (Legendary character) in literature. 3. Literature, Medieval—History and criticism. 4. Boccaccio, Giovanni, 1313–1375. Filostrato. 5. Dante Alighieri, 1265–1321. Vita nuova. 6. Influence (Literary, artistic, etc.) 7. Trojan War in literature. 8. Authority in literature. 9. Rhetoric, Medieval. 10. Intertextuality. I. Title. II. Series.
PR1896.S84 1992
821'.1—dc20 92-28021
CIP

821.1 Sti

Contents

Acknowledgments

Several libraries and a large number of people have generously helped me in this work. The Newberry Library in Chicago provided a grant and boundless research support; I did my research there and at the libraries of Cornell University and the University of Chicago. The Bodmer Library in Geneva and the Bodleian Library in Oxford sent me photographs from their manuscript collections, with wonderful promptness, as well as permission to reproduce those photographs. Chapter 4 appeared, in slightly different form, in *Stanford Italian Review* 9 (1990). Throughout this project, I have profited from the encouragement and advice of Lee Patterson, Winthrop Wetherbee, and Giuseppe Mazzotta. I read *Troilus and Criseyde* with Patterson and Wetherbee before their Chaucer books were out, and my reading is indebted to theirs in ways my notes cannot fully reflect. Mazzotta introduced me to Boccaccio, and brought me back into medieval studies when I thought I had left it. In addition, he served on the committee for the Cornell doctoral dissertation on which this book is based, along with Alice Colby-Hall, the late Robert Kaske, and, as director, Thomas D. Hill; my debt to them, and to Cornell's medievalist community and English Department, is profound. Before Cornell, at what now seems like an early age, I was introduced to Dante by John Freccero; my approach to literary interpretation was shaped (I hope) by Freccero's inspiring teaching. My own students at the University of Chicago and Northwestern University have sharpened my thinking. I have been helped in various memorable ways by Teodolinda Barolini, Howard Bloch, Mary Carruthers, Natalie Fisher, Debra Fried, Paul Gehl, Alan Hager, Claudia Johnson, Victoria Kirkham, Ronald Martinez, Gina Psaki, Braxton Ross, R. A. Shoaf, Janet Smarr, Elissa Weaver, and especially Barry Weller. Jerome Singerman has been the ideal editor. Kristina Bross and Beatriz Santiago Muñoz assisted ably in the final checking of references. Albert Ascoli has been a source of friendly counsel and peer pressure since seventh grade. In different ways, Jack Stillinger and Shirley Stillinger provided early and lasting models of an engagement with books; I have more recently taken encouragement from a younger bibliophile, Mary A. McCarthy. I thank all of the above; above all, I thank Lauren Berlant.

A Note on Texts and Translations

I list here my texts and translations for some frequently cited works; for full information, see the Bibliography.

Boccaccio, *Filostrato*, ed. Branca; translations adapted from apRoberts and Seldis.
Boccaccio, *Teseida*, ed. Limentani; translations mine.
Chaucer, *Troilus and Criseyde*, ed. Barney.
Dante, *Convivio*, ed. Simonelli; translations adapted from Lansing.
Dante, *Vita Nuova*, ed. De Robertis; translations mine, except for passages from Chapter 19, for which I have borrowed from Durling and Martinez, *Time and the Crystal*, Appendix 4.

References to these works are parenthetically identified according to the method of the cited editions: for the *Vita Nuova*, the numbers refer to chapter and sentence (even for the poems); for the *Filostrato*, "part" and stanza (or sentence, for the Proem); for the *Teseida*, book and stanza; for *Troilus and Criseyde*, book and line. Translations of the Vulgate Bible are based on the Douay-Rheims Bible. All other translations are mine, except where noted. In Latin quotations, I have normalized u's and v's. "*PL*" stands for J.-P. Migne, ed., *Patrologia Latina* (Paris: Garnier, 1844–64); references are to volume and column.

Introduction
"Of Making Many Books . . ."

Bonaventure, in the proem to his commentary on the *Sentences* of Peter Lombard, says that there are four ways to make a book.

> [Q]uadruplex est modus faciendi librum. Aliquis enim scribit aliena, nihil addendo vel mutando; et iste mere dicitur *scriptor*. Aliquis scribit aliena, addendo, sed non de suo; et iste *compilator* dicitur. Aliquis scribit et aliena et sua, sed aliena tamquam principalia, et sua tamquam annexa ad evidentiam; et iste dicitur *commentator*, non auctor. Aliquis scribit et sua et aliena, sed sua tamquam principalia, aliena tamquam annexa ad confirmationem; et talis debet dici *auctor*.[1]

> [The way of making a book is fourfold. For someone writes the words of others, adding or changing nothing, and he is simply called the *scribe*. Someone else writes the words of others, adding, but not of his own, and he is called the *compiler*. Someone else writes both the words of others and his own, but with those of others as the principal part and his own annexed for the purpose of clarifying them, and he is called the *commentator*, not the author. Someone else writes both his own words and those of others, but with his own as the principal part and those of others annexed for the purpose of confirmation, and such must be called the *author*.]

Modern scholars, making their own books, have more than once copied out this passage; it offers a useful glossary of medieval terms.[2] One striking feature of the passage, however, is an assumption about writing that underlies all four definitions. In each of the four cases, "aliquis" [someone] is dealing with "aliena" [things belonging to others]. The four writers differ in the ways they treat the *aliena*: the scribe copies them just as they are, the compiler excerpts and rearranges them, the commentator adds his own words to them, and the author adds them to words of his own. The *aliena* are always there. The fourfold definition does not include a writer who creates *ex nihilo* or from his own imagination. Bonaventure assumes that the only original, autonomous, definitive *auctor* is God.[3] Within the created world, as the preacher of Ecclesiastes notes with some dismay, "Faciendi plures libros nullus est finis" (Eccles. 12:12) [Of making many books there is no end]. For Bonaventure, authorship is merely one way of making a book, and books are made—in one way or another—from other books.

This book is a study of the intertextual and formal strategies employed by certain medieval writers in search of new ways to make a book. My principal texts are Dante's *Vita Nuova*, Boccaccio's *Filostrato*, and Chaucer's *Troilus and Criseyde*. Each of these texts describes itself as a *little* book: a "libello," a "picciolo libro," and a "litel bok," respectively.[4] Together, they lend support to the idea that books arise from books, for they form a sequence in which each becomes an essential *alienum* to its successor. But Bonaventure's account of the "modus faciendi librum" only hints at the revisionary modes of these acts of writing. *Troilus and Criseyde* is a free translation of the *Filostrato*, and I shall argue that the *Filostrato* is an inventive rewriting of the *Vita Nuova*. Dante describes the *Vita Nuova* as a scribal copy of his own Book of Memory; as he writes, however, Dante responds to a virtual library of precursor texts, including another book by Peter Lombard, a commentary on the Book of Psalms.

In the chapters that follow I take up each of my principal texts in chronological order, beginning with a chapter on Peter Lombard's Psalm commentary. My local aim is always to explicate the text I am discussing, but I am also concerned with the dynamics of the sequence: this book is an essay on late-medieval and early-Renaissance intertextuality, an inquiry into the complex ways in which books can be made from books. More than other periods, the Middle Ages and the Renaissance have long inspired kinds of reading that can broadly be called intertextual: there is a (sometimes uneasy) continuity between traditional philology, with its commitment to identifying sources and cataloguing topoi, and the more recent critical and theoretical inquiry into problems of influence, imitation, and cultural transformation. Among medieval/Renaissance intertextual readings, an exceptionally rich body of work has been produced by scholars studying Chaucer's relations to his Italian predecessors.[5] My own book is intended in part as a contribution to this already flourishing field. I take as axiomatic, for example, a principle that has become a commonplace among Chaucerians: the idea that, to read Chaucer's deployment of a prior text, we must read the prior text as carefully, and as intertextually, as we read Chaucer. But I would not call this book a *Troilus* book; it is equally a study of the *Vita Nuova* and the *Filostrato* on their own terms, and a study of the *kinds* of relationships that operate within and around the sequence of three.

One abiding concern is the intertextual aspect of literary form: I try to describe a mode of formal revision or reconfiguration, in which a writer rewrites not only ideas, plot matter, and tropes, but also the very constitution of the *alienum* he or she confronts.

At the same time the textual sequence I consider here has implications for other, larger sequences: the history of late medieval culture and, in particular, the history of the institution of authorship. *Auctoritas*—authorship and authority—has emerged in the last two decades as a dominant topic in medieval and Renaissance studies. Drawing on the earlier findings of cultural historians, and spurred by the post-structuralist claim that "the author" is a textual construct, scholars have begun to trace the gradual consolidation of the institutions that constitute modern, vernacular, secular authorship.[6] Such work has included both careful surveys of medieval intellectual theory and practice[7] and close readings of individual, often idiosyncratic, literary texts.[8] My own work belongs to the latter category. The *Vita Nuova*, the *Filostrato*, and *Troilus and Criseyde* all imagine a kind of writer that would have seemed quite alien to Bonaventure. This writer may be described in general terms as an autonomous human *auctor*; my three texts take part in the process that produces modern literature as such. But the innovative *auctoritas* constructed in different ways within these texts can be characterized more specifically as well. It is what I call "lyric authority": a model of authorship that deploys and transforms the structures of Latin learning set out by Bonaventure, but that draws equally from the vernacular tradition of the courtly love-lyric.

I

To introduce the interpretive problems raised by an *auctoritas* that is vernacular, amorous, and formally experimental, I want to begin a reading of a very brief second passage. This passage is drawn from a text with close ties to my trio of principal texts, Boccaccio's *Teseida*; it appears within a stanza describing the new love of both Arcita and Palemone for Emilia.

> E da' sospiri già a lagrimare
> eran venuti, e se non fosse stato
> che 'l loro amor non volean palesare,
> sovente avrian per angoscia gridato.
> E così sa Amore adoperare

a cui più per servigio è obligato:
colui il sa che tal volta fu preso
da lui e da cota' dolori offeso. (*Teseida* 3.35)

[And from sighs now to weeping
they had come, and if it had not been
that they did not wish to reveal their love,
often they would have cried out in anguish.
And this is how Love knows to behave
toward one to whom he is most obligated by service:
he knows this, who once was seized
by him and afflicted with such sorrows.]

This stanza is the culmination of the *innamoramento* that occupies the first part of Book Three. The two Theban youths have caught sight of Emilia from their prison window, and their delight in her beauty has given way to sensations of being wounded, copious sighs, and now muffled weeping. The stanza's special status as a culmination is signaled by the sententious and summary quality of the last four lines. The passage I wish to consider, however, is not part of the verse, although it literally appears within the boundaries of the stanza. It is a gloss consisting of three words, inserted above "preso" [seized] in the seventh line: "che sono io" [which is I].

Modern commentators have responded to this comment by asking: who is speaking? Who is the "I" that refers to himself between the lines, affirming that he is one who knows love's sorrows? For Giuseppe Vandelli, it is Giovanni Boccaccio himself: the three words are "a little eruption that bursts out from the enamored heart of the poet."[9] Vandelli writes, in 1929, as one who has just identified an autograph manuscript of the *Teseida* and has thereby ascertained Boccaccio's authorship of the glosses. When he treats this particular gloss, manuscript description and psychological speculation interpenetrate: Vandelli writes that "che sono io" is written in an extremely fine hand, even finer than that of the other glosses, "as if it were a matter of words that should be displayed as little as possible, a matter of private disclosure."[10] Vandelli assumes that the entire poem is addressed to a certain Fiammetta, as the dedicatory epistle says that it is, and he reads "che sono io" as a uniquely explicit declaration to her. More recent critics, however, have viewed Fiammetta as a poetic fiction addressed by a carefully crafted persona. Since this persona avows in the dedication that he is in love, he might plausibly be the "io" of the gloss. There is yet another possibility, suggested by Robert Hollander. The *Teseida* has a full program of glosses, both marginal and interlinear, and perhaps we are to understand these glosses as the work of a separate Boccaccian persona.[11] If the bookish, prosaic glossator is to be distinguished from the epic poet, then the "che sono io" gloss is an exclamation from an unexpected source: just as Arcita and Palemone heave tortured sighs from within, like winds bursting from caves (3.27), so in one brief phrase the glossator opens his heart.

All of these readings apply a modern standard of authorship to a medieval text. In our century we expect literary words to be the work of an identifiable writer: if the "io" of "che sono io" is not Boccaccio himself, he must be one of the fictive authors created within the text. It is worth considering another approach to the problem. The "io" might be the medieval "poetic I" described by Leo Spitzer, the first-person "representative of mankind." In the Middle Ages, Spitzer writes, "It was a trifling matter who the empirical person behind this 'I' actually was."[12] In this reading, "che sono io" would not be the utterance of an empirical man, a "gentleman who narrates and who says 'I' " (in a phrase Spitzer borrows from Proust);[13] rather, it would be an annotation grammatically constructed in the first person, referring to no particular person inside or outside the book. Logically, Boccaccio might intend the gloss to be the utterance of someone entirely distinct from the fictional poet of the *Teseida*, or the fictional glossator, or the real Boccaccio. It could be, for instance, an interpolation from an impressionable reader, an imagined Francesca (or an imagined Fiammetta?) who inscribes a "how true!" in the book while reading it. But to psychologize the anonymous "io" in this way would be to return to our modern habits of reading: the more radical possibility I am associating with Spitzer would describe the "io" as no one in particular, an Everyreader. The point of the gloss, then, would not be to characterize any individual person, but rather to confer an objective authority upon the description of love in the stanza: this is an account in which *any* lover instantly recognizes his or her own experience.

My own view, however, is that the meaning of "che sono io" is to be sought in the dialectic between these two ways of reading, between a modern insistence that words have individual authors and a tranquil medieval anonymity. Historically Boccaccio writes at a time when the "empirical author" is, to quote Spitzer again, "*in statu nascendi*":[14] he belongs to the long transitional period in which the modern institutions of literature are under construction. Boccaccio certainly knows the medieval "representative I," yet his own master Dante has self-consciously explored the possibility that a living vernacular writer might become an *auctor*. The *Teseida* as a whole can fairly be described as a transitional work in the history of authorship. On the one hand, by writing out his own poem, complete with dedication, rubrics, summarizing sonnets, and marginal and interlinear gloss, Boccaccio anticipates the project of a slightly later writer like Machaut, who "raise[s] the codex to the level of literary artifact, making it function as an inherent part of his poetic production."[15] On the other hand, Boccaccio (unlike Machaut) does not sign his book, and there is no evidence that anyone before Vandelli recognized the commentary as Boccaccio's own work: the commentary may be, in effect, a counterfeit anonymous text.

The indeterminate status of authorship in the *Teseida* as a whole may arise partly from our own ignorance about its reception, but I would suggest that the "che sono io" gloss is clearly and deliberately indeterminate. The gloss mimics the gesture of an author stepping forth from behind his text, yet it preserves an impenetrable anonymity. Certainly the gloss has something in common with the "author-function" described by Michel Foucault. In "What Is an Author?" Foucault treats "the manner in which a text apparently points to [a] figure who is outside and precedes it."[16] Foucault writes that the author-function is neither the proper name affixed to a text nor the first-person pronoun within the work, but rather "arises out of their scission—in the division and distance of the two" (129). The "che sono io" gloss points to *someone* who speaks from outside the text, and by prodding us to think about the various writers within the text (the glossator, the poet, Boccaccio) it evokes a scission. But there is no proper name, and no clear declaration of the need for an authorial identification. We begin by asking "who is speaking?" but end up instead with the question (from Beckett) that closes Foucault's groundbreaking theoretical essay: "What matter who's speaking?"

I am suggesting, then, that the "che sono io" gloss reflects upon the transitional period in which Boccaccio writes: it is a miniature portrait of the modern author *in statu nascendi*. I would further suggest that a powerful logic attaches this authorial half-emergence to the discourse of love in particular. As Foucault observes, the problem of the author is part of a larger problem in need of historical analysis, the problem of the subject (137–38): that is, the modern idea that "literary works are totally dominated by the sovereignty of the author" (126) depends upon, and may also serve to confirm, a fundamental belief in "the absolute nature and creative role of the subject" (137). And a number of scholars have argued, in a number of ways, that love-literature is the arena for the development of a historically new kind of subject, or subjectivity, or individuality. Joel Fineman, for example, argues that the *Sonnets* of William Shakespeare inaugurate "a genuinely new poetic subjectivity," and that "the Shakespearean subject is *the* subject of our literature, the privileged and singular form of literary subjectivity since the Renaissance."[17] The view that the modern subject is *somehow* invented in the Renaissance—a view supported with variations by a number of Renaissance scholars—accords well with the sort of medievalism that supposes an absolute chasm between medieval and post-medieval self-understanding. But some medievalists have objected forcefully to arguments like Fineman's,[18] and there is another tradition that associates a decisive transformation in the constitution of the subject to the writing of the later Middle Ages, and in particular to the new genres, romance and lyric, that deal with *fin' amors*.[19] Most recently, Paul Oppenheimer has made the claim—as sweeping as Fineman's—that "Modern thought and literature begin with the invention of the sonnet," in the early thirteenth century.[20]

Whatever the validity of these historical claims, there is no doubt that medieval literature often *represents* love as the agent of a stunning new psychological interiority. An exceptionally clear example of this phenomenon occurs in Guillaume de Lorris's *Roman de la Rose*, in the speech in which Love, having delivered the ten commandments of love, proceeds to predict the subjective life of the new Lover (2221–2566).[21] Love ordains the Lover's very thoughts, along with his sorrows and doubts, and goes so far as to prescribe whole speeches that *will* be uttered by the Lover:

> lors comanceras a plorer
> et diras: 'Dex! qu'ai ge songié?
> Qu'est or ce? Ou estoie gié?
> Ceste pensee, dont me vint?' (2436–39)
>
> [then you will begin to weep,
> and you will say: "God! What have I dreamed?
> What is this? Where was I lying?
> This thought, where did it come from?"]

— and so on, for fifty more verses. The experience of love is here presented as a pre-existent discourse that is taken up and adopted as the individual lover's own inner life.

The "che sono io" gloss, together with its stanza, illustrates the same process. According to the stanza, Love is a sovereign power, administering certain sorrows in a certain order: it is thus possible to specify a rich and complex inner experience by pointing to the universal lot of lovers and saying, "and I am one." Arcita and Palemone have undergone identical *innamoramenti*; likewise it is temporarily impossible to draw a clear line between the experiences of the protagonists, the poet, the glossator, and the historical Boccaccio. Are we to imagine that the "io" is some distinct individual who here signals his surrender to a more powerful force, or are we to imagine that this subject comes into being as a speaking subject through the very gesture of self-identification? The gloss fails to specify a clear answer. In general the first-person pronoun is a deictic or shifter, a word whose meaning in a text is fixed by the situation of the text's utterance. In this case, however, all we know for certain about the situation of the utterance is that it includes the utterance: there is nothing to stop the shifter from shifting indefinitely. Just as the "che sono io" is the zero degree of Foucault's author-function, so it is the zero degree of the "subjectivity effect" described by Fineman: rather than constructing the illusion of an unconstructed and capacious subjectivity, as in Shakespeare's *Sonnets*, Boccaccio's gloss takes a minimal first step toward subjective self-construction. Love is the force that makes possible—and makes problematic—authorship, authority, and subjectivity.

To understand the special *auctoritas* of Boccaccio's "che sono io" gloss, we might set it beside an equally cryptic modern inscription. Roland Barthes's *Fragments d'un discours amoureux* begins with a preface entitled "Comment est fait ce livre" [How this book is constructed], and this preface is followed by a page containing only a half-sentence, in unusually large type:

> C'est donc un amoureux qui parle et qui dit:
>
> [So it is a lover who speaks and who says:][22]

The colon points ahead to the heading on the next page: "Je m'abîme, je succombe . . ." (15) [I am engulfed, I succumb]. In Barthes's text, the large-print declaration partly counts as a revelation about Barthes: he writes the book as a lover, as the lover he is. Yet the phrase simultaneously has the effect of denying individual authorship. As Barthes will make clear in the entry headed "Identifications," the fragments of amorous discourse could be spoken by any lover, and—because identification is structural, not psychological—any lover can identify with any other lover in the act of utterance. "Tout réseau amoureux, je le dévore du regard et j'y repère la place qui serait la mienne, si j'en faisais partie" (153) [I devour every amorous system with my gaze and in it discern the place which would be mine if I were a part of that system]. The book is made of "paquets de phrases" (11) [bundles of sentences], assembled according to an arbitrary principle of alphabetization; the lover who speaks "n'intègre pas ces phrases à un niveau supérieur, à une oeuvre" (11) [does not integrate these sentences on a higher level, into a work]. In another well-known essay, Barthes says that a work is something that has an author; the *Fragments* would seem to be a "text," an unauthored discourse.[23] Even the marginal references to sources "ne sont pas d'autorité, mais d'amitié" (12) [are not authoritative but amical].

It would be tempting to identify Barthes's *amoureux* with the "io" of "che sono io." As Barthes writes, "Un longue chaîne d'équivalences lie tous les amoureux du monde" (155) [A long chain of equivalences links all the lovers in the world]. I have no wish, however, to collapse the historical distance that separates the moment of the *Teseida* from the moment of the *Fragments*. I do want to suggest that the two moments mirror each other. Barthes writes as a writer at the end of authorship; by denying specific individual attachment to the impassioned utterances that make up the *Fragments*, while refusing to take up an objective position outside them, Barthes presumably means to be both witnessing and advancing the process he elsewhere describes as "the death of the author."[24] For Boccaccio, history is moving in the opposite direction: literary *auctoritas* generates ambiguity and complexity not because it is coming apart but because it is coming together. This does not mean, however, that the "che sono io" gloss should be taken as a mere signpost on the road to a fully realized authorial identity. Boccaccio's engagement with a set of conflicting and unstable cultural expectations is as playful and as serious as Barthes's. (Another modern commentator, Alberto Limentani, describes the "che sono io" as "the point of greatest coquettishness in the fanciful edifice of Boccaccio's autobiography."[25]) In both texts, a universal discourse of love is the field that allows a partly formed authorial subjectivity—inchoate in Boccaccio, succumbing in Barthes—to half-emerge.

2

Several features of the "che sono io" gloss raise particular issues that have been studied in other contexts by other critics, issues that will recur throughout this book. Following the example of Barthes's disjointed *amoureux*—or the example of the medieval preacher, who unfolds different aspects of a single scriptural verse without consolidating a unified reading—I shall isolate four of these issues here for separate discussion.

Commentary as a Form

In the autograph manuscript, Boccaccio assumes all four of the writing roles described by Bonaventure. He is the scribe of the manuscript. As the writer of the poem, he twice describes his writing as an act of "compilation."[26] He writes a commentary to the poem—and this commentary affirms that the poet is truly, despite his self-description as a *compilator*, an *auctor*. The commentary makes this affirmation in a literal way, continually referring to the poet as "l'autore"; it implies an even grander claim to literary authority through its own presence outside and within the text. As many critics have noted, the paratextual materials attached to the stanzaic narrative—the rubrics and summaries and above all the commentary—make the book resemble a medieval edition of a classical epic poem.

The special local effect of the "che sono io" gloss depends in large part on the conventional subordination of commentary to text. We may understand the poet and the glossator to be different persons, or a single person employing different modes, but in any case the book is represented as the result of two distinct acts of writing: first the composition of a poem; second, and secondarily, the addition of a pedantic explication.[27] Without this literary division of labor, the sudden revelation of an identifying "I" would lose much of its force. The gloss is an eruption, an outburst, because it breaks through a *structure*; that structure is the form of commentary.

Commentaries—on the Bible, on legal texts, on classical poetry, and even on vernacular poems—have provided material for many scholarly investigations. Scholars have repeatedly mined these commentaries for information about medieval thought and medieval ways of thinking; in addition they have often remarked on the pervasiveness of commentary in the Middle Ages as a mode of intellectual production. The *Teseida* shows, however, that medieval commentary also provided a hierarchical structure that could be taken up and adapted and subverted by a formally inventive writer. There have been relatively few attempts to explore the implications of commentary as a deliberately chosen literary form. In Chapter 1 I offer a formal reading of one of the most influential of scriptural commentaries, the *Glossa Ordinaria*; this reading establishes a starting point for the sequence of revisionary vernacular forms that is my primary topic.

The Lyric Genre

Neither the "che sono io" gloss nor its stanza is literally a lyric text. The gloss is prose, and the verse stanza is part of a long narrative: the initial verbal phrase, "già . . . eran venuti" [now they had come], locates the stanza in the linear time of the *Teseida*. But this passage is surrounded by references to lyrics. Part of Emilia's seductive beauty is her constant singing of love-songs: she is described as "cantando / amorose canzon" (3.8) [singing amorous songs], "sempre cantando be' versi d'amore" (3.10) [always singing beautiful verses of love]. Both Arcita (3.13) and Palemone (3.23) mention this singing as one of her charms.[28] And one of their first responses to falling in love is to produce amorous lyrics of their own, "versi misurati" (3.38) [measured verses], which the glossator helpfully glosses as "sonetti e canzoni" [sonnets and *canzoni*]. These mentioned songs find an echo, I would suggest, in Boccaccio's own writing: the "che sono io" gloss is not a lyric text, but it constitutes a lyric moment within the narrative text.

The last four lines of the stanza, the summary statement of Love's dominion, could indeed appear in a courtly love-lyric. And the "io" of the gloss, in its very indeterminacy, resembles the first-person pronoun of lyric poetry. Literary theorists have described the "lyric I" as a merely virtual subjectivity: within the context of a lyric, the pronoun is stripped of its normal deictic function and, as Käte Hamburger has argued, the distinction between a fictive speaker and an empirical speaker becomes irrelevant.[29] Roland Greene, here building on Hamburger's work, writes that "this 'I' and its statements, which constitute 'an open structure,' are entertained by the reader as elements in his or her own life, are tried on and 're-experienced' from the inside."[30] Structural openness is especially a feature of the medieval lyric. Critics of the Old French "grand chant courtois" [great courtly song] such as Roger Dragonetti and Paul Zumthor have provided the most powerful discussions of the medieval lyric I. Zumthor, for example, describes lyric as, in its purest form, a "mode of speaking entirely and exclusively referred to an *I* that, although often having no more than a grammatical existence, nonetheless fixes the plan and the modalities of the discourse."[31] All these descriptions apply well to the "io" of the gloss. "Che sono io" is a minimal lyric, a first-person utterance that any reader may voice as a personal declaration of love.

Zumthor adds that the *I* of the "grand chant courtois" is "outside of all narration."[32] The particular "io" of "che sono io," however, appears poised at the edge of a narrative poem. We may understand this positioning in several ways: the gloss may underline a lyric quality in the text, or offer a lyric alternative to it, or suggest a lyric way of reading. Once again the gloss, in its enigmatic brevity, raises a problem and permits a range of solutions. The problem is one that is explored at greater length in my three principal texts: it is the problem of the relationship between lyric and narrative.

The *Vita Nuova*, the *Filostrato*, and *Troilus and Criseyde* are all books that combine lyric and narrative modes of writing. This is a description that has been offered, as we shall see, by critics of each text.[33] Again, however, we must turn to Old French specialists for the most sustained analysis of the relations between lyric and narrative. Beginning with Zumthor's structuralist investigations, the opposition "lyric/narrative" has emerged as a crucial analytic tool for understanding both the total system of medieval literature and an array of individual hybrid forms.[34] In the century that precedes Dante's composition of the *Vita Nuova*, an extraordinary number of texts attempt to bridge the generic gap between lyric and narrative. These include French romances that contain inset *chansons*,[35] or that present themselves as narrative elaborations of *chansons*,[36] as well as Provençal *chansonniers* that include prose *vidas* and *razos*,[37] and single-author *chansonniers* that imply a personal narrative through their disposition of lyric texts.[38] I would suggest that all these innovative forms contribute to a single literary project, and that one motive for this project is the special problem of *auctoritas* faced by the medieval lyric poet.

Within the domain of vernacular literature, the "grand chanson courtois" is a well-defined and prestigious mode. Yet the lyric poem is understood to be an oral composition, only incidentally set down in writing, and this limits its status in a culture that assigns the highest authority to writing and the book. As long as lyric collections are assembled by scribes rather than poets, the lyric poet can never truly be an *auctor*. The French and Provençal texts that I have mentioned attempt to remedy this situation by gathering lyric songs into unitary, book-length narratives. Their common project is at once to produce vernacular books charged with the social prestige of the "grand chant courtois," and to elevate the lyric poet's craft into a "modus faciendi librum" [way of making a book]; in the process, the lyric I is redefined as an authorial subjectivity. The Italian and Middle English texts that I shall discuss extend the tradition of the lyrical book in new directions: by experimenting with the possibilities of structural hierarchy within the literary text, each finds a new way to construct the relation between lyric and narrative.

SEXUAL DIFFERENCE

Before leaving the question of the lyric genre, we should note a certain asymmetry in the lyric utterances of Book Three of the *Teseida*. Emilia is repeatedly described as singing, and the emphasis falls entirely on the quality of her voice. For example, the valet who names Emilia to Arcita and Palemone says that she

> canta me' che mai cantasse Appollo,
> e io l'ho già udita, e così sollo. (3.40)
>
> [sings better than Apollo ever sang;
> I have heard her, and so I know it.]

The glossator notes that the poet here conflates singing and playing: Emilia's vocal ability is being compared to Apollo's skill with instruments. Certainly Emilia's singing involves verbal texts, "amorose canzon" and "be' versi d'amore" (3.8, 3.10), but there is no indication of the origin of these songs: they might be songs that Emilia has heard, or songs that she has composed, or songs that she improvises. The question of authorship does not arise; what matters is the act of singing, and the pleasure it brings.

By contrast, the lyrics of Arcita and Palemone are described in terms of their composition:

> in lor conforto versi misurati* *sonetti e canzoni
> sovente componean, l'alto valore
> di lei cantando; e in cotale effetto
> nelli lor mal sentieno alcun diletto. (3.38)
>
> [to comfort themselves, measured verses* *sonnets and *canzoni*
> they often composed, singing the high worth
> of her; and through such a result
> in their suffering they felt some delight.]

These lines repeat and transform the terms that describe Emilia's musical performance. "Cantando" may mean "singing out loud," as it always does in connection with Emilia, but it is more likely to carry here a classical connotation. The two Thebans sing Emilia's worth in the same way that Virgil sings arms and the man: they celebrate it in verse.[39] Apart from this one use of "cantare," there is no indication that they actually perform the songs they compose. Again, both Emilia's songs and those of the young men are "versi," but hers are "be' versi" [beautiful verses], the emphasis falling on the aesthetic effect of the finished text, while theirs are "versi misurati" [measured verses], with stress on the poet's measuring (and metric) technique. "Canzoni" too shifts its connotations: Emilia's "amorose canzon" are love songs in a general sense, but the phrase "sonetti e canzoni," in the gloss, refers to two particular poetic forms. Finally, both Emilia and the young men derive pleasure from their own singing, but her pleasure is as direct and clear as her voice—

> cantando cominciava a dilettarsi
> in voce dilettevole e arguta (3.29)
>
> [singing she began to take delight
> in her delightful, high voice]

—while their pleasure comes as the result ("effetto") of a process and is mixed with pain, "measured" in another sense of the word.

Emilia's singing, then, is pure voice—spontaneous music that inspires immediate delight—while the singing of Arcita and Palemone is a matter of deliberate composition, careful technique, fixed forms, and the sober comfort that comes from artistic self-expression. This contrast accords well with other contrasts in the scene: Emilia wanders at will in a lovely meadow, while Arcita and Palemone are left to their own resources in a prison inside a palace. She is associated with nature and liberty (she is "tirata da propria natura / non che d'amore alcun fosse constretta" [3.8; drawn by her own nature, not constrained by any love]); *they* are subject both to love and to the law, and they show themselves to be the bearers of a sophisticated literary culture. I would further suggest that the contrast between the two modes of singing is powerfully connected to the most obvious contrast between Emilia and the two Thebans: the fact that she is a woman and they are men.

It would be hard to prove this from the one scene alone, but we do not need to look far for support. The *Teseida* begins with a literal war between the sexes—Teseo's attack on the rebellious and courageous Amazons in Book One, which ends with Teseo's victory and the reformation of the Amazons' manners:

> e ora in lieti motti e dolci canti
> mutate avean le voci rigogliose,
> e' passi avevan piccioli tornati,
> che pria nell'armi grandi erano stati. (1.132)
>
> [and now into cheerful sayings and sweet songs
> they transformed their exuberant voices,
> and they made their steps little again,
> that before, in arms, were big]

In her childish playing and lovely singing, Emilia exhibits proper feminine behavior. And Arcita and Palemone are properly masculine—not because they have exuberant voices and take large steps, but because their literary activity parallels Teseo's imposition of cultural norms. Their singing arises as a response to Emilia's singing, and effects a transformation of it: they take her beautiful sound as the driving force for a system of measured lines, conventional forms, and conscious authorship. They build a palace, or a prison, around Emilia's voice.

The emerging *auctoritas* that is the subject of this book is characteristically a masculine institution: Isidore of Seville notes discouragingly that *auctor* has no feminine form.[40] Likewise, as David Aers and others have observed, the discourse of courtly love belongs to, and helps to define, the "courtly male";[41] women are usually its objects and its readers. The lyric scene in *Teseida* 3 suggests, however, that constructions of masculine authority and identity may involve a complex assignment of gender roles, and may well assign a particular positive value to that which is defined as feminine.

In recent years, the pairing of "genre" and "gender" has become a critical and theoretical commonplace. For students of genre, the linkage is worthwhile not only because it connects a formal problem to an intrinsically interesting thematic field,[42] but also because the feminist understanding of gender as a socially constructed system can illuminate (in Mary Jacobus's formulation) "not the genre of literature, but the literariness—the fiction—of genre."[43] The feminist investigation of gender and genre is another collective endeavor to which I hope to contribute here.[44] It has been suggested more than once that the lyric, as a genre, is typically characterized as feminine,[45] and I shall make the same suggestion in connection with the *Vita Nuova*. But in the *Filostrato* and in *Troilus and*

Criseyde, and here in the *Teseida*, the gender-genre system is more complicated. Emilia and the two Theban youths are both associated with the lyric, but the lyric in different aspects: she embodies a simple but powerful impulse—pure lyric—which they systematize as a genre and personalize as a form of authorship. And *their* willing subscription to a set of cultural conventions parallels their subjugation to Love's dominion: in submitting as they do, they establish the discursive field that enables the emergence of an incipient individual subjectivity in "che sono io." When I say that my three principal texts find new structures for the relationship between lyric and narrative, I mean in part that they gender their generic components differently.

The Question of History

I have spoken of the "che sono io" gloss as a lyric response to the narrative of the *Teseida*. It engages the story of how the two young men fall in love with Emilia, appearing at the end of that story, at the moment when the brief sequence of events can be summarized and stabilized as a universal truth about Love. But there is another narrative that is emphatically excluded from the amorous experience of Arcita and Palemone. That is the story of their own past lives, of their ancestors, and of Thebes.

> Era a costor della memoria uscita
> l'antica Tebe e 'l loro legnaggio,
> e similmente se n'era partita
> la 'nfelicità loro, e il dammaggio
> ch'avevan ricevuto, e la lor vita
> ch'era cattiva, e 'l lor grande eretaggio;
> e dove queste cose esser soleano
> Emilia solamente vi teneano. (3.36)

> [From their memory had fled
> ancient Thebes and their lineage,
> and likewise had departed
> their unhappiness, and the harm
> they had received, and their life
> that was wretched, and their great heritage;
> and where these things used to be
> they held only Emilia.]

What Arcita and Palemone have forgotten is history, both personal and dynastic, and indeed the very world of history.

This willful forgetting matches a deliberate poetic exclusion announced at the beginning of Book Three. According to the Book's argument, "a Marte dona alcuna posa / l'autore" (3.sonnet) [the author gives Mars a respite]; the poet himself declares in the book's first octave that he now sings of Cupid's battles rather than those of Mars. Mars has presided over the wars that dominate Books One and Two (1.14–15, 2.54, 2.94–95); moreover, as a figure for the human "appetito irascibile" (7.30 gloss) [irascible appetite] he is the source of the violence that stains the Theban heritage of Arcita and Palemone. In temporarily excusing Mars from the poem, therefore, the poet opens the possibility of a refuge from epic narrative and from history. The *innamoramento* scene is such a refuge, and its resistance to the dominion of Mars comes into clear focus in the passage immediately preceding the stanza just quoted in full—that is, the half-stanza glossed by "che sono io." In those four lines, Love (or Cupid) rules absolutely, without competition. And one effect of the gloss is to prove, once and for all, that the experience of love transcends history. Whoever the "io" is, he or she belongs to the time in which the *Teseida* is written—but the centuries and the momentous changes that separate two Thebans from a fourteenth-century Italian vanish in the face of an unmediated transhistorical identification. The palace-prison of lyric offers more than mere amnesia: it offers access to a force beyond worldly time.[46]

Mars will reappear, with some fanfare, at the beginning of Book Five, and the poet will close his poem by claiming proudly that he is the first Italian poet to make the Muses "cantare / di Marte . . . gli affanni sostenuti" (12.84) [sing the troubles sustained from Mars]. Although Mars is not the only reigning deity in the *Teseida*—he is paired with Venus, as Victoria Kirkham has argued[47]—it is the abiding presence of Mars that gives the *Teseida* its special character; the dismissal of Mars is thus a mere interlude. Even within Book Three, the lyric sanctuary is short-lived. Teseo sets Arcita free, introducing difference and jealousy between the two cousins; Arcita puts on armor and goes into exile from Athens; in Book Four he will return to Thebes to look upon its ruins. The escape from history and from martial narrative turns out to be a brief episode within the poem. There is a paradox here: if the identification with Love transcends time, it is not so much an episode as a presence, and its temporal duration is irrelevant to its power. But it is certainly the case that the *Teseida* as a whole is deeply concerned with the very matters—history, politics, and the epic—that are evaded in the lyric scene surrounding the "che sono io" gloss.[48]

The local evasions of this brief passage become global issues in the three "little books" I shall be discussing. Indeed, certain echoes provide a specific link between the lyric scene of *Teseida* 3 and the very opening of the *Filostrato*—a work composed in the same half-decade as the *Teseida* and in many ways a companion piece to it. As Alberto Limentani observes, the stanza describing Emilia's singing (3.40, quoted above) ends with the same unusual pair of rhyme-words as the second stanza of the *Filostrato*:

> tu mi se' Giove, tu mi se' Apollo,
> tu mi se' mia musa, io l'ho provato e sollo.
>
> [you are Jove to me, you are Apollo to me,
> you are my muse, I have proved it and I know it.]

This purely verbal echo points to other connections. The poetic persona who speaks here in the *Filostrato* has substituted a single woman for an epic universe; in this he is like Arcita and Palemone. And, as Limentani also notes, the deliberate poetic strategy announced in the *Filostrato*'s dedicatory letter resembles the adaptive behavior of Arcita and Palemone: all three young poets derive pleasure from singing about pain they cannot express directly. The two Thebans compose "sonetti e canzoni" within a carefully framed lyric scene; "Filostrato" (as he calls himself) establishes a lyric scene as a frame in which to compose the entire *Filostrato*.[49]

It might be possible to move directly from the *Teseida*'s lyric scene to the *Vita Nuova* and *Troilus and Criseyde* as well. I suspect that "preso" [seized] in *Teseida* 3.35 is meant to recall the opening of the first sonnet in the *Vita Nuova*, "A ciascun' alma presa" [To every captive soul]. That is the phrase Dante uses to address "tutti li fedeli d'Amore" (3.9) [all the faithful of Love], in a poem that asks for written responses; when the word "preso" appears as a characterization of lovers in the *Teseida*, one of Love's faithful inscribes his own response above the very word. And I suspect that Chaucer was thinking of *Teseida* 3 when he invented a garden scene of his own, at the beginning of the second book of the *Troilus*. When Pandarus finds Criseyde listening to "the geste / Of the siege of Thebes" (2.83–84), and urges her to "Do wey youre book" (2.111) and speak about love, he is asking her to do what Arcita and Palemone do: forget about Thebes. I shall have more to say about the *Vita Nuova*'s first sonnet and the Theban context of *Troilus* later in this book. Here I shall merely assert that all three "little books" explore the question of how love poetry may be framed within worldly time. In each text, the dialectic of lyric and narrative—which is both a structuring opposition and a problem for investigation—has powerful affinities with other enduring dialectic relationships: between love and temporality, and between the individual literary text and history.

This last pair of terms points to a doubleness in my own book. *The Song of Troilus* is both a series of close textual explications, addressing a set of distinct interpretive and philological problems, and a serial narrative of formal transformation and cultural change. This double constitution requires a dialogue between formalist and historicist modes of reading. As Paul de Man and others have observed, critical practice is continually being reshaped by a dialectic movement between these two modes.[50] In recent years historicism has come to seem dominant, at least in Anglo-American criticism. "New Historicism" and Marxian materialism have been slow to arrive in medieval studies, but they have now clearly arrived.[51] I am very much influenced by this trend: each of my textual readings features an emphatic "turn to history." In each case, however, the turn to history opens into an examination of the ways the very notion of historical context is subjected to a critique from within the individual text. My work does not aspire to a full historicism or a pure formalism, but rather seeks to investigate the engagement and disengagement of the two modes. To the extent that I ground this dialectic within individual texts, I may seem to be a formalist after all—I point to a text's divided self-understanding and say, "che sono io." But to the extent that I attempt to see what is willfully forgotten in the text, I work as a historicist. I do not claim to have escaped or transcended the dialectic, merely to be exploring it.

3

I have laid out, synchronically and rather schematically, some of the problems that will dominate the chapters that follow: I may list them even more schematically here as problems of intertextuality, *auctoritas*, subjectivity, the discourse of love, exegetical practice, lyric, narrative, gender, history, form. To summarize the diachronic narrative of the book, and to tabulate some of the philological questions to be addressed, I want to conclude with a more specific account of the book's makeup.

In Chapter 1, "*Sacra Pagina*," I interpret a manuscript page from Peter

Lombard's twelfth-century Psalter commentary. I suggest that text and gloss are laid out as a visual image of hierarchy patterned on the Neoplatonic cosmos as described in Augustine and Pseudo-Dionysius: the authority of the prophet-poet David descends in orderly fashion through the writings of the prophet-scribe Esdras, the Patristic commentators, and the medieval *compilator*. This hierarchy of *auctoritas* defines and establishes a certain *auctoritas* for the living human writer by subordinating him to Scripture in a dynamic structure. The textual hierarchy of the Psalter commentary will be a crucial formal model for the *Vita Nuova* in particular, but all of the vernacular books I discuss are powerfully drawn to the sort of lyric authority possessed by David. A. J. Minnis has traced the emergence of the human *auctor* by documenting the increasing exegetical interest in the life of David. David's multiple roles—as prophet, poet, lover, and wielder of political power—will be condensed to very different effect in the person of the young Dante or the doomed prince Troilus.

The next two chapters offer a reading of the *Vita Nuova*, focusing on the problem of the *divisioni*. Chapter 2, "Dante's Divisions: Structures of Authority in the *Vita Nuova*," examines the deployment of hierarchical models within the *Vita Nuova*. I argue that Dante complicates the text/gloss hierarchy of Psalter commentary by drawing an analogy between his two primary modes of writing, lyric verse and narrative prose, and his two main characters, Beatrice and Dante himself. As the relationship between those characters changes, so the formal constitution of the book undergoes revision in the course of the book. For example, Dante's third chapter, with its erotic dream and inaugural sonnet, opens the possibility of a reciprocal attraction between lyric and narrative, Beatrice and Dante. But the *divisioni* that Dante attaches to his lyrics help define the book as a textual hierarchy. The *divisioni* are usually seen as reflexes of a Thomistic Scholasticism, but I show that they refer as well to the much older tradition of the *divisio psalmi*. The stable hierarchy of the glossed Psalter has great appeal both for Dante and for his readers—I argue that Charles S. Singleton's theological reading of the *libello* implicitly celebrates this model—but the text subjects the atemporal hierarchy to the temporal vicissitudes of Dante's life.

Chapter 3, "Dante's Divisions: The History of Division," further explores the temporality of form within Dante's *libello*. I explore division as a crucial theme within the *Vita Nuova*, and show that this theme intertwines with the technique of *divisio textus* in unexpected ways. As a protagonist, Dante is divided by his temporality, and his divisions are themselves subject to change. In the course of the *Vita Nuova*, the method of the *divisioni* undergoes a shift that corresponds to the thirteenth-century rise of Scholasticism. But the final section of the *libello* demonstrates the dangers of Scholastic division, as the *divisioni* begin to infect the lyrics, producing fragmentary and ambivalent texts. The book's ending seems to resolve these instabilities in favor of the Scholastic hierarchy, but in fact it opens the text to a variety of revisionary responses: Dante's own *Convivio*, Petrarch's *Canzoniere*, Boccaccio's *Filostrato*, and of course the *Divine Comedy*.

Chapter 4, "The Form of *Filostrato*," describes the *Filostrato* as a polemical response to the *Vita Nuova*. There are many verbal and thematic echoes, but the *Filostrato* is above all a formal reconstitution of the earlier work. Where Dante takes pains to separate lyric and narrative as distinct textual components, Boccaccio fuses the two. He does this by providing an elliptical but complex frame for his poem, and by employing an octave stanza that functions equally well for lyric and narrative discourse. Similarly, the analogy between textual components and personal relationships has changed: where Dante structures lyric and narrative as a heterosexual dyad, Boccaccio assigns both roles to similar male figures, Troiolo and Pandaro. The point of this, I argue, is to define a new kind of *auctoritas*. Dante strategically claims a subservient status, projecting a quasi-divine Other and assuming a derivative inspiration, while Boccaccio envisions an autonomous and self-validating lyric authority.

Chapter 5, "The Form of Troilus: Boccaccio, Chaucer, and the Picture of History," explores the relationship between the personal lyric and political authority. Boccaccio raises this issue by setting his poem in Troy and emphatically eliminating the splendid martial displays associated with that setting. My focus here is the figure of the noble poet-protagonist Troiolo. I show that Boccaccio's portrayal of this figure must be understood as a complex response to classical and medieval traditions in which Troilus is the visual embodiment of political power. The *Filostrato* is strikingly devoid of epic ekphrasis and visual imagery in general, yet it defines itself as a single complex image: as it fuses lyric and narrative modes of writing, so it fuses the verbal and the visual. Boccaccio seems willfully apolitical in the *Filostrato*, but in fact he attempts to borrow the illustriousness of political authority for a literary kingdom beyond politics and beyond history. Yet the poem demonstrates, through its narrative, that this escape cannot succeed; the denial of history must be undone in time. In a final section, I discuss the visual depiction of Troilus in *Troilus and Criseyde*. Chaucer reinserts the pictures that are missing from *Filostrato*, rejecting its radical simplifications; but in Chaucer's text the conventional gestures have become (in part because of Boccaccio's challenging unconventionality) both problematic and newly meaningful.

Chapter 6, "Sailing to Charybdis: The Second *Canticus Troili* and the Contexts of Chaucer's *Troilus*," continues the discussion of *Troilus and Criseyde* as, in itself, a "narrative of formal transformation." I focus on two lyrics labeled "Song of Troilus," and their textual settings. The first *Canticus Troili* (1.400–20) is generally held to be the only English translation, before Thomas Wyatt, of a Petrarch sonnet. I show that the second *Canticus Troili* (5.638–44) is a much looser rendition of another Petrarch sonnet. Taken together, the two passages stage a contrast between two modes of literary imitation and two modes of literary framing. For the first lyric, Chaucer, who probably did not know the *Vita Nuova*, reverses Boccaccio's polemical revision of that work; he restores a clear textual hierarchy, framing the lyric as a privileged space of clear expression and faithful translation. My reading of this passage seems to support C. S. Lewis's claim that Chaucer "medievalizes" the proto-Renaissance *Filostrato*. But in Book Five of the *Troilus* the frame around the lyric text has broken down. Rather than containing a definite content, or containing contradictions, the song is a fragment that points inconclusively to a set of very different contexts. The song's "ship" drifts between the narratives that define the literary space of the *Troilus*: narratives that include the *Filostrato*, the *Thebaid*, and the turbulent history reflected in contemporary political poetry. Chaucer rejects Boccaccio's vision of a self-validating and apolitical *auctoritas*, yet he cannot rely on either old poetry or new politics to provide a stable basis for his writing. The second *Canticus Troili* points to an uneasy solution: an endless negotiation between imposing models and a new *auctoritas* that derives its power from the spectacle of its own careful dismantling.

An "Afterword" reframes some of the issues of the book as problems of personal and cultural memory.

1. *Sacra Pagina*

1

The early history of modern authorship is a history of experimentation with literary form. Medieval writers often disavowed originality, as we are often reminded, but their claims of conventionality typically refer to narrative material or philosophical wisdom; assertions of originality in style, mode, or structure are not at all uncommon. The literary production of the later Middle Ages is marked, in fact, by a proliferation of inventive and idiosyncratic forms, and by a sustained exploration of the very idea of form. In this disorderly workshop, the institutions of modern literature—notions of author, work, reader, genre, and "literature"—are under construction.

The subject of this book is the construction of a vernacular *auctoritas* in three formal experiments: the *Vita Nuova*, the *Filostrato*, and *Troilus and Criseyde*. Before turning to the sequence of three, it will be useful to consider a fourth work, the Psalter commentary of Peter Lombard. In the next chapter I shall argue that this is one of the books that Dante had most in mind when he wrote the *Vita Nuova*. Peter's commentary, then, belongs with the sequence under discussion; it is the first term in a sequence of four. This text, however, has a special status. Unlike the other three, it is not "literary" in the modern sense. More important, in the Middle Ages it was a far more influential and authoritative book than any of the three *libelli*. Peter's commentaries on the Psalms and the Pauline Epistles were called the "magna glosatura," and they became part of the *Glossa Ordinaria*, the standard compilation of interpretations for the entire Bible. The original Gloss had included commentaries on the Psalms and Pauline Epistles composed by Anselm of Laon in the late eleventh century. Around 1130, this "parva glosatura" was supplemented by a "media glosatura" by Gilbert of Poitiers (or Gilbert de la Porrée). Peter Lombard's commentaries, composed around the middle of the twelfth century, effectively replaced the earlier two versions by the last quarter of the century.[1] Thus Peter's text was part of the glossed Bible that could be found in any center of learning; it was part of the cultural heritage shared by my three lay writers, and for all three it represented a powerful model of established authority.

The *Glossa Ordinaria* has usually been treated as a research tool. In the Middle Ages it was an inexhaustible source of reliable biblical interpretations; in the twentieth century it has been an inexhaustible source of medieval ideas and images. In addition, some modern scholars have studied the Gloss *as* a medieval reference book: they have discussed its textual history, its manuscript layout, its exegetical practice, its intellectual context. In this chapter, drawing on the findings of those scholars, I want to suggest another way of reading the Gloss: as a text in its own right, a signifying form. Much of what I say here will be applicable to the glossed Bible as a whole, but my particular topic is Peter's Psalter commentary—and specifically the visual form of a single manuscript page of that commentary.[2]

As the text of the Gloss was stabilized in the twelfth century, the scribal layout of the page was stabilized as well. In certain respects the *mise en page* for the books glossed by Peter Lombard—the Psalter and the Pauline Epistles—represented a refinement of the *mise en page* employed for the other books of the Bible.[3] Modern photographic reproductions of typical twelfth-century examples are not hard to find; I take as example a plate accompanying an essay by M. B. Parkes[4]—an important essay that primarily treats, however, thirteenth-century developments in the form of the book.

Parkes describes the typical page succinctly:

> The full text of the Psalter or Epistles was disposed in a larger, more formal version of twelfth-century script in conveniently sited columns, and the size of the columns was determined by the length of the commentary on that particular part of the text. In the commentary itself the *lemmata* were underlined in red. Each of the *auctores* quoted in the commentary was identified by name in the margin, again in red, and the extent of the quotation was also marked. As the final refinement each of the *auctores* was given a symbol consisting of dots or lines and dots which was placed both against the name in the margin, and against the beginning of the *auctoritas* or quotation in the body of the commentary.[5]

I have little to add to this description. It seems important, though, to specify the location of the "conveniently sited columns" of text. In the plate that accompanies the essay, reproduced here as Figure 1, the scriptural text appears in two separate rectangles, separated by commentary: the end of Psalm 45 occupies a rectangle in the upper left-hand corner of the page,

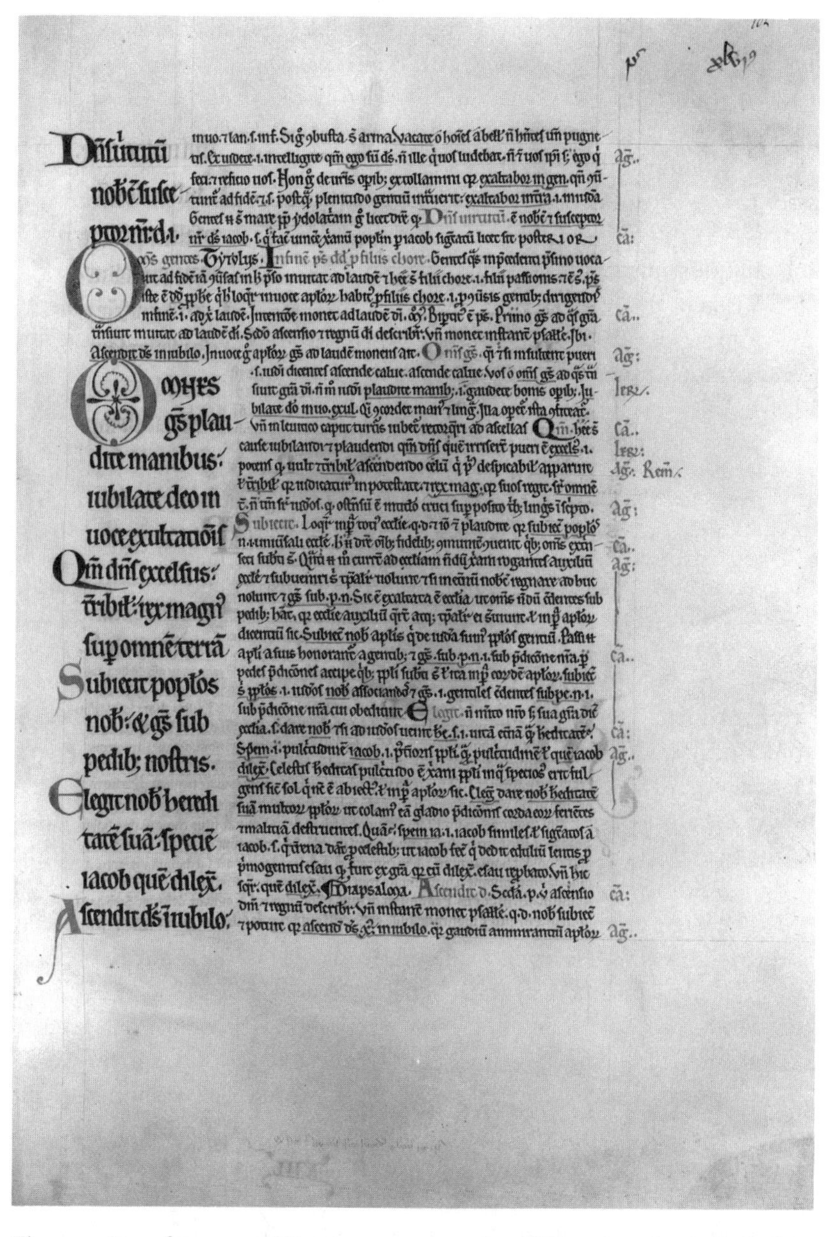

Figure 1. Page from a twelfth-century manuscript of Peter Lombard, *In Psalmos Davidicos Commentarii*. Bodleian MS Auct. D.2.8, fol. 105r. Used by permission of the Bodleian Library, Oxford.

while the first verses of Psalm 46 occupy a wider and taller rectangle fitted into the lower left-hand corner. This is a recto page, however, so the left-hand margin is also the center of the open book. In earlier Gloss manuscripts, the scriptural text occupies the center of the individual page, flanked by two columns of commentary.[6] One would have to see this page along with the verso of the previous page to recognize that the scriptural text is still in the center; the right-hand margin, where the apparatus for identifying citations appears, is the outer margin.

Visually, the most striking feature of the page is the contrast between the large script of the text and the smaller script of the commentary. The contrast implies a hierarchy. Parkes remarks that the *mise en page*

> reflects in practical and visual terms a dominant attitude to the ordering of studies found in the first half of the twelfth century, and expressed in statements like the following from the prologue to the *De sacramentis* of Hugh of St. Victor: "omnes artes naturales divinae scientiae famulantur, et inferior sapientia recte ordinata ad superiorem conducit" [all the natural arts act as servants to divine knowledge, and lower wisdom, rightly ordered, leads to higher].[7]

Parkes's argument pursues the idea of *ordinatio*: he notes that the gloss is "recte ordinata" [rightly ordered] because it follows the *ordo narracionis* [order of narration] of the text. (It is thus a *glossa ordinaria*.) But the verb "famulantur" [act as servants] also implies a powerful metaphor of hierarchy, as Parkes observes: "the *auctoritates* were subordinated to the study of the sacred page."[8] Dante, in the *Convivio*, uses the same metaphor: the gloss is a servant to the text.[9]

The page, then, is a visual emblem of hierarchy. This in itself is hardly surprising: as is well known, medieval people valued clear hierarchies and constructed them almost by force of habit. Not all hierarchies are identical, though.[10] As a way of defining more precisely the particular character of *this* hierarchy, I would compare it to two other images of hierarchy involving Scripture. These two images are drawn from the beginning of the Middle Ages, from the writings of Augustine and Pseudo-Dionysius.

Augustine's meditative gloss on the opening verses of Genesis, in the last three books of the *Confessions*, concludes with the vision of a cosmos: God's created universe, allegorized as a hierarchy connecting God and humanity. The image begins to come into focus with the word *firmamentum* (Gen. 1:6), which Augustine explains as a symbol for Scripture itself:

> quis nisi tu, deus noster, fecisti nobis firmamentum auctoritatis super nos in scriptura tua divina? caelum enim plicabitur ut liber et nunc sicut pellis extenditur super nos (13.15.16)[11]
>
> [who except you, our God, made the firmament of authority above us in your divine scripture? For the sky will be folded up like a book, and now is extended like a skin above us]

This "firmament of authority" is extended "super nos" [above us] but beneath God. The space between God and Scripture is inhabited by angels, those "aliae aquae super hoc firmamentum" (13.15.18) [other waters above this firmament] who have no need to read Scripture because they can read God directly, atemporally:

> ibi legunt sine syllabis temporum, quid velit aeterna voluntas tua. legunt, eligunt et diligunt . . . non clauditur codex eorum nec plicatur liber eorum, quia tu ipse illis hoc es (13.15.18)
>
> [there they read, without syllables of time, what your eternal will desires. They read, choose, and love . . . their codex is never closed nor is their book folded up, since you yourself are this to them]

Scripture acts as a mediating boundary between the atemporal and the temporal because its own status is ambiguous: it can be understood as a sequence of words, sounds to be spoken in succession, or as a unitary object.[12] In time to come, this sky will be folded up like a book (Apoc. 6:14) and we will be able to understand God's word as a timeless whole; for now, it is extended in time, and we must read "in aenigmate nubium et per speculum caeli" (13.15.18) [in the riddle of the clouds and through the mirror of the heavens]—"in signis et in temporibus et in diebus et in annis" (13.18.23) [in signs and in times and in days and in years].

Humanity is located below the firmament of Scripture, but there is a hierarchy here as well. The waters which are gathered together (Gen. 1:9) are the souls of those who seek worldly ends, who "innumerabili varietate curarum fluctuent" (13.17.20) [waver in an innumerable variety of cares]. The dry land represents the souls of those who thirst after God (13.17.21). There is yet a higher class within humanity: certain holy ones are called to be "luminaria in mundo cohaerentes firmamento scripturae tuae" (13.18.22) [luminaries in the world, adhering to the firmament of your scripture].

These are the saved, a "genus electum" (13.19.25) [chosen people]; they are illuminated variously by the gifts of the Spirit and shine on the world below (13.18). This group of "spiritales" [spiritual people], distinguished from the body of the faithful, is figured again in the "animam viventem" [living soul or creature] brought forth upon the earth in Genesis 1:24 (13.21.29); and again in unfallen man, man with dominion over the earth (13.23). The "spiritales" are God's messengers (13.21.29); they serve the faithful by bringing them the Word and exciting them to imitation (13.21.30). Augustine states that the "spiritales" may be either leaders or followers within the Church (13.23.33), but he goes on to describe the spiritual man as though he were a bishop:[13] he administers the sacraments, and he reads and expounds the Scriptures to the congregation, exercising judgment

> in verborum signis vocibusque subiectis auctoritati libri tui tamquam sub firmamento volitantibus, interpretando, exponendo, disserendo, disputando, benedicendo atque invocando te, ore erumpentibus atque sonantibus signis, ut respondeat populus: amen. (13.23.34)

> [in signs of words and in sounds subject to the authority of your book like the flying birds under the firmament, by interpreting, expounding, discoursing, disputing, praising, and invoking you, with signs breaking forth from the mouth and sounding, so that the people may answer: amen.]

At this point it appears that the human community has a visible hierarchy corresponding to the cosmic order.

Certainly Augustine's discourse in these chapters should not be reduced to a map: it is a complex and nuanced meditation, so that, for example, some terms in the Scriptural text receive more than one spiritual gloss. But there is an underlying map; it is summarized in a single paragraph near the end of the book (13.34.49).[14] God, angels, Scripture, the spiritual, the faithful, and the worldly are terms in a single hierarchy. Each pair of terms is separated vertically, but the hierarchy is not merely a ranking; it is a dynamic structure, through which the divine light descends to a fallen world. The firmament of Scripture, like the human "luminaria" that adhere to it, plays a crucial role in the chain of mediations: it receives the light from above and transmits it below.

The *Ecclesiastical Hierarchy* of Pseudo-Dionysius provides a more systematic map of the same territory: the Church is the hierarchy that distributes God's light to individual Christians. The structure that Pseudo-Dionysius outlines has much in common with the allegorized cosmos at the end of the *Confessions*. There are differences: notably, the "hierarchy" that Pseudo-Dionysius describes does not extend directly to God. The Church is headed by the order of bishops; the angels are higher still, but they belong to a different hierarchy, that which Pseudo-Dionysius describes in the *Celestial Hierarchy*. The ecclesiastical hierarchy is situated between two other hierarchies, celestial and legal, but it is not merely a segment in a super-hierarchy; it has an identity and a wholeness of its own. This formal wholeness is important to Pseudo-Dionysius; the ecclesiastical hierarchy is the material reflection of a spiritual reality, and the analogy between the two worlds is part of God's order. (The bishop functions as a mediator between God and the ordinary Christian, but in his own hierarchy he is the analogue of God.) "Our own hierarchy is itself symbolical"[15]—not only because it is full of symbols, but also because the entire hierarchy is a unitary symbol.

Augustine's allegorized cosmos is not, then, identical to the intricately detailed set of hierarchies described by Pseudo-Dionysius. The differences may arise in part from the difference between two modes of writing, between Augustine's densely figured and self-reflexive meditation and Pseudo-Dionysius's more systematic exposition. Still, the two models show a general similarity. They reflect the Neoplatonism that helped to shape both writers: the One, the Verbum, radiates downward to the Many, with the aim of drawing the Many back up through the hierarchy toward its own divine state.[16]

Like Augustine, Pseudo-Dionysius assigns the Bible a crucial role. Again, there are differences. For Pseudo-Dionysius the Bible is not itself a term in the ecclesiastical hierarchy, which is made up of human beings and rites. In one striking passage, however, the Bible is symbolically located within the ecclesiastical hierarchy:

> the hierarch carries on his head—in a holy manner—the sacred scriptures. Since the perfecting power and understanding of all the clergy were given to the hierarchs, men of God, by that divine goodness which is the source of every consecration, it is only proper that there should be placed on the heads of the hierarchs the scriptures which God himself handed down and which reveal to us all that we can know of God, all his works and words and manifestations, every sacred word and work, everything, in short, which the divinity has so generously wished to pass on to the human hierarchy, every sacred thing done and said by God. The hierarch who lives in conformity with God and who has a full and complete share of the hierarch's power is not simply content to enjoy the true and divinely enlightening understanding that comes from all the words and acts of the hierarchic rites. He also hands them on to others in accordance with their place in the hierarchy.[17]

In Augustine's reading of Genesis, Scripture is created before its readers: it has a kind of logical priority and an agency of its own. Pseudo-Dionysius assigns it a role that is both larger and smaller. On the one hand, "the being of our hierarchy is laid down by the divinely transmitted scriptures."[18] On the other hand, the Bible does not stand alone: it is inseparable from the oral teachings passed down by tradition,[19] and it appears as an object within the ecclesiastical hierarchy rather than as an agent. Again, though, there is a general similarity between the two images of Scripture: whether it is symbolically located in the sky or on the bishop's head, Scripture is a mediator between God and humanity, both transmitting and transmitted.

The hierarchy represented visually on the page of the Gloss is closely related to the hierarchies described verbally by Augustine and Pseudo-Dionysius. One striking difference should be mentioned immediately: the new role played by writing. In both of the earlier versions of hierarchy, the only written thing is the Bible. The divine text is involved in a hierarchy of living beings, both divine and human; it nourishes humanity by being rendered vocal, in public reading and oral teaching. In the hierarchy of the page, all is written. The Scripture is still a "firmamentum auctoritatis" [firmament of authority], and Augustine himself, as a holy expositor of Scripture, is accorded a position just below the firmament. But this firmament is part of a textual cosmos: the commentary is made up of *auctoritates* in another sense, "texts rather than persons,"[20] and the marginal notation "Ag." stands for a body of writing rather than a living man.

Despite this crucial difference, the manuscript page depicts a hierarchy in something like the full Pseudo-Dionysian sense of the term. It is a multi-leveled structure in which *auctoritas* diffuses from the central scriptural text to the outer margin.

The subordination of commentary to text is only the beginning of the hierarchy. The page, after all, contains three different kinds of writing, separated into distinct spaces. The large script of the Psalms occupies two rectangles on the left. The small script of the commentary fills the rest of the main area of the page. And the right margin is punctuated, but not filled, by a third type of writing: the small script of the apparatus, which differs from that of the commentary in that it is entirely red and consists of brief notations (two- and three-letter abbreviations, reference symbols, and vertical lines marking the extent of quotations in the commentary) rather than continuous prose.

Three types of script, then, are partitioned into areas that proceed from left to right across the page—or from the center of the open book to its outer margin. The three scripts correspond to three modes of composition: three of Bonaventure's four ways of making a book. In the terms of the passage with which I opened the Introduction, the Psalms are the work of an *auctor*, whether that *auctor* is understood to be God or David.[21] The commentary consists almost entirely of quotations from the Fathers and other well-established writers; this particular page includes a half-dozen passages from both Augustine and Cassiodorus, two from Jerome, and one from the ninth-century Remigius of Auxerre. These writers are *commentatores*; when they write their own words, those words are supplementary to the scriptural text, "tamquam annexa ad evidentiam" [annexed for the purpose of clarifying them]. Finally, Peter Lombard is a *compilator*: rather than presenting a personal interpretation of the Psalms, he has selected and copied passages from many volumes of commentary (in Bonaventure's phrase, Peter "scribit aliena, addendo, sed non de suo" [he writes the words of others, adding, but not of his own]). His achievement is not the formulation of new ideas but rather the new arrangement of old ideas, and the contours of this arrangement are visible at a glance in the marginal apparatus.

Bonaventure's fourfold account of the making of books presents a hierarchy in a limited sense of the term: it is a ranking, with the four modes of writing listed according to their increasing originality. Similarly, the three kinds of writing on the manuscript page can easily be ranked in terms of *auctoritas*, or, more concretely, certitude: as Bonaventure says, of the *Sentences*, "alius modus certitudinis est in sacra Scriptura et alius in hoc libro" [one mode of certitude is in holy Scripture and another in this book].[22] The hierarchy of the Gloss page is not, however, simply a static array, with less authoritative writing placed next to more authoritative writing by way of contrast. In this hierarchy, *auctoritas* descends from one level to the next.

Dante speaks of the descent of authority in a passage from the *De Monarchia*.[23] In order to refute the Decretalists, who assert that Christian faith is grounded in the traditions of the Church, he distinguishes between those traditions, the Church itself, and the Scriptures, and he ranks the three according to their authority. Logical priority is reflected in historical priority; although traditions, Church, and Scriptures all exist in the moment of Dante's writing, they arose at different times. First comes the Bible ("Ante quidem Ecclesiam sunt vetus et novum Testamentum" [3.3.12; prior to the Church are the Old and the New Testament]). Then the Church—and with the Church we are to place the "concilia principalia" (3.3.13) [principal councils] and also the writings of the Fathers, "Scripture doctorum, Augustini et aliorum" (3.3.13) [the teachers of Scripture, Augustine and others]. The Fathers were aided ("adiutos") by the Holy Spirit, though presumably not directly inspired in the same way as the writers of the Bible. Finally there are the "traditiones quas 'decretales' dicunt" (3.3.14) [traditions which are called "decretals"]. These traditions have their own "auctoritas apostolica" [apostolic authority], which must be subordinated to the authority of God's own word (3.3.14). We are dealing, then, with three forms of authority—not, however, three essentially different kinds but rather three degrees of a single authority. *Auctoritas* flows ("accedat . . . manat" [3.3.16; descends, flows]) from Scriptures to Church to tradition.[24]

Likewise the Gloss page presents a historical sequence of acts of writing (Scriptures, Fathers, Peter Lombard), and translates this historical sequence into a synchronic structure. The three bodies of writing are not, of course, merely juxtaposed on the page, but intimately connected. The web of connections is represented visually in a set of repetitions: the text of the Psalm is fragmented into the *lemmata* that appear in red in the commentary, and the reference symbols in the commentary, red dots and lines scattered through the prose, appear again in the marginal apparatus. As in the Neoplatonic cosmos, a central presence radiates outward through the successive levels of a hierarchy—and what is transmitted is inspiration, certitude, or *auctoritas*. The authority of the compilation derives from the greater authority of Patristic writings, and the authority of the Fathers derives from the greater authority of Scripture. Along with this outward motion there is—as a Neoplatonist would expect—another motion back towards the center. Dante alludes to this second motion: he argues that true philosophers should return to Scripture, "hanc veritatem venantes" (3.3.16) [hunting this truth], and his evidence for the priority of Scripture to Church is, appropriately, a scriptural citation: a verse in which the Church asks to be drawn toward her Bridegroom ("trahe me post te" [Cant. 1.3; *Monarchia* 3.3.12]). In the Gloss page, the motion that draws a reader from the margin to the center is the very activity of reading: the marginal apparatus points to the commentary, and the commentary points to the Psalm text.

Here, then, is a twelfth-century image of hierarchy to place next to those described by Augustine and Pseudo-Dionysius.[25] Its relation to those earlier hierarchies is like the relationship of the ecclesiastical hierarchy to the celestial hierarchy in Pseudo-Dionysius: it is not simply an extension of those hierarchies, but rather a fully-developed analogue operating in a world of its own, a world of written texts.

I would add two refinements to this account of the textual hierarchy.

First, returning to Bonaventure's fourfold definition of writing, is there a place for the "scriptor" on the page? Naturally the work of the scribe is immanent in the materiality of the manuscript: it is visible in all the writing. Occasionally, though, the producer of the individual book signals his presence in a distinct gesture. Some Gloss manuscripts of the late twelfth century feature elaborate illuminated initials, done in bright colors, depicting grotesque intertwined animals and naked human beings.[26] And the scribe himself sometimes elaborates on the vertical lines which are part of the marginal apparatus:

> Sometimes the lines are made into part of the book's decoration and they sprout flowers and foliage and one splendid copy from St-Victor has some lines in the form of comic pictures: on one leaf a worried-looking peasant at the foot of the page balances the line on his nose and on the top of the line he balances a striped pot; another, even funnier, has a monk's head at the top of the line and a pair of boots at the bottom.[27]

These pictures, when they appear, are part of the visual totality of the page, yet they possess no *auctoritas*. And they occupy an ad-hoc marginal space rather than a distinct block of the page. There *is* another distinct area, however, to which one might assign yet a fifth character, the *lector*: in the new *mise en page* employed for the commentaries of Peter Lombard, writes C. F. R. De Hamel, "there was no longer room for the reader to add his own personal glosses and an extra blank column was therefore ruled in the outer margins for reader's notes."[28] The textual hierarchy extends from the Bible through the Fathers to Peter Lombard and then beyond, to the mostly anonymous individuals who make and use particular manuscripts.

Second, another intermediate stage should be added to the hierarchy. On the manuscript page reproduced here, the text of Psalm 46 begins "Omnes gentes plaudite" [O clap your hands, all nations]. The commentary, however, includes another beginning: "Omnes gentes. Titulus. In finem psalmus david pro filiis chore" [All nations. Title. Unto the end, a psalm of David for the sons of Core]. The *titulus*, like the incipit, is written entirely in red. As Peter Lombard explains in the Preface to his commentary, the titles of the Psalms are part of the Scriptures and are divinely inspired, but they are not properly part of the Psalms they accompany: their human author is not David but the prophet Esdras.

> Esdras . . . propheta, qui Psalterium et totam bibliothecam a Babyloniis combustam instinctu Spiritus sancti reformavit, eodem Spiritu revelante, psalmos ita disposuit, eisdem et titulos apposuit (*PL* 191.60)

> [the prophet Esdras, who by the prompting of the Holy Spirit reconstructed the Psalter and the entire library burned by the Babylonians, with the same Spirit guiding him arranged the Psalms and added titles to them.]

Even within the Bible there are degrees of authority. Esdras is a prophet, but David is the "prophetarum eximius" (*PL* 191.55) [most excellent of the prophets]; in the Psalter, Esdras is (to use a modern term) an editor rather than an author. Accordingly, the *titulus* is assigned a special intermediate status, excluded from the central text but marked as biblical within the commentary. The idea of the *titulus* appears again at a higher level of organization. The first Psalm lacks a title of its own, because it *is* a title for the whole Book of Psalms: "iste psalmus, quasi titulus et prologus est sequentis operis. Continet enim summam et materiam totius libri" (*PL* 191.60) [this Psalm is like a title and prologue to the following work. For it contains the sum and subject-matter of the whole book]. And the relationship of Psalm 1 to the Psalter is mirrored in the relationship of the Psalter to the entire Bible: "Notandum quoque hanc Scripturam plus caeteris in ecclesiasticis frequentari officiis, quod ideo fit, quia in hoc libro consummatio est totius theologicae paginae" (*PL* 191.57) [It should be noted also that this Scripture is employed in the offices of the Church more often than others, because in this book is the sum of the entire field of theology]. On the manuscript page, Psalm 46 appears as a unitary text, but only because it is the closest approach to an ultimate Unity. The textual hierarchy of the Gloss develops a hierarchy that is already to be found in the Bible.

2

My account of the Gloss page has deliberately been "formalist" in two senses: unthematic and ahistorical. I have ignored the content of the words on the page, the ideas they express.[29] And I have—despite repeated references to "the twelfth century"—treated the page as an object outside of time. This second kind of formalism is, I think, invited by the object itself. The manuscript page spatializes a historical sequence as a visual structure, and makes no reference to its own historical moment; as Guy Lobrichon observes, the Gloss "belongs to the heaven of abstraction, apparently without date and place."[30] But of course the Gloss does exist in time. It can usefully be placed in several different historical narratives. Within the history of authorship, the Gloss, even considered purely as a form, represents an important new stage in the definition and validation of the human *auctor*.

The layout of the Gloss page asserts the inferiority of human writing to the divine Word; the elaborate textual hierarchy grows out of this basic subordination. At the same time, however, the hierarchy, precisely because it is well-defined and complete, accords the commentary a status that it might not otherwise have. Human writing was *always* understood to be inferior to the divine Word; here it has at least a place of its own. The absolute, categorical distinction between the Bible and all other texts is here reconceived as one vertical step in a hierarchy that operates even within the Bible. The commentary is indeed ancillary to the text—but then the *titulus* is ancillary to the Psalm and the marginal apparatus is ancillary to the commentary. Augustine's commentary and Peter's compilation lack the authority of Scripture, but they do possess authority, and the claim to authority is visible along with the acknowledgment of subordination.

The form of the *Glossa Ordinaria* was not achieved in a single leap of the imagination. As Anselm's commentaries on the Psalter and the Pauline Epistles were replaced by those of Gilbert of Poitiers and Peter Lombard, the manuscript layout of these books underwent a series of refinements. De Hamel presents this story succinctly.[31] He describes it in terms of efficiency and clarity—the Gloss *was* a marvelous research tool—but it is also possible to see a gradual consolidation of the position of human writing in the textual hierarchy. For the gloss of Anselm, the scribe first wrote the scriptural text in a central column on the page; then the gloss was added, both in the margins and between the lines, expanded or compressed to fit into the available space. Here the book is essentially a Bible with accidental notes. The "media glosatura" of Gilbert of Poitiers was originally designed as a separate book to accompany Anselm's glossed Bible; it was written in a continuous style, with scriptural phrases underlined for purposes of reference. After Gilbert's death, scribes expanded these phrases until most of the biblical text was included; later still, they copied out the biblical text, in a larger script, in a separate column at the center of the book. Now, however, it was the text that had to be expanded or compressed to follow the commentary. In this "very distinctive and clumsy form of page layout,"[32] the book is essentially a book of commentary, with the (intrinsically more important) scriptural text inserted as a supplement. Finally, for the "magna glosatura" of Peter Lombard, the scribes, after a period of experimentation, developed the layout I have been discussing. Both text and commentary were written together, so that the space of the page could be accurately apportioned between them. As a last refinement, a single set of horizontal lines was used to rule both text and commentary, with the letters of the text occupying two lines for each single line of commentary.

The "magna glosatura" no longer contained interlinear glosses. Lobrichon notes that the interlinear gloss was an invention of Latin Christianity: "The holy zeal of the Jewish copyists of the Torah does not seem to be relaxed to the point of introducing glosses in a human hand in the space reserved for the Bible,"[33] and Byzantine Christians observed the same restraint. In the layout of the Peter Lombard commentaries, the space of Scripture is again a sacred preserve. Certainly the unmarked area showing between the large letters of the text gives this space a bright look that contrasts visually with the more closely worked space of the commentary. At the same time, the clarification of the boundary between text and commentary gives the commentary—ancillary though it is—an integrity of its own.

So the textual hierarchy of the Gloss page can be understood as the culmination of a historical process. Earlier in the Middle Ages, the phrase "sacra pagina" [sacred page] had referred to the text of the Bible. By the time of Peter Lombard, "sacra pagina" usually meant theological instruction, *divinitas* as a branch of study.[34] The manuscript page of the Gloss is an emblem of the "sacra pagina" in this later sense: the human endeavor that includes, at its center, the Bible. The human writer has entered the sacred page.[35]

The textual hierarchy also provides, I believe, a useful tool for describing the history of authorship subsequent to the invention of the Gloss. The increasing independence and rising status of the human *auctor* in the late Middle Ages has been traced in several studies that analyze the ways the terms "auctor" and "auctoritas" were used.[36] The same development can be understood formally as a passage from the margins of the textual hierarchy toward the center. Before the Gloss, the books that received written commentaries were almost always ancient, canonical books—notably the Bible, Justinian, and the classical poets and philosophers.[37] There was, then, a categorical difference between the writing that could function as *textus* and the modern writing that defined itself as commentary. In the Gloss, however, "text" and "commentary" become relative terms rather than essential categories: *auctoritas* becomes a matter of degrees. And once text and commentary are understood as different kinds of writing, distinguished by position within a single book, it becomes possible to put new writing in the place of the text. The emergence of the human *auctor* in the world of medieval learning is visible in a sequence of some of the most important

Latin works—a sequence in which, repeatedly, commentary is elaborated and elevated to become the text for a new commentary.

In the last quarter of the twelfth century, as Beryl Smalley writes, "lectures on Scripture began to take the form of glossing the *Gloss*."[38] The subject of the lecture is still biblical truth, but now the Gloss is the text explicated in the lecture. The gloss-on-the-Gloss in turn becomes an independent text within the career of Peter Lombard. In the *Sentences*, Peter offers an abstract of the truth of Scripture and draws many of his *auctoritates* from the Gloss, including the parts of the Gloss that he himself had compiled. The *Sentences*, however, is structured by the logical sequence of its own topics rather than by the *ordo narracionis* of the Bible. The *Sentences* is a set of *quaestiones*, and the *quaestio* itself had emerged from occasional appearances in biblical commentary to stand alone as a systematic mode of discourse.[39] Around 1230, the *Sentences* became the official text of theology at the University of Paris, and the composition of a commentary on it became the regular exercise of a young professor.[40]

The textual hierarchy of the Gloss still operates in a commentary on the *Sentences*, but its dimensions have been adjusted: the commentary rises to a new status with respect to its text. The commentary is still subordinate, of course, but Bonaventure (for example) is closer to Peter Lombard than Peter Lombard is to David or Paul. In the passage which opened my Introduction, Bonaventure defines the *auctor* as a kind of writer in order to support his argument that Peter can justly be called an *auctor*: although the truth of the *Sentences* derives from God, the "doctor sive auctor doctrinae" [teacher or author of the Doctrine], Peter is the book's "alium, creatum auctorem" [other, created author].[41] Bonaventure does not characterize his own mode of writing, but by the definition he offers he would have to be called an *auctor* himself. His commentary includes a passage-by-passage exposition of the *Sentences*, but it consists largely of Bonaventure's own *quaestiones*.[42] Text and commentary use the same mode of discourse, and the text has become a structuring device, an occasion for more writing.[43] In the next stage of the process, the text is once again set aside and the writer treats his own work as a text in its own right: a systematic exposition of theological truth, a *summa*. M.-D. Chenu notes the connection between the definition of theology as a science, "increasingly independent of pastoral, spiritual, and moral preoccupations," and the development of the *summa* as a thirteenth-century genre.[44] Thomas Aquinas wrote one commentary on the *Sentences*; he is said to have abandoned a second in favor of writing the *Summa Theologiae*.[45]

This account is, of course, schematic. The *summa* did not simply replace the scriptural gloss: there were twelfth-century *summae*, and biblical commentaries continued to be written throughout the Middle Ages (by Aquinas, for example). At any one moment, a wide variety of discursive forms is available to the writer. The universe of available forms does change, however, and one way of describing this change is by abstracting a sequence of typical forms. The sequence I have sketched—the Gloss, lectures on the Gloss, the *Sentences*, commentaries on the *Sentences*, *summae*—is both a collection of influential works and an abstract of the history of learning in the twelfth and thirteenth centuries. I take the manuscript page of Peter Lombard's Psalm commentary as a powerful emblem of stable textual hierarchy; the sequence that transforms this hierarchy by repeatedly substituting commentary for text is an emblem—a kind of narrative synecdoche—of the gradual establishment of *auctoritas* for the living writer.

3

The living writer I have been discussing is a Latin, theological writer. The vernacular *auctor* has a separate history, or a complex of intertwined histories, only partially dependent on the fortunes of the Latin *auctor*. It is worth asking, though, how a vernacular *auctoritas* might emerge from the conceptual matrix provided by the Gloss page. Since the hierarchy on the page is constructed entirely from Latin sentences and abbreviations, the vernacular *auctor* cannot advance through the ranks; instead, what we find is a single decisive transformation, achieved in various ways, in which vernacular poetry moves directly to the center of the hierarchy.

The most powerful example of this transformation is, I believe, Dante's unfinished *Convivio*. There are earlier works that can be described as commentaries on vernacular texts. The Provençal *vidas* and *razos* gloss troubadour lyrics by supplying information about the lives of the troubadours.[46] Guido Cavalcanti's *canzone* "Donna mi prega" received a commentary in Latin.[47] The *Vita Nuova*, as we shall see, is an extraordinarily syncretic form; it engages a number of possible models, including the Gloss and Scholastic commentaries. In the *Convivio*, however, Dante unequivocally and explicitly follows the pattern of learned *expositio textus*. His prose is an elaborate gloss ("comento," 1.5.6) on certain of his own *canzoni*, employing the terminology and the form of a thirteenth-century Latin commentary.[48] Like Bonaventure's commentary on the *Sentences*, Dante's commentary on his own poems goes far beyond line-by-line exposition to become an independent, encyclopedic display of learning.

What is the effect of employing the hierarchy of text and commentary in a vernacular work? One might suppose that the *auctoritas* of the whole work would be diminished: if the authority of the commentary derives from the authority of the text, and in place of Scripture or the *Sentences* Dante offers only contemporary Italian love-lyrics, the commentary might seem doubly trivial. The actual effect, however, is just the opposite. The textual hierarchy is not merely a map of the diffusion of authority—it is itself, through its association with Latin learning, an authoritative form. Albert Ascoli has shown that Dante's discussion of *autoritade* in *Convivio* 4 implies a claim to a personal, specifically literary authority;[49] the form of the entire work ratifies this claim. In glossing his own *canzoni*, Dante asserts that they deserve to be treated as authoritative texts. When he explains that he writes his commentary in Italian, rather than Latin, so that it may remain subordinate to the lyrics (1.5), he does not so much degrade the commentary as elevate the lyrics—and as the lyrics are elevated, so, paradoxically, is the commentary.

In its exegetical form, the *Convivio* resembles many other medieval commentaries, including commentaries on the author mentioned in the *Convivio*'s first sentence, "lo Filosofo," Aristotle. The model of Psalter commentary has a special relevance for the *Convivio*, however. The texts that Dante glosses are not prose treatises but lyric poems, and in this they resemble the Psalms. Medieval literary theory had no single term corresponding to our "lyric,"[50] but like lyrics in the root sense the Psalms were understood to have been originally sung, to the accompaniment of a kind of lyre known as the decachord or *psalterium*.[51]

In recent criticism of medieval literature, "lyric" is often opposed to "narrative,"[52] and according to this opposition the Psalms—as they are understood by medieval commentators—again qualify as lyric. The Psalms define themselves against the narrative of Old Testament history: they were written by David, and they allude to events in David's life,[53] but they do not themselves present historical events in narrative form. Thomas Aquinas distinguishes between several different "modes or forms" of writing in the Bible; the mode of the Psalter is "deprecativus vel lauditivus" [full of blame or praise], and it is distinct from the "narrativus," which "in historialibus libris invenitur" [narrative, which is found in the historical books].[54] According to Peter Lombard, the Psalter as a whole is not arranged according to the order of its composition or the order of the events it describes.[55] And the individual Psalm, though it may not contradict the historical sequence, does not primarily refer to that sequence.[56] The grammatical tenses that locate the Psalm in a historical moment are only part of their literal clothing; rightly understood, the Psalms are prophecies, referring to Christ and to all the truths of the Bible.[57] There is thus a qualitative difference between the temporality of the Psalms and the temporality of the historical books. One of the clearest statements of this idea comes from the eleventh-century Bruno the Carthusian: "Notandum vero est quod nimia sancti Spiritus agilitate, prophetae de futuris quasi de praesentibus et praeteritis loquuntur. Omne namque futurum Spiritui sancto praesens est, et quasi praeteritum notum" (*PL* 152.639) [It is indeed to be noted that, with the extraordinary agility of the Holy Spirit, prophets speak of future things as of present and past things. For every future thing is present to the Holy Spirit, and known as if it were past]. The Psalm represents a moment—literally a moment drawn from the narrative of David's life, and spiritually a moment outside of time.

In Latin the Psalms are evidently not metrical, but Peter Lombard notes that this is an effect of translation: the Psalms are "apud Hebraeos metrice scripti: quod in translatione servari non potuit" (*PL* 191.58) [written among the Jews in meter, which could not be preserved in translation]. On this ground Dante himself draws an analogy between the Psalms and the *canzoni* of the *Convivio*. The beauty of his *canzoni*, he says, is beyond the reach of readers who cannot read Italian, for all poetic "dolcezza e armonia" [sweetness and harmony] is lost in translation: "E questa è la cagione per che li versi del Salterio sono sanza dolcezza di musica e d'armonia; ché essi furono transmutati d'ebreo in greco e di greco in latino, e ne la prima transmutazione tutta quella dolcezza venne meno" (1.7.14–15) [And this is the reason why the verses of the Psalter are without the sweetness of music and harmony; for they were translated from Hebrew into Greek and from Greek into Latin, and in the first translation all their sweetness was lost].

How far should we extend the analogy between Dante's lyrics and the Psalms? One way to answer this question would be to consider the figure of the Psalmist. As a poet whose biography includes political power and political exile, saintly love of God and adulterous love for a woman, sin and repentance and prophecy, David is always a potential model for Dante. Teodolinda Barolini has argued that Dante implies a parallel between the Psalms, for which he coins the word "tëodia" (*Paradiso* 25.73) [divine song], and his own "poema sacro" (*Paradiso* 25.1) [divine poem], the *Commedia*.[58] And there are psalmic echoes in the *Vita Nuova*, perhaps most strikingly in the episode of mysterious inspiration in which Dante's "lingua parlò quasi come per sé stessa mossa" (19.2) [tongue spoke as if moved by itself].[59] Dante never entitles himself a *novus David*; it remained for Boccaccio to draw an explicit comparison between the two, in his life of Dante.[60] Yet Boccaccio refers to David not as Dante's poetic precursor but as an illustrious repentant sinner. Dante's analogy between the *canzoni* of the *Convivio* and "li versi del Salterio" (1.7.15) [the verses of the Psalter] is both more limited and more audacious than Boccaccio's typological biography: Dante matter-of-factly sets his own poetic work next to David's.

A. J. Minnis has traced the emergence of the human *auctor* by documenting the increasing exegetical interest in the life of David. This book will describe a transformation in the figure of the lover-poet, a progressive humanization: we pass from David, the prophetic King of Israel, to Troilus, the doomed prince of doomed Troy, by way of an inspired but fallible Florentine citizen. My central topic, however, is not the figure of the poet but rather a series of formal strategies for constructing books from lyric poems. I want to conclude this chapter by suggesting that the glossed Psalter offers not only a version of lyric authority but also a literary form with special advantages for the vernacular maker of a lyric book. To describe these special advantages, I shall compare the glossed Psalter to two other prestigious Latin forms that include lyrics but do not involve an exegetical structure: the Psalter without a gloss, and the *prosimetrum*.

The Psalter is itself a book made from lyrics. Peter Lombard insists on the unity of the *Liber psalmorum* (*PL* 191.58); although it contains one hundred and fifty separate pieces, that very number is a symbol of wholeness (*PL* 191.56–57). The book has a wholeness that might be called organic: its parts work together like the strings of the instrument called "psalterium" in Greek and in Latin "organum" (*PL* 191.55). The vernacular counterpart of this unitary form would be the lyric sequence—Petrarch's *Canzoniere* and the Renaissance sonnet sequences that follow. But the *Canzoniere*, as has often been observed, is itself a formal transformation of the *Vita Nuova*. Petrarch's ability to constitute his "fragmenta" as an authored book, rather than a merely scribal anthology, depends in part upon the existence of a prior Italian book that enfolds lyric poems within a continuous prose context.[61] To say this rather too simply, before poets could imitate the Psalter they had to imitate the glossed Psalter.

Another kind of book that contains lyric poems is the *prosimetrum*, the form of, for instance, Boethius's *Consolation of Philosophy* and Martianus Capella's *De nuptiis Philologiae et Mercurii*. The *Vita Nuova* has often been described as a *prosimetrum*, but the *Convivio* is clearly not one. The example of the *Convivio* suggests certain limitations of the *prosimetrum* form. In the *prosimetrum*, prose and verse alternate, but both are written by a single person treating a single body of material. As the *Consolation* commentary once attributed to Thomas Aquinas explains, Boethius combines two different *modi scribendi* to achieve a purely rhetorical effect:

> Boethius uses in this book both prose and meter . . . For just as a medicine that is bitter would be taken with more pleasure, if it were mixed with some sweetness, so the arguments of philosophy communicated in prose would be received from Boethius more willingly if they were sweetened with the pleasantness of meter. And for this reason Boethius now uses meter, now prose; since to use them in alternation is more delightful.[62]

In Peter Lombard's glossed Psalter, verse and prose are not two alternating modes of a single voice; instead, they proceed from different writers, writing at different times. Even in the *Convivio*, where the text and commentary explicitly share a single author, two different moments of writing are systematically juxtaposed. For the lyric poet seeking to produce an authoritative book, the text-commentary structure has two advantages over the *prosimetrum*. As I have argued, the textual hierarchy itself establishes a certain authority for the work; and the hierarchical disjunction between verse and prose allows the lyric to retain its specifically "lyric" qualities. The *Consolation* contains *metra*, but to the extent that these *metra* are part of a book they are highlighted passages within a larger utterance rather than individual, integral poems.[63] The Gloss on the Psalter shows how lyrics may be developed into a book without losing their identity as lyrics. By closely following the model of Latin commentary, Dante claims an *auctoritas* for the prose of the *Convivio* and an even higher *auctoritas* for the separate *canzoni* that give rise to the book, without needing to present the *canzoni* as anything other than vernacular lyrics.

The glossed Psalter, then, provides an authoritative model for the construction of a hierarchical structure around lyric poetry. And it may serve, as well, as a conceptual framework for describing the emergence of vernacular *auctoritas*. Earlier I used the form of the manuscript page as the starting-point for a schematic account of the Latin *auctor*'s emergence through a gradual series of substitutions of commentary for text. In the domain of vernacular literature, a number of different works repeat the same daring substitution: a vernacular poem is installed in the place of the *textus*. Boccaccio's gloss to the *Teseida*, discussed in the Introduction, provides an interesting case. Boccaccio refers to Virgil once (6.53 gloss), and often mentions the classical poets as a group—"i poeti"—but he cites only one literary text by name: "la canzone di Guido Cavalcanti *Donna mi priega, etc.*, e le chiose che sopra vi fece Maestro Dino del Garbo" (7.50 gloss, p. 464) [the *canzone* of Guido Cavalcanti, "Donne mi prega," and the glosses that Master Dino del Garbo made upon it]. Here we can see two mutually confirming instances of authorization-by-gloss, one nested inside the other: Dino del Garbo's Latin commentary contributes to the authority of Guido Cavalcanti's Italian lyric—helps to make it worthy of citation among the *poeti*—and this emphasis on the importance of commentary adds to the authorizing power of Boccaccio's own marginal gloss.

A catalogue of the commentaries attached to vernacular texts might reveal an irregular progression in the boldness of the claim to authority. For the works of Dante, the progression is rather regular: the *Vita Nuova* gestures towards Latin commentary as one model among several; the *Convivio* offers a confident, vernacular *expositio textus*; for the *Divine Comedy*, the "Letter to Can Grande" borrows another learned exegetical form, the *accessus*, imitated this time *in* Latin. The "Letter to Can Grande" is probably by Dante himself, but other readers continue the sequence for the *Divine Comedy*: the first public lectures on a vernacular poem were Boccaccio's lectures on Dante in 1373, and these lectures, along with numerous full-length humanist commentaries, helped to establish the *Divine Comedy* as a modern classic.

The chapters that follow describe a more complex, and perhaps less exemplary, line of development. The *Vita Nuova* opens the possibility of a scholastic commentary for vernacular lyric poetry. The *Convivio*, unfinished though it is, develops the full implications of this possibility, but my own argument turns instead to Boccaccio's *Filostrato*, which responds to the *Vita Nuova* by emphatically refusing any hierarchy of text and commentary, collapsing Dante's multilevel structure to produce a single authorial discourse. Chaucer's *Troilus* begins by restoring a hierarchy of lyric poetry and narrative explication, but then enacts its own drama of form, staging a tragic collapse of structure. C. S. Lewis's claim that Chaucer "medievalizes" the *Filostrato* implies a certain reversibility in the direction of history, and I take this implication seriously: I shall argue that the *Filostrato* is a more forward-looking work than *Troilus and Criseyde*. Yet by committing itself to the reverses of history, the compromises and mediations inherent in literary adaptation, the *Troilus* defines a mode of self-critical authorship that doubles back upon, and moves beyond, the radical simplifications of the *Filostrato*.

2. Dante's Divisions: Structures of Authority in the *Vita Nuova*

1. Chapter Three

The *Vita Nuova* is a book that looks beyond its boundaries. The first chapter evokes a pre-existent book, the "libro de la mia memoria" (1.1) [book of my memory], and a rubric in that book "dinanzi a la quale poco si potrebbe leggere" (1.1) [before which little could be read]; the final chapter predicts a period of silence and a text that cannot yet be written. Beginning in recollection and ending in anticipation, the *Vita Nuova* defines itself as a decisive episode in a larger narrative it cannot fully specify. In fact, there are several narratives in which the *Vita Nuova* marks a turning point; these narratives include the life of Dante, Italian literary history, and the story of the founding of modern authorship. At the same time, the *Vita Nuova* is emphatically a "libello" (1.1 and passim)—a little book, a self-contained textual universe.

The familiar contrast between open-ended temporality and fixed form resounds in unexpected ways within the *Vita Nuova*. The book brings together several kinds of writing, and its two most prominent components are a continuing autobiographical narrative and a series of finished lyric poems. These two elements suggest, in turn, two distinct ways of reading the entire book. As Domenico De Robertis writes,

> la "forma del libro" . . . è una narrazione inframezzata di poesie o, se si vuole, poesie accompagnate, illustrate, commentate . . . dalla prosa . . .[1]
>
> [the "form of the book" is a narration with poems interpolated or, if one prefers, poems accompanied, illustrated, commented upon by the prose]

This is an elementary observation, but it offers a choice between two different formal hierarchies. The *Vita Nuova* is a work that subjects discrete lyric poems to a governing narrative, breaching their separateness—or else, "if one prefers," it is a work that employs Dante's life as secondary matter in a lyric anthology. It might seem that this is merely a question of emphasis, a matter to be resolved by some extratextual preference. In the reception history of the *Vita Nuova*, for example, we can make out a shift from one reading toward the other: early readers, such as Boccaccio, tend to treat the *libello* as a "compilation" of lyrics,[2] and Dante's prose emerges as an object of critical interest only in this century.[3] In any case, both of the readings suggested by De Robertis are logically tenable: either verse or prose might be construed as the center of the *Vita Nuova*'s textual hierarchy.

But a textual hierarchy is a kind of power structure; in the *Vita Nuova*, decisions about literary form have profound consequences. The choice that De Robertis offers, almost in passing, is not merely a choice between neutral, external descriptions. Within Dante's text the "form of the book" is raised as a fundamental problem, deeply connected to issues of authority, temporality, love, and knowledge. In this chapter I shall explore the relationship of the *libello*'s two primary textual components, lyric poetry and narrative prose; I shall argue that this relationship is complex and dynamic, and that it is decisively shaped by a marginal third component, the *divisioni*.

The basic ambiguity of the *Vita Nuova*'s prose/verse structure has attracted little critical comment. Yet I would suggest that the modern criticism has conducted an unacknowledged debate over the relative centrality of lyric and narrative modes in the *libello*, thus playing out a dialectic that begins in the text's own self-division. As a token demonstration of this claim, I shall mention here two recent studies that respond, in different ways, to Charles S. Singleton's 1949 *Essay on the Vita Nuova*. In *The Body of Beatrice*, Robert Pogue Harrison argues that Dante moves from lyric *to* narrative; the two modes are two successive stages, and so the text itself is essentially a narrative, a narrative that culminates in narrative.[4] This story of progress is told with great eloquence and subtlety; what remains unstated is its analogy to Harrison's own critique of Singleton's *Essay*. Harrison begins his book by dissenting from Singleton's "theologizing and artifactualizing approach" (3). Singleton, he writes, imposes a "totalizing framework" (5) upon the *libello*, in which the linear narrative of Dante's life is tied into a neat "circle of intelligibility" (6); in claiming to break out of this enormously influential "Singletonian paradigm" (4), Harrison draws an implicit parallel between his own critical project and Dante's escape from the "lyric circle of incorporation" (44). (Harrison does not associate Singleton's reading with the lyric form that Dante learns to transcend, but Singleton does in fact place the poems at the center of the *libello*, as we shall see.) Meanwhile, Singleton's description of the text as a circular totality has been defended and amplified in Robert M. Durling and Ronald L. Martinez's *Time and the Crystal*, a study of Dante's *rime petrose* that begins with an important chapter on the *Vita Nuova*. Durling and Martinez find a Neoplatonic cosmos in the *libello*, in an analysis that focuses, significantly, on a single *canzone* and its non-narrative prose accompaniment;[5] in effect they provide a circular, lyric alternative to Harrison's linear, narrative *Vita Nuova*.

I shall return to all three of these critical readings, and to the large question of the *kind* of totality created by Dante's little book. I want to begin exploring the form of the *Vita Nuova*, however, by considering the form of one brief passage: the first chapter containing a poem, Chapter 3. Chapter 3 plays a special role in defining the relationship of prose and verse in the text, yet it is in crucial ways uncharacteristic of the *Vita Nuova*.

Chapter 3 describes a series of events in Dante's life: he encounters Beatrice by chance on the street, returns to his room and dreams a marvelous dream, writes a poem about the dream addressed to the "famosi trovatori" (3.9) [famous poets] of his day, and receives a number of responses to this poem, including one from Guido Cavalcanti, who will become the first of Dante's friends. These events are recounted in prose, but the chapter also includes the text of the poem that Dante says he wrote, a sonnet beginning "A ciascun'alma presa":

A ciascun'alma presa e gentil core
 nel cui cospetto ven lo dir presente,
 in ciò che mi rescrivan suo parvente,
 salute in lor segnor, cioè Amore.
Già eran quasi che atterzate l'ore
 del tempo che onne stella n'è lucente,
 quando m'apparve Amor subitamente,
 cui essenza membrar mi dà orrore.
Allegro mi sembrava Amor tenendo
 meo core in mano, e ne le braccia avea
 madonna involta in un drappo dormendo.
 Poi la svegliava, e d'esto core ardendo
 lei paventosa umilmente pascea:
 appresso gir lo ne vedea piangendo. (3.10–12)

[To every captive soul and noble heart
into whose sight comes this present speech,
so that they may write back to me how it seems to them,
greetings in their lord, namely Love.
Already divided in thirds were the hours
of the time when every star is shining,
when Love appeared to me suddenly,
the memory of whose being fills me with horror.
Love seemed joyful to me, holding
my heart in his hand, and in his arms he had
a lady wrapped in a cloth, sleeping.
Then he woke her, and of this burning heart
the fearful lady he humbly fed:
then I saw him leave, weeping.]

There is a certain redundancy in the conjunction of prose and verse in Chapter 3. The text of the sonnet is not strictly necessary for the sense of the narrative; it may serve as evidence or illustration, but the story requires only the statement that a sonnet was written. On the other hand, the sonnet makes sense by itself, and renders a good deal of the prose narrative unnecessary. The chapter seems to be made up of two distinct texts, either one of which could stand alone.

If the two texts are similar in represented content, they are nonetheless different, and the difference is a difference in form. The juxtaposition establishes an opposition between two modes of writing: the mechanical distinction between prose and verse is recast as a contrast between "narrative" and "lyric." These terms must be supplied by a modern reader, and they may seem forced in the context of Chapter 3, however well they apply to other parts of the *Vita Nuova*. "A ciascun'alma presa," taken by itself, would hardly be called non-narrative, since its last ten lines recount the events of a dream in straight chronological order. But I think the terms are useful—if they are understood to represent not essential qualities but a differential pair, each term defining itself against the other. It is the sonnet's *difference* from its prose counterpart that qualifies it as non-narrative, as lyric.

The pairing of "narrative" and "lyric" has many possible connotations, but the close correspondence between prose and verse in Chapter 3 (unusual for the *Vita Nuova*) has the effect of severely limiting such connotations. The prose text and the verse text form what is called in linguistics a "minimal pair," foregrounding one salient contrast: a contrast, I believe, between two ways of treating time. Although the sonnet recounts most of the prose dream, there are several striking omissions—notably at the beginning and the end. The sonnet doesn't mention the "nebula di colore di fuoco" (3.3) [cloud the color of fire] from which Amore appears, or his opening words in Latin, "Ego dominus tuus" (3.3) [I am your lord]; it omits the direction of Amore's final departure with Beatrice, "verso lo cielo" (3.7) [toward the sky or heaven]. One effect of these omissions is to define the sonnet's account of the dream as a limited passage within a longer narrative. When we turn again from the poem to the prose, we notice that the dream extends further in both directions, and indeed that the story of the dream extends beyond the dream's boundaries, both back to the encounter that seemed to cause the dream and forward to the beginning of a new friendship as a distant consequence of the dream. We are reminded forcefully of the fixed frame of the quatorzaine, and of the capacity of prose to be continued indefinitely.[6]

The sonnet does not entirely erase the narrative context, however; it collapses and incorporates a part of the larger story. In the prose, the dream is followed by the writing of a poem and the appearance of responses from other poets. The sonnet lays out the dream in chronological order, but it also implies the two later events in its first quatrain, which calls attention to the poem's existence as a text and asks for responses. The dream is still, of course, an event prior to the writing and the reading of the poem, but it is no longer (as in the prose) *mentioned* first. The sonnet's opening complicates the temporal position of the sonnet as a whole: the words on the page are "present" both to the poet who writes them and to the other poets who will later read them; an implicit future audience of troubadours, pens poised to write, attends upon the past-tense account of the dream.

Narrative and lyric in Chapter 3 are not merely two different styles or attitudes; they are two different modes of textual existence. Both prose account and lyric poem define themselves as reflections of a pre-existent reality, a series of events. But they respond to the series in two distinct ways. The prose mimes the temporality of its object: it patterns its own discursive sequence upon the unfolding of history. The sonnet implies a temporal order without adopting this order as its own: it locates itself in a complex, self-defining moment of utterance. Paul Zumthor has described a related phenomenon in connection with the "grand chant courtois": he writes that the *trouvère* lyric typically dismantles the structures of narrative, to the point that they are thoroughly deconstructed ("dé-construits") and narrativity itself becomes purely virtual.[7] "A ciascun' alma presa" does something significantly different: it preserves events from the prose but moves later events to the beginning of the text, reshaping the narrative line to form a circle. The structuring principle of the sonnet is not the temporality of the world but rather, apparently, the "arte del dire parole per rima" (3.9) [art of speaking words in verse] that the young Dante has taught himself.[8]

The two texts that make up Chapter 3 thus face each other across an ontological divide: they derive their being from a single extratextual reality in two contrasting ways. They do face each other, however, and even mirror each other. They are linked by more than the common ground of their dramatic material, the overlapping of content that highlights their formal divergence. Beyond this shared affiliation, there are verbal echoes that imply a specularity between the two texts. The double use of "cominciare" [begin] in the sentence that introduces the sonnet—"cominciai allora questo sonetto, lo quale comincia . . ." (3.9) [I then began this sonnet, which begins . . .]—balances two very different kinds of beginning, the unrepeatable beginning of an event in a life and the perpetual beginning of line 1 of a poem. And Dante seems to suggest a spurious etymology when he wakes from his "deboletto sonno" (3.7) [feeble sleep], considers "ciò che io avea nel mio sonno veduto" (3.9) [that which I had seen in my sleep], and writes a "sonetto" (3.9) [sonnet]—as though *sonnet* meant *little sleep*. Indeed, there is a kind of parallel between the poetic form of a sonnet and the experienced form of a dream. If this sonnet happens to be an unusually narrative lyric, the dream in the prose account—a framed vision, located in the temporality of daily life but taking its own separate time—might be called a prose lyric.

I have pulled apart Chapter 3, discussing the sonnet and the prose narrative as separate texts in order to describe the complex relationships that the chapter creates. What is the structure that holds these two texts together? The obvious answer, I suppose, is that the lyric is contained within the prose narrative. And not merely spatially: from the perspective of the prose, the lyric is an object caught up in a story, a material text less important for its content than for its functional value. One might even speak of its *exchange* value: it stands in for a dream, and is replaced in turn by the alternative accounts of the dream offered by other poets, thus serving to mediate between a private erotic vision and an entrance into a poetic fraternity. But the perspective of the prose is not the only perspective. If we begin with the sonnet, and from this vantage point look around, it appears that the larger narrative is in fact contained by the sonnet. The sonnet is "lo dir presente" (3.10). This "present speech" refers to other *less* present language; it invites written judgments or interpretations from other poets, and in making the invitation it contains these new writings within its own referential domain. The later rewriting by Dante himself, the prose account in Chapter 3, is likewise contained in advance. The relationship of prose to verse in Chapter 3 goes beyond similarity and difference to a more active engagement: the two texts mirror each other, though they are separated by contrasting modes of existence, and each incorporates the other.

The verb "incorporate" brings us, at last, to the events that are represented in both prose and verse. The dream features an act of literal incorporation: Beatrice is made to eat a burning object that Amore says is the dreamer's heart. Yet Beatrice is herself enveloped: in a red cloth, in Amore's arms, in a cloud of flame, in the dream. The incorporation is mutual. Amore enforces reciprocity by bringing Beatrice into Dante's sleep and bringing his heart to her mouth.

We are so accustomed to thinking of Beatrice as the object of Dante's one-sided amorous gaze that it is surprising, I think, to imagine reciprocity between the two. Chapter 3 must be granted its own fantasy, however; it is not merely a microcosm of the *Vita Nuova*. Critics have rarely treated the chapter as an independent passage;[9] they have not commented upon the mutual incorporation fantasized in the dream, or pointed out certain ways in which Dante and Beatrice mirror each other. The chapter includes two greetings: on the street, Beatrice "mi salutoe molto virtuosamente, tanto che me parve allora tutti li termini de la beatitudine" (3.1) [greeted me with such a power that the entire extent of bliss appeared to me then], and Dante in turn offers his audience of love-poets "salute in lor segnor, cioè Amore" (3.10) [greetings in their lord, namely Love]. These two greetings frame the event that is central to both prose and verse, the dream, and here Dante and Beatrice—for all their many differences—find themselves in rather similar positions.

Both Dante and Beatrice are asleep; both are rudely awakened, and the same verb, "disvegliare," is used in both instances (3.6, 3.7). This similarity is underscored by imagery that evokes, as Barbara Nolan has shown, the prophetic books of the Old Testament. Several aspects of the dream, beginning with the appearance of a figure in a cloud the color of fire, suggest that Dante is in the position of an Ezechiel receiving a vision. But Nolan also notes that the reluctant consumption of the burning heart is like the reluctant eating of a book in the visions of Ezechiel and John. In this analogy, Beatrice is the one who receives revelation.[10] In the fantasy of the passage, Dante and Beatrice are revelations to each other; as Beatrice consumes the book of Dante's heart, she becomes the heart of his book.

I am suggesting that the relationship between prose and verse in Chapter 3 is analogous to the relationship between Dante and Beatrice. Like the two texts, the two human characters mirror each other and incorporate each other. To complete the analogy, all that remains to be specified is the ontological divide that separates Dante and Beatrice. If the two are segregated by social convention in the episode of the greeting, in the episode of the "maravigliosa visione" (3.3) [miraculous vision] it is clear that they *exist* in very different ways. Beatrice is a figure within a dream. Dante is a figure within the same dream, but he is also the dreamer, and the writer who transcribes the experience retrospectively.[11] The Dante who mirrors Beatrice is not the figure of Dante in the dream (as would happen if, for instance, the vision showed the two exchanging hearts) but rather the Dante who dreams. Both Beatrice and Dante are violently awakened, but Beatrice sleeps and wakes within the vision, while Dante, sleeping in actuality, dreams the vision from which he awakes. The mutual embrace imagined in Chapter 3 must bridge a chasm.

2. Models for the *Vita Nuova*

Critics tend to treat the *Vita Nuova* as a fascinating totality, as a formal puzzle. The same *lectura Dantis* that wanders at will through the *Divine Comedy*, glossing images and ideas along the way, stands back from the *Vita Nuova* and attempts to solve the whole work at once. When Charles S. Singleton speaks of "the reader of the *Vita Nuova* who is seeking to grasp *the* principle of its unity and *the* secret of its form"[12]—my emphasis—he could be describing most of its modern professional readers.[13]

The *Vita Nuova* itself encourages this interpretive effort, not merely by *being* a puzzling form, but by describing itself as such. Consider, for example, a famous crux from the chapter that announces Beatrice's death. Dante offers three reasons for refusing to describe the event; the first is "che ciò non è del presente proposito, se volemo guardare nel proemio che precede questo libello" (28.2) [that this is not part of the present plan, if we wish to look at the proem that precedes this little book]. Generations of readers have dutifully turned back to the first chapter to find the statement of intention that would rule out an account of what is arguably the central event of the book. But such a statement is not easy to find there.[14] Critical efforts to gloss the proem so as to accommodate the later statement have yielded contradictory and inconclusive results.[15] I would compare this interpretive impasse to another authorial intervention at another Dantean threshold, the gates of Dis:

> O voi ch'avete li 'ntelletti sani,
> mirate la dottrina che s'asconde
> sotto 'l velame de li versi strani. (*Inferno* 9.61–63)

> [O you who have sound understanding,
> mark the doctrine that is hidden
> under the veil of the strange verses.][16]

John Freccero has called this passage "something of a scandal," since the hidden doctrine has in fact remained well-hidden. He argues that Dante means to direct our attention to the very *act* of looking; what matters is not a particular hidden truth, but the process, a process of conversion, that would lead to Truth.[17] Similarly, the "prima ragione" [first reason] of *Vita Nuova* 28 confidently asserts that a particular question can be answered by merely looking, yet the answer may matter less than the act of looking and the form of the question.

The two passages convey very different assumptions about the texts that contain them and about the proper way of reading these texts. One passage speaks of "versi strani" [strange verses]—perhaps a variant of *alieniloquium*, the standard etymology of *allegoria*—that form a concealing veil to be pierced by wise readers. The exact referent of "versi strani" is not clear: possibly the entire *Divine Comedy* or all of *Inferno*, but more likely some segment of Canto 9, with the implication that different strategies of reading are required for different parts of the text. In this poem some verses are exceptionally strange, exceptionally freighted with alienated *dottrina*.[18] The other passage, in contrast, refers to a *libello*: the text here is a single, manageable object. This *libello*, moreover, is consistent and unified, governed throughout by a single "proposito" [plan]—a "proposito" that is not only "presente" to the whole text but also plainly announced in the rhetorically correct place, the proem, for anyone who will look there. It is striking, though, that the *proposito* is made the object of a hermeneutic quest, however trivial that quest is supposed to be. Where the reader of the *Inferno* is instructed to find *dottrina*, not only for the sake of reading *Inferno* but presumably also for *dottrina*'s own sake, the reader of the *Vita Nuova* is encouraged to uncover the rules of the game, the principles of exclusion and inclusion for the *Vita Nuova* itself. The critic who tries to solve the *libello* is responding to a challenge laid down by Dante.

The solutions proposed are usually models for the work. Two senses of "model" are relevant: "model" as theoretical explanatory structure and "model" as particular historical exemplar. In *Vita Nuova* criticism it is difficult to maintain the distinction between the two types of model, because the effort to describe the form of the work often proceeds as a search for sources.

Pio Rajna realized, at the turn of the century, that a single exemplar would not suffice. In 1890 he argued that Dante found his essential "schema"—the alternation of lyric poems with explanatory narrative prose—in Provençal *chansonniers* that included prose *vidas* and *razos*.[19] In 1902 he turned to the inessential remainder of the text, the *divisioni*; in what has remained almost the last word on the subject, he stated that these derive from Thomas Aquinas's commentaries on Aristotle and from Scholastic writing and pedagogy in general.[20]

Rajna concludes:

> Let us now briefly turn our attention to the overall plan of the *Vita Nuova*. Its two constitutive elements derive from quite opposite origins. One comes from minstrelsy, from courts, from celebrations: the other from the world of the learned, from the cold halls of the schools, from the austere life. But all is reconciled within the mind of Dante, all produces harmony.[21]

Rajna's account of the *Vita Nuova* as a fusion of divergent "worlds," a unitary form constituted within a contradictory plurality, has set the tone, I think, for subsequent formal analysis. Critics who attempt to read the work strictly on its own terms, without reference to Dante's sources, tend to describe its structure as a set of overlaid structures: "poetic structures and prose structures,"[22] or "the overlapping of two perspectives,"[23] or again "a deep adversity of paradigms."[24] More commonly, a plurality of theoretical models is described in terms of a plurality of historical models—models not merely juxtaposed but interwoven or superimposed, co-present throughout the "overall plan" of the work. Where the *Divine Comedy* seems to journey between different modes, styles, and genres, the *Vita Nuova* is of a piece throughout, "a work born all at once,"[25] yet it must be understood as a "gathering and concentration of models."[26] By consensus, diverse

LORETTE WILMOT LIBRARY
NAZARETH COLLEGE

models—in both senses, theoretical and historical—coexist in the work from beginning to end.

The dynamics of this coexistence have remained relatively unexamined: the syncretic economy of the text (or of Dante's harmonizing mind) has been more appreciated than analyzed. Critical effort has concentrated on revising and extending the list of "constitutive elements." A dizzying array of texts and traditions has been said to contribute to the formation of the entire *Vita Nuova*. Besides the Provençal *vidas* and *razos*[27] and the Scholastic *divisio textus*[28] proposed by Rajna, these models include the *Consolation of Philosophy*;[29] the *Consolation of Philosophy* with a thirteenth-century gloss;[30] the *prosimetrum* as a classical genre[31] or as a medieval school exercise;[32] medieval commentaries on the Bible and the pagan *auctores*;[33] Augustine's *Confessions*;[34] "the arts of memory described in classical and medieval rhetorics, the literary idiom of Cavalcanti, and the apocalyptic prophecies of Sacred Scripture";[35] Cicero's *De Amicitia*, Brunetto Latini's *Rettorica*, the *De Amore* of Andreas Capellanus, and the Book of Psalms;[36] "sonnet narratives" by Guittone and possibly (the *Fiore*) the younger Dante;[37] Provençal single-author lyric collections;[38] Bonaventure's *Itinerarium Mentis ad Deum*;[39] Franciscan hagiography;[40] the Catholic liturgy;[41] medieval church architecture.[42]

In my discussion of *Vita Nuova* 3, I have proposed one more model for the form of the *libello*. My model is drawn from a strange world indeed: the world represented within the *libello* itself. I have argued that the relationship between prose and verse is presented as a formal analogue to the human relationship between Dante and Beatrice. I believe that this analogy is maintained throughout the work. The prose narrative is circumstantial and temporal, divided unevenly into stages to match the twists and turns in Dante's life. It is Dante who repeatedly changes: the adjective "nuovo" [new] is most often applied to the various desires, mental and physical states, and poetic projects through which he passes.[43] The prose has a past and a future, both within the book and beyond its boundaries; this past and future are Dante's. Beatrice has no real story. She herself is (like the last poem in the *Vita Nuova* [41.1]) a "cosa nova" (19.11) [new thing],[44] but she does not change. In dying, and thereby entering a "secol novo" (31.15) [new world], she only becomes more fully herself; her newness, like that of the biblical "canticum novum" [new song], will not become old. Likewise the poems exist as fixed and self-contained creations, transcendent and atemporal.[45]

This proposal, however, complicates as much as it explicates. The other models that have been suggested for the *Vita Nuova* attempt to clarify a puzzling form by mapping it onto other, prior forms. My internal model, in contrast, plays one aspect of the work against another. One can propose an analogy between two relationships (prose is to verse as Dante to Beatrice) without specifying the structure of either relationship. The formal question I posed earlier, "is this a narrative with poetic interpolations or a lyric collection with prose commentary?" is merely rephrased as a thematic question: "is this the story of a time in Dante's life or a celebration of Beatrice's eternal virtue?" And since the relationship of Dante to Beatrice changes in the course of the story, my proposal implies that the form of the *libello* is itself subject to change. We may be dealing not with a single total structure but with a series of possible structures projected successively by the text.

Chapter 3 imagines one structure for the relationship between prose and verse, Dante and Beatrice. Prose and verse are absolutely distinct, yet they mirror and embrace each other. They are not simply equal partners, since it is clear that one is subordinated to the other, but the direction of subordination is unclear. At this point, the two basic models described by De Robertis seem equally valid: in Chapter 3 the prose narrative supplements, and is supplemented by, the poem. The power structure of the human relationship is similarly ambiguous: dreaming, Dante objectifies and strips Beatrice so that he can imagine being, to her, a naked object, "una cosa la quale ardesse tutta" (3.5) [a thing entirely burning]. This is a relationship of reciprocal subjection, reciprocal desire.

Chapter 3 is unique in the *Vita Nuova*, however, precisely in its vision of reciprocity. Dante will, of course, continue to observe and imagine and describe Beatrice throughout the *Vita Nuova*—but never again will we see so clearly the lover's fantasy of being an object to his beloved. And Beatrice will never again play the role she plays in Chapter 3. If her reluctant consumption of Dante's burning heart in the dream stands out as an unusual moment in the *libello*, it is in fact no more unusual than the greeting that gives rise to the dream. Never again will Beatrice take a positive action toward Dante, even a positive action as mild as acknowledging him on the street. She will *appear*, above all, in public places, and of course her appearance will have miraculous effects on all who see her; in addition she will deny Dante her greeting, laugh at him, weep for her dead father, and die. After Chapter 3, Dante's investment in Beatrice seems to be precisely an investment in one who will look upward rather than back; this redirection of her gaze allows her to function as a divine mediatrix.

This shift in the personal relationship has its formal counterpart. In discussing Chapter 3, I have laid stress upon the sonnet's reference to future rewritings of the events it describes ("in ciò che mi rescrivan suo parvente" [3.10; so that they may write back to me how it seems to them]). After Chapter 3, no poem will refer to the possibility of other writing. In the *Vita Nuova* as a whole, the prose directs its interpretive and admiring gaze toward the poems, but the poems do not know that the prose exists. A hierarchy is installed in the text.

For a picture of this hierarchy, as staged in a Florentine church, we might turn to Chapter 5:

> Uno giorno avvenne che questa gentilissima sedea in parte ove s'udiano parole de la regina de la gloria, ed io era in luogo dal quale vedea la mia beatitudine; e nel mezzo di lei e di me per la retta linea sedea una gentile donna di molto piacevole aspetto, la quale mi mirava spesse volte, maravigliandosi del mio sguardare, che parea che sopra lei terminasse. Onde molti s'accorsero de lo suo mirare; e in tanto vi fue posto mente, che, partendomi da questo luogo, mi sentio dicere appresso di me: "Vedi come cotale donna distrugge la persona di costui"; e nominandola, io intesi che dicea di colei che mezzo era stata ne la linea retta che movea da la gentilissima Beatrice e terminava ne li occhi miei. (5.1–2)

> [One day it happened that this most gracious lady was sitting in a place where words about the Queen of Glory were heard, and I was in a position from which I saw my bliss; and halfway between her and me, along a straight line, sat a gentlewoman of very pleasing appearance, who looked at me many times, marveling at my gaze, which seemed to end with her. And many noticed her looking, and such a thought came to them that, as I left this place, I heard someone say behind me: "See how that lady ruins his appearance"; and when she was named I understood that the lady mentioned was the one who had been halfway along the straight line that began from the most gracious Beatrice and ended in my eyes.]

Dante here hits upon the stratagem of using a screen-lady to write about Beatrice without seeming to, and the screen-lady's status as a medium or means, a *mezzo*, is literalized in the emphatic geometry of the scene: the screen-lady is the midpoint, the "mezzo," in the straight line drawn from Beatrice to Dante's eyes. The line continues figuratively in both directions. Beatrice herself is attending to words about the Virgin, the mediatrix who in turn looks directly upon God. In the other direction, there are the "many" who observe Dante and the *donna dello schermo*. Because this chain of gazes involves mediation, it allows misrecognition: the crowd mistakes the object of Dante's gaze, and Dante himself does not yet realize the extent to which he loves Christ in Beatrice. But the direction of the gaze is unmistakeable; the spatial plotting defines a hierarchy.

I locate the first sign of a textual hierarchy even earlier, however: in the very chapter that envisioned reciprocity. In describing Chapter 3 as a complex balance of two primary texts, I ignored one brief passage. This passage introduces a third mode of writing, a marginal textual component that is, I shall argue, decisive for the relationship of the central dyad.

> Questo sonetto si divide in due parti; che ne la prima parte saluto e domando risponsione, ne la seconda significo a che si dee rispondere. La seconda parte comincia quivi: *Già eran*. (3.13)

> [This sonnet is divided in two parts; for in the first part I offer a greeting and ask for a response, in the second I indicate what it is that requires a response. The second part begins here: *Already were*.]

3. The *Divisioni* and the *Divisio Psalmi*

The *divisioni* in the *Vita Nuova* have never been popular with editors or critics. Antonio D'Andrea opens a historical review with this observation, and concludes even more strongly: despite a few scattered insights in the criticism, "it can be said that the *Vita Nuova* continues to be read as if the divisions did not exist."[46] The work's first editor was Boccaccio, who literally relegated the divisions to the margins of his important early copy. This emendation accounts for the most important set of variations in the manuscript tradition: in the large family of manuscripts derived from Boccaccio's, some follow the new arrangement, others omit the *divisioni* entirely, and still others clumsily reintegrate them into the text. In the nineteenth-century editions the *divisioni* are marginalized or italicized if they appear at all. The manuscript situation was not understood until Michele Barbi's 1907 critical edition, which placed the *divisioni* firmly in the text—where they could still, of course, be all but ignored.[47]

Boccaccio defended his quite deliberate deviation from authorial intention in a marginal comment of his own—perhaps the first modern editor's note. His argument, though it may have encouraged a simple devaluation of the *divisioni*, is subtle. Of the two reasons given, the first associates the scribal *mise en page* with a structure of subordination. Boccaccio does not erase or banish the *divisioni*, but rather puts them in their proper place.[48] I quote from the beginning:

> Maraviglierannosi molti, per quello ch'io advisi, perchè io le divisioni de' sonetti non ho nel testo poste, come l'autore del presente libretto le puose; ma a ciò rispondo due essere state le cagioni. La prima, per ciò che le divisioni de' sonetti manifestamente sono dichiarazioni di quegli: per che più tosto chiosa appaiono dovere essere che testo; e però chiosa l'ho poste, non testo, non stando l'uno con l'altre bene mescolato.[49]

> [Many will be astonished, I think, that I have not placed the divisions of the sonnets into the text, as the author of the present little book did; but to this I answer that my reasons have been two. The first is that the divisions of the sonnets are clearly declarations of them: so that they appear to be gloss rather than text; and thus I have placed them as gloss, not as text, since one is not properly mixed together with the other.]

Because the divisions are devoted to explication, they are commentary, and commentary should not mix with text. The clear opposition between commentary and text is immediately complicated by a possible objection.

> Se qui forse dicesse alcuno—e le teme de' sonetti e canzoni scritte da lui similmente si potrebbero dire chiosa, con ciò sia cosa che esse sieno non minore dichiarazione di quegli che le divisioni—, dico che, quantunque sieno dichiarazioni, non sono dichiarazioni per dichiarare, ma dimostrazioni delle cagioni che a fare lo 'ndussero i sonetti e le canzoni. E appare ancora queste dimostrazioni essere dello intento principale; per che meritamente testo sono, e non chiose.

> [If at this point someone were to say, "the explications of the sonnets and the *canzoni* he wrote could similarly be called glosses, in that they are no less declarations of them than are the divisions," I say that, insofar as they are declarations, they are not declarations made to declare, but expositions of the reasons that led him to write the sonnets and *canzoni*. And these expositions still seem to belong to the principal intention; so that they are deservedly text, and not gloss.]

Boccaccio appears to privilege the poems as the focus of the book; he is content to describe the narrative prose as "le teme de' sonetti e canzoni" [the explications of the sonnets and *canzoni*].[50] At the same time, however, he recognizes that the relation of narrative to lyrics is not a simple subordination. The prose narrative does indeed explicate the poems, as much as the divisions do, but it is only a gloss *per accidentiam*: its true responsibility is not to the lyric texts but to the extratextual *cagioni* that prompted the writing of those texts. Thus it is "deservedly text, and not gloss." Boccaccio's copy does not mix text with gloss; clearly, however, it does mix two very different kinds of text, poems caused by certain events in Dante's life and prose that recounts those events.[51] For Boccaccio, the relationship of narrative and lyric is open to discussion; the *divisioni* are unambiguously glosses.

The *divisioni* are indeed marginal to the *Vita Nuova*. The site of the margin varies, however, according to the way the work as a whole is mapped. If the *libello* is (in De Robertis's phrase[52]) "una narrazione inframezzata di poesie" [a narration with poems interpolated], the *divisioni* are certainly not part of the narrative; they must have entered the work along with the lyric interpolations. On the other hand, if the book consists of "poesie accompagnate, illustrate, commentate . . . dalla prosa" [poems accompanied, illustrated, commented upon by the prose], then the *divisioni* must belong with the book's supplementary prose. In De Robertis's phrasing the slippage between "*narrazione*"/"poesie" and "poesie"/"*prosa*" is scrupulous. The choice between the two descriptions is not merely a choice between two ways of disposing two stable elements: the line between the two parts of the text shifts, and according to either reading of the book's structure the *divisioni* belong to the part that is added.

This suggests that the *divisioni*, marginal as they are, have a special role to play in the structure of the *libello*. Twice marginal, they function as a sort of hinge between narrative prose and lyric poetry. It is not just that they represent an overlapping of the two primary components of the work—though textually they amount to a grafting of words from the lyrics (the incipits) into the present-tense discourse of the retrospective writer. Nor are they simply an excluded third type of writing—though they are indeed non-narrative and non-poetic. Rather, the *divisioni* belong to whichever half of the work is described as supplementary. If the *divisioni* represent the most intimate contact of prose and verse—the most direct expansion of the verse into prose, the most focused examination of the verse by the prose—they also link the two textual elements by serving as a shifting bar between them.[53]

The *divisioni* do seem mechanical—formulaic in style and literal-minded in method. Still, even as pure *techne*, the *divisioni* contribute to the meaning of the work.[54] If they stand outside its philosophical exploration and its psychological drama, they nonetheless contribute significantly to its structure—or to the problem of its structure. Even if they are *merely* structural, a sort of complex floating hinge or internal scaffolding, my argument has been that the *Vita Nuova* charges merely structural questions with thematic weight.

We have already seen, however, that the *divisioni* are more than a colorless, *ad hoc* apparatus: they carry connotations of their own. As Rajna first observed, they summon up a world of associations, deriving as they do "from the world of the learned, from the cold halls of the schools, from the austere life."[55] (In the more pejorative words of another scholar, they bring with them "the harsh rod of the schoolmaster."[56]) But it is not enough to view the *divisioni* all at once, as so much quaint machinery; like any texts, they must be read. I will not argue that they are richly expressive texts, or that they rise very often above the mechanical either in style or method. They are, however, evocative precisely in their technique, and I hope to show that they are somewhat more nuanced than is usually noticed. If they do not escape the realm of *techne*, this realm is the domain of an investigation conducted throughout the *Vita Nuova*, an examination of techniques and structures of knowing and writing.

For Rajna, the link between the *divisioni* and Scholasticism is nearly self-evident; opening the commentaries of Thomas Aquinas, one finds Dante's method everywhere, and Aquinas is cited only as a "conspicuous example" of a widespread procedure.[57] Other critics cite individual Scholastic commentaries as illustration, but follow Rajna's lead in identifying the *divisioni* with an intellectual movement rather than with particular texts. Singleton, for instance, offers a parallel chosen "at random," from Bonaventure's commentary on the *Sentences* of Peter Lombard, but discourages attempts to find a particular source: "Far too much has been made of specific sources for the *divisioni*."[58] D'Andrea, who provides by far the most thorough examination of the *divisioni*, discusses Albertus Magnus's commentary on the *Sentences* and Pseudo-Thomas Aquinas's commentary on the *Consolation of Philosophy* as possible models, but affirms that Dante's divisions "follow the plan common to the scholastic commentaries of the thirteenth century."[59]

Without question, Dante's *divisioni* evoke the world of thirteenth-century Scholasticism. I believe, however, that the place of Scholasticism in the *Vita Nuova* is complicated by the existence of a second model for the *divisioni*. The *divisioni* adapt the characteristic terminology of contemporary Scholastic interpretation, but they also imitate a much older exegetical practice: the practice of dividing the Psalms.

In the next chapter we will consider the history of the *divisio psalmi*. Here it will suffice to say that Cassiodorus includes in his sixth-century *Expositio Psalmorum* a division for each Psalm, and that this precedent is followed by many (though by no means all) subsequent Psalter commentaries. "Psalm division" and "Scholastic division" are not two mutually exclusive categories: they merge in the thirteenth century, as we shall see, when the *divisio psalmi* becomes Scholastic. But the long tradition of dividing Psalms has special relevance for the *Vita Nuova*. This becomes clear when we set the *divisione* of *Vita Nuova* 3 (quoted above) against a thirteenth-century Scholastic *divisio textus* and a twelfth-century *divisio psalmi*. The Scholastic example here will be the Scholastic example offered by Singleton; the psalm-division comes from the work discussed in Chapter 1, the twelfth-century Psalter commentary of Peter Lombard.

Here is the passage Singleton cites, from Bonaventure's commentary on the *Sentences*:

> Unde liber iste secundus, qui incipit: *Creationem rerum*, etc., dividitur in duas partes. In prima agit de hominis conditione; in secunda de lapsu eius et tentatione, infra distinctione vigesima prima: *Videns igitur diabolus*, etc. Prima pars habet duas; quia enim homo communicat cum omnibus creaturis, et cetera facta sunt propter hominem, ideo primo agit de conditione rerum in generali, secundo vero in speciali, infra distinctione secunda: *De angelica vero natura*, etc.
>
> Prima pars habet duas. In prima determinat de conditione rerum quantum ad principium efficiens, in secunda vero quantum ad finem, ibi: *Et quia non valet eius beatitudinis*, etc. Prima pars habet tres particulas. . . .[60]

> [And this second book, which begins *The creation of things*, etc., is divided into two parts. In the first he treats the condition of man; in the second his fall and temptation, starting at Distinction 21: *The devil therefore seeing*, etc. The first part has two parts; for, since man shares some things with all creatures, and other things are done on account of man, therefore he first treats the condition of things in general, second in particular, starting at Distinction 2: *Concerning the angelic nature*, etc.
>
> The first part has two parts. In the first he treats the condition of things according to their efficient cause, in the second according to their end, there: *And because no sharer of his beatitude could*, etc. The first part has three subparts. . . .]

Here is Peter Lombard's division of the third Psalm:

> [B]ipartitus est psalmus. Primo, ponit duas partes oppositas a simili praeliantium, ex una parte persequentium multitudinem, ex altera, Christum oratione armatum, et Deo susceptore securum. Secundo, finis rei ostenditur, id est resurrectio, quae est consummatio passionis; unde proponit non esse timendum, ibi, *Ego dormivi*. (*PL* 191.78)[61]

> [The Psalm is bipartite. First, it posits two opposing parties in the likeness of fighters: from one side the multitude of persecutors, from the other, Christ armed with his speech and secure in God the Defender. Second, the end of the matter is set forth, namely the Resurrection, which is the completion of the Passion; whence it shows that it is not to be feared, there: *I have slept*.]

Now, which of these two *divisiones* more closely resembles the sonnet division in *Vita Nuova* 3? On the basis of verbal style alone, one would easily choose the first. Bonaventure's Latin might be the original for Dante's Italian ("Questo sonetto si divide in due parti; che ne la prima parte . . ." [3.13; This sonnet is divided in two parts; for in the first part . . .]). Peter uses other terms: "bipartitus est" instead of "dividitur in duas partes"; "primo" and "secundo" as adverbs, not adjectives modifying *partes*. (The "duas partes oppositas" are not textual sections but elements of the Psalm's represented content.) While Dante's division is recognizably related to both the Latin examples, an analysis of intrinsic stylistic features supports D'Andrea's claim that Dante follows the Scholastic mode of the thirteenth century. There is another basis, however, on which one can argue that Peter's Psalter commentary is the superior model for the *Vita Nuova*. The two Latin commentaries differ not only in the language they employ for dividing but also in the structural role they assign to the *divisio textus*. It is necessary to map the exegetical work as a whole.

In Bonaventure's commentary on the *Sentences*—and in the other commentaries previously adduced as models—the *textus* that is divided is quite long. Bonaventure treats each of the four books of the *Sentences* as a unitary whole.[62] For each book, he provides, in the course of his commentary, an extremely elaborate division. The division is parceled out into separate sections, each labeled "Divisio textus," but the *divisiones* are not self-contained; they are carefully linked to each other, so that together they constitute a single structure, a logical diagram of the book. The first "Divisio textus," of which Singleton quotes the beginning, is itself only a beginning. Book 2, we are told, has two parts; the second part begins at *Distinctio* 21 (using a standard reference system for the *Sentences*). Each of these parts is, of course, further divisible. At the beginning of Book 2 there is no need to subdivide the second part; this can be postponed until *Distinctio* 21, some five hundred printed pages away ("sequitur secunda pars principalis . . . pars ista habet tres partes" [here follows the second principal part . . . this part has three parts][63]). The first part of Book 2 *is* subdivided here, and the first of these subdivisions is subdivided. Now that the book has been whittled down to a manageable passage—*Distinctio* 1, *Pars* 1—we are given a complete *divisio* of the passage. (It has three "particulae," each divided in two.) All of Book 2 will be analyzed in this way; the separate "divisiones textus" could be extracted from the commentary and printed together as one coherent, if unwieldy, outline of Book 2.

The division also serves as a framework for Bonaventure's book of commentary. The sections labelled "Divisio textus" together constitute a complete exposition of Peter Lombard's text. In addition, each passage of division, by focusing attention on a small part of Peter Lombard's text and identifying its central topics, opens the way to a more expansive form of response: a set of *quaestiones* exploring the theological issues discussed in the *Sentences*. Thus the "Divisio textus" is followed by a section headed "Tractatio quaestionum," which typically begins, "Ad intelligentiam vero eorum quae in hac parte dicuntur, quaeritur hic de . . ." [For the understanding of the things said in this part, we inquire here concerning . . .].[64] The "Tractatio" is also structured as a *divisio textus*, but now it is an anticipatory outline of Bonaventure's own discussion, which consists of *articuli* subdivided into *quaestiones*. These *quaestiones* could stand alone as a theological treatise, but the elaborate scaffolding of "Divisio textus" and "Tractatio quaestionum" provides a complex linkage between Bonaventure's argument and the text of the *Sentences*.

In other thirteenth-century commentaries, the *divisio textus* assumes an even larger role. It is still the case that the division performs the work of textual exposition, but now *all* of the commentator's contributions to knowledge are expressed as textual exposition.[65] For example, the *Consolation* commentary of Pseudo-Thomas Aquinas, recommended by D'Andrea as a possible model for the *Vita Nuova*, begins by dividing the Boethian *liber* into five primary parts, the five "libros partiales quos continet" [partial books which it contains].[66] The first of these parts contains thirteen parts: seven *metra* and six *prosae*. The commentator calls attention to the modal distinction between verse and prose,[67] but wherever possible he treats the *metra* just as he treats the *prosa*—he subdivides.[68] At no point is there an isolated *divisio textus*; rather, the entire commentary is a single, capacious division. The articulated hierarchy of sub-headings and sub-sub-headings is unveiled gradually, as a concurrent parallel to Boethius's articulated text. This is also the pattern of, for example, Thomas Aquinas's commentary on the *Nicomachean Ethics*.[69]

Dante did produce a vernacular example of this Scholastic genre: the unfinished *Convivio*. After the first book, each book of the *Convivio* is constituted as an elaborate comment on one of Dante's own *canzoni*. The "literal" exposition that makes up the bulk of these books takes the form of *divisio textus*. The divisions are carefully and explicitly hierarchized, and extended over many *capitoli*. (In Books 2 and 3, the literal exposition is followed by a less regimented allegorical exposition [2.12–15, 3.11–15]; in Book 4, twice the length of the other books, only a literal exposition is offered. It might be added that the prefatory first book, which does not treat a *canzone*, is exactingly outlined in the manner of the divisions that follow.) Dante's encyclopedic banquet of philosophy follows the pattern of Scholastic exposition: its most salient structuring device is *divisio textus*.

In contrast, the *Vita Nuova* more nearly follows the plan of Peter Lombard's commentary on the Psalms. Peter, adhering to the tradition begun with Cassiodorus, assigns the *divisio psalmi* a well-defined place quite different from the overarching position of the *divisio textus* in thirteenth-century Scholastic commentaries. To begin with, each Psalm is treated as a text in its own right, rather than as a *lectio* chosen from a larger unitary text. Thus each *divisio psalmi* stands alone; there is no attempt to construct a larger structure from the separate *divisiones*.[70] Moreover, the *divisio psalmi* is isolated within the comment on each Psalm. It is a brief, self-contained statement; it represents one approach to the Psalm among several offered in the prefatory section of the comment. Occasionally the *divisio* will be cited later on in the verse-by-verse exposition of the Psalm,[71] but there is no further subdivision. The *divisio psalmi* may be intended as a structuring aid for the reader of the commentary, but it does not noticeably structure the commentator's discussion. Similarly, in the *Vita Nuova*, individual lyrics are treated as separate texts, and each *divisione* is a brief, self-contained section within the prose.

My aim in comparing these two possible models for Dante's divisions has not been simply to promote one set of texts at the expense of another. The scholarly consensus is undoubtedly correct: the *divisioni* evoke, in style and method, the discourse of thirteenth-century Scholasticism. This observation is essential to my larger argument; in the next chapter, I shall return to the question of the place of Scholasticism in the *Vita Nuova*. My claim here is merely that the *divisioni* imitate, in addition, the *divisiones* found in Psalter commentaries. In one sense, this new model does not require any substantial remapping of the *Vita Nuova*'s cultural contexts. As I have mentioned, Scholasticism and Psalter commentary do not form a mutually exclusive pair. And, in any case, biblical exegesis belongs to the same "world of the learned" as Scholasticism in general; Rajna's 1902 account of the *libello*'s two worlds receives no new challenge here. Still, there is something to be learned from the tradition of the *divisio psalmi*. Dante's *divisioni* make a more powerful connection with the world of Latin commentary than is usually claimed. They call to mind not only a discursive universe but also a particular textual model for the form of the whole *Vita Nuova*: the model of the glossed Book of Psalms.

4. The *Vita Nuova* and the Glossed Psalter

If the only models for the *divisioni* in the *Vita Nuova* are the Scholastic expositions traditionally cited, then the *rest* of the *Vita Nuova* remains virtually untouched by the association. Placing the *libello* next to Bonaventure's commentary on the *Sentences*, one feels that the *divisioni* do indeed come from a different world than the poems and the narrative prose. The analogy between Dante's text and Bonaventure's operates only for intermittent brief stretches: the *divisioni* offer glimpses of a discursive realm that is, in effect, *all* division. D'Andrea extends the scope of the analogy in two ways. He argues, convincingly, that four of Dante's relatively abstract digressions are presented as *quaestiones* in the Scholastic manner—so that the other half of a work like Bonaventure's is evoked, again intermittently.[72] Moreover, when he proposes the pseudo-Thomistic *Consolation* commentary as a possible model, he is perhaps motivated by the desire to find an exemplary book containing verse, prose, and *divisio*. Yet he seems to present this proposal somewhat speculatively, and he does not argue for any detailed correspondence between the *Vita Nuova* and the glossed *Consolation*. The analogy with the great model of Scholasticism remains limited, confined to discrete sections of the *libello*.

My claim for the *divisio psalmi* as a model for Dante's *divisioni* depends in part on the intrinsic features of the divisions (there is, of course, a *general* similarity in style and method), but it depends even more on the positioning of the divisions within larger textual structures. The analogy, if it operates at all, joins not merely discrete sections from two different books but rather the books themselves—and once the two books are placed next to each other, it becomes clear that the connection between the divisions is only the most salient in a system of connections. A Psalter commentary such as Peter Lombard's—more precisely, the *liber* containing both text and commentary—is a model for Dante's whole *libello*.

Along with the relatively marginal *divisioni*, each of the two primary modes of writing in the *Vita Nuova*—lyric verse and narrative prose—finds a counterpart in the glossed Psalter. In the last chapter I suggested that the Psalms were understood to be lyrics: metric, non-narrative poems, originally sung to instrumental accompaniment. Certain features of the Psalms, moreoever, are especially relevant to the lyrics of the *Vita Nuova*. The Psalms are described both as prophecies and as poems of praise. For Peter the *titulus* of the Psalter is "liber Hymnorum, vel Soliloquiorum Prophetae de Christo" (*PL* 191.58) [Book of Hymns or Soliloquies of the Prophet Concerning Christ]. *Soliloquium* is one kind of *prophetia* (*PL* 191.58); certainly some of the lyrics in the *Vita Nuova*—those recounting visions, and foretelling the death of Beatrice—could be described as prophetic.[73] *Hymnus* means "laus Dei cum cantico" (*PL* 191.58) [praise of God accompanied by a song]; in the *Vita Nuova*, the "stilo de la sua loda" (26.4) [style of her praise] is the mode of poetic composition that Dante most valorizes.

The connection between Dante's lyrics and the Psalms has been noticed before. J. A. Scott cites a phrase from a sermon attributed to Hugh of St. Victor, "Canticum est vita, canticum novum vita nova" (*PL* 177.926) [Song is life; new song, new life], and goes on to state that Dante too echoes

> the psalmist's "Et immisit in os meum canticum novum, carmen Deo nostro" [Ps. 39:4; And he put a new canticle into my mouth, a song to our God], for the song of praise he sings to Beatrice is, within the limits of the work, *carmen Deo nostro*.[74]

And De Robertis uses Augustine's explication of the Psalter to explore "the theme of beatifying praise" in the *Vita Nuova*.[75] These arguments are entirely thematic; they are strengthened by the general but striking *formal* resemblance between two lyric collections. In this respect the *divisioni*, by pointing to the glossed Psalter as a possible model, underline a connection that is clear enough in itself. What has not been suggested before, however, is that Dante's narrative prose has a counterpart in Psalter commentary.

The Psalms themselves are not narratives, but they are intimately associated with narrative. For Peter Lombard, the narrative dimension of the Psalter is provided by the first commentator on the Psalms, the prophetic scribe Esdras. Esdras not only rescued the texts from the burning library and arranged them in their present order, he also opened up their meaning by attaching individual titles: "titulos apposuit, qui sunt quasi claves psalmorum, Sicut enim per clavem intratur in domum, ita per congruas titulorum expositiones, subjectorum clarescit intelligentia psalmorum" (*PL* 191.60) [he added titles, which are like keys to the Psalms, for just as one enters a house with a key, so, through apt explanations of the titles, the understanding of the Psalms placed below them is clarified]. Often, as in Psalm 3, the *titulus* explicates the Psalm by referring to David as a historical figure, and indeed by referring to a particular passage of David's history. This is the first topic Peter takes up in his comment on the third Psalm.

> Titulus: *Psalmus David cum fugeret a facie Absalonis filii sui.* De historia sumpsit Esdras velamen mysteriorum; legitur enim in libro Regum quod Absalon filius David persequens patrem suum, quaerebat eum occidere. Cui David cessit cum suis, exiens de civitate Jerusalem, nudis plantis: intelligens hoc sibi contingere propter peccatum adulterii commissi cum Bersabee, et homicidii de Uria perpetrati, sicut Natham propheta praedixerat ei dicens: *Non recedet gladius de domo tua, et suscitabit Dominus semen tuum contra te* (*II Reg.* xii). Dum autem Absalon persequeretur David converso contra eum exercitu, Absalon terga vertit in fugam, atque impetu muli ductus est in ramosam quercum: ramis cujus circumnectentibus collum ejus, ibique capite intercepto pendens, ab Joab principe militiae David interfectus est. Quod mortuo David restitutus in regnum, in pace regnavit. (*PL* 191.77)

> [Title: *The Psalm of David when he fled from the face of his son Absolom.* From history, Esdras took a veil of mysteries; for we read in the Book of Kings that Absolom the son of David, pursuing his father, sought to kill him. David retreated from him with his followers, going forth from the city of Jerusalem, with bare feet: understanding that this was happening to him because of the sin of adultery committed with Bathsheba, and his murder of Uriah, just as Nathan the prophet predicted to him saying: *The sword shall not depart from your house, and the Lord will raise up your seed against you* (2 Kings 12). When David however was pursuing Absolom, with an army turned against him, Absolom turned his back in flight, and by the force of his mule was led into a branching oak: and with his neck tangled around with branches, hanging there with his head caught, he was killed by Joab, the leader of David's army. With Absolom dead, David, restored to his kingdom, ruled in peace.]

The *titulus*, which briefly identifies a historical moment (2 Kings [2 Samuel] 15:14), is enough to evoke a richly circumstantial historical narrative (drawn from 2 Kings 11–18). Peter begins his explication of the poem by writing a chapter in the life of the poet.

The Old Testament historical referent is often theorized, in medieval commentary and in modern accounts of medieval commentary, as the "literal" meaning of the text: "littera gesta docet" [the letter teaches what happened].[76] One must avoid simply conflating the two terms, however.[77] In 2 Kings, the literal and the historical do indeed coincide; in the Book of

Psalms the equation is problematic. As Peter recognizes, the letter of the Psalm refers only indirectly to the history and makes no mention of the historical particulars. David's bare feet and Absalon's long hair must be supplied from somewhere other than the letter of the text; they are part of an imported "velamen mysteriorum" [veil of mysteries]. The historical narrative is extratextual, however, only in the sense that it belongs to a *different* text: the branching oak that catches Absalon is planted not in a nonlinguistic realm of hard facts but rather in another book of the Bible. The Second Book of Kings here serves as a canonical *libro della memoria*.

Here, then, is the analogy between the *Vita Nuova* and a glossed Psalter such as Peter Lombard's. The two hybrid books have in common three modes of writing: lyric, *divisio*, and narrative. In the last few pages I have treated each of the three modes separately, but the analogy depends on the configuration of three modes rather than on a point-by-point correspondence. I do not claim that 2 Kings, or Peter's summary of a passage from it, is very much like the narrative of the *Vita Nuova* in either style or substance; there are obvious differences, just as there are differences between the Psalms and Dante's love-lyrics. There may be suggestive similarities, too: the lyrics have some of the qualities of the Psalms, and there are resonances of the life of David in Dante's autobiography.[78] My concern here, however, is with textual structure. In each book, a series of lyric poems is supplemented with *divisiones textus* and with a prose account of the poet's life.

Earlier I argued that the *Vita Nuova* is fundamentally ambiguous in structure and that Chapter 3 demonstrates the ambiguity. In Chapter 3, the two models for the *libello*—prose narrative with inserted poems and lyric anthology with explanatory prose—are held in a careful suspension; each of the two modes of writing, prose and verse, claims a position of centrality, a position that renders the other mode supplementary. Similarly, Dante and Beatrice face each other in an erotic stasis of mutual subordination. In making this argument, I set aside the brief sonnet-division—following the critical tradition that has always neglected the *divisioni*. Yet the seemingly negligible *divisioni*, introduced to the *libello* in Chapter 3, bring with them the possibility of a stable hierarchy. By their very marginality, they prompt a sensitive reader like Boccaccio to produce a copy of the *Vita Nuova* that looks, indeed, like a book of commentary. And they evoke one kind of commentary-book in particular, a powerful textual model that may tip the balance toward one of the two possible structures for the *libello*. To the extent that we read the *Vita Nuova* as a version of the glossed Psalter, the lyric poems (and Beatrice) move to the center.

In the glossed Psalter, narrative is subordinate to lyric. It is subordinate first of all because it is a kind of commentary: 2 Kings possesses an authority of its own, of course, but excerpted in Peter's gloss it becomes ancillary. The historical narrative is subordinate in another sense as well. Although it is part of the meaning of the Psalm, its importance is carefully circumscribed. The discovery of the underlying narrative is only a first step in the hermeneutic process. We have seen that the interpreter of Psalm 3 must begin by supplying a historical context, but he is not allowed to rest there: the historical referent must itself be interpreted. I resume the prefatory comment where I earlier left off:

> Huic historiae alludit titulus, de quo tamen non agit psalmus, sed de significato historiae, id est de passione et resurrectione Christi . . . David enim, Christus est: Absolon filius ejus, Judas est quem cum aliis apostolis filium vocat Christus in Evangelio . . . (*PL* 191.77)

> [The title alludes to this history, but the Psalm is not concerned with this but with the signified meaning of the history: that is, with the passion and resurrection of Christ . . . For David is Christ: Absolom his son is Judas, whom Christ calls "son" with the other apostles in the Gospel . . .]

The passage from 2 Kings, with all its interesting details, has served its purpose. It was, after all, only a "velamen mysteriorum" [veil of mysteries]. According to Second Corinthians, the entire Old Testament conceals its truth beneath a "velamen," and Christ has removed the veil, allowing Christians to look directly upon the truth.[79] By itself, the Psalm had no allegorical covering; yet its true meaning could not be seen clearly until a veil was placed upon it and then removed. Having established that the speaker of the poem is Christ, Peter Lombard can discard the Old Testament narrative.[80] What replaces the story of David is not exactly the Gospel story of Christ (Judas, mentioned here to support the David-Christ parallel, appears only once, in passing, in the comment that follows) but rather the timeless facts of Christ's passion and resurrection. The verses of the Psalm can be understood, in effect, as straightforward statements about the relationship of God to men, non-narrative renderings of atemporal truths. The recourse to 2 Kings is an analytic detour that permits the Psalm to be read literally after all.

The model of the glossed Psalter thus offers the reader of the *Vita Nuova* a structure for the whole work—a stable textual hierarchy, with the lyrics at the center—and also a method for interpreting the different parts of the structure. The results of reading the *libello* according to this model can be seen, I believe, in one of the most important modern interpretations: Singleton's *Essay on the Vita Nuova*. Singleton does not discuss the Psalms or their commentators. He does, however, draw an explicit analogy between the form of the *Vita Nuova* and the graphic image of a single page of a medieval glossed book, with different scripts used to distinguish "those parts which are done by different authors or at different times."[81] "That is the whole picture," he writes: "a text of poems with a gloss and then yet another gloss" (53). Singleton's model here is *any* medieval glossed book, but the glossed Psalter seems an especially apt instance, not only because the Psalter is "a text of poems" but also because a commentary like Peter Lombard's shows how a seemingly self-sufficient narrative can function as a gloss to a lyric text.

In Singleton's mapping of the work, the first "gloss" is Dante's life-story, a sequence of events that is metaphorically verbal but is in fact a narrative authored by God. Like Peter Lombard, Singleton draws a simple but powerful analogy from the historical narrative—Beatrice (like David) is a figure of Christ.[82] Singleton is in no hurry to discard the historical narrative: equipped with a complex figural hermeneutic, he spends much of the early part of his analysis exploring the concrete details of the prose narrative.[83] For Singleton as for Peter, however, the exploration of history is only a necessary detour on the way to a more direct apprehension of the truths expressed literally in the lyrics. In his penultimate chapter, entitled "Vita Nuova," Singleton turns to the content of the poetry as if returning to something that should have been clear all along:

> In this manuscript Book of Memory the poems are, after all, the primary text; the rest is either a gloss to the poems or a gloss on that gloss. Hence, if there are three stages in the poet's love, that fact ought to be visible first in the poems. And so it is, although were there no gloss in prose to point out that fact, we might easily fail to see it. (80)

A new examination of the poems reveals "Three stages in love, three subject matters for poems" (105). Like Psalm 3, which treats first the Passion and then the Resurrection, Dante's poetic collection takes up each of the three stages in turn, but the sequence of stages is not so much a narrative as an always-available *itinerarium*.

Singleton describes the form of Dante's *libello* as a stable hierarchy of lyric text and narrative gloss; he places his emphasis on the unity of the whole rather than on the subordination of one element to the other, but both aspects of hierarchy—unity and subordination—emerge clearly in his account. This well-defined model allows him to assume, without ever quite stating, two analogies that connect the textual hierarchy to other hierarchies. First, he draws an implicit parallel between the privileged position of Beatrice in Dante's life and the privileged position of the lyrics in the *libello*: he writes that the Book of Memory has the death of Beatrice at its center, and "this Book becomes a book with a multiple gloss revealing the true meaning of her life and death (and the causes and the meanings of the poems)" (55). Both as a textual construct and as a drama of persons, the *Vita Nuova* is, in Singleton's account, structured by a dyadic hierarchy. Second, Singleton describes the *libello* as an image of the cosmic hierarchy: he speaks of "that little world of the *Vita Nuova* where Beatrice is, as Christ is in the real world whose author is God" (24).[84]

Singleton thus reads the *Vita Nuova* as if it were a Dantean version of the glossed Psalter. I have associated Singleton's theoretical model with a particular medieval text, as he does not, for two reasons. First, although his argument obviously does not stand in need of my help, I have tried to support and develop it. A fine recent essay on the *Vita Nuova*, Robert Pogue Harrison's *The Body of Beatrice*, argues eloquently against Singleton's totalizing, theological, allegorical reading and in favor of a more flexible and phenomenological account of the *libello*.[85] Yet the *divisioni*, which Harrison treats very briefly, urge precisely the sort of reading that Singleton provides: they evoke the powerful model of the glossed Psalter and thereby invite us to see the book as a hierarchical totality.

My second reason is in a sense the contrary of the first: by objectifying Singleton's theoretical model in a textual exemplar, I hope to limit its authority. Singleton derives his textual hierarchy from medieval thought in the broadest sense; the layout of the manuscript book is only an emblem for a cultural pattern. Singleton is by no means guilty of the "ruthless totalizing" Lee Patterson attributes to Robertsonian exegetical interpretation:[86] he recognizes contradictory tendencies in medieval culture. Yet he describes the original context of the *Vita Nuova* as a macrocosm analogous to the book's microcosm: "What can the little world of the *Vita Nuova* mean unless it is rounded (in us) by some sense of that larger world which was standing around it at birth?" (5). The "larger world" here may be the "Book of the World," the divinely ordained cosmos celebrated by the Middle Ages, or it may be the real world of the Middle Ages, where people believed in such a cosmos.[87] Scholars frequently make an imperceptible (but logically suspect) transition from the medieval commitment to an idea of universal order, expressed in various ways in various texts, to a modern idea of medieval thought *as* a universal order. Even in Singleton's understated formulation, the medieval cosmos is so imposing and so huge a model that it can all too easily assimilate any particular text to its own totality. The glossed Psalter is somewhat less intimidating. It is an important book, and it does present an image of hierarchy, but it is only a book.

To read the *Vita Nuova* without imagining it as a microcosm, a stable textual hierarchy, is to miss part of its point. But to settle on this image as a final model for the work is to endorse one of the text's self-representations more fully than the text itself does. Within the *Vita Nuova*, the glossed Psalter provides only one possible structure. In arguing that Chapter 3 presents a glimpse of another possible structure, I have suggested that the picture of totalized hierarchy is offered as contingent—that totalization is not a precondition but rather a process enacted within the book. Again, the linear plotting of the church scene in Chapter 5—the hierarchy of Virgin, Beatrice, screen-lady, Dante, the others—turns out to be unstable. It undergoes a series of substitutions: one screen lady is replaced by another (9); Dante learns to address Beatrice directly, using his own words as a "mezzo" (12.8); Beatrice's greeting is denied so that Dante must find a new end of love in his own praise (18); the mediator Amore vanishes (after chapter 24); the living Beatrice is herself removed (28); the Donna Gentile (35) attracts Dante's attention without finding a place in the chain.

The mutability of the *Vita Nuova*'s personal hierarchy is matched by a formal instability. As we shall see in my own Chapter 3, the *divisioni* undergo shifts in procedure and position; as they change, the projected formal constitution of the book changes. The *Vita Nuova* evokes the stable hierarchy of the glossed Psalter as a model, but subjects this model to its own temporality. This raises questions: what does it mean to present an authoritative, logocentric totality as one possible gloss for a text, evidenced most clearly in the most marginal passages? Does the disjunction between vernacular courtly lyrics and Holy Scripture call into doubt the very authority that is implied by the analogy? To explore these questions, it is necessary to explore the temporality of the *divisioni*.

3. Dante's Divisions: The History of Division

divido -dis -si . . . quasi diversis modis videre
—Uguccione da Pisa

1. The Meaning of Division

Critics have had little to say about the thematics of division in the *Vita Nuova*.[1] Yet there are striking indications that "divisione" and "dividere"—terms that recur throughout the text, almost always in connection with the formal *divisioni*—are meant to resonate with meanings beyond their technical Scholastic sense.[2] In Chapter 31, for example, the first chapter after Beatrice's death to include a poem, Dante announces that henceforth the *divisioni* will appear before their poems and not after: "E acciò che questa canzone paia rimanere più vedova dopo lo suo fine, la dividerò prima che io la scriva" (31.2) [And so that this *canzone* may seem to remain the more widowed after its ending, I shall divide it before I write it out]. The metaphor of "vedova" describes textual components as human characters: if the poem seems widowed when it stands alone at the end of the chapter, then poems are married to prose. This metaphor is not precisely the same as the analogy I proposed in Chapter 2: the *canzone* is like Beatrice in being, at least grammatically, female, yet in the story it is not Beatrice who has been widowed but Dante—or Florence, "facta . . . quasi vidua" (28.1) [become a widow]. Nonetheless, the comparison clearly associates Dante's textual practices with the human events he is describing. "La dividerò" means, of course, "I shall write the division for it," but here it also suggests a more violent action; the aural resemblance of "vedova" and "dividerò" reminds us that widowing is one kind of dividing. Dante may even have known an etymology that relates the two words: "vidua, id est a viro divisa" [widow, i.e., divided from a man].[3]

"Dividere" escapes from its narrow technical sense again in Chapter 38. By now the new pattern is firmly established: Dante describes the occasion of a poem, provides the incipit, divides the poem in advance, and copies out the poem. Here, though, another sort of division intervenes between the incipit and the textual *divisione*:

> e dissi questo sonetto, lo quale comincia: *Gentil pensero*; e dico "gentile" in quanto ragionava di gentile donna, ché per altro era vilissimo.
> In questo sonetto fo due parte di me, secondo che li miei pensieri erano divisi. L'una parte chiamo cuore, cioè l'appetito; l'altra chiamo anima, cioè la ragione; e dico come l'uno dice con l'altro. . . .
> Questo sonetto ha tre parti . . . (38.4–7)

> [and I composed this sonnet, which begins, *Gentle thought*; and I say "gentle" in that it spoke of a gentle lady, for otherwise it was most base.
> In this sonnet I make two parts of myself, according to the way my thoughts were divided. One part I call my heart, that is desire; the other I call my soul, that is reason; and I say how one speaks with the other. . . .
> This sonnet has three parts . . .]

The effect is nearly comic: at the moment when we expect Dante to divide his sonnet, he pauses to divide, instead, himself.

What does "divisio" mean for Dante? The issue is not exactly the concrete meaning of the term—in the Middle Ages as now, to divide something is first of all to separate it into parts—but rather its range of applications and connotations. In medieval culture, "divisio" is something of a prestige term: it is used often, in many different contexts, and it can carry powerful judgments both positive and negative. I know of no critical attempt, either medieval or modern, to gather all the various meanings of "divisio" into a single complex concept. There is a logic to the multivalence of the term, however, that is part of the logic of medieval commentary.

Fundamentally, "divisio" has a double force, corresponding to the syntactic ambiguity that allows the noun to be understood as both a condition and an activity. As a condition—dividedness—*divisio* is a fall from unity, and ultimately a fall from the One that is God. Two different kinds of fall must be clearly distinguished, though. The Fall in Eden, in which humanity divided itself from God and (simply) divided itself, is the origin of the moral dividedness that besets the race: *divisio* is strife, heresy, disorder, sin. "Peccare nichil est aliud quam progredi ab uno spreto ad multa" [To sin is nothing other than to proceed from the scorned One to the Many], writes Dante in *De Monarchia* (1.15.3). The world is also characterized, however, by a necessary ontological dividedness, which stems from a very different sort of fall: the orderly descent of Being from God through his creation. In Neoplatonist thought, the material world is a divided and variegated reflection of its single creator.[4] The image of God as one who divides the world to create it is not confined to systematic theology, however; in the Bible, the God who "divisit lucem ac tenebras" (Gen. 1:4) [divided the light and the darkness] is "unus atque idem Spiritus, dividens singulis prout vult" (1 Cor. 12:11) [one and the same Spirit, dividing to every one according as he will]. Here there can be no negative judgment on the act of division, but the condition of having been created, of being divided, is understood to be a condition of ontological inferiority.

Dividedness, then, is contrasted to unity, and it can be contrasted in two distinct ways: as an outright negation and as a lower step in a hierarchy. To illustrate these familiar senses of the term, I offer a passage from (again) Peter Lombard's commentary on the Psalms. Here Peter, paraphrasing from Cassiodorus and Augustine, treats Psalm 21:19, "Diviserunt sibi vestimenta mea et super vestem meam miserunt sortem" [They divided my garments among them; and they cast lots upon my clothing]:

> Per vestimenta enim Christi Scripturae vel sacramenta Ecclesiae accipiuntur; per tunicam inconsutilem, super quam missa fuit sors, charitas vel unitas Ecclesiae intelligitur; per illos qui vestimenta diviserunt perversores Scripturarum intelliguntur. Sicut ergo illi actualiter vestes diviserunt: sic illi qui non tendunt ad unitatem, diviserunt sibi vestimenta mea, spiritualia sacramenta, et Scripturas sacras corrumpentes. Sacramenta enim illius et Scripturae potuerunt dividi per haereses; sed non tunica desuper, id est adeo per totum contexta. . . . Haec est charitas vel unitas Catholicae Ecclesiae, quam nemo potest dividere. (*PL* 191.235)

> [By the garments, the Scriptures of Christ or the sacraments of the Church are understood; by the seamless coat, over which they cast lots, charity or the unity of the Church is understood; by those who divided the garments, the perverters of the Scriptures are understood. In this way therefore they actually divided the clothes: thus those who do not seek unity have divided among themselves my garments, corrupting the spiritual sacraments and the holy Scriptures. For his Sacraments and Scriptures could be divided by heresies; but not the coat woven from the top down, that is, throughout. . . . This is the charity or unity of the Catholic Church, which no one can divide.][5]

In this passage the picture of sinful *divisio*, a violent negation of unity, is clear. "Unitas" is nearly interchangeable with "charitas"; the agent of division is heresy. At the same time, God's benign division of his creation is implied, I think, in the contrast between the plural garments of the Sacraments and Scriptures and the one seamless coat of Charity. The Sacraments and Scriptures are entirely holy, yet they are plural and *divisible* precisely because they mediate between an indivisible Love and a divided world.

The dividedness of the world is thus produced, in very different ways, by God and by sinners. Dividing is also, however, a normal human activity. Here we move to the second broad sense of *divisio*. It is necessary to speak of a family of meanings: especially in the thirteenth century, "divisio" is a technical term in a number of different contexts, used to denote a number of different specific activities, but its various applications are clearly related. All of these forms of *divisio* are positive and necessary parts of human cognition and discourse.

Division is part of science and logic. The distinctive *modus agendi* of the human sciences, as distinct from the divine sciences, is the "modus definitivus, divisivus, et collectivus" [definitive, divisive, and collective mode]:[6] in the words of Alexander of Hales, "such a mode must exist in human sciences because the apprehension of truth through the human reason is unfolded by divisions, definitions, and ratiocinations."[7] The human mind, seeking to understand any object, makes its own divisions. There are several different kinds of division, and logical divisions can be made properly and improperly; proper logical division is taught in Boethius's treatise *De divisione* and in the Scholastic classroom.[8] *Divisio* is not only a deliberately chosen activity of the trained mind, however; as the quotation from Alexander of Hales implies, it is a necessary part of any human intellection whatsoever. According to Thomas Aquinas, human intellection includes two complementary processes, *compositio* and *divisio*. *Compositio* and *divisio* are distinctively temporal, and are to be contrasted with the direct and atemporal intellection of God and the angels.[9]

Division is also part of reading. A systematic division of the text can be justified on purely practical grounds. Hugh of St. Victor, in the Prologue to "De Tribus Maximis Circumstantiis Gestorum," speaks of textual division as a useful aid to memory. He says that he memorized the Psalter by taking advantage of the divisions already present in the text: "by dividing and marking off the book by psalms, and then each psalm by verses, I have reduced a large amount of material to such conciseness and brevity." When a text is continuous, it is necessary to impose artificial divisions and subdivisions, because "the memory always rejoices both in brevity of length and fewness in number."[10] Even where memorization is not the goal, a systematic division of the text makes it more accessible to scholars. Richard H. Rouse and Mary A. Rouse discuss the imposition, in the twelfth and thirteenth centuries, of standard chapter-divisions and subdivisions in the Bible and other important texts; these divisions, made more visible by innovations in the *mise en page*, allowed for quick reference to particular passages.[11]

The division of the text can be a handy reference tool, a system imposed from without, but it can also arise from within the text and express its form. "Divisio textus" is one synonym for "forma tractatus" [form of the treatise].[12] To know the division of a text is to know a good deal about it; to divide the text—to identify the true *divisio textus*—is not only a preliminary to further study but also an important act of criticism in itself. The theoretical statements of this idea borrow from the related idea that all logical investigation proceeds by division. In a commentary on Aristotle's *Praedicamenta*, Robert Kilwardby writes, "Since we only know a composite from our knowledge of its parts, and of their nature, and since that book is composed of parts, therefore we must not be ignorant of what parts, and what sort of parts, it is composed."[13] More sweepingly, Hugh of St. Victor writes in his *Didascalicon*, twice, that "Modus legendi in dividendo constat" [The method of reading consists of dividing]. According to Hugh, division descends from universals to "singula"; since universals are better defined and more easily understood than individual things, to read by dividing is to investigate "occulta" [hidden things].[14]

Clearly there is some connection between these theoretical statements and the actual practice of the schools, in which explication by *divisio* was the constant exercise. A. J. Minnis writes that the new vocabulary for the *forma tractatus* "was one *result* of the desire to conceptualise about the current techniques of meticulously dividing and subdividing a text for teaching purposes."[15] On the other hand, G. Paré, A. Brunet, and P. Tremblay, in their eloquent description of Scholastic *divisio textus*, give the impression that the practice might have arisen in response to Hugh of St. Victor's general statement.

> The essential procedure of teaching, as of personal study, is *divisio*. "Modus legendi in dividendo constat." It is difficult to see what Hugh of St. Victor means by this investigation (*dividendo investigat*), which seems to begin with the parceled-out analysis of the text in its grammatical and logical structure (*partitio*), but which develops into a speculative inquiry exceeding the bounds of textual exegesis. *Dividere* is the proper work of the human spirit, of "reason," which descends from the universal to the particular . . .[16]

Undoubtedly theory and practice respond to each other. It is probably best to speak, as Judson Allen does, of a cultural "habit": *divisio* is a "pervasive . . . instrument of analysis,"[17] both employed and celebrated.

One other particular form of *divisio* should be mentioned here: division as a rhetorical mode. In classical rhetoric, the *divisio* was a particular section of a speech.[18] Late medieval *artes praedicandi* employ the term with a different, broader range of reference. In the thematic sermon, the homiletic form that came to dominate in the thirteenth century, the preacher chooses a verse of scripture—the "theme"—and finds within it a number (usually three) of distinct topics for his discourse. This *divisio* of the theme then provides the structure for the sermon as a whole. The division may correspond to a literal division of the words in the verse (*divisio intra*), or each of the topics may derive from the verse as a whole (*divisio extra*).[19] Within the *artes praedicandi*, "divisio" may begin as a term for the analytic procedure that finds multiple topics or meanings within a single theme, but it becomes a term for a way of producing discourse, and a versatile term at that. In the *Forma Praedicandi* of Robert of Basevorn (1322), "divisio" refers to the preacher's initial division of the theme, and to one of the "ornaments" of the sermon, and to one of the varieties of *another* ornament, *amplificatio*.[20] For the preacher, at least, to divide is to preach.

In the last few pages I have attempted to sketch out a division of *divisio*:[21] to organize the various applications of the term into two large groups with smaller subgroups. Is it possible to speak of a single medieval conception of division? There is an evident contradiction in the connotations of the term: dividing Scripture is wicked when the divider is a garment-rending heretic and virtuous when the divider is a preacher. Yet there is a logical relationship between these two views. To summarize my division: as a condition, *divisio* is characteristic of the world as distinct from God—the created world or the fallen world. As an activity, *divisio* is characteristic of the human subject seeking to understand and to explain. To state this even more schematically: *divisio* is, *in malo*, the condition that separates humanity from God and, *in bono*, one process by which humanity reaches toward God.

Both basic meanings of *divisio* are relevant to medieval biblical commentary. Again, a manuscript page of Peter's commentary on the Psalms (discussed in Chapter 1) provides an emblem. The multiplicity of glosses for a single text is a sign of their lower rank in the hierarchy of authority. As the Psalm text is literally divided into the *lemmata* of the commentary, so the single truth of Scripture divides itself as it radiates through the words of its interpreters. I have described the manuscript page as a Neoplatonic cosmos, in which text is to gloss as unity is to division. This cosmos incorporates a positive, Aristotelian kind of division, when (as in Peter's commentary) the act of dividing becomes part of the process of interpretation. Like a preacher, the commentator works no violence upon the text when he divides it; rather than reducing the text to the condition of dividedness, he opens it up, in its unity, to a divided world. Division proceeds in both directions: as a descent from unity, it radiates outward; as a part of the act of reading, it proceeds toward the center. The hierarchy represented in the page is both stable and dynamic, and "divisio" is one name for the vertical operation that differentiates levels and holds them together.

Both kinds of division operate in the *Vita Nuova* too, and Dante asks us to consider the relationship between them. When the *canzone* is "più vedova" (31.2) [more widowed], it is metaphorically subject to the tragic dividedness of the world; when Dante says, "la dividerò" [I shall divide it], he is not enforcing this dividedness but rather contrasting the unity of the text to the intellect that must read by dividing. Again, when Dante juxtaposes his own psychological division with the *divisione* of the sonnet in Chapter 38, he is juxtaposing a chaotic condition and a systematic process. The two kinds of division are not simply mixed in the *libello*, however: they are deployed in a regular pattern, and they work together to form a single structure. In the last chapter, I argued that the glossed Psalter is one possible model for the *Vita Nuova* and that the *divisioni* bring this model into view. Now I would add that the complex of ideas associated with *divisio* works to strengthen the dominance of a hierarchical model for the text. In its cast of characters and its formal constitution, the *libello* can be understood as a reflection of the Neoplatonic cosmos.[22]

In the human drama of the *Vita Nuova* it is always Dante who is divided, and the agent or occasion of this division is always Beatrice. In the first *canzone* after Beatrice's death, Dante refers to her as "quella che m'ha 'l cor diviso" (31.13) [she who has divided my heart].[23] It may be that Beatrice has now divided Dante's heart by her departure, but in fact her living presence was just as divisive. Perhaps the most striking instance of this is the moment in which the nine-year-old Dante first sees the nine-year-old Beatrice.

> In quello punto dico veracemente che lo spirito de la vita, lo quale dimora ne la secretissima camera de lo cuore, cominciò a tremare sì fortemente, che apparia ne li menimi polsi orribilmente; e tremando disse queste parole: "Ecce deus

> fortior me, qui veniens dominabitur michi." In quello punto lo spirito animale, lo quale dimora ne l'alta camera ne la quale tutti li spiriti sensitivi portano le loro percezioni, si cominciò a maravigliare molto, e parlando spezialmenta a li spiriti del viso, sì disse queste parole: "Apparuit iam beatitudo vestro." In quello punto lo spirito naturale, lo quale dimora in quella parte ove si ministra lo nutrimento nostro, cominciò a piangere, e piangendo disse queste parole: "Heu miser, quia frequenter impeditus ero deinceps!" (2.4–7)

> [At that moment I say truly that the vital spirit, which dwells in the most secret chamber of the heart, began to tremble so strongly that it showed alarmingly in my smallest pulses; and trembling it said these words: "Behold a god stronger than I, who will, coming, rule over me." At that moment the animal spirit, which dwells in the high chamber to which all the sensitive spirits carry their perceptions, began to wonder greatly, and, speaking especially to the spirits of vision, said these words: "Now your bliss has appeared." At that moment the natural spirit, which dwells in that part where our food is digested, began to weep, and weeping spoke these words: "O wretched me, for I shall often be disturbed from now on!"]

The anaphoric repetition of "in quello punto" [at that moment] emphasizes the simultaneity of the actions described in the three sentences: here are three immediate responses to a single event, three lines branching out from a single point. Seeing Beatrice, the juvenile Dante experiences a kind of subjectivity that is evidently new to him, an interior life defined by a plurality of "spiriti" [spirits]—three primary "spiriti" in charge of other, lesser "spiriti" and "polsi" [pulses]. Each of the three "spiriti" utters a Latin sentence that is inscribed in Dante's book of memory.

This moment establishes a pattern that is repeated throughout the *libello*. Dante is frequently the recipient of mysterious utterances—the cryptic messages of the personified Amore, for example, or the verse that his own tongue speaks "quasi come per sé stessa mossa" (19.2) [as if moved by itself], or the words that he hears in his nightmare (23). This plurivocal discourse, which ultimately refers to the silent Beatrice, is modeled on the language of Dante's own divided subjectivity. Repeatedly, Beatrice—or the sight of her, or the love she inspires, or her death—splits Dante into a plurality of speaking spirits or thoughts. When she is about to greet him,

> uno spirito d'amore, distruggendo tutti li altri spiriti sensitivi, pingea fuori li deboletti spiriti del viso, e dicea loro: "Andate a onorare la donna vostra." (11.2)

> [a spirit of love, destroying all the other sensitive spirits, drove out the feeble spirits of vision, and said to them: "Go and honor your lady."]

In a related formulation, Amore "fa li miei spiriti gir parlando, / ed escon for chiamando / la donna mia" (27.4) [makes my spirits wander, speaking, and they issue forth calling my lady]. When Dante thinks about his love, "mi cominciaro molti e diversi pensamenti a combattere e a tentare, ciascuno quasi indefensibilemente" (13.1) [many and diverse thoughts began to battle and struggle within me, each one as if unanswerably]; he goes on to paraphrase each thought separately. The Donna Gentile who attracts Dante's attention in the last part of the book has no such power to divide: when Dante makes two parts of himself in Chapter 38, it is because the memory of Beatrice has arisen to challenge his new desire.[24]

Dante's mutability, in the last part of the book and throughout, is another form of dividedness. In his frequent shifts in desire, mood, appearance, and poetic strategy—his repeated "newness" to himself[25]—we see the self-alienation of a plural subjectivity played out over time. The Love that can speak as a benign stranger within Dante's heart has the power to transform that heart, to estrange it for the better:

> Allora dico che mi giunse una imaginazione d'Amore; . . . e pareami che lietamente mi dicesse nel cor mio: "Pensa di benedicere lo dì che io ti presi, però che tu lo dei fare." E certo me parea avere lo cuore sì lieto, che me non parea che fosse lo mio cuore, per la sua nuova condizione. (24.2)

> [Then I say that a vision of Love came to me; . . . and it seemed to me that he joyfully said in my heart, "Remember to bless the day that I seized you, since you ought to do that." And indeed I seemed to have such a joyful heart, that it did not seem as though it were my heart, because of its new condition.]

This mutability arises from the temporality of Dante's life, and in the *Vita Nuova* temporality itself has an origin—in the same event that inscribes a multiplicity of interior voices.[26] The first sight of Beatrice (2) is the first marker of time in the *libro della memoria*, and it prompts the young Dante to project a past and a future. The three "spiriti" respond to the present moment of "quello punto" by speaking in three different tenses—or rather two different tenses, past ("Apparuit iam") and future ("ero deinceps"), along with an absolute, immediate interjection that is immediately extended into the future ("Ecce deus . . . qui veniens dominabitur . . . "). For

Dante, the present moment is not a time but rather the dividing-point between two stretches of time. As Augustine writes, "si extenditur, dividitur in praeteritum et futurum: praesens autem nullum habet spatium" [if it is extended, it is divided into past and future: the present however has no space].[27]

There *is*, for Augustine and for Dante, a present moment that is extended infinitely without being divided: the eternal present of God. In the *Vita Nuova*, this timelessness is represented by Beatrice. Beatrice does not essentially change: she is eternally new, but never new to herself, and when she dies only the desolate city she leaves behind is transformed. Likewise, Beatrice is not essentially divided. Dante may treat her different qualities and manifestations separately, as a theologian treats the different aspects of God separately, but she is never said to contain a plurality. Within the *libello*, Beatrice is the nearest approach to Unity. In Dante's numerology, she is a Nine, one step below the triune God:

> ella era uno nove, cioè uno miracolo, la cui radice, cioè del miracolo, è solamente la mirabile Trinitade. (29.3)
>
> [she was a nine, that is, a miracle, whose root, that is, the root of the miracle, is only the miraculous Trinity.]

The represented universe of the *Vita Nuova* embodies a Neoplatonic "metaphysics of light," with Beatrice radiating divine virtue to the world below her.[28] In the final sonnet, Dante's spirit climbs above the highest material sphere and sees Beatrice as pure splendor (41.11). Even in life, however, Beatrice exists to transmit God's light. The *canzone* "Donne ch'avete intelletto d'amore" describes her as a radiance located between the angels and mortal humanity. The angels say to God,

> Sire, nel mondo si vede
> maraviglia ne l'atto che procede
> d'un'anima che 'nfin qua su risplende. (19.7)
>
> [Lord, in the world is seen
> a marvel in the act that proceeds
> from a soul that shines back as far as up here.]

If the light is visible to the angels, however, its real effects are felt below:

De li occhi suoi, come ch'ella li mova,
escono spirti d'amore inflammati,
che feron li occhi a qual che allor la guati,
e passan sì che 'l cor ciascun retrova:
voi le vedete Amor pinto nel viso,
là 've non pote alcun mirarla fiso. (19.12)

[From her eyes, wherever she may move them,
issue forth flaming spirits of love,
which strike the eyes of whoever gazes on her,
and they pass within so that each one finds the heart:
you see Love portrayed in her face,
where no one can gaze fixedly.]

Occasionally Beatrice forms part of a plurality—a plurality of *donne*, in which the other women occupy a lower stage of the hierarchy. Ladies who accompany her share in her splendor: "ciascuna per lei riceve onore" (26.12) [each one receives honor through her]. When the beloved of Guido Cavalcanti walks ahead of her, one "maraviglia" [miracle] follows another (24.8), but Giovanna is a miracle *because* she precedes Beatrice; she receives her name from John the Baptist, the mortal who prepares the way for Love itself (24.4–5). The hierarchy beneath Beatrice is transitory, just as Dante's apprehension of her is imperfect and mutable. Beatrice's own place in the hierarchy connecting God and humanity is fixed. Within the limited domain of the *Vita Nuova*, Beatrice is the unity at the center.

In this Neoplatonic structure, dividedness is a sign of inferiority. But the *Vita Nuova*, like the Psalm commentary of Peter Lombard, also incorporates the other, more Aristotelian, sort of *divisio*, division as a positive human activity. The *divisioni* of the lyrics do not simply symptomatize dividedness. Rather, as tools to "aprire la sentenzia de la cosa divisa" (14.13) [open the meaning of the divided thing] for imperfect readers, they work to overcome dividedness. Likewise the narrative prose—sequential, circumstantial—is inferior to the relatively atemporal, relatively abstract lyrics, but its function is to serve them beneficially, to "aprire per prosa" (25.8) [open through prose] that which might remain inaccessible otherwise. If Dante as a lover is passively divided, as a writer he can divide constructively. And this applies not only to the ancillary parts of the *libello* but also to the lyrics themselves. The lyrics are divided reflections of their chief subject, Beatrice, yet they transmit part of her virtue to a divided world.

Thus the *Vita Nuova* can be read as a stable hierarchy on the model of the hierarchy embodied in a Psalm commentary. In this reading, Beatrice makes Dante feel his inferior dividedness, but he takes a step in her direction by "dividing" in another sense: authorized by his vision of her, he translates her timeless, unitary, silent radiance into a sequence of words, by writing first the lyrics and then the *Vita Nuova*. And the *Vita Nuova* is, in this reading, a textual counterpart to the human relationship that generates it: the subordination of Dante (and all of his writing) to Beatrice is repeated in the subordination of prose to verse. In the textual hierarchy, a transcendent lyric text radiates its meaning through two different levels of prose, and the *ragioni* and *divisioni* are divided servants that serve by dividing.

2. The History of a Method

Once again (as in Chapter 2) I have arrived at a stable and totalizing form for the *Vita Nuova*—with the intention of complicating it by exploring the temporality of form within the work. Critics generally treat all of the *divisioni* at once—"One example will serve to remind any reader of them all," writes Singleton[29]—and that has been my own method so far. The *divisioni* are not all identical, however; the rules for division change in the course of the *Vita Nuova*.

The *divisioni* fall into three phases. These phases correspond to the three main sections of the *libello*, when the book is divided according to the disposition of its lyric forms. Critics have long observed that the work's three completed *canzoni* are situated symmetrically:

10 – C – 4 – C – 4 – C – 10,

where "C" means completed *canzone* and the numbers stand for all other poetic forms. (The other poems are all sonnets, except for one *ballata* [12] and two unfinished *canzoni* [27, 33].) Singleton, reasonably noting "the exceptional importance of the number nine in this work," suggests that the central group of 4 - C - 4 be considered one unit, and that the first and last sonnets be considered a prologue and an epilogue. This yields the pattern

1 – 9 – C – 9 – C – 9 – 1.

Singleton goes on to associate the three 9s with "three stages in the poet's love."[30] My own division of the *divisioni* is grafted onto Singleton's pattern. In my view, the first phase of the *divisioni* extends over the first ten poems;

the second extends over the central nine; the third extends over the final ten; and the *divisioni* for the first and last *canzoni* are transitional. I shall return to the third phase; my concern in this section is the contrast between the first phase and the second.

Here are two *divisioni*, one from near the beginning of the book and one from near the middle:

> (1) Questo sonetto si divide in quattro parti: ne la prima parte chiamo la Morte per certi suoi nomi propri; ne la seconda, parlando a lei, dico la cagione per che io mi muovo a blasimarla; ne la terza la vitupero; ne la quarta mi volgo a parlare a indiffinita persona, avvegna che quanto a lo mio intendimento sia diffinita. La seconda comincia quivi: *poi che hai data*; la terza quivi: *E s'io di grazia*; la quarta quivi: *Chi non merta salute*. (8.12)

> [This sonnet is divided into four parts. In the first part I call Death by certain names proper to it; in the second, speaking to it, I say why I am moved to curse it; in the third I revile it; in the fourth I turn to speak to some unspecified person, although in my own understanding this person is specified. The second part begins here: *since you have given*; the third here: *And if I, of grace*; the fourth here: *Who merits not salvation*.]

> (2) Questo sonetto si divide in due parti: ne la prima dico di lui [Amore] in quanto è in potenzia; ne la seconda dico di lui in quanto di potenzia si riduce in atto. La seconda comincia quivi: *Bieltate appare*. La prima si divide in due: ne la prima dico in che suggetto sia questa potenzia; ne la seconda dico sì come questo suggetto e questa potenzia siano produtti in essere, e come l'uno guarda l'altro come forma materia. La seconda comincia quivi: *Falli natura*. Poscia quando dico: *Bieltate appare*, dico come questa potenzia si riduce in atto; e prima come si riduce in uomo, poi come si riduce in donna, quivi: *E simil face in donna*. (20.6–8)

> [This sonnet is divided into two parts. In the first I speak of Love as a potential; in the second I speak of it as a potential realized in action. The second begins here: *Beauty appears*. The first part is divided into two: in the first I say in what subject this potential resides; in the second I say how this subject and this potential are brought into being, and how the one is related to the other as form is to matter. The second begins here: *Nature makes them*. Then when I say: *Beauty appears*, I say how this potential is realized in action; and first how it is realized in a man, then how it is realized in a woman, here: *And likewise in a woman*.]

Each *divisione* divides its text into four parts quite independent of the spatial proportions of the poem. Certain differences between the *divisioni* appear at once: the second uses a technical philosophical vocabulary that is missing in the first, and the first reaches four parts in a single step, while the second subdivides two parts into two parts each. Beyond these differences, there is a fundamental difference in analytic method. The first *divisione* separates its "sonetto" into four different speech acts: "chiamo la Morte"; "parlando a lei, dico . . ."; "la vitupero"; "mi volgo a parlare a indiffinita persona" [I call Death; speaking to it, I say . . . ; I revile it; I turn to speak to some unspecified person]. The parts are distinguished according to the mode or recipient of Dante's discourse. The second *divisione* describes one complex speech act; the verb throughout is "dico." Here the parts of the poem correspond not to the various rhetorical gestures of the poet but to the various aspects of the poem's topic. The sonnet, apparently, presents these different aspects in a logical structure: first potential force, then the realization of potential force in action; under the first heading, first the subject of the potential force, then the relationship of subject and potential force; under the second heading, action in men and then action in women.

I shall call these two modes of division "rhetorical division" and "logical division." The two modes make different assumptions about the way a poem signifies. Rhetorical division posits no necessary connection between the sequence of a poem and the topic it treats. (The poet addresses Death in three different ways, then turns to speak to another person.) Logical division assumes a congruence between the form of a poem and its topic, so that in dividing the poem one divides the topic as well.

The *divisioni* of the first phase are rhetorical divisions. They describe their poems as sequences of utterances, or (for example in 15 and 16) as sequential notations of separate thoughts in no particular order. The *divisione* for the first completed *canzone*, "Donne ch'avete intelletto d'amore," is rhetorical in its main division: the poem consists of a "proemio" [proem], a "trattato" [treatise] and an envoi ("quasi una serviziale de le precedenti parole," 19.15 [like a servant to the preceding words]). The second part, however, which comprises three fourteen-line stanzas, is subdivided in an elaborate and ostentatiously logical fashion. This *divisione* (to which we shall return) marks the transition to the second phase, in which the *divisioni* are predominantly logical.

I will spare the reader a full documentation of this claim. To define my terms, I have chosen a pair of *divisioni* in which the contrast is especially pronounced. Not all the *divisioni* in the second phase are so systematically logical, and one or two might be exceptions to the pattern; not all the *divisioni* in the first phase use different verbs of discourse to distinguish each part. I believe the trend is quite clear, however. As the illustrative pair I have chosen suggests, logical divisions tend to be subdivided, and this at least can be objectively quantified: in the first phase, only one *divisione* contains a subdivision (15); in the second phase, only two *divisioni* lack them (both in 22).

The general pattern is maintained, paradoxically, when no division appears. Each of the first two sections of the *Vita Nuova* contains one finished but undivided sonnet. In both cases, Dante gives the same explanation for the omission: the meaning is clear enough from the prose *ragione* (14.13, 26.8).[31] In both cases, however, the lack of a division is in effect a comment on the poem itself. The two sonnets are what a Psalm commentator would call "atomus." Peter Lombard never attributes symbolic significance to the number of parts he finds in a Psalm, except when he finds no separable parts at all. He writes, for example, that Psalm 132 is about

> charitas proximi, quae facit fratres habitare in unum. Unde est benedictio et vita. Et est hic psalmus atomus, id est sine divisione, ubi charitas proximi commendatur, quae nullam admittit alienationem mentis seu divisionem.(*PL* 191.1181–82)[32]

> [the love of one's neighbor, which makes brothers live as one. From which comes blessing and life. And this psalm is *atomus*, that is, without division, since the love of one's neighbor is commended, which admits no alienation of the mind or division]

Similarly, the undividedness of these two sonnets reflects a certain absence of alienation in the text of the sonnet—but in two different ways, reflecting the attitudes about poetry that characterize the first two phases of the *Vita Nuova*. The first sonnet, "Con l'altre donne mia vista gabbate" (14.11–12), describes a moment of humiliation, when Beatrice joins a group of ladies in mocking Dante, but it has another distinction as well: it is the first poem to address Beatrice directly. What is undivided about it, and unmediated, is the act of speaking. The second sonnet, the famous "Tanto gentile" (26.5–7), is a third-person account of Beatrice's appearance. It describes a grace that reduces all who see her to silence: "ogne lingua deven tremando muta" (26.5) [every tongue, trembling, falls silent]. As Dante knew, the Greek word for *lingua* is *glossa*;[33] Beatrice's splendor, apprehended directly, makes commentary both impossible and unnecessary.[34] Here the poem is *atomus* because of the glory of its object. The two sonnets show, respectively, a rhetorical and a logical *lack* of division.

It is not difficult to relate these two theories of *divisio textus* to the poetic concerns of the *Vita Nuova.* In the first third of the book, Dante writes about his own condition: his poems are "narratori di tutto quasi lo mio stato" (17.1) [narrators of nearly all my condition]. With the crucial *canzone* "Donne ch'avete intelletto d'amore" (19), Dante begins to find solace in the praise of Beatrice (18.6); he develops a corresponding new style, "lo stilo de la sua lode" (26.4) [the style of her praise]. As De Robertis writes, Dante has found

> A new object of poetry, the lady; a new kind of poetry, praise; a new mode of setting forth these reasons: calling the listeners to amplify the range of his discourse, to collaborate in the triumph of this poetry.[35]

The *divisioni* of the first phase focus on the poet's utterance, as Dante himself attends to his own condition; the *divisioni* of the second phase focus on the object of the poems, as Dante turns his worshipful attention to Beatrice.

But I would also relate the changing method of the *divisioni* to the history of the *divisio psalmi.* When I argued, in Chapter 2, that the *divisioni* in the *Vita Nuova* evoke the *divisio psalmi*, I supported my claim by using the commentary of Peter Lombard as an exemplary text. The *divisio psalmi* is not a fixed form, however; it changes over the centuries. The shift from rhetorical division to logical division within the *Vita Nuova* reflects a trend in the history of Psalter commentary, which in turn reflects a larger trend in intellectual history.

Cassiodorus invented the *divisio psalmi.*[36] He describes his procedure in the preface to his commentary:

> unusquisque psalmus pro sua qualitate dividendus est, ne nobis intellectum permisceat aut occulta mutatio rerum, aut varietas introducta loquentium[37]

> [each individual psalm must be divided according to its nature, so that our understanding may not be confused either by a sudden change of subject, or by the introduction of different speakers]

and again in his commentary on the first Psalm:

> divisio facienda est, quae, si recte adhibeatur, ita illustrem et perspicuam nobis efficit dictionem, ut, priusquam legatur orationis textus, ante nobis eius relucere possit intentio[38]

> [a division must be made, which, if it is rightly applied, makes the words so clear and bright that, before the text of the prayer is read, its purpose can shine out before us.]

Cassiodorus assumes that a single "intentio" shines through the Psalm. But the Psalm is an imperfect medium for conveying the divine light to human eyes: it can conceal confusing shifts of subject (*res*) and of speaker. The commentator renders the Psalm "illustrem et perspicuam" [clear and bright] by dividing it.

When Cassiodorus divides a Psalm, he does not make distinctions within its *res*; rather, he describes a series of distinct speech acts. The *divisio* supplies the rhetorical context of the utterance of the text; the Psalm has a speaker, an addressee, a mode of speaking, and a topic, and any one of these can change at any point.[39] This is rhetorical division. Indeed, Ursula Hahner notes that Cassiodorus derives his idea of *divisio* from the *partitio* of Cicero, and that he frequently uses rhetorical terms to describe the different parts of a Psalm. In providing *divisiones* for the Psalms, Cassiodorus has a double aim: to clarify their meaning and to show that Scripture follows the laws of classical rhetoric.[40]

Cassiodorus's *Expositio Psalmorum* was read and quoted throughout the Middle Ages,[41] but his divisions do not seem to have attracted imitators until the twelfth century, when *divisiones psalmorum* become fairly common. For example, Honorius of Autun and Pseudo-Bede, both writing near the beginning of the century,[42] copy out Cassiodorus's *divisiones* into their own commentaries, with an important change: they abridge the text of the *divisio*, as might be expected, and they also insert scriptural lemmata into the *divisio* itself, something Cassiodorus did not do.[43] The addition of the lemmata suggests that the function of the *divisio* has now changed. There is presumably no longer any need to prove that the Bible is rhetorically sound; the *divisio* now serves a more immediate, practical purpose. In the commentary of Cassiodorus, the *divisio* stands alone as a prefatory overview of the Psalm, and one must read through the complete gloss to find out where the divisions actually fall within the text. (The stages are clearly marked: "Venit ad secundam partem,"[44] for example.) In the twelfth-century commentaries, the *divisio* serves as a brief index to both text and gloss.

Cassiodorus's *divisiones* had always been available; I assume that their reappearance after nearly six centuries reflects a change in the interests of the commentators—a new appreciation of *divisio textus* as both a formal principle and a practical research tool. The figure at the transitional point may be Anselm of Laon, Honorius's teacher, who wrote at the very beginning of the twelfth century. The *divisio psalmi* makes a sudden appearance midway through Anselm's commentary on the Psalter, which was part of the original *Glossa Ordinaria*: before Psalm 106, there is no *divisio psalmi*; beginning with Psalm 106, only one Psalm lacks a *divisio*.[45]

Peter Lombard revises the Cassiodorian *divisiones* still further. In general, he divides the Psalms at the same verses, but he describes the parts differently. To illustrate the difference, here are the two divisions of Psalm 3. Cassiodorus:

> Totus hic psalmus ad personam Christi Domini competenter aptatur. Persona vero eius est virtus omnipotentissimae deitatis et humilitas humanitatis assumptae, non sub permixtione confusa, et indivisibili adunatione subsistens. Primo itaque modo ad Patrem loquitur, persecutoribus exprobans, qui irreligiosa contra ipsum verba loquebantur. Secundo loco fidelis populus, ne mortem formidet, instruitur, quando eum exemplo auctoris sui spe resurrectionis certissimae consolatur.[46]

> [This whole of this Psalm is aptly attributed to the person of Christ the Lord. His person indeed is the strength of the almighty Godhead and the humility of the humanity which he embraced; but the two do not mix through intermingling, but exist in indivisible unity. To begin with, he speaks to the Father, reproaching persecutors who were speaking impious words against him. Secondly, the faithful people are instructed not to fear death, when he consoles them with the hope of most certain resurrection following the example of their Author.]

I have already quoted Peter Lombard's division:

> [B]ipartitus est psalmus. Primo, ponit duas partes oppositas a simili praeliantium, ex una parte persequentium multitudinem, ex altera, Christum oratione armatum, et Deo susceptore securum. Secundo finis rei ostenditur, id est resurrectio, quae est consummatio passionis; unde proponit non esse timendum, ibi, *Ego dormivi*. (*PL* 191.78)

> [The Psalm is bipartite. First, it posits two opposing parties in the likeness of fighters: from one side the multitude of persecutors, from the other, Christ armed with his speech and secure in God the Defender. Second, the end of the matter is set forth, namely the Resurrection, which is the completion of the Passion; whence it shows that it is not to be feared, there: *I have slept*.]

Both commentators agree that the Psalm treats first Christ's relationship to his persecutors and then (at verse 6) Christ's resurrection. Cassiodorus, however, describes the two parts as two different speech acts, addressed to two different audiences. He begins by stating that Christ is the speaker throughout and stressing that Christ's human and divine natures are not merely mixed but indivisibly united. This absolute unity manifests itself in a divided form, however: Christ's utterance, the Psalm, is *permixtus*, with human and divine placed side by side, as Christ addresses first God the Father and then humanity. Indeed, the Psalm *must* be divided, as Cassiodorus says in his preface, lest our understanding be *permixtus* in a different sense, confused ("ne nobis intellectum permisceat").[47]

In contrast, Peter focuses his own attention on the material that is treated in the Psalm. If there is a "speaker" it is either the prophet David or the Psalm itself (in context, either might be the subject of "ponit"), but the emphasis falls on what is said rather than on the act of speaking. And the Psalm does not simply turn from one topic to another; it makes a single statement that can be analyzed as bipartite. The first part, in Peter's account, shows a conflict between two forces, and the second part shows the "finis rei" [end of the matter]. Cassiodorus does not specify any connection between the two parts of the Psalm beyond the unity of the speaker. This is not an insignificant connection, of course: if one part corresponds to Christ's divinity and the other to his humanity, divinity and humanity are mystically one in Christ. But Cassiodorus does not make this logic explicit and does not use it to analyze the content of Christ's two utterances. For Peter, the text of the Psalm is logically coherent in itself; its very structure declares a real relationship between persecution and resurrection.

The contrast between Cassiodorus's *divisio* of Psalm 3 and Peter Lombard's is the contrast between rhetorical and logical division. For Cassiodorus, the medium of scriptural language is eloquent but potentially misleading; the task of the commentator is to account for the rhetorical variability of the text so as to point to a higher unity that lies beyond the text. For Peter Lombard, the form of the Psalm is meaningful in itself; the commentator only makes explicit a logical analysis that is already implied in the text. Peter rationalizes the Psalm—he shows it to be not only inspired and eloquent but also orderly and reasonable. The process of rationalization does not end with Peter Lombard, however; it continues in the thirteenth-century commentaries of, for example, Hugh of St. Cher (composed 1230–35) and Thomas Aquinas (composed 1272–73).[48]

Hugh of St. Cher takes over the *divisiones* of Peter Lombard and elaborates upon them. He begins his division of Psalm 3 thus:

> Et dividitur Psalmus iste in duas partes. In prima parte ponit partes oppositas a similitudine pugnantium. Secundo finis rei ostenditur, id est resurrectio, ibi, *Ego dormivi etc.*
>
> Prima pars dividitur in tres partes. In prima agit de persecutoribus. In secunda de persona adiuvantis, ibi, *Tu autem domine*. In tertia de persona pugnantis, ibi, *Voce mea*. In prima aggravat persecutionem inimicorum. Primo ostendendo eos esse multos, ibi, *Multiplicati sunt*. Secundo crudeles, ibi, *Qui tribulant me*. Tertio detractores, ibi, *Multi insurgunt*. Quarto invitantes ad desperationem, ibi, *Multi dicunt etc.*[49]

> [And this Psalm is divided into two parts. In the first part it posits opposing parties in the likeness of combatants. Second, the end of the matter is set forth, that is, the resurrection, there: *I have slept, etc.*
>
> The first part is divided into three parts. In the first it treats persecutors. In the second the person of the one who helps, there: *But thou, O Lord*. In the third the person of the combatant, there: *With my voice*. In the first it increases the persecution of enemies. First by showing them to be many, there: *They are multiplied*. Second, cruel, there: *Who afflict me*. Third, detractors, there: *Many rise up*. Fourth, inviters to desperation, there: *Many say etc.*]

In Chapter 2, I contrasted the *divisio textus* of thirteenth-century Scholasticism with the older tradition of the *divisio psalmi*, using Peter Lombard's commentary as my example. In the terms of the contrast I established there, the *divisio* of Hugh of St. Cher is fully Scholastic. It employs the same vocabulary as Bonaventure's commentary on the *Sentences* ("dividitur in duas partes" rather than "bipartitus est"). It is subdivided and subsubdivided. And it no longer occupies an isolated, prefatory position in the commentary. What I have quoted here is only the beginning of the division. Of the two primary parts, the first has three parts; of these three, the first has four parts—and the first of *these* parts is the beginning of the Psalm, so the verse-by-verse comment begins. Hugh subdivides the remaining subdivisions as he reaches them.

Peter Lombard's assumption that the Psalm is logical in its form is here carried to an extreme. For Hugh, the rationality of the textual ordonnance reaches down even to the level of the phrase. In a linguistic analysis, "qui tribulant me" would be described as a relative clause; it follows "quid multiplicati sunt" because it modifies the subject of the verb. But that would be a rhetorical explanation, relying on the accidental rules of Latin rather than the nature of the extra-linguistic matter being treated. In a logical division, "qui tribulant me" is the second part of the first part of the first part; it appears where it does because the sequence "multos," "crudeles," "detractores," "invitantes ad desperationem" shows a steady increase in evil ("aggravat persecutionem inimicorum").

The *divisio* of Hugh of St. Cher is still recognizably a *divisio psalmi*. Moving a step beyond Peter Lombard, Hugh has further rationalized, or "scholasticized," the original *divisio* of Cassiodorus. Thomas Aquinas starts fresh, constructing an entirely new division. I quote from the beginning of the second primary part:

> *Tu*. Haec est pars secunda. Ubi [David] ostendit sibi a Deo paratum auxilium. Et circa hoc duo facit. Primo ostendit sibi specialiter adesse divinum auxilium. Secundo generaliter omnibus, ibi, *Domini est salus*. Et circa primum tria proponit. Primo auxilium divinum. Secundo auxilii experimentum, ibi, *Voce mea*. Tertio securitatis conceptum, ibi, *Non timebo*. Dicit ergo, *Tu autem Domine* . . .[50]

> [*Thou*. This is the second part. Where David shows the help provided to him by God. And on this he does two things. First he shows that divine help has been present to him in particular. Second, in general to all, there: *Salvation is of the Lord*. And on the first he sets forth three things. First, divine help. Second, the experience of help, there: *With my voice*. Third, the receiving of security, there: *I will not fear*. He says therefore, *But thou, O Lord* . . .]

Formally, this division works in the same way as Hugh's: the division serves as an elaborate skeleton for the entire comment. But Thomas Aquinas's vocabulary is even more abstract than Hugh's. He uses colorless verbs ("ostendit," "facit," "proponit," rather than "aggravat"), and the topic of this second part is not a person, "persona adiuvantis," but "auxilium" itself. And Thomas has entirely rethought the structure of the Psalm, placing his primary division at verse 3 rather than verse 6. The *divisio* has escaped its origin in Cassiodorus's rhetorical analysis; Thomas Aquinas would have composed this Scholastic *divisio textus* even if there were no tradition of the *divisio psalmi*.

Thomas Aquinas's unfinished Psalter commentary is a small monument of Scholasticism. It exhibits, in the words of Erwin Panofsky,

> the much derided schematism or formalism of Scholastic writing which reached its climax in the classic *Summa* with its three requirements of (1) totality (sufficient enumeration), (2) arrangement according to a system of

> homologous parts and parts of parts (sufficient articulation), and (3) distinctness and deductive cogency (sufficient interrelation).[51]

And, treating the Psalm text as a coherent field of study like the *sacra pagina* of theology, this commentary applies its schematism in the service of *manifestatio*, the "elucidation or clarification" that Panofsky has called "the first controlling principle of Early and High Scholasticism" (30). Panofsky's *Gothic Architecture and Scholasticism* describes a "mental habit" (21) that extended beyond the faculties of theology to all the professional classes of the thirteenth century—a "modus operandi" (28) rather than a body of particular ideas.[52] The book is primarily a synchronic account of a single cultural moment, but Panofsky does devote a section to the gradual consolidation and gradual decomposition of High Scholasticism (3–20). The history of the *divisio psalmi* is a minor but telling index of the gradual consolidation. It shows that Scholasticism can be understood not only as an achieved system but also as a process—a "movement" in two senses, both a collective activity and a journey. The commentary of Peter Lombard is a precursor to the High Scholastic commentary of Thomas, but Peter Lombard is already "scholasticizing" the commentary of Cassiodorus.

The *divisioni* of the *Vita Nuova* also undergo a process of scholasticization. Modern readers tend to regard the *divisioni* as utterly static and uniform, but when they are read carefully, and read in the context of the *divisio psalmi*, it becomes clear that they have a dynamism of their own. They change, and their change reflects both a revision of Dante's personal aims and a broad trend in twelfth- and thirteenth-century intellectual history; they participate in the temporality of the *libello* and in the temporality of Dante's world. I do not see a gradual, regular transformation in the *divisioni*, nor would I connect them to specific moments in the history of Scholastic thought: rather, there is a single important shift, from the *divisioni* of the first third of the work to the *divisioni* of the middle third, and this shift is like the shift from Cassiodorus to Peter Lombard, or from Peter Lombard to Hugh of St. Cher. The passage from rhetorical division to logical division is a miniature image of the rise of Scholasticism.

3. The Critique of Division (I)

The microcosmic model of the *Vita Nuova*—the Singletonian vision of hierarchy that I have glossed with the glossed Psalter—combines two different forms of *divisio*, which we may loosely call Neoplatonic and Aristotelian: first, the radiation of divine unity through human multiplicity, which prompts the human soul to reach toward the truth of the One; second, one of the means by which the human soul makes that effort, namely intellectual analysis. The history of the *divisio psalmi* suggests, however, that some forms of Aristotelian division are more Aristotelian than others. The *divisioni* in the middle of the *Vita Nuova* are more forcefully analytic than the *divisioni* that precede them; rather than sorting out the rhetorical moments of the lyric text, they reach *through* this text to divide the object that the text represents. But when one force in a stable, dynamic structure is stepped up, there is at least the possibility of destabilization.

The *Vita Nuova* provides an image for the rise of Scholasticism, but I believe that it also implies a critique—a critique that combines two quite different counterreactions to the increasingly Scholastic tone of the *divisioni*. First, a counterreaction from the Neoplatonic position: when the rhetorical analysis of lyric poems is elevated into a "principle of progressive divisibility (or, to look at it another way, multiplicability),"[53] the Neoplatonist can reply that multiplicity is a degradation of Unity. Second, a counterreaction directed against the commentator's increasing abstractness, in which the erotic impulse behind the lyrics (played out in Chapter 3, and repressed by the vision of a divinely ordained hierarchy) returns to mock the pedantic language of "potenzia" and "atto." In two different ways, the divisive force that Dante attributes to Beatrice reasserts its power against the confident enterprise of Dante's own divisions. The critique of Scholastic *divisio textus* is most visible in two passages: the *divisione* for "Donne ch'avete intelletto d'amore" and the entire third phase of the *divisioni*.

The *divisione* that accompanies the *Vita Nuova*'s first *canzone* is the most elaborate in the book, and Dante calls attention to this fact:

> Questa canzone, acciò che sia meglio intesa, la dividerò più artificiosamente che l'altre cose di sopra. (19.15)

> [This *canzone*, so that it may be better understood, I will divide more carefully than the others above.]

This is partly, no doubt, a tribute to the special place this poem holds in the *Vita Nuova* and indeed in Dante's career. "Donne ch'avete" marks the beginning of a new mode of writing; it has been called "the true centre of the book";[54] we have seen that it provides an unusually clear picture of the hierarchy that locates Beatrice between the angels and the earth; Dante cites it as a special achievement both in the *De Vulgari Eloquentia* (2.8.8) and *Purgatorio* (24.51). The *divisione* itself is, as I have suggested, an opening into a new style: branching out from a rhetorical division, a most "artificioso" [careful] subdivision sets the pattern for the logical *divisioni* of the second phase. *This* logical division, however, makes a statement of its own—a statement that threatens to undo the achievement of the *canzone*.

Here is the subdivision of the second part:

> Poscia quando dico: *Angelo clama*, comincio a trattare di questa donna. E dividesi questa parte in due: ne la prima dico che di lei si comprende in cielo; ne la seconda dico che di lei si comprende in terra, quivi: *Madonna è disiata*. Questa seconda parte si divide in due; che ne la prima dico di lei quanto da la parte de la nobilitade de la sua anima, narrando alquanto de le sue vertudi effettive che da la sua anima procedeano; ne la seconda dico di lei quanto da la parte de la nobilitade del suo corpo, narrando alquanto de le sue bellezze, quivi: *Dice di lei Amor*. Questa seconda parte si divide in due; che ne la prima dico d'alquante bellezze che sono secondo tutta la persona; ne la seconda dico d'alquante bellezze che sono secondo diterminata parte de la persona, quivi: *De li occhi suoi*. Questa seconda parte si divide in due: che ne l'una dico de li occhi, li quali sono principio d'amore; ne la seconda dico de la bocca, la quale è fine d'amore. (19.17–20)

> [Then when I say *An angel cries out*, I begin to treat of this lady. And this part is divided in two: in the first I say what is understood of her in Heaven; in the second I say what is understood of her on earth, here: *Milady is desired*. This second part is divided in two: for in the first I speak of her in terms of the nobility of her soul, narrating some of her effective powers, which proceed from her soul; in the second I speak of her according to the nobility of her body, narrating some of its beauties, here: *Love says of her*. This second part is divided in two; for in the first I speak of some beauties that are according to her entire person; in the second I speak of beauties that are according to determined parts of her person, here: *From her eyes*. This second part is divided in two: for in one I speak of her eyes, which are the beginning of love; in the second I speak of her mouth, which is the goal of love.]

Rhetorically, the most striking feature of this text is its anaphora: the second part of the *canzone* is divided in two, and then "questa seconda parte si divide in due" [this second part is divided in two], three more times. This repetition calls attention to a regular, logical pattern. Each binary division, until the last, posits a hierarchical pair: heaven/earth; soul/body; whole/parts. For each of these pairs, the first term goes undivided while the second term "si divide in due."

The *divisione* might be said to mimic a pattern of division actually existing in the things named. In each hierarchical pair, the second term is ontologically inferior to the first, and part of this inferiority is a greater divisibility. To take the most obvious example, there is a logic to dividing the "bellezze che sono secondo diterminata parte de la persona" [beauties that are according to determined parts of her person] and leaving undivided the "bellezze che sono secondo tutta la persona" [beauties that are according to her entire person]. This is a logical division; in analyzing the text, it responds to the object that is represented in the text.

Now, I have mentioned a recent essay by Durling and Martinez that argues for a Neoplatonic cosmos embodied in the *Vita Nuova*. That essay is in fact a brilliant reading of Chapter 19, both the *canzone* and the *divisione*. Durling and Martinez observe the pattern in the second part of the division, and see a resemblance between its carefully articulated hierarchy and the Neoplatonist's "chain of being."[55] In addition they see a close fit between the division and the poem, a fit so close that it is possible to complete the division by dividing the *first* part at each stage and thereby produce an image of hierarchical ascent to match the descent that is explicit in the text. This argument leads them to several conclusions that I myself reached by a different route: for example, the idea that Beatrice "is an agent of reunification—or of an ultimate division"[56] and the idea that the term "divisione" has a metaphysical valence throughout the *Vita Nuova*.

Yet I am inclined to read the *divisione* of "Donne ch'avete" with a very different emphasis than Durling and Martinez. By focusing on a single *canzone* and its non-narrative explication, they arrive at a microcosmic model of Dante's text entirely in tune with Singleton's *Essay*. I would suggest, in contrast, that the lyric microcosm is endlessly engaged with an open-ended narrative temporality—and that the driving forces of Dante's life return unexpectedly in this most artificial of divisions. The second part of the *divisione* can be viewed as a spatial structure or as a temporal sequence, and as a sequence it moves decisively in one direction. At each point, the *divisione* leaves behind the higher term and lingers on the lower, as if expressing a preference. The focus shifts from Beatrice, to Beatrice as she is on earth, to Beatrice as she is visible on earth, and then to Beatrice as she is visible in close-up. This is an erotic journey, from the idea of Beatrice to her mouth. And the process could continue. (Like Durling and Martinez, but in quite another way, I suggest that the division invites completion.) *Occhi* and *bocca* do not seem to be an ontological hierarchy,[57] but this pair could be treated like the others; its "seconda parte" is literally a "diterminata parte," the mouth, and a careless reader, lulled by the anaphora, might add, "questa seconda parte si divide in due."

The image of a purely physical division, the parting of lips, seems coarse for the *Vita Nuova*. Dante seems aware, though, that some sort of coarse or careless reading is possible. In a sentence that Durling and Martinez do not cite, Dante immediately adds:

> E acciò che quinci si lievi ogni vizioso pensiero, ricordisi chi ci legge, che di sopra è scritto che lo saluto di questa donna, lo quale era de la operazioni de la bocca sua, fue fine de li miei desiderii mentre ch'io lo potei ricevere. (19.20)[58]

> [And so that any vicious thought may be avoided from this, whoever reads here should recall what is written above, that the greeting of this lady, which was among the operations of her mouth, was the goal of my desires as long as I could receive it.]

This is an unsatisfying disclaimer, and not merely because, like most warnings against vicious thinking, it can incite the very thinking it warns against. (The reader will at least wonder what the *vizioso pensiero* might be.) It is unsatisfying because it does not cohere well with the poem or the prefatory narrative. In the scene that precedes the writing of "Donne ch'avete," Dante tells a group of ladies that the "fine di tutti li miei desiderii" (18.4) [goal of all my desires] is no longer Beatrice's greeting; it is now the praise of Beatrice. If the *canzone* really does end its *trattato* by coming to rest on the "saluto," then the first poem in the new style has slipped back into the habits of the old style. Is this the case? The warning, dwelling as it does on the problem of the "bocca," prompts us to look again at the lyric text. The lines in question are:

> voi le vedete Amor pinto nel viso,
> là 've non pote alcun mirarla fiso. (19.12)

> [you see Love portrayed in her face,
> where no one can gaze fixedly.]

There is no mention of the "saluto" [greeting] here, and no mention of the "bocca" [mouth].[59] The *divisione* has translated "viso" [face] into a particular part of the "viso"—and has described this part with a word that is normally excluded from Dante's courtly lyric vocabulary.[60] When Francesca, in *Inferno* 5, replaces "disiato riso" [desired smile] with "bocca," there is at least the hint of a carnal sensibility.[61] This is not to say that the *divisione* is simply wrong: perhaps Dante was thinking of Beatrice's mouth when he wrote these rather general lines. Whether the *divisione* is revealing Dante's unstated intention or importing an idea of its own, however, it works a transformation on the lyric text.

The *divisione* eroticizes the *canzone*. The interpretation that the *divisione* offers is not flagrantly carnal, to be sure, but it is at least *more* carnal than the reading the text itself seems to invite. And this very act of interpretation has erotic overtones. In the envoi of the *canzone*, Dante addresses his song as a young woman, a "figliuola d'Amor giovane e piana" (19.13) [young and gentle daughter of Love]; the *divisione* treats the song as a textual body to be explored. It gazes directly at the place where "non pote alcun mirarla fiso" (19.12) [where no one can gaze fixedly], and reaches into the letter of the text to find, or supply, not "Amor" but a "bocca." The composition of the *canzone* began when Dante's "lingua parlò quasi come per sé stessa mossa" (19.2) [tongue spoke as if moved by itself]. As De Robertis notes, this image recalls several scriptural passages, including Ps. 50:16–17: "exultabit lingua mea iustitiam tuam. Domine, labia mea aperies; et os meum adnuntiabit laudem tuam" [my tongue shall extol thy justice. O Lord, thou wilt open my lips; and my mouth shall declare thy praise].[62] This Psalm text is relevant to the *divisione* as well. When the *divisione* engages the *canzone*, the *canzone* can be understood as the meeting-place of two mouths: in the beginning, the exultation of Dante's tongue; in the end, the wish that Beatrice's mouth might be opened.

I have argued that the *divisioni* in the *Vita Nuova* function collectively to stabilize the form of the *libello*. The ambiguous and reciprocal engagement envisioned in Chapter 3 is replaced by a univocal hierarchy modeled on the textual hierarchy of biblical commentary; the desires that seem to drive the fantasy of Chapter 3—erotic desire and the desire for revelation—are channeled through a pattern of *divisio* to make a dynamic structure of authority and praise. In the *divisione* to "Donne ch'avete," however, it appears that the program of stabilization has both succeeded and failed. The rapacious, seductive reciprocity of Chapter 3 has been repressed: Beatrice will neither eat nor address Dante again. But if her mouth is now closed, the possibility of its opening suffuses the text. The erotic violence of the first dream returns, transformed, in the very apparatus Dante has borrowed from the "fredde sale delle scuole" [cold school-halls].

And the *divisione* to "Donne ch'avete" offers a way of reading all the *divisioni* in the *libello*. The path that this *divisione* describes, a descent from the spiritual to the material, from a whole to its parts, is the path that all the *divisioni*, by their very nature, must take: they treat songs as written things, "cose," and treat these things as collections of parts. Such a division need not work any real transformation on its object: the separation into parts may be purely notional, leaving the original unity of the object unimpaired. This is the way that Scholastic *divisio textus*, like the older *divisio psalmi*, is supposed to work—standing apart from its object, not changing it but explaining it. Thomas Aquinas, for example, states that *compositio* and *divisio* belong solely to the human intellect, not to the objects that that intellect understands. It is true that the intellect understands by assimilation to its objects ("intellectus intelligit per assimilationem ad res"[63]), but intellectual composition and division are not themselves assimilated: they are part of the temporal process by which assimilation is achieved. The *divisione* of "Donne ch'avete", however, does change the object it divides—it revises the *canzone*—and this suggests that *assimilatio* may work in both directions. The dividing intellect may recreate the unitary object in its own divided image, according to its own desires.

4. The Critique of Division (II)

I have suggested that the *divisione* of "Donne ch'avete" seems to challenge the lyric, microcosmic stability of the text. But it should be recalled that Durling and Martinez read this very text as a confirmation of Neoplatonic order—and nothing that I have said can be taken as a refutation of their reading. In fact, Neoplatonic orders are nearly impossible to disprove, once they are plausibly suggested: any particular evidence of mutability, evil, or dividedness turned up by a skeptical investigator can be explained as a marginal negation of a central Unity. Even the "vizioso pensiero" (19.20) [vicious thought] that is mentioned as a possibility within the text could be recuperated as an indication of the chaos at the edge of the cosmos.[64] Like the "vizioso pensiero," the critical reading of the *divisione* is no more than a possibility, a possibility that can be, and perhaps should be, avoided.

If the *divisione* of "Donne ch'avete" suggests a negative reading of Scholastic analysis in general, this is nonetheless the very *divisione* that inaugurates the phase of logical, Scholastic division in the *Vita Nuova*. The critique of the new process does not seem to hamper its smooth functioning; in the second phase, Dante divides Amore (20), Beatrice and her effects

(21, 26.14ff), and his own experiences (22, 23, 24), without working any visible transformation on the objects divided. The sonnet "Ne li occhi porta" is divided according to "la nobilissima parte de li suoi occhi" [the most noble part of her eyes] and "la nobilissima parte de la sua bocca" (21.5) [the most noble part of her mouth], but this time the physical analysis is clearly justified by the text, which refers to the "occhi" and to the two actions of the mouth, speaking and smiling ("parlar," "sorride," 21.3–4). And "eyes" and "mouth" return in the text of the sonnet that receives no *divisione*, "Tanto gentile," in a careful chiastic pattern:

> ogne *lingua* deven tremando muta,
> e li *occhi* no l'ardiscon di guardare. . . .
> [Ella] dà per li *occhi* una dolcezza al core . . .
> e par che de la sua *labbia* si mova
> un spirito soave pien d'amore,
> che va dicendo a l'anima: Sospira. (26.5–7, emphasis added)

> [every *tongue*, trembling, falls silent,
> and *eyes* do not dare to look at her . . .
> She gives through the *eyes* a sweetness to the heart . . .
> and it seems that from her *lips* moves
> a gentle spirit full of love
> that goes saying to the soul: Sigh.]

The prose that framed "Donne ch'avete" reached into the lyric to make a connection between two mouths. Here, the lyric itself constructs a linkage between the mouth and eyes of someone who sees Beatrice and Beatrice's own eyes and mouth. Beatrice's observer is a general "altrui" (26.5) [other], one who looks ("la mira," 26.7) but who shies away from looking too directly or speaking. Yet this observer is granted a direct apprehension of Beatrice: the journey from mouth to mouth, by way of the eyes, is undertaken by Beatrice's miraculous virtue, which speaks directly to the observer's soul. (Here there is no need to warn against "vizioso pensiero" [vicious thought].) The effect, I think, is to confirm the objectivity and adequacy of Dante's vision throughout the second phase of the *Vita Nuova*, the direct vision expressed both in lyrics of praise and in logical *divisioni*. The "seems" of the sonnet—"Tanto gentile e tanto onesta *pare* / la donna mia" [So noble and so virtuous seems my lady], and again "par," "mostrasi," "par" [seems, appears, seems]—*might* introduce the possibility of error or uncertainty, but with Beatrice appearance is reality.[65]

The critique that I have discerned in the long transitional *divisione* could be extended to Dante's amorous Scholasticism throughout the second phase. If "Tanto gentile" retroactively justifies the surprising emphasis on eyes and mouth in the analysis of "Donne ch'avete," perhaps it is because Dante, as a lyricist, has assimilated Beatrice to his own critical understanding of her. The confirmation of objectivity offered by the sonnet could be called circular, a self-confirmation: Dante looks at Beatrice to see what she is like, and one of the things he discovers is that her true nature is visible to anyone who looks at her. Within the second phase, however, the critique remains theoretical—a *possible* skeptical reading of a project that is succeeding on its own terms. In the final third of the *Vita Nuova*, however, the negative effects of active, analytic division become visible within the text.

The final complete *canzone*, "Li occhi dolenti" (31), marks the transition between the second phase and the third. As Foster and Boyde note, this *canzone* is "closely linked to the first canzone in praise of Beatrice, *Donne ch'avete*, of which it is the completion."[66] Appropriately, the *divisione* of this lyric is in effect a revision of the earlier *divisione*. Again, there are three main parts, a "proemio" [proem] and an envoi and a long middle section treating Beatrice herself: "ne la seconda ragiono di lei" (31.3) [in the second I speak of her]. Again the middle section is subdivided and sub-subdivided. (These two are the only *divisioni* in the *Vita Nuova* to contain sub-subdivisions.) This time, however, the middle section changes course. It begins as a *trattato* about Beatrice, but it ends by returning to an earlier topic—"la mia condizione" [my condition]. Here is the subdivision of the second part:

> Poscia quando dico: *Ita n'è Beatrice*, ragiono di lei; e intorno a ciò foe due parti: prima dico la cagione per che tolta ne fue; appresso dico come altri si piange de la sua partita, e comincia questa parte quivi: *Partissi de la sua*. Questa parte si divide in tre: ne la prima dico chi non la piange; ne la seconda dico chi la piange; ne la terza dico de la mia condizione. (31.5–7)

> [Then when I say, *Beatrice has gone*, I speak of her; and concerning this I make two parts: first I state the reason for which she was taken; afterward I say how another weeps for her departure, and this part begins here: *She has left her*. This part is divided into three: in the first I say who does not weep for her; in the second I say who weeps for her; in the third I speak of my condition.]

As Giuseppe Mazzotta has observed, for Dante the "quest must pass through bodies."[67] The *divisione* to "Donne ch'avete" enacted a particularly literal version of this quest. Now, in Chapter 31, although Beatrice herself is in glory, her body is missing; as the *divisione* states, Dante's discourse about Beatrice is diverted toward the material world she has left behind, and returns to treat Dante himself. The subject of the final part of the *canzone* really is "quale è stata la mia vita" (31.15) [what my life has been]—Dante's life and his physical appearance, his parts: "mi tramuta lo color nel viso" (31.13) [my face has changed color]; "giugnemi tanta pena d'ogne parte, / ch'io mi riscuoto" (31.14) [so much pain comes to me from all sides, that I am shaken]. Beatrice is mentioned, in this last section of the *trattato*, only as the cause and the observer of Dante's condition. She is "quella che m'ha 'l cor diviso" (31.13) [the one who has divided my heart]; everyone observes "la mia labbia tramortita" (31.16) [my deathly face], but Beatrice alone can truly see, from Heaven, "qual ch'io sia" (31.16) [what I am].

Dante has begun to write, once more, poems that are "narratori di tutto quasi lo mio stato" (17.1) [narrators of nearly all my condition].[68] He has returned to the poetic mode of the first third of the *Vita Nuova*, but with an important difference. Before, Dante wrote about his own condition in the ultimate hope of winning Beatrice's love. Two other ladies figure in the lyrics from that phase: the two successive "donne-schermo" whom he pretends to admire in order to conceal his true feelings (5–7, 9–10). The lyrics of the first phase occupy a mediating position like that of the screen-ladies: Amore advises Dante, "Queste parole fa che siano quasi un mezzo, sì che tu non parli a lei immediatamente, che non è degno" (12.8) [Make these words a kind of intermediary, so that you do not speak to her directly, which is not fitting]. Dante's aim, though, is to speak to Beatrice, however indirectly: "per questo sentirà ella la tua volontade" (12.7) [from this she will understand your will]. Soon Dante begins addressing her directly, reasoning, "Se questa donna sapesse la mia condizione, io non credo che così gabbasse la mia persona, anzi credo che molta pietade le ne verrebbe" (14.9) [If this lady knew my condition, I do not believe that she would so mock my appearance; rather I believe great pity would come to her]. In these lyrics, Dante has not yet discovered "lo stilo de la sua loda" (26.4) [the style of her praise], but when he later writes the *Vita Nuova* he realizes that his subjective laments did imply praise for Beatrice; he transcribes only poems that contain "loda di lei" (5.4) [praise of her].

In the final third of the *libello*, Dante again writes about his condition, but now some of the poems are about Beatrice (that is, about Dante's grief over her death) and some are not. Again, there is another lady, the "donna gentile" [gracious lady] of Chapters 35–38. The Donna Gentile balances the screen-ladies in the first part of the book, but her role is strikingly different; rather than serving as a literary fiction, she is the real subject of four sonnets. She may ultimately be judged a "simulacrum" (as Amore terms the screen-ladies [12.3]), a noble but inferior substitute for Beatrice; this time, however, the substitution occurs not in Dante's deliberately chosen poetic rhetoric but in his confused thoughts. Dante's focus on his own condition is no longer a means to an end; it is an end in itself. Now that Beatrice's eyes have been removed from this world, he is seemingly fascinated with his own: beginning with "Li occhi dolenti," the word "occhi" [eyes] appears nine times in the lyrics, and in every instance but one the "occhi" in question are Dante's.[69]

Similarly, the third phase of *divisioni* recapitulates the first phase, with a difference. The *divisioni* in this final section are, in the terms I have defined, predominantly "rhetorical" rather than "logical." In the manner of the Cassiodorian *divisio psalmi*, they distinguish separate speech acts. Again, the presence or absence of subdivisions provides a quantifiable measure: like the first phase, the third phase contains only one subdivided *divisione* (34.4–6). What is new is the relationship between *divisione* and text. We have already encountered one alteration in the formal pattern: after Beatrice's death—and beginning with "Li occhi dolenti"—the *divisione* precedes the poem, "acciò che [la] canzone paia rimanere più vedova dopo lo suo fine" (31.2) [so that the *canzone* may seem to remain the more widowed after its ending]. This relocation seems emblematic of a change in Dante's strategy of division. In the first two phases, the lyric text is a complex unity, with a reader's division following after; in the third phase, division precedes, and appears to infect, the text. The *divisioni* themselves return to the method of the first phase, but the lyrics display a new kind of dividedness.

The third phase begins with a trio of experiments in split and fragmentary forms. The sonnet "Venite a intender li sospiri miei" is a complex speech act indeed: Beatrice's brother has asked Dante for a lament on a recently departed lady, pretending that he is not speaking of Beatrice (32.1–3), and Dante writes of his own grief, pretending that the sonnet is made "per lui" ("in his name, in his place," explains De Robertis). This is reminiscent of the strategy of the "schermo" [screen] in the first part of the *Vita Nuova*, but there the pretense concealed the identity of the poem's real subject; here, for the first time, the identity of the speaker is obscured—concealed like the purloined letter, since the "I" of the poem is Dante after all.[70] The two possible speakers of this sonnet return in the next poem, the incomplete *canzone* "Quantunque volte, lasso!, mi rimembra." In these "due stanzie d'una canzone" (33.2) [two stanzas of one *canzone*], one stanza is spoken by Beatrice's brother and one by Dante, although a reader who does not look closely ("chi non guarda sottilmente," 33.2) will miss the distinction. The sonnet that follows, "Era venuta ne la mente mia," has a single speaker throughout, and it ends by marking the completion of a cycle, the first calendar year since Beatrice's death. But the sonnet has, mysteriously, "due cominciamenti" (34.3) [two beginnings]—that is, two different opening quatrains—and this double beginning prompts Dante to divide the entire poem twice. No explanation is given for the textual anomaly; Dante does not, for example, speak of revision or of starting over. Clearly, however, there is a continuity between "Venite a intender," an utterance attributable to two different persons, "Quantunque volte," an unfinished beginning made up of two distinct and separately voiced utterances, and "Era venuta," a single utterance with two beginnings. In each case, but in different ways, the poetic text originates in dividedness.

These three poems are followed by the four sonnets to the Donna Gentile. The first two of these (35, 36) receive no *divisione*. Earlier in the *Vita Nuova*, I have argued, the lack of division points to an unalienated, *atomus* quality in the lyric text. These two sonnets, however, need no division because they are divisive in themselves: for the first time, Dante's affections are alienated from Beatrice. In the next two sonnets, Dante remembers Beatrice and his thoughts are truly divided. Dante introduces the last sonnet to the Donna Gentile by juxtaposing the "tre parti" [three parts] of the sonnet with the "due parti" [two parts] he finds in himself (38.5–7). The two opposing parts of Dante are here called "cuore" and "anima" (38.5) [heart, soul]. This presents a problem, since "nel precedente sonetto io fo la parte del cuore contra quella de li occhi, e ciò pare contrario di quello che io dico nel presente" (38.6) [in the preceding sonnet I make one party of the heart against that of the eyes, and this appears contary to what I say in the present one]. The problem is soon solved, but it is noteworthy that Dante himself has become a text to be variously divided.

The episode of the Donna Gentile has received relatively little critical attention.[71] It would seem to pose a special challenge to any reading of the *Vita Nuova* as a story of progress, spiritual or artistic. Dante himself calls attention to the importance of this episode in the *Convivio*, where he redeems the Donna Gentile as an allegorical figure of Philosophy (2.12); most treatments of the Donna Gentile are content to evaluate this revelation or revision as a key to the relationship between the *Vita Nuova* and the *Convivio*.[72] Within the *Vita Nuova*, though, the episode is a puzzling false start. After addressing four sonnets to the "donna gentile," Dante repents his "malvagio desiderio" (39.2) [evil desire] and returns to a wholehearted devotion to Beatrice. There is little evidence that the episode has contributed anything to the new understanding that is expressed in the last few chapters of the *libello*. Singleton treats the Donna Gentile in two brief paragraphs: in the third phase, Dante has found a new, upward-directed love, a synthesis of the kinds of love expressed in the first two phases, and his momentary attraction to the compassionate lady proves that his love proceeds from a fallible free will.[73] In my own reading, the episode of the Donna Gentile is precisely typical of the third phase, and the three phases together constitute a coherent story, though not a story of steady progress.

This story may be summarized thus: Dante's *divisioni*, non-narrative in themselves, together enact a formal drama that is closely entwined with the psychological, spiritual, and artistic concerns of the *Vita Nuova*. The three phases of the book represent three different structural accommodations of *divisio*, where *divisio* is both a particular exegetical technique and an aspect of the relationship between a human lover and a quasi-divine beloved.

In the first phase, the love-poet Dante responds to Beatrice by becoming absorbed in the phenomena of his own subjectivity, and the critic Dante is content to sort out the complications of his own poetic rhetoric. Division arises from the dividedness of the temporal, experiential, linguistic world in which the beloved manifests herself. Dante dwells on his own divisions as a way of beginning to approach the unity that divides him.

In the second, central phase, Dante turns to face Beatrice. He writes poems in the style of praise, and his *divisioni* analyze the objects of the poetry rather than the linguistic surface. This new direct gaze has the effect of elevating Beatrice: the theological structure of the *Vita Nuova* becomes more explicit, with Beatrice displaying God-like powers and the lyrics assuming the poetic mode of the Psalms. Dante too is elevated. He is no longer a blank page on which the effects of love are inscribed, but rather an active student in the new theology. Now it is Dante who divides.

The third phase of the *Vita Nuova* is a logical extension of the first two phases. The potential danger of Scholastic *divisio* has been demonstrated in the *divisione* to "Donne ch'avete": as the observer becomes more aggressive, his analysis may assimilate the beloved object to his own nature; the reader who divides "più artificiosamente" (19.15) [more carefully] may end up replacing the text he divides with the artifice of his own division. In the third phase, Dante divides more aggressively than ever. The *divisioni* return to the method of the first phase, but they now precede the "più vedova" (31.2) [more widowed] poetry. A new, visible dividedness enters the lyric text: the poems begin to look like fragments, and they are assigned multiple speakers and, most significantly, multiple objects. Dante's division, freed from its subservience to a unifying object, collapses upon itself.

5. The Fate of Division

There is one more stage in the story, a final moment of certainty that replaces the confusion of the third phase. After the sonnets about the Donna Gentile, Dante writes two sonnets expressing grief for Beatrice; he omits *divisioni*. These sonnets should perhaps be considered the conclusion of the Donna Gentile episode: in a passage of six chapters (35–40), four undivided sonnets—two about the Donna Gentile and two about Beatrice—frame two divided sonnets about Dante's divided heart. The final sonnet of the *Vita Nuova*, however, represents a triumphant return to the mode of the central phase, and a development upon it. In "Oltra la spera che più larga gira," the "sospiro" [sigh] that Beatrice inspires, as at the end of "Tanto gentile," climbs into Heaven to view Beatrice in glory: "Quand'elli è giunto là dove disira, / vede una donna" (41.11) [When it has arrived at the place it desires, it sees a lady]. The sonnet employs the poetic mode of the first phase, according to Dante—it is "uno sonetto, lo quale narra del mio stato" (41.1) [a sonnet that narrates my condition]. But at this moment subjective self-description and objective praise are fully synthesized: Dante's condition is inseparable from the vision of Beatrice.

Appropriately, the *divisione* of this last sonnet returns to the Scholastic mode of the central phase. The *divisione* contains no subdivisions, but Dante points out that it *could*; he ends by noting, "Potrebbesi più sottilmente ancora dividere . . ." (41.9) [It could be divided even more subtly], a comment that recalls the ending of the *divisione* to "Donne ch'avete."[74] Even without subdivisions, the final *divisione* is conspicuously logical. The first four parts (of five) isolate different aspects of the journey undertaken by the "sospiro" [sigh] which is glossed as "pensero" [thought]:

> Ne la prima dico *ove* va lo mio pensero . . .
> Ne la seconda dico *perché* va . . .
> Ne la terza dico *quello* che vide . . .
> Ne la quarta dico *come* elli la vede . . . (41.3–6, emphasis added)[75]

> [In the first I say *where* my thought goes . . .
> In the second I say *why* it goes . . .
> In the third I say *what* it sees . . .
> In the fourth I say *how* it sees her . . .]

This analysis is loosely patterned on the oldest type of *accessus ad auctores*, which specified the *circumstantiae* of a text by answering the questions "who," "what," "why," "in what manner," "where," "when," and "whence" (or "by what means").[76] In the *accessus*, these are questions about the rhetorical situation of a text; in Dante's logical *divisione*, they are questions about the event described in the text.

This *divisione* is Scholastic in another sense as well. It introduces into the *Vita Nuova* a distinguishing feature of Scholastic *divisio textus*: for the first time, a discursive comment is attached to the framework of the division. Indeed, since the brief *ragione* concerning the writing of the poem says virtually nothing about its content, the *divisione* contains all the *expositio textus* that Dante has to offer. Within its small compass, the *divisione* imitates the exegetical mode of Bonaventure and Thomas Aquinas as nothing else in the *Vita Nuova* does—especially since the interpolated comment is a citation of Aristotle.

> Ne la quarta dico come elli la vede tale, cioè in tale qualitade, che io non lo posso intendere, cioè a dire che lo mio pensero sale ne la qualitade di costei in grado che lo mio intelletto no lo puote comprendere; con ciò sia cosa che lo nostro intelletto s'abbia a quelle benedette anime sì come l'occhio debole a lo sole: e ciò dice lo Filosofo nel secondo de la Metafisica. (41.6)

> [In the fourth I say how it sees her to be such, that is of such a quality, that I cannot understand it: that it is to say that my thought ascends into the quality of this lady to such a degree that my intellect cannot comprehend it; for our intellect stands in relation to those blessed souls as the weak eye in relation to the sun: and the Philosopher says this in the second (book) of the *Metaphysics*]

In the final poem and final *divisione* of the *Vita Nuova*, the ambitious claim of the book's central phase is repeated and amplified. Again, both Beatrice and Dante are elevated. Within the sonnet, Beatrice is literally a celestial radiance, so bright that an observer must utter words that are (except for the name "Beatrice") unintelligible to an earthbound listener. The *divisione*, though, stresses the power of Dante's understanding. The "sospiro" [sigh] of the sonnet (or "peregrino spirito" [pilgrim spirit] in the eighth line) is rendered as "pensero" [thought], and Dante is concerned with his own active "intelletto" [intellect] rather than the "intelligenza nova" [new intelligence] mentioned in the sonnet, sent down by Amore to draw the sigh upward. If Dante cannot fully comprehend Beatrice, he can at least construct a logical account of the limits of his comprehension—an explanation cast in the form of Scholastic commentary and authorized by the Philosopher.

The penultimate chapter of the *Vita Nuova* is, in effect, the starting point for the *Convivio*. "Sì come dice lo Filosofo nel principio de la Prima Filosofia, tutti li uomini naturalmente desiderano di sapere" [As the Philosopher says at the beginning of the *First Philosophy*, all men by nature desire to know]. So begins the *Convivio*, and its first *canzone* begins, like the *Vita Nuova*'s last sonnet, in the spheres: "Voi, che 'ntendendo il terzo ciel movete" [You, who through understanding move the third sphere]. Now, I have described the *Convivio* as a work with a stable textual hierarchy: from beginning to end, it is formally patterned on a full-blown thirteenth-centry Scholastic *expositio*. One might suppose, then, that the drama of form in the *Vita Nuova* has a happy ending: the cosmic model of lyric text and Scholastic *expositio*, built up and then challenged within the *libello*, returns at the end to remain, standing, as the chosen structure for the work—and the structure outlasts the work, so that it can be employed again, more consistently and more ambitiously, in the *Convivio*.

The *Convivio* itself, however, complicates this reading of the *Vita Nuova*. The *Convivio* does indeed present itself as an elaboration of the final part of the *Vita Nuova*, but not in the way I have just suggested: Dante says that his new career as a student of philosophy began with his encounter with the "donna gentile," who is actually "figlia di Dio, regina di tutto, nobilissima e bellissima Filosofia" (2.12.9) [the daughter of God, queen of all things, most noble and beautiful Philosophy]. My formal analysis of the *Vita Nuova* lends a strange kind of support to this understanding of the "donna gentile." I have argued that the Donna Gentile episode is typical of the third phase of the *Vita Nuova*, and that Dante's dividing, in this phase, becomes more aggressive and self-sustaining than before. In this sense, the Donna Gentile might be a figure of active *divisio*, and an appropriate sponsor for the hyperactive *divisio* of Dante's philosophical discourse in the *Convivio*. *Within* the *Vita Nuova*, however, the Donna Gentile cannot possibly represent a final, privileged mode of understanding and writing. There, Dante's attraction to the Donna Gentile is a fruitless error; he repudiates her as an object of love and returns to his singleminded adoration of Beatrice. In the *Convivio*'s version of the story, this last event is missing, being replaced by an ending in which the devotion to Lady Philosophy continues indefinitely. The problematic difference between these two treatments of the Donna Gentile points, I believe, to a formal and intellectual problem that exists already, and remains unresolved, in the *Vita Nuova*.

The *Convivio* is not, of course, a simple book. Yet it strives to achieve a kind of simplicity, a purity of form. Dante begins by defining and justifying his new discursive mode in advance: he devotes the first Book of the *Convivio* to "cleansing the bread" for the philosophical banquet (1.2.1). This circumspect fastidiousness may be in part a response to the impulsiveness of the *Vita Nuova*, which seems to find its *modus procedendi* as it proceeds. Dante ends the very first chapter of the new work by comparing its spirit with that of its predecessor:

> E se ne la presente opera, la quale è Convivio nominata, e vo' che sia, più virilmente si trattasse che ne la Vita Nuova, non intendo però a quella in parte alcuna derogare, ma maggiormente giovare per questa quella; veggendo sì come ragionevolmente quella fervida e passionata, questa temperata e virile esser conviene. Ché altro si conviene e dire e operare ad una etade che ad altra . . . (1.1.16–17)

> [If in the present work, which is called *Convivio*, as I wish it to be, the subject is treated more maturely than in the *Vita Nuova*, I do not intend by this in any way to disparage that book but rather more greatly to support it with this one, seeing that it understandably suits that one to be fervid and passionate, and this one tempered and mature. For it is proper to speak and act differently at different ages . . .]

This statement asserts both continuity and contrast between the two works, and I believe that this relationship is visible throughout the *Convivio*. One thing that is cleansed in the *Convivio* is the mixed and problematic form of the *Vita Nuova*: in his relative maturity, Dante attempts to purge from his writing certain qualities only approximated by the adjectives "fervid and passionate."[77] Without attempting anything like a full reading of the later work, I shall conclude this chapter by suggesting that the deliberate, declared purity of the *Convivio* provides a revealing index of the *Vita Nuova*'s complexity.

The first *canzone* of the *Convivio* opens by addressing the spirits who move the third sphere, the sphere of Venus. The meaning of this address claims most of Dante's attention in the allegorical section of the exposition (2.12–15). There, Dante explains that each of the heavenly spheres stands for one of the "scienze," and that the sphere of Venus is a figure of Rhetoric. The *canzone* as a whole describes Dante's new devotion to Philosophy, which Dante will later define as the love of all the sciences, or indeed the sciences themselves (3.11.17). Rhetoric is not, then, discarded—but it is assigned a distinctly subordinate place in the scheme of the work. Dante says that he has addressed his poem to the third sphere because he was led to Philosophy by two masters of rhetoric, Boethius and Cicero (2.15.1). His own discourse in the *Convivio* moves from the evident beauty of the *canzoni* to the truths allegorically concealed within them, and in the final Book even Dante's poetic writing has lost its allegorical veil. Rhetoric is a step on the way to a higher destination;[78] the *Convivio* is largely occupied with "Morale Filosofia," which is allegorically represented by the crystalline sphere (2.14.14), far above the sphere of Venus.

Yet the *canzone* also describes—like the two divided sonnets in the *Vita Nuova*'s Donna Gentile episode (37–38)—a subjective conflict between the love of Beatrice and the love of the "donna gentile." In this version of the conflict, the new love, now defined as the love of philosophy, wins out. So the *canzone* simultaneously describes a passage from Rhetoric/Venus to Philosophy and a passage from Beatrice to Philosophy. Beatrice herself is not an allegorical figure in the *Convivio*, but the new gloss implies a three-way association between Rhetoric, Venus, and the love of Beatrice. As we know from the *Vita Nuova*, however, the love of Beatrice may be described either as an erotic attachment (the love of a woman) or as a divine adoration (the love of God, by way of a mediatrix). And the *Convivio* allows this second possibility as well. In the literal exposition, Dante explains that the Intelligences of the third sphere have transferred his love from Beatrice to the Donna Gentile because their influence does not extend to the glorious realm of souls after death (2.8.4–6). Beatrice is henceforth excluded from the *Convivio* as too exalted;[79] Dante permits himself one digression on the immortality of the soul as a way of closing the subject.

> però che de la immortalità de l'anima è qui toccato, farò una digressione, ragionando di quella; perché, di quella ragionando, sarà bello terminare lo parlare di quella viva Beatrice beata, de la quale più parlare in questo libro non intendo per proponimento. (2.8.7)

> [since the immortality of the soul has been touched on here, I will make a digression and discuss this topic; for with this discussion it will be well to finish speaking of that blessed living Beatrice, of whom as a matter of purpose I do not intend to speak further in this book]

Is the love of Beatrice to be placed in the third sphere, the sphere of Rhetoric and Venus, or in the highest sphere of all, the Empyrean sphere of Theology (2.14.19)? In the *Convivio*, there is no need to decide. Just as the *Convivio* defines in advance its own mode of discourse, so it claims a well-defined area of competence—the second-highest sphere, the domain of all that human intelligence can understand through its own investigation. The spheres above and below—the domain of human intelligence guided by divine revelation or aesthetic pleasure and the domain of other-than-intellectual experience—are treated respectfully, but they fall outside this text. In the *Convivio*, the question of Beatrice is set aside: the ambiguous or unstable status of Dante's love for her is referred to the pre-philosophical vagueness of the *Vita Nuova*.

As an emblem of the *Convivio*'s transformation of the *Vita Nuova*, I would cite the repeated image of the eyes and the mouth. The second *canzone* refers to the "occhi" [eyes] and "dolce riso" [sweet smile] of Lady Philosophy (3 canz. 57). The literal exposition describes "occhi" and "riso" as the two "balconi de la donna" (3.8.9) [balconies of the lady], and explains that the lady's soul shines through her eyes with absolute clarity (3.8.10), but is revealed in her smile "quasi come colore dopo vetro" (3.8.11) [almost like a color behind glass]. "Colore" suggests both the multiple refractions of a single light and the many "colors" of rhetoric. The allegorical comment makes this last suggestion explicit:

> li occhi de la sapienza sono le sue demonstrazioni, con le quali si vede la veritade certissimamente; e lo suo riso sono le sue persuasioni, ne le quali si dimostra la luce interiore de la sapienza sotto alcuno velamento. (3.15.2)
>
> [the eyes of wisdom are her demonstrations, by which truth is seen with the greatest certainty; and her smile is her persuasions, in which the inner light of wisdom is revealed behind a kind of veil]

The gloss on the "dolce riso" does contain a hint of Theology: persuasion may be inferior to demonstration, but by some reckonings a "luce interiore" [inner light] concealed beneath a veil is more desirable than the sort of truth that can be known with the greatest certainty. The *Convivio* is not prepared to develop this hint, however. From Dante's new perspective, the persuasion of the mouth is a subordinate power of Philosophy; it is associated especially with Boethius and Cicero, "li quali con la dolcezza di loro sermone inviarono me . . . ne lo amore, cioè ne lo studio, di questa donna, gentilissima Filosofia" (2.15.1) [who with the sweetness of their discourse guided me in the love, that is, in the study, of this lady, most gentle Philosophy].

The *Convivio* is above all a text for the eyes. The first *canzone* mentions only "occhi," and the gloss here is rhapsodic:

> li occhi di questa donna sono le sue demonstrazioni, le quali, dritte ne li occhi de lo 'ntelletto, innamorano l'anima, liberata de le condizioni. O dolcissimi e ineffabili sembianti, e rubatori subitani de la mente umana, che ne le mostrazioni de li occhi de la Filosofia apparite, quando essa con li suoi drudi ragiona! (2.15.4)

> [the eyes of this lady are her demonstrations, which when directed into the eyes of the intellect, enamor the soul that is liberated from its conditions. O most sweet and ineffable looks, sudden captors of the human mind, who appear in the demonstrations of the eyes of Philosophy when she converses with her lovers!]

The *Vita Nuova* makes repeated reference to both *occhi* and *bocca*, but, as the *divisione* to "Donne ch'avete" suggests, Dante's central focus is on the mouth: "la bocca, la quale è fine d'amore" (19.20) [the mouth, which is the goal of love]. The mouth, however, has a complex and changing appeal. Beatrice's smile is both an erotic object ("fine di tutti li miei desiderii" [18.4; goal of all my desires]) and a vehicle of divine inspiration (a "novo miracolo" [21.4; new miracle]); Dante's tongue is the source of songs that dominate his book as Beatrice dominates his life. The *Convivio* offers a set of terms for the "scienza" of the mouth in the *Vita Nuova*: Venus, Rhetoric, Theology. This is not really a clarifying terminology, however: in the *Convivio*, Dante makes no attempt to separate the various attractions of the mouth in the earlier *libello*, and such a separation would be difficult in any case. When "la mia lingua parlò come per sé stessa mossa" (19.2) [my tongue spoke as if moved by itself], are we to think of the autonomous actions of the physiological spirits, the enunciation of a new lyric facility, or the prophetic utterance of the Psalmist? It is hard enough to decide within the *Vita Nuova*, and the *Convivio* offers no new help. In the *Convivio*, the mouth is an unexplored problem; Dante can state that "la lingua non è di quello che lo 'ntelletto vede, compiutamente seguace" (3.3.15) [the tongue cannot completely follow what the intellect sees] and then turn his attention to what the intellect sees.[80] The exclusions of Dante's philosophical banquet reveal the forces at work in the *Vita Nuova* without attempting to explain how they work.

The *Vita Nuova* traces the effects of a ravishing, inspiring, sub- or super-intellectual force: the effects of Beatrice, considered as a beautiful woman, as a divine radiance, and—I have argued—as an image for Dante's own lyric voice. But the *libello* also records the history of Dante's response to Beatrice. And this response is above all reasonable:

> avvegna che la sua imagine, la quale continuatamente meco stava, fosse baldanza d'Amore a segnoreggiare me, tuttavia era di sì nobilissima vertù, che nulla volta sofferse che Amore mi reggesse sanza lo fedele consiglio de la ragione in quelle cose là ove cotale consiglio fosse utile a udire. (2.9)
>
> [although her image, which stayed with me continually, was Love's assurance of ruling over me, nonetheless it was of such extremely noble power that it never allowed Love to rule me without the faithful counsel of reason, in those matters where such counsel would be useful to hear.]

The "counsel of reason," Dante's active response to the force that dominates him, is visible already within the represented action of the *Vita Nuova*: he translates his baffling subjective experiences into poems written according to "l'arte del dire parole per rima" (3.9) [the art of speaking words in verse], and he applies these poems to social ends, using them to gain entry into a literary circle, to speak (less successfully) to Beatrice, and to satisfy the requests of friends. In the text of the *Vita Nuova*, moreover, the prose responds reasonably to lyrics that are frequently mysterious.[81]

In the "reasonable" prose of the *Vita Nuova*, Dante anticipates the mode of the *Convivio*. The stable form of the *Convivio*, however, results from a constitutive fact about the work: reason is applied to an entirely reasonable object. Philosophy is the sphere where the human intellect is precisely adequate—both sufficient and "equal to." The *Convivio* treats love as well as wisdom, but, as Dante's etymology of "filosofo" suggests,[82] love is here the love *of* wisdom, and the love of wisdom is wise in itself. In the *Vita Nuova*, love and wisdom are distinct and sometimes contradictory forces. I have claimed that the *divisioni* imply a structure that yokes both together: since the term "divisio" can apply both to Beatrice's conquering power and to Dante's discursive, cognitive response, it is possible to imagine the book as a single dynamic hierarchy on the model of a Psalm commentary, a textual cosmos combining Neoplatonic emanation outward with an Aristotelian quest to return to the center. This image of the text, however, though it is an image of stability, is an unstable achievement *within* the text. In the temporality of the *libello*, there is indeed a correlation between Beatrice's power and Dante's responsive vigor: his *divisioni* are most logical when the vision of Beatrice is clearest, in the middle third of the book and in the penultimate chapter. But the vision of Beatrice is not permanent for Dante; just as important, Dante's own analytic *divisio* is a progressive force, associated with a broad current in twelfth- and thirteenth-century intellectual history, so that it can attain a self-defeating autonomy in the Donna Gentile episode. The *Convivio* redeems this autonomy by applying philosophy to philosophy; the Donna Gentile episode becomes a celebration of the power of Scholastic investigation. In the *Vita Nuova*, the intellect is only temporarily adequate, and then only in part, to its object.

In Chapter 2 I argued that the fundamental ambiguity of the *Vita Nuova*'s form is a choice between two different ways of structuring lyric and narrative—a choice that also involves the relative centrality of Dante and Beatrice in the text. Is the book a story about Dante, lover and love-poet, or is it an annotated collection of Beatrician lyrics? In the final analysis, this ambiguity is the problem that renders the model of stable textual hierarchy unstable within the work. The prose arises in response to a collection of lyrics, yet the force of its narrative unity and analytic self-confidence threatens to overpower its first cause; Dante derives his authority as a love-poet from his vision of Beatrice, yet his increasing authority threatens to render derivative the vision that authorizes him. In making this rather schematic formulation, I have subordinated an atemporal hierarchical model to the temporality of the work that intermittently projects it. But the problem of narrative and lyric returns at this more abstract stage of the analysis. The Neoplatonic cosmos is an atemporal accommodation of temporality, and as an explanatory model, I have suggested, it is virtually impossible to prove wrong. Clearly the *Vita Nuova* projects for itself, at certain moments, a structure based on this model; a reader who is so inclined might argue that this is truly the constitutive structure of the work, manifested more and less clearly from chapter to chapter (manifested *more* clearly at the center and near the end, traditionally privileged sites of meaning). Is the *Vita Nuova* a temporal sequence that occasionally points toward a vision of timeless unity, or is it a cosmic order unfolding, explicating itself, in time?

My goal has not been to answer the questions posed by the *Vita Nuova*, but rather to show *how* they are posed. Any linguistic artifact can be described alternatively as a sequence or as a structure, of course; the *Vita Nuova* is unique in the way that it frames this inherent ambiguity as a problem of love, knowledge, and textual power. The *Convivio* is one solution to the problem: Dante purges certain aspects of the form of his *libello* to create a self-validating philosophical discourse. Along with Venus, Rhetoric, and Theology, one last excluded feature of the *Vita Nuova* is narrative itself; although the *Convivio* incorporates fragments of Dante's autobiography, the banquet is a spatial display, resolutely non-narrative. There are other solutions to the problem of the *Vita Nuova*. Petrarch creates his *Canzoniere* by removing the prose narrative from the form of the *Vita Nuova*; in the process, he raises new problems about the relationship of time and the lyric. In the next chapter I shall argue that Boccaccio, in the *Filostrato*, makes another crucial adjustment of Dante's problematic form, fusing the countervailing modes of the *libello*, lyric and narrative, into a single new poetic mode.

Each of these three books—*Convivio*, *Canzoniere*, and *Filostrato*—finds a way of preserving the form of the *Vita Nuova* by eliminating certain of its formal contradictions. The most complex response to the challenge posed by the *Vita Nuova* is, of course, the *Divine Comedy*. Readers have always recognized that the end of the *Vita Nuova* seems to look ahead to Dante's masterwork. I have claimed that the penultimate chapter of the *libello*, by combining visionary lyric with Scholastic exegesis, gives a parting glimpse of the most exalted possible structure for the work—and, in so doing, it offers a foretaste of the *Convivio*. The *Vita Nuova* as a whole, however, constitutes a critique of the structure as well as an embodiment of it. And the very last chapter asserts that the problem of writing about Beatrice has not yet been solved. In a brief paragraph, Dante tells of a "mirabile visione" (42.1) [miraculous vision] that he is not yet ready to treat, and he expresses the hope that, if he lives "alquanti anni" [some years], he may "dicer di lei quello che mai non fue detto d'alcuna" (42.2) [say of her that which was never said of any woman]. The *Divine Comedy* is the work that the *Vita Nuova* most seems to anticipate, and not only because it is the work in which Dante returns to the subject of Beatrice. Of the four successor texts I have mentioned, the *Divine Comedy* is the one that most boldly takes up the contradictions of the *Vita Nuova* and treats them *as* contradictions, exploring and developing and finding new resolutions, revising but not revising away. A vast critical literature testifies to the complexity of Dante's later treatment of terms that are already established in the *Vita Nuova*: love and reason; rhetoric, theology, and philosophy; human and divine *auctoritas*; language as temporal and language as spatial; affirmation and critique; unity and division.

Certainly, as Mazzotta and others have argued, the *Vita Nuova* should not be read as a mere "prolegomenon" to the *Divine Comedy*.[83] My own reading, centering on the most marginal passages of the *libello*, has assumed the work's right to dictate its own terms. Yet this reading paradoxically confirms that the *Vita Nuova* would be a "prolegomenon" even if Dante had not lived to write the *Divine Comedy*, both because of its open ending and because of its formal instability—or more precisely its ambiguous mixture of stability and instability. In retrospect it can be considered a crucial and immediate precursor to at least four quite different books. The *libello* that simultaneously follows a multiplicity of models becomes in turn a privileged model to an array of divergent sequels; it stands alone in its willingness to enter so many narratives.

4. The Form of *Filostrato*

The Proem of Boccaccio's *Filostrato* describes the discovery of a form. In fact, the word "forma" appears twice, with two very different applications: it refers first to the poem's protagonist, Troiolo, and second to the text of *Filostrato* itself. The two forms raise different interpretive problems and point to different intertextual affiliations; they will receive separate treatment here. In this chapter, after a brief introduction, I address the question of the literary form of the *Filostrato*; in the next I return to the form of Troiolo. My claim in both chapters, however, is that the *Filostrato* is a self-conscious experiment that sets forth a distinctive new form of lyric authority—in each of its two "forme," and in the analogy briefly suggested by the double application of the term, the analogy between a noble youth and a new book.

The Proem, a prose epistle from "Filostrato" to his beloved "Filomena," recounts an erotic and poetic crisis: when Filomena leaves Naples, Filostrato cannot safely contain his grief and desire, yet he cannot express himself directly because he is "vinto dal volere il vostro onore più che la mia salute guardare" (19) [overcome by the desire to protect your honor more than my health]. He decides he must express himself anyway, and immediately a solution occurs to him, as if by divine inspiration. "E il modo fu questo: di dovere in persona d'alcuno passionato sì come io era e sono, cantando narrare li miei martiri" (26) [And the way was this: I wanted to be able, in the person of someone emotionally overcome as I was and am, to relate my sufferings in song]. Accordingly, Filostrato recalls the "antiche storie" (27) [old stories] and finds, in the Trojan prince Troiolo, a form: "della persona di lui e de' suoi accidenti ottimamente presi forma alla mia intenzione" (29) [from his person and from his fortunes, I took a form excellently suited to my intention].

Clearly, this discovery solves a problem for Filostrato: it allows him to write the poem that he sends to Filomena. Troiolo's sorrows are "utili" (29) [useful] to Filostrato. Yet Filostrato's own account of this utility seems implausible. Late medieval literature offers a well-established way of expressing transgressive desire discreetly; Filostrato could write courtly love-lyrics. And it is hard to accept his claim that he chooses a historical persona in order to protect Filomena's honor, since he punctuates his narrative with references to the personal desire that drives him (e.g., 1.1–6, 3.1–2, 9.5–8)—and since he prefaces the narrative with the explicit Proem.

Filostrato's attachment to his form should be understood in the light of his other preoccupations. From the beginning, the Proem is concerned with the desire for a visible person. Filostrato says that he once held that the sight of one's beloved was less important than thoughts about her (1–5); the deprivation of his own vision of Filomena brings the truth to his clouded intellect, and he realizes that sight is primary (6–9). Now he turns from this absent presence to Troiolo. In the "antiche storie" Filostrato seeks not a story but a "persona"; the phrase "la persona di lui e . . . suoi accidenti" (29) [his person and his fortunes] transforms the temporal vicissitudes of a life into the secondary qualities, the Aristotelian accidents, of a primary substance. Despite his historical distance, Troiolo is immediately accessible to Filostrato as a figure of "similissima" (28) [very similar] grief. Troiolo himself is the "scudo . . . del mio segreto e amoroso dolore" (27) [shield for my secret and amorous suffering]; he is an arresting new form.

Critics have described the *Filostrato* itself as a formal innovation. They have adopted the phrase "cantando narrare li miei martiri" (26) [to relate my sufferings in song] as an apt formulation for what is new in the verse: the way it conjoins two distinct modes of writing, lyric and narrative. Often the conjunction is associated with the *ottava rima* stanza. David Wallace, for example, writes: "This fine hendecasyllabic phrase . . . suggests some conscious appreciation of the *ottava*'s double capabilities: his work is to be at once narrative and lyrical."[1] This simultaneity may be achieved through a subordination of one mode to another, but critics have seen two opposing structures of subordination: one speaks of Boccaccio's "bold and novel subordination of 'antiche storie' to the private business of the love lyric,"[2] while another claims that "Boccaccio subordinates lyric to narrative through versification."[3]

These discussions have remained largely descriptive; they have tried to characterize the poem's formal method without considering its representations of form as, precisely, representations.[4] But the text's markings of generic affiliation, in the Proem and throughout, are—like all generic labels—performative as well as informative.[5] The Proem is a perceptive piece of early criticism, as modern critics have realized, but it is also the opening of Filostrato's seductive gift to Filomena, a gift that depicts, among other things, the seductiveness of unitary forms. The familiar first move of formalist interpretation seems justified here: the meaning of the formal frame can be referred to the signifying body of the text. And the implications of this in-folding extend outward as well: Filostrato's "cantando narrare" reflects upon Boccaccio's own authorial practice. Like the "forma" of Troiolo's person, the new-found "modo" of writing enters into an economy of desire within and surrounding the text.

To understand the relations between lyric and narrative in the *Filostrato*, we must explore the Proem's second "forma." Once Filostrato has found a way to write, his writing assumes a form of its own: "queste cotali rime in forma d'uno picciolo libro . . . ridussi" (32) [I composed these rhymes into the form of a little book]. Filostrato's "picciolo libro" is a formal invention that radically reworks its nearest precedent: Dante's "libello," the *Vita Nuova*.

Janet Smarr has outlined a pattern of Dantean allusion in the *Filostrato*, in which an orderly series of echoes from the *Divine Comedy* in the body of the poem is framed by echoes from the *Vita Nuova* that appear in the direct discourse of Filostrato in the Proem and the Envoy. She concludes that the fictional speaker is meant to represent a less enlightened sensibility than that of the real author: Filostrato remains arrested at the earliest stage of Dante's ascent to divine truth, while the poem ironically points to the path not taken.[6] This is a suggestive and important argument, but it contains a serious imbalance. The *Vita Nuova* appears first and last in the *Filostrato*—and it is present throughout. Vittore Branca notes a dozen verbal echoes in the body of the poem.[7] Certain events in Boccaccio's narrative recall episodes from the *Vita Nuova*: Troiolo's first sight of Criseida in the temple of Pallas (1.18–31) is a variation on the episode in which Dante sees Beatrice in church (*Vita Nuova* 5); Troiolo's dream, in which a boar tears out Criseida's heart without causing her distress (7.23–24), clearly evokes the dream in which Amore feeds Beatrice Dante's heart (*Vita Nuova* 3).[8] Finally, there is a general but striking resemblance between the *Vita Nuova*'s represented world—the strangely abstract city, the solitary chamber—and *Filostrato*'s.

These additional references to the *Vita Nuova* need not weaken Smarr's reading of the *Filostrato* as a deliberately non-transcendent version of Dante's autobiographical myth, and in fact they may strengthen it. Surely we are meant to notice the difference between the two temple meetings: in both scenes, the lover observes his beloved without his gaze being observed, but Troiolo's discovery of Criseida is patterned on the *Vita Nuova* scene in which Dante first discovers not Beatrice (whom he has seen before) but the temporary ruse of the screen-lady. Again, Dante's dream of the burning heart is an exalted mystery, while Troiolo's dream of the boar is carnal and all too legible. One might further support Smarr's thesis by noticing a different pattern: *Filostrato*'s allusions to the *Divine Comedy* occur almost entirely in similes and prayers, suggesting that Dante's journey to the stars can only be a figurative speculation for this poem of the flesh. My aim here is not to support or challenge Smarr's overall reading, but rather to emphasize the insistent presence of the *Vita Nuova* in Boccaccio's text. Smarr writes, "It seems that Boccaccio was reading the *Vita Nuova* as a promise of a tale rather than as the tale itself,"[9] but it would be just as fair to say that in the *Filostrato* the *Vita Nuova* is precisely "the tale itself."

The *Vita Nuova* is not, of course, the source of the Troiolo-and-Criseida plot, nor of the idea of using a historical persona. But it is the most visible model for the formal decisions that Filostrato makes *after* he has chosen Troiolo: when "susseguentemente in leggier rima e nel mio fiorentino idioma, con stilo assai pietoso, li suoi e li miei dolori parimente compuosi" (29) [subsequently in light rhyme and in my Florentine idiom, with a style which would excite pity, I composed his sorrows equally with my own] and again when he gathers his rhymes together to make a little book. For Boccaccio, the *Vita Nuova* is a rich source of dramatic detail and stilnovistic diction; more important, it is provocative as a whole, as a *libello*. Here is another book that combines lyric and narrative modes of writing, *cantare* and *narrare*.

We have seen that the form of the *Vita Nuova* has been an interpretive crux, in part because of the text's own insistent but inconsistent self-representations; an extensive critical literature testifies to the singularity and overdetermination of this form. From the perspective of the *Filostrato*, the problem is somewhat simplified. The Proem's "cantando narrare" invites us to see the *Vita Nuova* as a unique solution to the technical problem of making an extended literary work out of brief love-poems. Other solutions include the French romances that contain inset *chansons*, and the Provençal *chansonniers* that include prose *vidas* and *razos*.[10] Carlo Muscetta suggests that the *Roman du Chastelain de Couci* is the "modello strutturale" for the *Filostrato*,[11] and I do not wish to deny the importance of the French tradition for Boccaccio; it is in the modern study of French medieval literature that the opposition "narrative/lyric" has emerged as an important analytic tool.[12] But the *Vita Nuova*'s evident centrality in Boccaccio's text urges a Dantean approach to the "lyrical book." Whatever the motives behind the French and Provençal innovations, Dante would have understood the problem as a question of *auctoritas*.

The topic of literary authority has been raised, in *Filostrato* criticism, by Giulia Natali. She argues that Boccaccio presents his poem as a kind of lyric utterance because he wishes to elevate it within the existing literary hierarchy. "The literary framework in which the young Boccaccio inscribed his first narrative attempts—I speak of *Filostrato*, *Filocolo*, and *Teseida*—is without doubt hegemonized by lyric experience, which has already achieved the highest levels of perfection and codification."[13] Then why write a narrative at all? Natali mentions the "demands of fantasy,"[14] but her concept of a literary hierarchy can—with only a slight complication—suggest another sort of answer. The lyric had a certain hegemony in vernacular literature, but its status was sharply limited in a culture that assigned the highest authority to writing and the book. The "lyrical book," in its various experimental forms, attempts to remedy this situation. The seven *chansons* composed by the fictional Chastelain de Couci become part of a structure of authorship: they are registered as the works of a single poet, and the romance as a whole is signed in an acrostic near the end by a certain Jakemes.[15] Dante in turn takes responsibility for both his lyrics and his book: the deliberate construction of a personal *auctoritas*, more explicit in the *Convivio*, begins in the *Vita Nuova*.

Dante extends the lyric not only in the direction of the vernacular romance (as do his French and Provençal predecessors, in different ways) but also in the direction of Latin models—toward the Boethian *prosimetrum*, and, more important, towards the tradition of theological and philosophical exegesis. In casting his prose narrative as a running commentary on the lyrics, he evokes an authoritative Latin form. Moreover, the prose, primarily devoted to a memorial narrative, lends the lyric collection the unity and stability of a book. It remains a collection of lyrics, but it becomes at the same time a single narrative work. Finally, Dante establishes another kind of unity by identifying the "I" of the framing prose with the "I" who has written the various lyrics and the "I" who appears within them. A single "Dante," occupying different temporal positions, is projected for the whole *libello*; at once lyric poet, scribe, commentator, and historian, he is a new sort of author.

The *Filostrato* is frequently described as a work that is simultaneously lyric and narrative. Filostrato's "cantando narrare" must be understood, however, as a polemical revision of Dante's formal invention. The *Vita Nuova* constructs its unity out of sharply distinguished components, defining "narrative" and "lyric" as an oppositional pair of modes that alternate neatly in the work. In contrast, the *Filostrato* presents itself as a fusion—not an orderly collocation or a graceful compromise, but a forceful yoking—of two distinct modes.

Natali has stressed the extent to which the Proem describes the poem as a lyric utterance; when Filostrato announces a lament for an absent lady, he could be introducing any number of *chansons courtois*.[16] His language, I would emphasize, specifically echoes phrases that Dante uses to introduce lyrics in the *Vita Nuova*.[17] But Natali seems to assume that the poem is actually a narrative, dressed up to resemble a lyric. In fact, the Proem affirms that the poem will be a lyric *and* that it will be a narrative, and I believe the nature of the poem is never definitively settled; hence the critical disagreement on the direction of subordination between lyric and narrative. Filostrato's epistle is marked by an oscillation between narrative and lyric impulses, between sudden events and static emotional plights. The ideal opening scene of the Court of Love is disrupted by the lady's departure; a new bitter understanding of love's truth creates an insupportable pressure from within to write; the written text is meant to bring about a new event, the lady's return. Like the *Vita Nuova*, the Proem subjects lyric experience to the temporal domain of narrative and simultaneously views temporal experience from a lyric perspective; here, though, the engagement of the two modes issues in a single poem in a new mode.

Filostrato consistently uses the plural to describe his own passionate utterances both before and after his discovery of a literary form. His "sospiri . . . multiplicati in molti doppi di gravissima angoscia," his "voci," his "amorosi canti e . . . ragionamenti pieni di focoso amore" (15–16) [sighs multiplied in many duplications of the gravest anguish; words; amorous songs and discourses full of ardent love] are translated into "le . . . voci, le lagrime e' sospiri e l'angosce" (34) [words, tears, sighs, and distresses] of the poem. But the translation is made possible by the unitary "forma" drawn from the old books, and Filostrato's expression of feeling is complicated by the integrity of Troiolo's story. Some parts of the story—Troiolo's sighs, Criseida's beauty—reflect the poet's own situation "apertamente" (34) [clearly]; other parts must be understood obliquely (Troiolo's "felice vita" [happy life] with Criseida stands for Filostrato's purely ocular gratification [30–31]); still other parts are irrelevant to Filostrato but must be included "perciocché la storia del nobile e innamorato giovane ciò richiede" (35) [because the story of the noble young lover requires it]. The insistent narrative unity of the work stands in contrast to its multiple and variegated lyric expressiveness. But narrative and lyric cannot be isolated as discrete parts of the work: the "picciolissimo dono" (33) [very small gift] that Filostrato sends Filomena is at once a collection of lyrics in the form of a narrative and a narrative charged with the expressive and seductive function of a lyric.

In the body of the poem, the fusion of love-story and love-song is achieved, as critics have noted, by the *ottava rima* stanza. The appearance of this stanza in the *Filostrato* and in the *Teseida*, written within a few years of each other,[18] is a formal innovation of some consequence for European literature. It has been explained in two different ways. According to Branca, *ottava rima* derives from the popular Italian romances called *cantari*; Boccaccio employs the stanza, along with certain other stylistic and thematic features of the *cantari*, in a poetry that is equally influenced by refined courtly forms such as the French romance and the Dantean lyric.[19] Dionisotti and others have argued that all the *cantari* postdate and emulate the *Filostrato*, and that the *ottava* is borrowed from French lyric poetry.[20] This account of the *cantari* has been convincingly refuted,[21] but clearly *trouvère* verse remains another possible source for Boccaccio's stanza-form.

According to either account, Boccaccio finds the ABABABCC stanza and transforms it by translating it from one literary realm to another—from popular to learned, or from brief song to extended romance. In the *Filostrato*, the stanza makes possible another kind of transformation: the conflation of narrative and lyric writing. In the French romances that contain inset lyrics, the interpolations are marked prosodically: octosyllabic couplets briefly give way to more complex rhyme schemes and longer lines.[22] The *Vita Nuova*, of course, makes an even sharper distinction between lyrics and context. The *Filostrato* does not offer such boundaries. Troiolo's soliloquies (e.g., 1.50–56) and letters (e.g., 2.96–106) could pass for *trouvère* lyrics: they follow the stanza-form of a Gace Brulé poem included in the *Roman du Chastelain de Couci*.[23] But they are metrically indistinguishable from their context; they appear without frames, "ponding on the surface of the narrative."[24] One might try to divide the *Filostrato* into relatively narrative passages and relatively lyrical passages, but the form of the poem lends no help to the effort. In the experience of reading, the *ottave* march past, and it is impossible to predict whether the next stanza will advance the plot or lament its failure to advance; narration, soliloquy, and dialogue possess a common vocabulary and a common shape.

Moreover, the stanzaic form allows the whole poem to stand as both an extended narrative and a single *canzone*. In Dante's definition, a *canzone* is "the linking together in the tragic style of equal stanzas without a 'reprise' with the meaning expressed as a unity."[25] Filostrato's Envoy (Part 9) supports both classifications of the work. The metaphor of the poem as a ship arriving in port (9.3–4) is associated with longer, especially epic, works;[26] the end of the journey here is the end of the story, the place where the narrative stops. After a brief rest, though, the poem is instructed to continue to a further destination, the lady who will read it (9.5–8). This second journey is not the temporal sequence of a story but the idealized speech act of a lyric poem. Branca notes repeated echoes of a Cavalcantian or Dantean *congedo*: in an echo not signaled by Branca, Filostrato's address to his poem as "canzon mia pietosa" (9.1) ["my piteous song"] recalls Dante's parting address to the first poem he writes after Beatrice's death: "Pietosa mia canzone, or va piangendo . . . (*Vita Nuova* 31.17) [my piteous song, go weeping now].[27] The work is sealed as both a narrative and a lyric poem.

"Cantando narrare," then, conflates into a single term two formal elements which are neatly distinguished in the *Vita Nuova*. What does the conflation mean? What is at stake for Boccaccio when he rewrites the constitution of Dante's *libello* to make his own "picciolo libro"? Again, I think, it is a question of *auctoritas*—of authority and authorship. One way to approach this large theme is to move further into the two texts, to explore the connections between literary form and represented content.

I have argued that the *Vita Nuova* implies a continuing analogy between two constitutive dyads—two primary modes of writing, narrative prose and lyric verse, and two primary characters, Dante and Beatrice. Although the *libello* experiments with different structures for these dyads, one structure is central, the structure of biblical commentary. In imitating a book such as Peter Lombard's Psalter commentary, the *Vita Nuova* evokes a book that carries authority in part because it *structures* authority. According to this model, both dyads in the *libello*, formal and personal, are hierarchies that resemble the hierarchy of text and gloss. An absolute separation of modes, and of characters, is required by the hierarchy: the genre division becomes a gender division. The hierarchy in turn lends authority to each of its components. Dante, by establishing Beatrice as a figure of divine privilege above him, claims a place in heaven for her and divine inspiration for himself; by treating his own poetic compositions as though they were Psalms, he elevates both the verses and the ancillary text that explicates them. The *Vita Nuova* asserts its authority by creating an image of authority, pointing to it, and declaring its own subordination.

Now, I have also argued that the *Vita Nuova* provides a critique of this exegetical order by subjecting the timeless hierarchy to its own temporality of form. The stable Neoplatonic cosmos of text and gloss is "central" because it comes into being in the course of the work and is subsequently challenged. In particular, it is challenged by the uneven fit between two countervailing forces, each a kind of *divisio*: the force of love, erotic or divine, that radiates from Beatrice, and Dante's own responsive effort to understand Beatrice and translate her effects into the clear language of Scholastic analysis. Dante's own *Convivio* removes this potential instability by applying philosophical methods to philosophy itself: as his etymology of "filosofo" (3.11.5) implies, "love" is subordinated, and fused, to "wisdom." Boccaccio implies an alternative resolution of the instability when he recalls this etymology in the rubric of his own poem: "Filostrato tanto viene a dire quanto uomo vinto e abbattuto d'amore" ["Filostrato" is as much as to say "a man conquered and laid prostrate by love"]. In this book, love conquers reason. Dante's two modes of writing are reduced to one, and, although Troiolo and Criseida are separated at the beginning and end, they are literally *not* separated in the middle of the narrative, with disastrous results. The denial of hierarchy can be understood as a collapse.

Yet the collapse is strategic, and the form of the *Filostrato* defines a new form of authority. Like Dante, Boccaccio implies an analogy between modes of writing and dramatic characters. The figure most associated with the lyric is Troiolo. "Era contento Troiolo, ed in canti / menava la sua vita" (3.72) [Troiolo was happy, and in songs led his life]. Troiolo's life is equally a song in his periods of anguish. Left to himself, it is hard to imagine that he would have much of a story. In Criseida's presence, he is "fiso" (1.28) [fixed] in his gaze; in her absence, he is repeatedly described as "sospeso" (2.15, 2.121 rubric, 4.17, 7.6, 8.8) [suspended]. Above all, he is the site of a self-sustaining passion that finds utterance in an endless stream of words and sighs:

> diceva molte altre parole
> piangendo e sospirando, e di colei
> chiamava il nome . . .
> . . . ma tutte eran fole
> e perdiensi ne' venti . . .
> . . . onde il tormento
> multiplicava ciascun giorno in cento. (1.57)

[he said many other words,
weeping and sighing, and called
her name . . .
. . . but they were all vain
and lost themselves in the wind . . .
. . . and so his torment
multiplied a hundred times each day.]

Of course, Troiolo is not left to himself: Pandaro repeatedly leads him out of his stasis. Pandaro differs from Troiolo primarily in his relationship to action. He is one of the "compagni in simili disiri" (2.13) [companions in similar desires] whom he himself recommends; though he is powerless to help himself (4.57–58), in his role as friend he can propose to Troiolo both a "fatica" [labor] (for himself) and a "dolce fine" [sweet result] (for Troiolo [2.32]). Pandaro is a mediator who urges a strategically unmediated utterance, as in his advice on letter-writing: "s'io fossi in te, intera scriverei / ad essa di mia man la pena mia" (2.91) [if I were in your place, I would write to her in my hand about my entire suffering].[28] He translates Troiolo's lyric sensibility, his life led in songs, into a narrative.

The poet Filostrato speaks a language in which lyric and narrative are fused; he synthesizes and transcends the divided functions of Troiolo and Pandaro. His fundamental connection to the story, however, is a specular identification. Like Pandaro, he sees himself in Troiolo. The three men are *all* "compagni in simili disiri" [companions in similar desires], equals placed in different relations to a single center of feeling, Troiolo's heart. They speak for one subjectivity from three grammatical positions—they are first person, second person, third person, and they are associated respectively with lyric soliloquy, dramatic dialogue, and narration. Each of these discourses, however, mirrors the other two: lyrics are staged as dramatic utterances within a narrative that is actually an oblique lyric cry.

There is at least one more version of specularity to consider. The text of the *Filostrato* is described, in the Proem, as a little book (Proem 32), a "picciolissimo dono" (Proem 33) [very small gift]; moreover, in the Envoy, "l'autore parla all'opera sua" (9 rubric) [the author speaks to his work], treating it as a messenger. The text is an object, a person, or—as I shall argue in Chapter 5—a unitary image. The proper name of this embodied totality is the name that is applied as an epithet to Troiolo and employed by the author himself as a pseudonym.[29] The *Filostrato* is founded upon a narcissistic economy of multiple reflections: with the aid of Troiolo and Pandaro, Filostrato sees himself in *Filostrato*.

Where are Filomena and Criseida in this structure? I have argued that the *Filostrato* is structured on relationships between men, in contrast to the heterosexual dyad that structures the *Vita Nuova*; within this homosocial economy, women occupy an essential but problematic position.[30] Filomena's counterpart in the body of the poem is Criseida: Criseida's "bellezza e' costumi, e qualunque altra cosa laudevole in donna" (34) [beauty, good manners, and any other thing praiseworthy in a lady] are compliments to Filomena. But there is more than this to Criseida, and though Filostrato says vaguely that "altre cose" (35) [other things] should be disregarded, at no point does he deal with the obvious problem that his story as a whole is a very odd compliment to send a lady. Criseida, as a character, is flawed by moral doubleness; as a sign for Filomena, she is semiotically double.

Filomena herself appears in the book in a confusing variety of roles. In the Proem, she is the intended audience, the person upon whom the poem is meant to act. In the first stanzas of the poem (1.1–5), she is still the absent lady, but she is also the Muse who can help Filostrato write a praiseworthy poem: his prayer now is for the successful completion of the work rather than for his lady's return. A second invocation (3.1–2) asks for "lume duplicato" [redoubled light]. Filomena is still addressee and Muse, and now she is Filostrato's primary topic as well: he describes himself as continually singing her praises ("le lodi tue continue cantando" [3.2]). But when Troiolo learns that Criseida must leave Troy, a rubric notes that "L'autore che della sua donna suole l'aiuto chiamare, qui il rifiuta" (4.23 rubric) [The author, who usually calls on his lady for aid, here refuses it]. In three disorienting stanzas (4.23–25), Filostrato says that he no longer needs his lady's inspiration; that he will not mind if she ceases to listen; but that if she should happen to encounter the poem he hopes she will be moved by it. Yet this is the moment in the story that, according to the Proem, most corresponds to Filostrato's own state, the moment that ought to be most directly addressed to Filomena.

A list of Filomena's appearances in the poem must include one dramatic non-appearance. Criseida's betrayal of Troiolo (6.8ff) either destroys her equation with Filomena or drastically qualifies the praise of Filomena, but here the author is silent. This is especially striking when the *Filostrato* is compared to one of its primary sources for the Troiolo story, the *Roman de Troie* of Benoît de Sainte-Maure. There, the news of Briseida's betrayal prompts a double intervention from the author: he rails against the faithlessness of women in general (13438–56), and then, because he says he fears the blame of his own beloved lady, he devotes even more space to *her* virtues as an individual (13457–94).[31] Muscetta notes the importance of this unique dedication occurring precisely here in the *Roman de Troie*;[32] Boccaccio may have been influenced by the conjunction of the Troilus story and an amorous address. Yet this particular address is significantly missing at this point in the *Filostrato*. The body of the poem ends with a discussion of women in general, in which "Criseida villana" (8.28) [base Criseida] figures as the type of the "rea donna" (8.33) [evil woman] young men should avoid. This discussion is less bitterly misogynist than Benoît's outburst, since it admits the existence of women worth loving, but Filostrato does not say which group Filomena belongs to; unlike Benoît, he makes no effort to reconcile a general antifeminism with the praise of a particular lady. These stanzas are followed directly by the Envoy, which rededicates the work to Filomena.

Just as Criseida, even in her soliloquies, mirrors a succession of men—Pandaro, Troiolo, Diomede—so Filomena assumes a series of rhetorical roles successively required by the poem. The various appearances of these women are evidently epiphenomena to the central specular relationships between men; the women play Echo to the male Narcissus. (It is almost enough to say, at one point, "Criseida seco facea il simigliante" [3.55; Criseida did likewise to herself].) Filomena is a version of Dante's Beatrice, but she is a Beatrice whose functionality has been laid bare. Boccaccio will not follow Dante's strategy of positing an Other from whom authority can descend. He collapses the hierarchy of Dante's *libello*—the structure that guarantees both the Otherness of authority and its orderly descent--into a specular fusion. The Other is divided and degraded, while the authority of the self is self-authenticating. In the *Filostrato*, Boccaccio writes the author who writes himself.

In the Italian *trecento*, the paradigmatic "author who writes himself" is Petrarch; John Freccero provides the classic account of Petrarch's "literary self-creation" in the *Canzoniere*.[33] It is instructive to place the *Canzoniere* alongside the *Filostrato*, as another lyric book that revises the form of the *Vita Nuova*.[34] To repeat a reductive but not entirely mistaken formula, the *Canzoniere* is the *Vita Nuova* without its prose.[35] I earlier claimed that the prose narrative is the very means by which Dante constructs a personal authority of his own. But the *Canzoniere*, deprived of such a discourse, does not revert to the condition of the medieval lyric anthologies produced by scribes; rather, interconnections and metastatements within the separate poems invite the reader to find a unifying gloss that is all the more powerful for being implicit. In the *Vita Nuova*, the figure of the author is textually localized, inscribed in autobiographical passages interspersed with the lyrics. The author of the *Canzoniere* is located nowhere except in the book as a whole: the absent and transcendent gloss for this totality is the proper name that never appears, "Petrarch."[36]

Boccaccio, in contrast, provides a fictional name for the self-authoring and -authorizing author: the name that appears in rubrics and refers to writer, poem, and protagonist, "Filostrato."[37] This visible inscription points to a crucial difference between the *Filostrato* and the *Canzoniere*. Each of the two texts derives a powerful new mode of writing from the divided form of the *Vita Nuova*. (The power of the new modes is suggested by their subsequent codification as Renaissance genres: the *Canzoniere* becomes the model for later sonnet sequences, while the *Filostrato*, along with the *Teseida*, inaugurates the tradition of the courtly stanzaic narrative poem.) But the *Canzoniere* preserves and even heightens the dualities of the *Vita Nuova*. Petrarch produces his lyric book by isolating lyric from narrative; the oppositional pairs in Dante's hierarchical structure (narrative/lyric, male/female, lover/beloved, writer/text) have become polarities of absence and presence.[38] The *Filostrato* collapses the Dantean hierarchy, imagining the fusion of lyric and narrative, the physical union of lover and beloved, and the identification of writer and text. It foregrounds the self-construction of the new author.

That Boccaccio himself felt a certain critical distance from "Filostrato" is suggested by Filostrato's reappearance as one of the ten noble young storytellers in the *Decameron*. Several textual echoes confirm that the name is meant to evoke the specifics of the earlier work: for example, Filostrato becomes the king of the Fourth Day, as if to commemorate Criseida's betrayal of Troiolo, which also occurred on the "quarto giorno" (6.9) [fourth day] of the ten-day period before her promised return to Troy.[39] In the *Decameron*, Filostrato is the only storyteller who seems to have any grasp of his own status as a fictional character: he says that he expects his own love to end unhappily, "né per altro il nome, per lo quale voi mi chiamate, da tale che seppe ben che si dire mi fu imposto" (3 concl. 6) [nor was it for any other reason that I was given (by one who knew what he was talking about) the name by which you address me]. Filostrato's awareness of the fictional name that Boccaccio will assign him breaks the narrative frame. Yet such uncanny self-consciousness brings Filostrato no special wisdom; he is gently mocked as one who demands to hear only stories that apply to him personally.[40] The earlier Filostrato also looked through stories to find an image of himself; his deliberate writing strategy has become, for the *Decameron*'s Filostrato, a consumer's addiction to a genre.

Is the Filostrato of *Filostrato* already an object of satire? Robert Hollander and Janet Smarr both claim that he is: Hollander writes that Filostrato is, like all the narrators in Boccaccio's early works, "a foolish lover, a target of Boccaccio's ironic attack upon the religion of love."[41] Yet I have tried to show that Filostrato embodies a powerful and historically ascendant model of authorship. Certainly Hollander and Smarr are right to see Filostrato as a carefully constructed persona; it would now seem naive to read the Proem as Boccaccio's own straightforward autobiography.[42] But the Proem specifically outlines the logic that would lead a sophisticated writer to construct a character quite unlike himself to express his own longings. If Hollander is right that Boccaccio does not share Filostrato's religion, it is equally true that Filostrato does not share Troiolo's religion[43]—yet Filostrato does not, on that account, refuse to consider Troiolo an adequate and useful image of himself. We might imagine a kind of meta-proem in which Boccaccio chooses Filostrato to choose Troiolo. But there is nothing to prevent us from imagining a frame-story that mocks the self-absorption of an amorous youth. The text allows both possibilities because its own attention, its own projection of authorship, is turned inward. As a matter of biography, Boccaccio doubtless felt some attraction to the masculine laureate authority that Petrarch would claim for himself and make available to modern literature. The *Filostrato*, however, invites a critique of that authority—precisely because it offers a visible inscription of the authorial proper name, and renders poetic self-creation as itself an appealing form.

5. The Form of Troilus: Boccaccio, Chaucer, and the Picture of History

The *Filostrato* has suffered from two inevitable comparisons: it looks like a minor work whether it is placed next to Chaucer's treatment of the same story or next to Boccaccio's own masterpiece the *Decameron*. In the last chapter I treated the *Filostrato* as a sophisticated and self-conscious portrayal of a new kind of literary *auctoritas*—but I would not deny that there is something thin, something shallow, about this book. Critics usually explain this quality by referring to its author's age (about twenty-five); one Chaucer critic who devotes many perceptive pages to the *Filostrato* describes it as "a youthful piece written in haste."[1] It is possible, though, to read the apparent deficiencies of the work as deliberate choices. Another Chaucerian, Donald Howard, takes this approach when he describes the *Filostrato* as "a poem from which has been excised, as by a surgeon's scalpel, all that might give it the aura of legend or myth."[2] Perhaps Howard was thinking of William Carlos Williams's picture of Marianne Moore, "wiping soiled words or cutting them clean out, removing the aureoles that have been pasted about them or taking them bodily from greasy contexts."[3] The pairing of Moore and Boccaccio seems unlikely, but I do believe that the *Filostrato* is an avant-garde work: a challenge to the existing institutions of literature and a formal experiment that, through its very negations, organizes around itself a set of less reticent traditions. In the phrase that Moore placed at the front of her collected poems, "Omissions are not accidents."

The formal transformation described in the last chapter amounts to an excision or omission. Boccaccio bases his "forma d'uno picciolo libro" (Proem 32) [form of a little book] on the form of the *Vita Nuova*, but through a prosodic innovation he eliminates the distinction between lyric and narrative. This is a gesture of polemical simplification: rather than deriving authority from a complex arrangement of authoritative forms, Boccaccio collapses Dante's hierarchy and writes a self-defining, self-authorizing lyric book. In this chapter I return to the first "forma" mentioned in the

Proem to the *Filostrato*, the form of Troilus: "della persona di lui e de' suoi accidenti ottimamente presi forma alla mia intenzione" (29) [from his person and from his accidents, I took a form excellently suited to my intention]. I have suggested that this "forma" is the form of a visible person; now I want to complicate that suggestion by exploring an obvious and puzzling omission in Boccaccio's text. The *Filostrato*, though it is set in ancient Troy, is strangely lacking in the illustrious and exotic imagery associated with that setting and strangely lacking in visual imagery in general.

The exploration of a textual absence requires a comparative method, and here my comparisons will be diverse. In effect, I will be reading the *Filostrato* against the background of two art galleries, both located in Naples and both now lost: a private collection from the Roman Empire described by a Greek writer and a royal hall with murals painted by the medieval master Giotto. More concretely, I will be juxtaposing Boccaccio's nearly imageless text to a series of verbal pictures found in the tradition of Trojan history. Although most of my book examines the relations between narrative and lyric modes of writing, this chapter hinges on two other, but related, dialectic oppositions: between narrative and ekphrasis, and between text and image.[4] The topic is still *auctoritas*, but here the authorship of the vernacular poet is brought into contact with the authority of secular power: in the *Filostrato*, I shall argue, the visual is political.

Since my argument involves a certain indirectness—reading a lack of pictures by looking at pictures—I want to indicate its divisions in advance. In section 1, "Pictures of Troy," I explain my assertion that the omissions of the *Filostrato* include both Trojan material and visual imagery, and I argue that these omitted things are fundamentally connected. In the two sections that follow, "Unhappy Boy" and "Famous Men," I discuss two versions of the form of Troilus known to Boccaccio: the form of the dying Troilus in the *Aeneid* and the form of the living Troilus in the medieval histories that are Filostrato's most immediate "antiche storie" (Proem 27) [old stories]. I shall summarize my conclusions about the *Filostrato* at the end of the third section. Finally, in section 4, "The Book of Troilus," I add a post-Boccaccian wing to the gallery of Trojan portraits by discussing the visual depiction of Troilus in Chaucer's *Troilus*. My intention here is not at all to move "beyond" Boccaccio's minor poem to a more enlightened treatment of the same material, but rather to use the *Filostrato*'s powerful unconventionality as an entry into the complex and self-critical conventionality of the *Troilus*.

1. Pictures of Troy

In *Filostrato*'s Proem, the "persona" of Troilus is presented as a pre-existent form: Filostrato says that he discovered it by turning over the ancient stories in his mind. Yet the choice of this form raises problems. Why go to Troy for narrative material? Filostrato explains that he could not simply speak his own anguish, for fear of causing even more anguish, yet he could not keep silent; the story of Troiolo is a "scudo" [shield] for his "segreto e amoroso dolore" (27) [secret and amorous suffering]. Yet, as I have suggested, this explanation is hardly adequate, since the writer declares his amorous preoccupations both in the Proem and in addresses to his beloved throughout the poem. In addition, the reasons that medieval writers normally cite for retelling ancient stories do not apply here: there is no announcement of a generalizable moral lesson, and it is not clear that the Troilus story features true deeds that ought to be held in memory, since Filostrato himself casts doubt on its reliability ("*se* fede alcuna alle antiche lettere si può dare . . ." [28; *if* any credence can be given to the ancient writings]). Finally, the sheer glamor of epic narrative, the colorful martial trappings and splendid royal displays—features that might recommend a Trojan story to any writer—are all but missing in the *Filostrato*.

James H. McGregor has recently argued that Troy is a crucial presence within the *Filostrato*: the well-known history of the Trojan war provides a moral commentary on the romance of Troiolo and Criseida.[5] My own claim here deals with a more superficial matter—not Troy's meaning but rather its material manifestations in the text. If the Trojan narrative is a partner to the love story it is effectively a silent partner. Boccaccio has pieced together an amorous plot from separate episodes within the voluminous medieval Troy books, eliminating battle scenes, and he has gone beyond this to minimize the suggestions of epic grandeur within the love scenes. The story may serve as a "shield" to Filostrato, but it contains no shield—and no arms, no horses, no ramparts, no tombs.[6] The scene in which Criseida first sees Troiolo from a window, for which Chaucer will arrange a victory parade and Shakespeare a procession of Trojan princes, is here a glance between two people that could occur on any Italian street. The Proem speaks of "il valoroso giovane Troiolo, figliuolo di Priamo nobilissimo re di Troia" (28) [the valorous young Troiolo, son of Priam, the most noble king of Troy], and this is a description that might plausibly occur in the poem, perhaps when Pandaro speaks to Criseida on Troiolo's behalf—but Troiolo is introduced into the narrative simply as one of the Trojan "giovinetti" [young men], and Priam is not mentioned until midway through the poem.[7]

To see what "aura of legend or myth" (in Howard's phrase) is missing from the *Filostrato*, it is enough to turn to the *Teseida*, which Boccaccio wrote within a few years of the *Filostrato*. This stanzaic narrative is full to bursting with epic trappings: battle scenes, duel scenes, arming scenes, descriptions of exotic places including the houses of Mars and Venus, and elaborate ekphrases, notably the frame-by-frame description of the pictures on Arcite's tomb, which retell in visual form the entire *Teseida* (11.69–91).[8] As McGregor acutely observes, the appearance of this last description in the text "makes the whole of *Teseida* an *ekphrasis* on the tomb of that hero."[9] Now, to speak of ekphrasis is to point to another pronounced omission from the *Filostrato*. This is a text virtually free of visual description. Not only are specifically Trojan sights left unspecified; even the pictures that might accompany any love story are missing. Here we find no painted wall, such as Dante leans on at one point in the *Vita Nuova*, no sketch of an angel like the one he draws when he daydreams about Beatrice. Criseida is described very generally and never given a full *effictio*. (The most vivid description of her appearance, a line that appears twice in Part 1, pointedly refuses to describe *her*: "sotto candido velo in bruna vesta" [1.26, 1.38; under a white veil in a black habit].) Troiolo is never described visually at all. This is a text of passionate and persuasive utterances and not at all a text of sights.

In its indifference to the world of epic, and the larger world of visible things, the *Filostrato* seems to mirror its protagonist. When Troiolo is first stricken by love, Criseida entirely dominates his thoughts, so that

> Ciascun altro pensier s'era fuggito
> della gran guerra e della sua salute. (1.44)
>
> [Every other thought had fled,
> of the great war and of his well-being]

These lines evoke a passage in the *De Vulgari Eloquentia* in which Dante defines three fundamental subjects for poetry (2.2.7). The first is the "salus" [well-being] that is achieved through "armorum probitas" [prowess in arms]. Troiolo has ceased to care for this martial "salute" and has devoted himself instead to Dante's second subject, "venus" or "amoris accensio" [the burning of love]. (Apparently Dante's third subject, "virtus" [virtue] or "directio voluntatis" [the direction of the will], does not enter the picture for Troiolo.) At the end of the *Teseida*, Boccaccio refers to the same Dantean passage to make the claim that he is the first Italian poet to take up the subject of Mars and his works.[10] Here, Troiolo's all-consuming love is presented as a generic preference, and it is the generic preference of the *Filostrato* as well. Like Arcita and Palemone in the lyric scene of *Teseida* 3, discussed in the Introduction, Troiolo has substituted a woman for a war story; but the Theban cousins make their substitution in an interlude within a martial poem, while Troiolo's substitution is an abiding obsession matching that of his narrator.

Troiolo's relation to the larger visible world is complex. It is of course the sight of Criseida that causes him to fall in love, and he continually recreates her beauty in his mind (e.g., 1.33). But as long as Criseida remains in Troy—and this is a qualification to which we shall return—he has no interest in seeing anything else. His attitude toward his surroundings is indicated in the passage in which he first travels to her house:

> Era la notte oscura e tenebrosa
> come Troiol voleva, il quale attento
> mirando andava ciascheduna cosa,
> non forse alcuna desse sturbamento
> poco o assai alla sua amorosa
> voglia . . . (3.24)
>
> [The night was dark and cloudy
> as Troiolo wished, who attentively
> went watching each thing,
> that not even one might give a disturbance
> little or great to his amorous
> will . . .]

Troiolo is looking here, but he views the city in which he lives as a collection of nondescript objects, mere things whose value is determined by whether or not they impede his amorous progress. When he enters Criseida's house, he waits in a "certo loco remoto ed oscuro" (3.25) [certain remote and dark place], and

né gli fu l'aspettar forte né duro,
né 'l non veder dove fosse palese. (3.25)

[the waiting was not hard or difficult for him,
nor the not seeing clearly where he was.]

Troiolo imagines that when Criseida arrives he will be happier than if he were "sol signor . . . del mondo" (3.25) [sole lord of the world]; but he is already exercising an autocratic dominion over all that he sees, subjecting it to the priority of his will and wishing it into darkness. The narrative seems to second Troiolo's wish: the places and things that fail to attract Troiolo's attention remain vague and unvisualized in the text.

Yet the Proem, as we have seen, leads one to expect that vision will be a crucial theme in the *Filostrato*. It begins with a *question d'amour* debated in a Court of Love: which is best, to see one's beloved, to speak of her, or to think of her? Filostrato says that he used to uphold the advantages of pure thought, partly on the grounds that thought can dispose the beloved ("la cosa amata" [Proem 5; the loved thing]) according to its own desires. The same cannot be said of vision and speech (5), presumably because vision and speech involve an interaction with a potentially resistant external world.[11] Now, however, the departure of his own beloved from Naples to Sannio has changed his mind. The removal of Filomena's "graziosa e vaga vista" (9) [gracious and beautiful sight] has paradoxically brought the truth into Filostrato's "tenebroso intelletto" (7) [darkened intellect]; the preeminence of vision is proved through its absence.[12]

The Proem's explicit celebration of sight helps to qualify Troiolo's "non veder" as an emphatic negation. It is a negation experienced by Filostrato as well. Filostrato has moved from one kind of non-seeing to another: from a misguided reliance on "falso parere" (4) [false appearance], which led him to argue a foolish position, to the literal "privazione" (8) [privation] of the only sight that matters to him. And Filostrato's account of his personal experience helps us to understand his non-visual narrative style in psychological terms. After Filomena's departure, Filostrato's eyes

> si sono . . . spontanamente ritorti da riguardare li templi e le logge e le piazze e gli altri luoghi ne' quali già vaghi e disiderosi cercavano di vedere, e talvolta lieti videro, la vostra sembianza (12)

> [spontaneously turned away from looking at the temples and the loggias and the squares and the other places in which formerly, longing and desirous, they sought to see, and sometimes joyfully saw, your countenance]

Similarly, in the imagined city of Troy—among exotic pagan temples, ancient palaces, epic battlefields—Filostrato's eyes turn away from the sights they might see.

I have been speaking of Troy and the visual as two distinct subjects, two fields of poetic material that happen to be linked through their omission from the *Filostrato*. But I believe the link is stronger than that: there is a tradition that associates Troy and images. In *Laocoön*, Lessing chose a statue of a dying Trojan priest to stand for the visual arts in general; long before the eighteenth century, however, Trojan material had a special status for artists and for writers about art. In the Middle Ages, the Troy story was a favorite subject for "mural decoration whether in paint or tapestry."[13] As a topic for literary ekphrasis it appears in a variety of settings: on the pavement of the Terrace of Pride in *Purgatorio* 12, where it caps an acrostic series; on a saddle presented to Enide in Chretien's *Erec et Enide*; on the walls of the allegorical castle in the twelfth-century Italian poem *Intelligenza*, where the pictures occupy nearly fifty stanzas and are later explained as figures for "beautiful memories"; on the wall of the Temple of Venus in Chaucer's *House of Fame*—as it will appear later in Shakespeare's *Rape of Lucrece*.[14] A medieval writer, Richard of Fournival, reveals a habit of thought when, in a general discussion of words and images, he speaks of "an illustrated story, whether about Troy or something else."[15]

So the choice of a Trojan story, along with the narrator's opening discourse on vision, establishes a strong expectation from the outset of the *Filostrato*. This is a text that could employ its stanza-form as *Intelligenza* and the *Teseida* do, to frame pictures drawn from epic narrative. Yet the dominance of erotic desire, in both Filostrato and Troiolo, has produced a text with very little epic and almost no pictures.

To summarize these particular omissions—to say in a word what the *Filostrato* is *not*—I would mention yet another ekphrastic writer: Philostratus. There were actually three or four Greek writers by that name, probably related and still not clearly sorted out, in the second and third centuries C.E. The texts attributed to various Philostrati include several on Troy and on paintings: the *Heroicus*, a strange retelling of the fall of Troy with special attention to the appearances of heroes; a Greek Anthology epigram on an image of Telephus, wounded by Achilles when the Greek chieftains were travelling to Troy; and the *Imagines*, a series of brief essays on the paintings in a private gallery in Naples, a gallery once thought to be real but in fact probably fictional.[16] The paintings in the *Imagines* depict many different subjects, but Troy appears repeatedly and has the pride of place, as the first painting shows a scene from the *Iliad*. "Here"—writes Philostratus—"is the lofty citadel, and here the battlements of Ilium."[17]

When Boccaccio entitled his poem "Filostrato," was he thinking of the Greek Philostratus? The possibility cannot be ruled out. There is no positive evidence that Philostratus was known in Naples in the early fourteenth century. But his works, especially the *Imagines*, were well known in Byzantine circles at this time;[18] Naples was a center of Greek culture, and numerous Greek translators were attached to the court of King Robert, although their work has mostly not survived;[19] Boccaccio was interested in Greek language and culture (clearly titles like "Filostrato" and "Filocolo" are meant to *look* like Greek);[20] later in his career Boccaccio quotes two other epigrams from the Greek Anthology, although it is not known how he learned them.[21] In the *Genealogy of the Gentile Gods* Boccaccio mentions several scholars with whom he studied in the Naples of his youth: the Greek monk Barlaam; Barlaam's Greek pupil, Leontius Pilatus; and Paul of Perugia, whose mythological compendium *The Collections*, destroyed within Boccaccio's lifetime, drew Greek learning from Barlaam and from another lost authority, Theodontius.[22] Any of these scholars would have been most interested in the writings of Philostratus. Certainly Coluccio Salutati was interested, at the beginning of the next century. In a letter to Pandolfo Malatesta, who has requested a physical description of the Trojan hero Hector for a painting, Salutati cites Homer, Dares, Dictys, Guido delle Colonne, and finally, as the richest source of visual detail, a certain Greek named Philostratus, whose book he has just obtained with difficulty.[23]

It is at least possible that Boccaccio, although he could not read Greek, knew of a Philostratus who wrote about Troy and the images of heroes.[24] If he did, then he may have intended the name "Filostrato" ("Philostratus" in Italian) to announce a Trojan subject, and to support the Proem's emphasis on visible forms.[25] (The other name in the Proem's rubric, "Filomena," also carries an association with pictures: the mythical Philomena wove a tapestry telling her story.) But I should stress that this is no more than a possibility. Salutati's book, imported from Constantinople around 1400, is the first Philostratus manuscript that can be placed with certainty in Italy;[26] it is of course possible that Boccaccio never heard of his Neopolitan predecessor and coined or derived the name "Filostrato" independently.[27] In either case, I take "Philostratus" as a rubric for the omissions of the *Filostrato*. Whether by coincidence or by design, Boccaccio's Filostrato is an anti-Philostratus: a writer who draws his material from the story of Troy but emphatically leaves out the images contained in that story.

To explore the meaning of this non-accidental omission, we must enter into a tradition that Boccaccio seems to evade, although he clearly knew it: the tradition of the visible form of Troilus.

2. Unhappy Boy

Troilus appears only once in the *Iliad*, in Priam's lament for his dead sons in Book 24; he appears only once in the *Aeneid*, as a painted image in Book 1. Aeneas has landed in Carthage and, veiled by invisibility, he surveys a wall in a temple of Dido that contains pictures from the fall of Troy. The third picture in the series is that of Troilus:

> parte alia fugiens amissis Troilus armis,
> infelix puer atque impar congressus Achilli,
> fertur equis curruque haeret resupinus inani,
> lora tenens tamen; huic cervixque comaeque trahuntur
> per terram et versa pulvis inscribitur hasta. (1.474–78)[28]
>
> [elsewhere the fleeing Troilus, his weapons flung away—
> unhappy boy, and ill-matched in conflict with Achilles—
> is carried along by his horses and, fallen backward, clings to the
> empty car,
> yet clasping the reins; his neck and hair are dragged
> over the ground, and the dust is inscribed by his reversed spear.]

Troilus was in fact a common theme for ancient art. The surviving images refer to a story that can be reconstructed, in various versions, from other literary sources as well: Troilus accompanies his sister Polyxena to a fountain; Achilles, hiding nearby, chases Troilus and kills him, usually by beheading him. As Piero Boitani has suggested, Troilus is first of all a tragic victim.[29] In some pictures, his miniature corpse dangles like a doll from the hand of a much larger Achilles; in some, his severed head becomes a missile thrown by Achilles against a cohort of Trojans. Virgil is evidently alluding to a slightly different story—Troilus has entered into battle with Achilles—but he conveys a similar pathos. The participial verb "fugiens" [fleeing] suggests the sweep of an epic action, but the verbs that follow gradually bring the action to a halt: "amissis" [flung away]; "fertur" [is carried along]; "haeret" [clings]; "tenens" [holding]; "trahuntur" [are dragged]; "inscribitur" [is inscribed]. Within the pathetic sequence of Troilus's dying, the image of his death bears down in a moment of self-inscription.

Critics have observed that Troilus has special importance in the series of paintings. He is the first individual Trojan to be described and the only one to be described at such length. Moreover, his death has special consequence for Troy: the legend was that Troy would never fall if Troilus lived to be twenty. Troilus is thus a counterpart to the Palladium, the image of Pallas Athena that also guarantees Troy's safety;[30] the connection is suggested by the next painting on the wall, which depicts the temple of Pallas (1.479–82).

Aeneas is stupefied, lost in his gaze, but his revery ends with the entry of another beautiful form, that of Dido ("forma pulcherrima Dido"; 1.495–96); soon he devotes himself to producing his own narrative account of the Fall of Troy, which occupies Book 2. Lee Patterson, in an essay on "Vision and Narration in the Epic," writes,

> The point is not simply that full knowledge cannot be mediated by images, but that the gaze is one pole of a dialectic of which the other is some form of discursive exposition. The gaze implies a nostalgic evasion of understanding, a lowered state of consciousness that is figured by a trance-like stupor that must be broken, both to disarm its dangerous seductions and to unlock the riches its object contains.[31]

Patterson here seems to unbalance the dialectic he describes, by privileging discursive exposition over visual image.[32] Yet the end of the *Aeneid* reverses this priority. When Aeneas has Turnus in his power, Turnus makes a plea for mercy which stays Aeneas's arm:

> et iam iamque magis cunctantem flectere sermo
> coeperat, infelix umero cum apparuit alto
> balteus et notis fulserunt cingula bullis. (12.940–42)

> [and now more and more as he paused, these words began
> to sway him, when high on the shoulder was seen the luckless
> baldric, and there flashed the belt with its well-known studs.]

What Aeneas sees is the belt that Turnus ripped from young Pallas, the son of Evander, after killing him. The belt was described then: it depicts the slaughter of the fifty sons of Aegyptus by their brides, and when Turnus takes it he takes both its weight and the crime engraved on it ("impressumque nefas" 10.497). The belt is now a "trophy" of Pallas, and a "memorial of cruel grief" ("monumenta doloris," 12.945) in two senses.[33] And Pallas himself seems to condense at least two images from Dido's wall: he is a warrior who has died in his youth, like Troilus, and his name suggests the totemic image of Pallas Athena. This visual reminder of the mortal Pallas tears Aeneas out of the trance caused by Turnus's words, and the poem ends six lines later with the notoriously unassimilated image of a dying warrior. It would appear that images and speeches engage in a true dialectic, something like the dialectic of *punctum* and *studium* that Roland Barthes describes in connection with photographs:[34] the image is the point, the pricking, which spurs both meditation and narrative action.

But what is the point of such an image? In the *Aeneid*, pictures are associated with the past, as in the examples we have just considered, and the future, as in the shield made by Vulcan in Book 8 which sets out a pictorial account of the coming rise of Roman power. (It is customary to contrast this shield with Homer's shield of Achilles, which depicts the entire world in a timeless present tense.) Visual images are thus signs of the trajectory of historical destiny. Even images of the past, images that prompt what Dante in *Purgatorio* 12 calls "la puntura de la rimembranza" (12.20) [the pricking of memory], point to the future: when Aeneas sees the pictures of fallen Troy in Carthage, his first thought is that the story of his grief has spread over the earth, and that such fame brings with it a kind of salvation (1.459–60, 463). But the image as a *form* has a special power that distinguishes it from discursive renderings of the past and future. We return to the form of Troilus.

Françoise Meltzer has described the scene in the temple as a *mise en abîme*, because Aeneas sees himself ("se quoque," 1.488) in one of the later images.[35] The abyss first declares itself, however, in the Troilus picture. Aeneas's own gaze is mirrored within the image. Aeneas is said to feed his soul on the empty picture ("animum pictura pascit inani," 1.464), and twelve lines later the adjective *inanis* is reused to describe the chariot to which Troilus vainly clings: "curruque haeret resupinus inani" (1.476) [fallen backward, he clings to the empty car]. This latter phrase—the center of the Troilus passage—is linked in turn, through a repetition of *haeret*, to a subsequent description of the way Aeneas clings with his look ("obtutuque haeret defixus in uno," 1.495 [he hangs fixed in a single gaze]). The text thus signals an analogy between Troilus dying and Aeneas looking at the image of Troilus dying. At the same time, the verb *inscribere*, used to describe what Troilus's spear does to the dust, connects Troilus's dying action with the making of a picture *and* the writing of a poem: as Aeneas reads one kind of inscription, we read the other. Meltzer argues, in connection with this passage, that "the text of the *Aeneid* colonizes the image and gives writing the dominance,"[36] but one might just as reasonably argue that the image is given unique importance, as the place in the text where the action of the poem and the action of writing the poem can meet. The picture is a puncture through the constitutive fictions of the *Aeneid*, uniting the fall of Troy, Aeneas's reaction to this fall, and our reaction to his reaction, into a single fixed gaze.

Troilus himself makes another powerful connection: with Troy. I have stated that Troilus's death is causally related to the fall of Troy; he is in effect a totem for the city. Yet Troilus stands for Troy in other ways as well. He is a synecdoche, a typical Trojan youth, one among many. He is a metaphor, in that his fall is like the larger fall. And his name implies an even stronger natural bond. It could be "Troia" plus the dimunitive suffix *-ulus*: "Troilus" could mean "little Troy." Or Troilus could stand to Troy as Romulus to Rome: he could be an imaginary founder. Alternatively, as Boitani has suggested, we might read the name as "the sum and conflation of 'Tros' and 'Ilos,' Troy's founders."[37] Since Ilus is the son of Tros, the name would thus fuse father and son. "Ilus" is also known to readers of the *Aeneid* as the other name of Aeneas's son Ascanius, the name that becomes "Iulus" after the fall of Troy, and then—for a descendant, by a logical continuation—"Iulius," the Caesar of the second Troy.

Troilus is thus multiply connected with Troy: he is an image of Troy, where "image" implies a powerful natural connection, figurative and figural and totemic, between representation and object. The picture of Troilus—the image of the image of Troy—introduces into the *Aeneid* not only a theory of Troy but also a theory of this kind of imaging. Imaging both fixes and transfixes: it makes a unity by piercing generations of father and sons and generations of writers and readers; it connects the present moment to the line of history, and connects the individual to the collective, the city. Troilus stands for the possibility of a second Troy; and more generally for the possibility that a person and a city can stand for each other. The *Aeneid* is framed between the image of Troilus and the sight of Pallas's belt because the space of the poem is the space between cities—between Troy and Rome, and more immediately between Carthage and Latinus.

What is the special power of the image of a youth at the moment of dying? If the image stands as the embodiment of Trojan power, the power that Aeneas carries with him and will reestablish for Rome—as I think it does—why not show Troy in its glory, Troilus alive and well? Clearly, wounds serve to secure a viewer's attention: witness the appearance of the dead Hector in Aeneas's prophetic dream in Book 2, which prompts the cry, "cur haec volnera cerno?" (2.286) [why do I see these wounds?]. In a painting, however, wounds serve a more specific function: they are the mark of a historical narrative within the static image. As Philostratus says in his *Imagines*, the proper response to a historical picture is to turn away and recall a text. His first painting is a battle scene based on Homer, and he writes, "let us try to get at the meaning of it. Turn your eyes away from the painting itself so as to look only at the events on which it is based. Surely you are familiar with the passage in the *Iliad* where . . ."[38] Later he has the student return to the picture and notice the ways in which it differs from Homer. The image derives its power from its dialectic relationship to a canonical narrative, and this relationship is called into play by the violence within the picture. Without their various wounds and agonies, the heroes would be interchangeably beautiful.

The signifying force of wounds is greater still when the painting has a Trojan subject: by connecting the image to the narrative of Troy's destruction, they give it a unique authority. Virgil's Troilus undergoes a tragic annihilation, becoming an empty image clutching at emptiness. But the finality of his fate is the very source of the power he makes available to Aeneas and to Virgil. Troy is an authorizing precedent for Rome, and later for virtually every medieval state that cared to fabricate a mythical origin,[39] both because it was great and because it now exists no more. It can stand outside history as the fantasy of a totality that gives meaning to history because its own history has arrived at a total destruction; it could not function as a totemic image if it were more than an image. As Guido delle Colonne states, "Though Troy itself was completely destroyed, it rose again, and its destruction was the reason that the city of Rome, which is the chief of cities, came into existence, being built and extended by the

Trojan exiles."[40] And Guido goes on to provide a list of all the modern European cities founded by the exiles, including Boccaccio's own Naples.

At this point we can attempt a first reading of the "form of Troilus" in the *Filostrato*. Boccaccio alludes to Virgil only sparingly; the one direct quotation that Vittore Branca notes is the phrase "Palladio fatale" (1.18) ["fateful Palladium"] used to characterize the temple where Troiolo first meets Criseida (compare *Aeneid* 2.165–66).[41] The Palladium itself, the image of Pallas, goes undescribed, as does Troiolo himself. Yet the choice of Troilus as a persona, as a form, inevitably evokes the single most famous encounter with Troilus's visible shape.[42] It would seem that Boccaccio's concerns are very different from Virgil's; his work does not tend toward the founding of a city. The most salient meaning of Virgil's Troilus, namely Troy itself, seems to have surprisingly little to do with the *Filostrato*. But Virgil's Troilus may be significant as a *mode* of signifying, as the form of a form. Virgil's ekphrasis focuses a multiple analogy between an ancient drama, an observer within that drama, and an observer *of* that drama. A similar analogy is the very precondition of the *Filostrato*: it is focused in the name "Filostrato," which connects poem, protagonist, and poet.

Another medieval reteller of the Troy story, Albert de Stade, recognized that the name "Troilus" has the form of a title; he concludes his dull hexameter poem, *Troilus* (1249), with the couplet:

> Troilus est Troilus Troiano principe natus
> Et liber est *Troilus* ob Troica bella vocatus.
>
> [Troilus is Troilus, the son of the Trojan prince,
> And the book is called *Troilus* on account of the Trojan war.][43]

The tautology "Troilus is Troilus"—a phrase that reappears in Shakespeare's *Troilus and Cressida* (1.2.64)—unfolds into a statement about the book that contains the war. Boccaccio omits the war, but maintains the totalizing equation: Filostrato is Troilus, and the book, and the writer.

If Boccaccio seems uninterested in the totalization of the city within the individual, the individual within the city, he is nonetheless interested in totalization: the totalization of the literary work. Earlier I described the *Filostrato* as a book without images, but it would be equally correct to say that it is a book with one striking image: the complex image offered by the Proem, the form of Troilus that becomes the form of a little book and then a "very small gift" ("picciolissimo dono") to send to the absent beloved. Again, the *Teseida* provides a useful contrast: it contains pictures and pictures *within* pictures, such as the historiated tomb of Arcite, while the visible object constituted by the entire *Filostrato* has no competition from within the poem. Similarly the *Teseida* is a book made up of twelve "Books," in the classical manner, but the nine divisions of the *Filostrato* are labeled "Parts," as if to suggest that the work possesses unity at one level alone, the level of the whole work. In this respect, Boccaccio's picture of Troilus surpasses even Virgil's. The Virgilian Troilus is an emblem of totalizing unity, but it is only one picture among eight on a wall, one totem for Troy among several; Boccaccio's "form of Troilus" is removed from this economy, set apart as unique. Paradoxically, it has also been removed from the realm of the visible, sublimated into a disembodied title. Where Virgil offers a visual representation of destruction, Boccaccio goes a step further by destroying visual representation. The form of Troilus is an absent, transcendent figure for totality; the privation of vision contains the truth of vision.

3. Famous Men

The picture is complicated, however, when we turn to the medieval texts. Boccaccio's source for the narrative of Troilus and Criseida is not, of course, Virgil, but rather the medieval Troy story. Two texts are of special interest: Benoît de Sainte-Maure's *Roman de Troie* and Guido delle Collonne's *Historia Destructionis Troiae*. The *Roman de Troie* is one of the three "romans antiques"—that is, one of the three French mid-twelfth-century retellings, in thousands of octosyllabic couplets, of classical stories. Benoît's own sources are the pseudo-eyewitness accounts, in late-classical Latin prose, of Dares and Dictys. Guido's book is a 1287 Latin prose adaptation of Benoît. Medieval readers generally assumed the reverse order of transmission, naturally guessing that a Latin work was older and closer to the source than a French romance;[44] Boccaccio's own evaluation is impossible to determine, and he draws on both versions. For my own argument the differences between Benoît and Guido are not very important, and I shall draw my illustrations from Guido. What *is* important is the difference between classical epic and medieval history, between the ways they treat images. To see the difference, it will be useful to begin with one of the other French romances, the *Roman d'Eneas*.

Visual images are crucially important in the *Eneas*, but they are handled rather differently than they are in the *Aeneid*. For Virgil, images refer to the past or future; for the French writer, they are emphatically *present*. The historical mural in Dido's temple is gone, and in place of Virgil's ekphrasis we find a description of the stones that make up the walls of her wondrous castle: marble in all colors, gray, white, indigo, and red, and three rows of powerful magnets that render armed attack ineffective (422–47).[45] Again, the final encounter between Aeneas and Turnus is significantly modified. It is still the case that Aeneas hesitates before killing Turnus and acts only when he sees the visible reminder of Pallas's death (9775–9814). But now the reminder is a ring made of gold, with a jacinth carving of a lion cub (5763–74). Gone is the ominous mythic picture of the fifty murdered bridegrooms; it has been replaced by a medieval heraldic image, an image not *of* any past event but an image *for* a living person, a living line. That line has come to an end with Pallas's death, but the memorial of death is also a striking visual display: an elaborate tomb in which the body is preserved in its royal clothes, kept from corruption through an embalming system that pumps balm and turpentine from vessels of gold and sardonyx. The tomb is topped by a gold plaque with an epitaph:

> An cest tombel gist ci dedanz
> Pallas li proz, li biaus, li genz,
> qui fu fiz Euander lo roi:
> Turnus l'ocist an un tornoi. (6491–94)
>
> [Here within this tomb lies
> Pallas the brave, the handsome, the noble,
> who was the son of Evander the King:
> Turnus killed him in single battle.]

As a text, this epitaph is unremarkable; what is remarkable is its textual setting. The epitaph is inscribed directly into the octosyllabic medium, and the medieval reader sees exactly the words that the grieving survivors are supposed to have seen.

For Virgil, the visual image is both other to the text and crucially involved in it, as Troy is both tragically lost to Aeneas and the source of his power. The medieval romance is transparent to its images; the visual traces of dead warriors take their place in the bright scenery of the revived epic narrative. It is not hard to find a broad historical explanation for this shift. For Virgil, the Roman Empire is a going thing, an available and inescapable context for his poem; the poem's desire is not so much for the lost city of Troy as for a historical dimension in which both Troy and Rome have meaning. For the medieval writer, both Troy and the Roman Empire are gone, and making-present becomes an essential activity. The impulse to make the Empire present derives not merely from nostalgia or a love of the exotic, but also from the twelfth-century desire to establish new states and new lines of legitimate descent.[46] The recourse to transparent representation of ancient warriors is of a piece with the twelfth-century development and systematization of heraldry, which R. Howard Bloch has described as "the most obvious European example of a universal totemic activity by which a particular sign or logos is, within a differentiated system of similar interrelated symbols, associated with a particular family or clan."[47] I do not claim that Pallas's lion cub is the sign of any particular twelfth-century family, though it was a common heraldic symbol, but that it is a token of the *kind* of image that is valued. We have moved from classic ekphrasis, which traverses an ontological gap dividing word from image, to blazonry: that is, to the verbal description of heraldic signs, where the verbal description has the same legal force as the coat of arms and the coat of arms must be reducible to a short verbal description.[48]

The *Roman de Troie*, probably written a few years after the *Eneas*, exhibits the same interests, with a kind of one-upmanship at work that is visible as well in Guido's translation. Again there are elaborate tombs; but the most important tomb, that of Hector (whose epitaph is saved for the very end), is in fact a double image of Hector. On top, according to Guido, there is fixed

> a certain golden statue, representing a likeness of Hector, with his naked sword in his hand, and his glance and expression were toward that place where the Greek army was staying in its tents, so that he seemed to offer threats to the Greeks with his naked sword.[49]

Beneath this is the corpse itself, preserved by an embalming system even more elaborate than that envisaged for Pallas: a preparation of balsam flows from a vase lodged in an "ingeniously constructed aperture in his head," down "first to the front of the forehead, through the inner parts, then to the eyes and nose" and so through the rest of the corpse to a second vase located in the feet.[50]

I take this double image to be an emblem of the work as a whole—for the narrative has indeed a hinged double theme. The *Roman d'Eneas* crucially adds a continuous erotic theme to Virgil's narrative: Dido receives no more space than before, but now Lavinia is a second love interest, and extended Ovidian scenes of love-at-a-distance become the emotional cores of the second half of the story. Where the *Eneas* writer can achieve an erotic narrative by expanding plot elements already found in Virgil, Benoît adds an entirely new set of episodes to the Dares and Dictys narrative, producing an interlace of two different modes.[51] The continuous martial story derived from Dares and Dictys—the story of a warrior with a naked sword, a man threatening other men—is now punctuated with scenes from four different love-stories, those of Jason and Medea, Paris and Helen, Troilus and Briseida, and Achilles and Polyxena. It may seem fanciful to read the preserved corpse of Hector as an emblem for the twelfth-century erotic subject—that complex of interior spaces and abundant fluids—but I find confirmation in the very next episode, in which Achilles, visiting Troy during a truce, first sees Polyxena. She is grieving at the tomb of Hector, and in her description—her "blazon," in a second sense of the term[52]—she seems to mirror both parts of the tomb:

> The vivid color of her cheeks which colored her face with the redness of roses was not at all faded from its vivid brightness and freshness on account of the anguish of her grief, nor was the natural rosy color removed from her lips, nor did the floods of tears flowing from her eyes darken the splendor of her eyes. In fact, it seemed to the onlookers that the tears flowing down her cheeks seemed to have the appearance of a tablet of new ivory, gleaming with milk-white radiance, which someone had bedewed with drops of brilliant clear water; so also her beautiful golden blond hair scattered in many strands looked like gold, so that it almost seemed to be not hair but rather threads of gold bound together.[53]

The alternating structure of the Trojan romance suggests a dialectic relationship between war and love, but these images—Polyxena and the tomb of Hector—fuse the two spheres. Once again, the medieval writer has brought into the world of the poem that which must remain essentially Other in the *Aeneid*. For Virgil, love is a seductive alternative to imperial destiny; it is confined to Book IV, the section that medieval literary critics understood to be a fictional addition to the historical narrative. For Benoît and Guido, war and love are on a footing, both part of the story, both visible. Similarly, Troilus is no longer a unique, mysterious totem image: drawing on Dares and Dictys, Benoît makes Troilus a major actor. He is the second Hector, a copy of Hector, but not a reflection cast into a non-textual realm of historical image; he is simply the second warrior in the land.

The single most striking moment of the making-visible of heroes is a static series of descriptions that appears fairly early in the narrative. Both Benoît and Guido cite Dares as the source of the descriptions:

> Dares the Phrygian wished in this place to describe the form and appearance of several of the Greeks and Trojans, and, although he did not mention all, at least he described the most famous. For he asserts in the book which he made, written in Greek, that he saw them all with his own eyes. For very often during truces made between the armies he went to the Greek tents, and he observed the nature of each of the chief people, gazing at them so that he would know how to describe their characteristics in his work. For he said first of all that Helen shone with excessive loveliness . . .[54]

Here, finally, we find the living form of Troilus.

> Troilus, although he was large of body, was even larger of heart; he was very bold but he had moderation in his boldness. He endeared himself to young girls, since he was pleased to maintain a certain reserve toward them. In strength and valor for fighting he was another Hector, or second to him. Moreover, in the whole kingdom of Troy, no young man was celebrated for such great strength and such great daring.[55]

This description is not especially informative, nor especially visual, but what is crucial is its presentation: it is the result of direct vision. As with Aeneas's gaze within the temple, the visual image pierces through the historical distance separating readers from the ancient dead, but now the ancient dead are recovered *as* living people. The set of images occupies the space of a truce, a public space in which an inquisitive reporter or reader can simply wander and look. And the availability of this ancient knowledge to modern readers is figured in the transparency of visual images to writing. Another writer in the tradition, Joseph of Exeter, exclaims upon the power of writing to equal the power of images; he expresses what W. J. T. Mitchell has called "ekphrastic hope"[56]:

> O that the power of my eloquence might bring back faces that have been snatched from us, and that kings who have been hid from our eyes might, when proclaimed by my words, live in men's hearts. As silent paintings present warriors long buried to an admiring people, so do pages adorned with words speak aloud of kings. The one art charms the eye, the other charms the ear.[57]

In one manuscript of Guido, the images are literally realized as images (see Figure 2).[58] Although this manuscript was produced too late to have influenced the *Filostrato*—around 1370, in Venice—it provides a telling reading of the catalogue of descriptions. Generally the illustrations in Guido manuscripts are placed on separate pages, or at the beginning of major sections, or in the margins; here they break into the textual columns in unusual numbers. The hope expressed by Joseph of Exeter has been fulfilled: the pages adorned with words literally contain pictures.

These pictures differ from the other pictures in this manuscript in several important ways. They do not depict scenes from the narrative but rather portraits devoid of context: the characters are temporarily freed from their story, as in a temporary truce, and seen as whole beings. With one exception, the portraits are presented frontally, in contrast to the profile action scenes. (The exception is Diomede, the only character to be described in the text as deceitful; he is in profile.[59]) Meyer Schapiro has demonstrated that frontality itself implies power in medieval art: frontal portraits tend to be reserved for hieratic figures or for demonic idols posing as hieratic figures. He comments on the difference between frontal and profile images:

> The profile face is detached from the viewer and belongs with the body in action . . . in a space shared with other profiles on the surface of the image. It is, broadly speaking, like the grammatical form of the third person, the impersonal "he" or "she" with its concordantly inflected verb; while the face turned outwards is credited with intentness, a latent or potential glance directed to the observer, and corresponds to the role of "I" in speech, with its complementary "you." It seems to exist both for us and for itself in a space virtually continuous with our own, and is therefore appropriate to the figure as symbol or as carrier of a message.[60]

Moreover, in medieval art the gesture of pointing with the index finger—the gesture performed by most of these figures—usually signifies an act of speaking.[61] It is precisely the gesture of messengers or of characters in dialogue. *These* characters, however, speak directly to the viewer. Finally, although some illustrated manuscripts provide verbal identifications for every character depicted, this manuscript does not generally label characters, even in potentially confusing narrative scenes. Names *are* provided here, even though—because of the systematic spacing of portraits in the text—there is no possibility of confusion. The names are not marginal captions; they appear prominently within the picture, and the characters stand inside or in front of their own names. At the same time, they point

Figure 2. Page from a fourteenth-century manuscript of Guido delle Colonne, *Historia Destructionis Troiae,* fol. 27. Bodmer Library, Geneva. Used by permission of Fondation Martin Bodmer.

to their names: the names are both objects and utterances. In effect, these historical figures declare themselves to the reader of the book.

Hugo Buchthal has connected these particular manuscript pages to a larger trend in fourteenth-century Italy.

> Undistinguished as this gallery of portraits is artistically, it is not without interest when it is viewed in conjunction with the various fresco cycles of famous men which became popular as decorations of princely castles and palaces in the course of the Trecento.

The most striking parallel, according to Buchthal, is

> the decoration of the *Sala degli uomini famosi* executed about 1332 by Giotto for King Robert of Naples in the Castel Nuovo. Among its nine famous figures from antiquity were four heroes of the Trojan War: Hector, Aeneas, Achilles, and Paris.[62]

Giotto's work is now lost and is known to us only through written texts—notably an anonymous corona of nine sonnets, each devoted to one of the portraits.[63] These sonnets suggest that the effect of the portraits was like the effect of the manuscript pages: the historical figures speak directly to the viewer, announcing their names. Each uses the present tense to declare his identity and the past tense to describe his life:

> I' son Paris dell'alto re Priamo
> Qui figurato e fui 'l suo quinto figlio.
>
> [I am Paris of the high king Priam
> Here depicted and was his fifth son.]

This is the very scene in which Boccaccio wrote the *Filostrato*—in Naples, in the court of King Robert, in 1335 or a little later.[64] Giotto's hall was part of a political project. Pierluigi Leone de Castris has written that the Hall of Famous Men belongs to a new chapter in the history of art, a chapter opened when King Robert returned to Naples from Provence in 1324, "with the double desire of expanding Angevin political hegemony on the peninsula and creating a learned and 'modern' court that would be the mirror and the justification of this hegemony."[65] One other connection between the Neapolitan court and Trojan history should be mentioned: Hugo Buchthal has linked the manuscript depiction of Hector's tomb with the tomb of King Robert's only son, Duke Charles of Calabria.[66] The tomb, produced in 1332 by Tino di Camaino, represents the dead ruler twice, as a recumbent corpse and as a reigning monarch. The second depiction—what Erwin Panofsky has called "the activation of the effigy"[67]—was quite rare in fourteenth-century Italy but was historically ascendant; it became common in the fifteenth century. The manuscript illustration modifies Guido's text, bringing it into line with Charles's tomb, by showing Hector's corpse lying down rather than seated. Buchthal notes that the Angevins claimed direct descent from Priam and suggests quite plausibly that "[P]opular imagination may have associated Hector and Duke Charles."[68]

Such a context complicates the meaning of "the form of Troilus." Boccaccio's omission of visual display from his Troy story is not merely a response to ancient stories; it must be read as a polemical exclusion of the very element in his sources that would have seemed most potent and prestigious at the moment of his writing. The images of famous men are not degraded—as in, say, Shakespeare's *Troilus and Cressida*—but simply left out. Now, the explanation for this cannot be Boccaccio's general taste: he elsewhere praises King Robert, and he dresses the *Teseida* in epic trappings, and he later writes a book on Illustrious Men. Rather, his strategy here must be referred to the special project of the *Filostrato*—which is, I have claimed, to write a book that can stand alone as whole and self-authorizing.

A portrait of a Trojan hero serves to establish authority, whether it appears in a history book or a courtly hall. The *Filostrato* refers to no portrait except the complex verbal portrait constituted by the entire work; and the refusal of authorizing imagery is called into being as a salient fact about the text by the choice of Trojan subject matter. We can see this strategy again in the interplay of love and war. In the medieval histories, love and war are analogous, intertwined subjects. The *Filostrato* draws its narrative line from these histories, but emphatically discards any "pensier . . . della gran guerra" (1.44) [thought of the great war]. Through this double gesture, Boccaccio succeeds in writing a book about love that is positively *not* about war, and his insistence on the self-sufficient value of love as a subject amounts to an argument for the autonomy of courtly literature.

Yet the image of King Robert's Castel Nuovo should warn us that the rejection of political concerns can never be absolute. I have argued that Boccaccio takes from Virgil the form of Troilus rather than, as it were, the content: he is interested not in Troy but rather in the structure of self-confirming totalization represented by the relationship between Troy and its personified image. Yet presumably a similar logic contributes to King Robert's interest in Trojan heroes: the figures that Giotto painted are important for their particular identities, but equally important for the *kind* of fame, the kind of self-declaring illustriousness, they represent. They define not an ideological position but a mode of collective identification, in order to confirm the place of king and court in the expanding kingdom. This is to say that even the form of totalization has political import. Boccaccio does not merely pass through his medieval sources to appropriate the founding structures of Virgil; Virgil's Troy has already been put to contemporary uses, and Boccaccio's project must be to appropriate an existing structure of appropriation.

Boccaccio accomplishes this meta-appropriation, I would argue, by presenting the *Filostrato* as an unprecedented fusion of disparate elements. He responds to the medieval Troy books as he responds to Dante's *Vita Nuova*, by collapsing distinctions. I suggested in Chapter 4 that the poem constructs a specular equation between first-person, second-person, and third-person discourse: in Meyer Schapiro's terms, it is both a profile and a frontal portrait. The tomb of Duke Charles and the tomb of Hector—in the manuscript illustration—also combine profile and frontal depictions, but they do this by offering two images, partitioned into separate registers. The *Filostrato* combines the image of Troilus living and the image of Troilus dead into a single image. But to call the poem a single image is to collapse an even more basic opposition, the opposition between image and text. The poem has no images, yet it *is* an image; it is a public shield for personal misery, and it carries a single indivisible mark of identity. Like the characters in the Guido manuscript, the poem points to its own name as its essential truth. Rather than gratifying the ekphrastic wish by juxtaposing real pictures with real letters, the *Filostrato* claims to subsume the opposition into a single metaphorical equation.

Does the *Filostrato* succeed in using the form of Troilus to establish a new kingdom of the book? The question is posed for us, I believe, but cannot be decided. On the one hand, the Proem and the author's final envoy seal the poem as a totalized whole, and the tautological equation implied by the name "Filostrato" cannot be shaken. On the other hand, the story that is told within this stable form documents the disruptive entry of political identification into the utopian private space of love.

The figure most associated with this repoliticization is the figure who can never quite be assimilated to the work's internal economy of homosocial identifications, Criseida. It is Criseida who crosses the border of Troy, and in so doing she brings into the poem the idea of Troy—for example, in the flirting dialogue where she and Diomede compare Trojan manners with Greek (6.14ff). She is the first Trojan character to have a view of Troy as a whole, and she is associated with this view even when the viewer is Troiolo; it is her impending departure that prompts him to address a lament to his city ("tu città") and to Priam (4.123). (Priam is first named in the poem when Calchas is negotiating for Criseida's transfer [4.4].) After she leaves, he seems to see Troy for the first time; we do not see what he sees, but we see *that* he sees:

> Quando sol gia per Troia cavalcando,
> ciaschedun luogo gli tornava a mente;
> de' quai con seco giva ragionando:
> "Quivi rider la vidi lietamente,
> quivi la vidi verso me guardando,
> quivi mi salutò benignamente,
> quivi far festa e quivi star pensosa,
> quivi la vidi a' miei sospir pietosa." (5.54)

> [When he went riding through Troy alone,
> each place returned to his mind;
> of these places he would go about speaking to himself:
> "Here I saw her laugh joyfully,
> here I saw her looking toward me,
> here she graciously greeted me,
> here I saw her rejoice and here stay thoughtful,
> here I saw her full of pity for my sighs."]

The substitution that Troiolo originally made, Criseida *instead of* Troy, is here being reversed, as the memory of Criseida leads him to the sights that the ancient histories offered all along.

The conjunction of Troiolo with Troy must be fatal for him, and one minor index of his downfall is the textual juxtaposition of the two cognate names. When Troiolo returns from handing Criseida over to Diomede, we are told,

> *Troiolo* in *Troia* tristo ed angoscioso,
> quanto fu mai nessun, se ne rivenne. (5.15)

> [*Troiolo* returned to *Troy*, sad and distressed
> as much as anyone ever was.]

The aural play of that first line will be familiar to readers of Chaucer; Chaucer establishes the relationship between Troilus and Troy in the second line of his poem, where he calls Troilus "the kyng Priamus sone of Troye." But Boccaccio has avoided precisely this effect until this point in the poem, and where Chaucer rhymes "Troye" with "joie," Boccaccio continues the alliteration from Troiolo and Troy to "tristo" [sad]. For Troiolo, to return to Troy is to return to himself as alienated. The verbal juxtaposition reappears twice. Diomede seduces Criseida, and "'n brieve spazio ne cacciò di fore / *Troiolo* e *Troia*" (6.8) [in a brief space he expelled *Troiolo* and *Troy*]. Later Deiphebo captures a garment of Diomede's and "mentre che portarlosi davanti / facea per *Troia*, *Troiol* sopravvenne" (8.9) [while he was having it carried before him through *Troy*, *Troilo* came up unexpectedly]. "Troiolo in Troia"; "Troiolo e Troia"; "Troia, Troiol": in a brief space, the two terms collapse toward each other.

The last of those three scenes is especially interesting: the incident in which Troiolo recognizes a brooch on Diomede's garment, recognizes it as a token that he gave to Criseida, is an invention of Boccaccio's, and it transforms the scene in which Aeneas recognizes the belt of Pallas at the end of the *Aeneid*.[69] Once again, *we* do not see the brooch (what is depicted on it?), but we see that it is being seen. The entry of Trojan material into the poem is accompanied by a new preoccupation with looking at things in general. The most striking instance of this is the one straightforward *effictio* in the poem, the one exception I have been suppressing to make my general claim. It occurs in the stanza just before the stanza that announces Criseida's betrayal of Diomede, and it is a description of Diomede:

> Egli era grande e bel della persona,
> giovane fresco e piacevole assai,
> e forte e fier, sì come si ragiona,
> e parlante quant'altro greco mai,
> e ad amor la natura avea prona. (6.33)

> [He was tall and handsome in his person,
> young, fresh, and very pleasing,
> and strong and proud, as they say,

and as well-spoken as ever any other Greek,
and he had a nature prone to love.]

Like Guido's description of Troilus, quoted earlier, this does not seem especially visual; it is, however, the one remnant of the set-piece descriptions in Boccaccio's "ancient stories." Appropriately enough, it is located, like those descriptions, in a time of truce—because, in a modification of his sources, Boccaccio has made Criseida's departure the consequence of military negotiations during a truce. In the *Filostrato*, the public space of clear vision is the space of death.

So the *Filostrato* succeeds in defining itself as a totalizing image on the model of Virgil's picture of Troilus; yet within its own narrative it compromises the autonomy of the form of Troilus. We can make at least one more reversal: the compromise, the collapse of Troilus into Troy, is part of the process of his death, and his death is what originally constitutes him as an image. Does the *Filostrato* achieve an illustrious new form of literary authority? The question is undecidable—because of the paradox that founds totality on wounding—and thus productive. This may be the reason Boccaccio chose as his literary form a dying youth rather than one of King Robert's healthy, picturesque heroes.

4. The Book of Troilus

As a coda to this chapter and an introduction to the next, I want to set the *Filostrato* against two more pictures of Troilus, taken from Chaucer's *Troilus*. Given what I have said about Boccaccio's response to earlier images of Trojan history, *Troilus and Criseyde* can be characterized briefly and somewhat anticlimactically: Chaucer reinserts the pictures that Boccaccio emphatically omits. As C. S. Lewis suggested in 1932, Chaucer rejects the avant-garde impulse he found in his primary source and returns the narrative to the mainstream of medieval Trojan historiography.[70]

One obvious contrast between the two poems has already been mentioned. The *Filostrato* treats the deep connection between Troy and Troiolo as an open secret—something known to everyone, certainly, but never mentioned in the poem until Troiolo's amorous sanctuary is violated. The narrator of the *Troilus*, by contrast, calls attention to the relationship from the beginning. His purpose, he says, is

> The double sorwe of Troilus to tellen,
> That was the kyng Priamus sone of Troye. (1.1–2)

The syntactic construction allows the momentary suggestion that Troilus is not only the son of King Priam of Troy but also the son of Troy itself. Chaucer's narrator is, as Lewis pointed out, "an 'Historial' poet"; he does what he can to foreground the political and historical aspects of his material, and when the shape of the story makes it seem digressive to narrate "the Troian gestes" (1.145) at length, he tells his readers where that material may be found, "In Omer, or in Dares, or in Dite" (1.146).

This change is not only a displacement of emphasis, but also a revaluation of Troy itself. When "Troye" appears as a rhyme-word in the *Troilus*, it invariably rhymes with "joye"; just as strikingly, "joye" invariably rhymes with "Troye."[71] Certainly it is possible to read this coupling ironically, as Eugene Vance suggests: "there can be no 'joy' in 'Troy.'"[72] But Troy *is* the place of joy for most of the poem; to say that there can be no joy in Troy is to say, in effect, that there can be no joy in joy, no lasting bliss in temporal human pleasure. For Boccaccio's Troiolo, Troy is fatal even in its unfallen condition; for Chaucer's Troilus it is the ground, however unstable, of happiness. In rhyming "Troye" and "joye," Chaucer implies an understanding that is explicit in a historiographer like Guido delle Colonne: the idea that Troy, "that most noble and marvelous great Troy,"[73] is a city whose fall richly deserves to be lamented.

Chaucer is of course consistently skillful in his rhyming. Within the *Troilus*, the "Troye/joye" rhyme is just one instance of a sophisticated technique that establishes a network of signifying patterns on the formal surface of the text.[74] But this rhyming technique merely develops a feature of the *Filostrato*. Boccaccio does not seem to employ complex rhyme-patterns throughout the *Filostrato*, but he does have a preferred rhyme for "Troia": "gioia" [joy] is far less frequent than "noia" [annoyance, grief]. Troy is coupled with trouble even when the explicit theme is happiness, as in Hector's invitation to Criseida:

> e tu sicura, lieta e senza noia,
> con noi, mentre t'aggrada, ti sta' 'n Troia. (1.13)
>
> [and you—safe, happy, and without grief—
> stay with us, as long as it pleases you, in Troy.][75]

The contrast between these two ways of rhyming Troy suggests, almost too neatly, the difference between two poetic approaches to the matter of Troy. For Boccaccio, the name of the city calls forth grief; for Chaucer, joy. If we were to describe Chaucer's treatment of the *Filostrato* on the basis of this feature alone, we might say that he elaborates, to an extraordinary degree, his predecessor's technical devices, but that he rejects the most daring implications of those devices. Surely Boccaccio's reading of Troy is the *difficilior lectio*. Medieval moralists often described Troy as a sinful city, doomed by its pride or its moral laxity,[76] but I do not think it was ever described as, before its destruction, a place of grief. Chaucer's pattern may be more powerful because it is more expected; my point is simply that it *is* more expected. This is one of the places where, as Lewis states, Chaucer "did not hesitate . . . to *amenden* and to *reducen* what was *amis* in his author."[77]

We might understand Chaucer's portraits of Troilus (to which I shall shortly turn) in this light. The *Troilus* contains far more Trojan material than the *Filostrato*, and in general it is a far more visual text: it is richly attentive to the phenomenal world—the world of colors, clothing, birds, gestures, architecture—that holds so little interest for Troiolo and his narrator. B. A. Windeatt adopts the phrase "paynted proces" (2.424) as a metaphor for Chaucer's method of literary adaptation: "It is as if stronger light is thrown over the original and a more deeply etched picture emerges, with lighter lights, deeper shadows, and a whole range of intervening shadings."[78] Windeatt is not speaking here of specifically visual description, but using a suggestive visual metaphor to describe a more general "'thickening' of the texture of language and idea";[79] vivid description is part of this "in-eching." In filling out the visual world of the poem, however, Chaucer is not adding anything new; rather he is adding something old, returning Boccaccio's under-imaged narrative to the visually oriented mode of the *Roman de la Rose* or the *Teseida*. For Chaucer, there seems to be no reason *not* to describe Troilus.

The first extended description of Troilus shows the value given to martial machinery and visual display in Chaucer's poem, and I want to quote it at length. Criseyde is alone in her room, having just learned from Pandarus that Troilus loves her, when she hears a public clamor outside; Troilus is returning victorious from battle.

> This Troilus sat on his baye steede
> Al armed, save his hed, ful richely;

And wownded was his hors, and gan to blede,
On which he rood a pas ful softely.
But swich a knyghtly sighte trewely
As was on hym, was nought, withouten faille,
To loke on Mars, that god is of bataille.

So lik a man of armes and a knyght
He was to seen, fulfilled of heigh prowesse,
For bothe he hadde a body and a myght
To don that thing, as wel as hardynesse;
And ek to seen hym in his gere hym dresse,
So fressh, so yong, so weldy semed he,
It was an heven upon hym for to see.

His helm tohewen was in twenty places,
That by a tyssew heng his bak byhynde;
His sheeld todasshed was with swerdes and maces,
In which men myghte many an arwe fynde
That thirled hadde horn and nerf and rynde;
And ay the peple cryde, "Here cometh oure joye,
And, next his brother, holder up of Troye!" (2.624–44)

This is indeed, as the narrator says, Troilus's "happy day" (2.621). He has triumphed in battle, and he is about to receive Criseyde's responsive attention. For Boccaccio's Troiolo, war and love were mutually exclusive fields of endeavor, but here both realms—military glory and amorous "heven" (2.637)—have been condensed into a single passage.

The passage effects another kind of condensation as well: it combines two strains in the tradition of Troilus portraiture, showing him both as a triumphant warrior and as the victim of a brutal assault. The two framing stanzas emphasize wounds, blood, the breaking of armor, the piercing of skin: but all of this destruction attaches to Troilus's horse and to his protective shell of "horn and nerf and rynde" (2.642). Troilus's person is miraculously untouched, and is described both without wounds and without armor in the central stanza of the three. In that stanza, "armes" become a moral attribute (he is "So *lik* a man of armes and a knyght," 2.631), and the narrator's emphasis falls on the qualities that belong to Troilus all by himself. Given Criseyde's curious gaze, and the notorious vagueness of the phrase "to don that thyng" (2.634), we might say that

Troilus is imaginatively stripped naked; the stripping reveals, however, not flesh but rather essential qualities—high prowess, might, hardiness, freshness and youth and wieldiness. These qualities make Troilus wholly admirable, but clearly the signs of deadly combat are also a crucial part of his appeal for Criseyde, for the crowd, and for Chaucer's audience.

Troilus appears here healthy and whole, yet paradoxically arrayed in the very wounds that originally gave his image such power. Chaucer, unlike Boccaccio, does not attempt to construct a seamlessly unitary image: this picture is partitioned, as the stanzaic text is partitioned. For the picture the line of division is the line between Troilus's unhelmeted head and his battered armor and horse. We remember, uncomfortably, that most of the histories describe Troilus's eventual death as a decapitation; here, however, head and body make a whole person. Chaucer has gone back through the *Filostrato* to discover the world of Trojan history, and the authority and attractiveness of that world are made present again.

I would suggest, however, that Boccaccio's wholesale rejection of certain conventions has transformed the meaning of those conventions for Chaucer: they are no longer merely givens, but rather have become contested elements, charged with local significance. In the triumphant description just discussed, the contest seems to be over: Troy and its visual splendor have been retrieved in full force. But it is characteristic of Chaucer—as I shall argue at greater length in the next chapter—to reestablish a traditional form and then pull it apart. The picture of Troy becomes visibly problematic for Chaucer in the textbook *effictio* of Troilus in Book 5. As many readers have observed, this description is awkwardly located: it comes absurdly late in the poem, and it intrudes on a private scene between Diomede and Criseyde. Indeed, it follows upon set-piece descriptions of those two, and in the sequence we can see a progressive wrenching of poetic logic. Diomede is a new character, and so a brief portrait (one stanza, not translated from the one-stanza *effictio* in the *Filostrato* but clearly substituting for it) is appropriate. The three-stanza portrait of Criseyde that immediately follows expresses many forms of ambivalence and anxiety ("Tendre-herted, slydynge of corage; / But trewely, I kan nat telle hire age" [5.825–26]), but what is strangest about it is its very mode, cataloguing Criseyde's physical and moral traits at this late date as if we were just being introduced to her. Still, there is a certain appropriateness to the pairing of these first two portraits, since they describe the two characters we have just seen talking. Troilus's portrait, on the other hand, can have no justification other than some urgent wish on the part of the narrator: perhaps the wish that Criseyde would look in both directions and see Diomede and Troilus as the narrator sees them, or perhaps a desire to ward off the danger of the moment by returning nostalgically to a more familiar, more conventional form—both the form of the triumphal parade in Book 2 and the form of Trojan history books in general.

These three portraits are derived from the portrait sequences in Benoît, Guido delle Colonne, and possibly Joseph of Exeter. In the portrait of Troilus, however, the commonplaces take on a new force. Here is the text:

> And Troilus wel woxen was in highte,
> And complet formed by proporcioun
> So wel that kynde it nought amenden myghte;
> Yong, fressh, strong, and hardy as lyoun;
> Trewe as stiel in ech condicioun;
> Oon of the beste entecched creature
> That is or shal whil that the world may dure.
>
> And certeynly in storye it is yfounde
> That Troilus was nevere unto no wight,
> As in his tyme, in no degree secounde
> In durryng don that longeth to a knyght.
> Al myghte a geant passen hym of myght,
> His herte ay with the first and with the beste
> Stood paregal, to durre don that hym leste. (5.827–40)

I have remarked that Guido delle Colonne's description of Troilus is not especially visual, but neither is it markedly *non*-visual; like the other Troy-book descriptions, it relies on general moral language with a few physical attributes mixed in. Chaucer's description, however, makes an issue of visual specification. Criseyde's portrait included vivid evocations of her appearance, for example her "maner" of going

> ytressed with hire heres clere
> Doun by hire coler at hire bak byhynde,
> Which with a thred of gold she wolde bynde. (5.810–12)

This detail oddly echoes a phrase from the earlier description of Troilus:

> His helm tohewen was in twenty places,
> That by a tyssew heng *his bak byhynde*. (2.638–39)

The echo suggests the range of material excluded from the final *efficitio* of Troilus, which represents Troilus only in the most general and approving terms, as if any particular details would detract from the ideal image the narrator is intent on creating. In the earlier picture of Troilus, the particularities of torn sinew and dashed shield were part of his appeal, part of his attractive masculine "maner"; here, the realm of the military and the realm of the particular have both become areas to be avoided. The narrator is attempting to return, in effect, to the protective frame of the earlier passage's central stanza.

For Diomede, the narrator describes qualities and habits but creates an impression of imposing physicality (most notably, "he was of tonge large" [5.804]). In addition, the Diomede portrait stresses a theme that is missing from the Troilus portrait. Diomede's lineage is mentioned twice in seven lines: he is "lik his fader Tideus," and "heir . . . of Calydoigne and Arge" (5.803–5). Although the narrator usually, in a departure from the *Filostrato*, stresses Troilus's noble family, here he seems willfully determined to describe Troilus as standing alone. This determination accounts for the wordy awkwardness of the second stanza of the portrait: the narrator makes the banal assertion that Troilus is second to no one and cites "storye" as support, but *this* story has repeatedly praised Troilus as second only to Hector. (Even the crowd, in the earlier scene, felt obliged to qualify their praise of Troilus with a parenthetical "next his brother," 2.644.) Hence the flustered concession that some "geant" might conceivably be mightier.

In itself, Chaucer's final *effictio* of Troilus is not very different from those to be found in the tradition of Trojan history. But it works to very different effect: the stock ingredients of the tradition have been activated as signifying elements in a complex drama of authorial psychology and literary form. This activation is made possible for Chaucer, I suggest, by Boccaccio's self-conscious disruption of the tradition. In reviving the old forms of Trojan history as new problems, Chaucer does not turn entirely away from Boccaccio's more radical response to those forms. By its very presence in the *Troilus*, Trojan portraiture contributes to the overturning of Boccaccio's polemical self-authorization; paradoxically, however, this last portrait of Troilus seems to express a longing for the ahistorical, nonvisual autonomy of the *Filostrato*. The description is both idealistic in its absoluteness and pathetic in its disconnectedness. In a characteristically ambivalent gesture, Chaucer has pasted Boccaccio's "form of Troilus" back into the book from which he removed it, but on the wrong page.

6. Sailing to Charybdis: The Second *Canticus Troili* and the Contexts of Chaucer's *Troilus*

1. The Second *Canticus Troili*

In the final book of his tragedy, Chaucer's Troilus, in order to "shewe / Th'enchesoun of his wo" (5.631–32), composes a song:

> O sterre, of which I lost have al the light,
> With herte soor wel oughte I to biwaille
> That evere derk in torment, nyght by nyght,
> Toward my deth with wynd in steere I saille;
> For which the tenthe nyght, if that I faille
> The gydyng of thi bemes bright an houre,
> My ship and me Caribdis wol devoure. (5.638–44)

In many of the manuscripts, this song receives a rubric: "Canticus Troili," "Cantus Troili," or "The song of troilus."[1] Two earlier passages in the *Troilus* are marked similarly: the lyric beginning "If no love is" (1.400–420), and—somewhat less often—the hymn to Love in Book 3 (3.1744–71). In the recent editions of Barney and Windeatt, "Canticus Troili" appears as a rubric for all three passages; in Root and in Robinson, it is reserved for the songs in Books 1 and 5. Thus "O sterre" is either the second or the third *Canticus Troili*. Although I shall be stressing the difficulty of pinning down this brief text, the terminological ambiguity has to be resolved, and I shall refer to "O sterre" as "the second *Canticus Troili*." I do this partly to stress the close connections between Troilus's final song and his first.[2] These connections include not only thematic similarities (such as the ship metaphor) and roughly symmetrical placement in the *Troilus*, but also a shared status as consciously crafted poems. The central hymn to Love is a song, but we are not told that Troilus chooses his words (as at 1.386–87) or *makes* a song (as at 5.633); he simply sings (3.1743). The first and last *Cantici Troili* are the two songs that Troilus actually composes in the course of Chaucer's narrative.

If the last *Canticus Troili*—henceforth "the second"—invites comparison with the first, the comparison appears to work entirely to the disadvantage of the later effort. The first *Canticus Troili* has always been recognized as a moment of literary achievement exceptional even in the *Troilus*. Early readers copied it separately;[3] in 1720, it was modernized and praised by George Sewell;[4] a modern critic has called its first stanza "one of the most beautiful stanzas of love poetry in the language."[5] Moreover, the song is an object of special fascination for literary historians. It is a direct translation of a sonnet by Petrarch: the only appearance of Petrarch's vernacular poetry in English, it is commonly stated, before the English Renaissance. The first *Canticus Troili*—often called simply "the *Canticus Troili*"—is "an isolated landmark in literary history."[6]

Placed next to this poetic monument—an unfair setting, perhaps, but one suggested by the text—the second *Canticus Troili* seems unremarkable and somewhat awkward. It has occasioned little scholarly commentary and, to my knowledge, no special praise. Yet Chaucer can be a poet of artful awkwardness. We have learned to read his gaucherie as grace by finding new contexts for it: where the narration of the *Troilus* appears clumsy, for example, the depiction of an troubled Narrator is complex and moving.[7] Perhaps the inferiority of the second *Canticus Troili* to the first is part of the meaning of Chaucer's poem. Is Troilus's third sorrow a loss of poetic skill? Such an idea may be suggested in passing: note that Troilus now sings "With softe vois" (5.636) and that when he has finished singing he falls "soone . . . ayeyn into his sikes olde" (5.645–66). And the song itself may refer to a loss of inspiration: it expresses the fear of a certain failure, and (as we know from the proem to Book 2) it is conventional to compare poetic progress to a sea-voyage.[8] I believe the situation is more difficult than this, however. No single context will rescue the song; what is remarkable about the second *Canticus Troili* is the way it raises precisely the problem of contexts.

It is possible to define more carefully the "awkwardness" of this writing. The stanza is almost ostentatiously unified—by nautical imagery from the first line to the last; by subordinating connectives (*of which*, *That*, *For which*, *if that*) that structure the entire stanza as a single sentence; and by a sound-pattern in which the first end-rhyme (*light*/*nyght*) appears internally in the fifth and sixth lines (*nyght*, *bright*) and the final end-rhyme (*houre*/

devoure) is anticipated by a series of "-r" sounds (*sterre*, *herte soor*, *evere derk in torment*, *steere*). Yet this symbolic, syntactic, prosodic unity is contradicted by a certain fragmentation in the argument of the stanza. Many readers have stumbled, I suspect, over the *if* clause in the fifth and sixth lines: "the tenthe nyght, if that I faille / The gyding of thi bemes bright an houre." If Troilus has lost all the light of his star, how can he doubt that he will lack this light for an hour? It is possible to rationalize the apparent discrepancy through rather tortuous paraphrase, in at least two ways: "If, on the tenth night, I lack your guidance for even a single hour (as I lack it continually now)"; or "if I fail to have your guidance—if it fails to return to me—for an hour on the tenth night." The logical sound of the causal conjunction, "For which," encourages some such rationalization, but I believe that the effort is troubling.[9] An outright contradiction would be less confusing—we would recognize a change of heart. This uneasy consistency is characteristic of the second *Canticus Troili* as a whole.

It is instructive to remove "For which" and break the stanza into two parts. Consider this Chaucerian fragment:

> O sterre, of which I lost have al the light,
> With herte soor wel oughte I to biwaille
> That evere derk in torment, nyght by nyght,
> Toward my deth with wynd in steere I saille.

The logic of this allegory seems clear enough. Against his will, Troilus is sailing toward death. We have seen this language before:

> God wold I were aryved in the port
> Of deth, to which my sorwe wol me lede! (1.526–27)

and again,

> Love . . . With disespeyr so sorwfulli me offendeth,
> That streight unto the deth myn herte sailleth. (1.603–6)

In our fragment are we to imagine death as a "port" or as a less hospitable destination? In either case, the voyage is out of Troilus's control, and the course is set. In Chaucerian usage, one "bewails" an irrevocable situation or something that is irrevocably lost.[10] The second line of this fragment is somewhat problematic, it is true. The redundancy of "With herte soor" makes one ask the reason for the entire line—why is Troilus saying that he ought to lament rather than simply lamenting, as he has been doing at length and unself-consciously throughout Book 5? Is this an act of "bewailing," or is it a preface to such an utterance, or a substitute? And exactly what is to be lamented—the loss of the star (as one might expect, this being a song "of his lady deere" [5.636]), the fact of imminent death (as a strict reading of the syntax would demand), or the tormented darkness of the voyage? These alternatives are not mutually exclusive, however: it is entirely possible to lament and speak of lamenting in the same breath, to grieve and bewail dying of grief. This fragment is consistent, both in the situation it describes and in the rhetorical effect it aims to produce. Yet it seems somewhat sketchy, perhaps not complete in itself but drawn from a larger context.

Consider this second fragment:

> O sterre . . .
> . . . if that I faille
> The gydyng of thi bemes bright an houre,
> My ship and me Caribdis wol devoure.

Again, the allegory, though it is merely sketched, is clear enough. A sea-voyage is threatened by Charybdis. The voyage presumably has another destination (one doesn't normally sail *to* Charybdis); and for the threat to matter the voyage must be happy, or at least worthwhile, in itself. The success of the voyage depends on guidance from the lady; apparently she is guiding the ship now, but her guidance may fail at the crucial moment. This happier voyage is one we have met in several forms. Criseyde has been imagined as the port:

> [Pandarus to Troilus:] Stond faste, for to good port hastow rowed (1.969)

and as a fellow sailor:

> For out of wo in blisse now they flete (3.1221)

and as the pilot (or rudder):

> [Troilus to Criseyde:] [God] wol ye be my steere,
> To do me lyve, if that yow liste, or sterve. (3.1291–92)

The rhetorical point of this fragment too seems clear. As a guiding star, Criseyde becomes a benevolent celestial being, and her distance from Troilus is an aspect of her power; moreover, Troilus can now hope to reach her through prayer. For clearly this utterance is not a flat statement of possibilities: Troilus is asking his star not to fail.

Each of these two "fragments," then, can be read as a statement drawn from an allegorical account of Troilus's situation:

1. Because you are gone, I am sailing toward death.
2. If I lose you, my ship will sink.

These two sentiments cannot easily be combined. If the ship's destination is death and the voyage is tormented, the threat of Charybdis loses most of its force; either the loss of the guiding star is settled or it is not; finally, (1) is a lament, while (2) is a plea. But of course neither part of the stanza makes its statement so explicit—the "port of death" is not mentioned, for example—and it is just possible to combine the two into a coherent, if complicated, statement:

3. Since you left I have been sailing in the direction of my death (that is, Charybdis), and I will surely end up there unless you return to guide me past the danger.

I have omitted one phrase from this analysis, "the tenthe nyght." This would seem to belong to the second half of the stanza—but does the sailor, still days away from Charybdis, know to the nearest night the time of his greatest danger? Probably not. I assume that most readers take the temporal indicator *sensu literale*, as a token of Troilus's real situation that is incorporated into the allegory of the ship without itself being allegorized. Again, though, it is possible to paraphrase the entire stanza:

4. Since you left I have been sailing in the direction of my death, i.e., Charybdis, where I will surely end up unless you are here on the tenth night without even an hour's absence (*or*, unless you are here for one hour on the tenth night) to guide me past the danger.

The second *Canticus Troili*, with its appearance of unity and its logical syntax, demands to be put together into something like (4); yet it continually threatens to split into (1) and (2), incompatible fragments held together by the unlikely glue of "For which the tenthe nyght."

The shifting sense of the second *Canticus Troili* can be explained in terms of Troilus's feelings: the stanza can be read as a psychological narrative of composition. Troilus sets out to express his woe, by pathetically addressing his absent lover, stressing her absence, and describing his own situation in the most extreme terms. After the bleak acknowledgment of imminent death, there seems to be nothing left to do but to "biwaille" in earnest. Yet the phrase "nyght by nyght" has reminded Troilus that his fate is not settled. Temporizing, he appends a "for which" clause and mentions "the tenthe nyght," the night so much depends on. He recalls that he is addressing Criseyde and that he has something to say to her more urgent than mere lamentation. Wishing to exhort Criseyde to return, but not wanting to question her integrity, Troilus again dramatizes his own plight, now seen as conditional. Now he has reached a second ending, a second cadence of emphatic closure, in the space of seven lines; his original poetic project, moreover, has been effectively sabotaged. With the impatience characteristic of Troilus in this part of the romance, he abandons the song and goes back to sighing.

This psychological account is defensible but incomplete, I think. What it leaves out is the uncertainty, the nervousness, of the reading experience; it describes a poem that simply moves from (1) to (2) without ever invoking (4), without ever demanding—and authorizing—a logical but tortured paraphrase. The play of unity and contradiction in this song can best be understood, perhaps, by contrast with the first *Canticus Troili*. Here is the third and final stanza of the earlier song:

> And if that I consente, I wrongfully
> Compleyne, iwis. Thus possed to and fro,
> Al sterelees withinne a boot am I
> Amydde the see, bitwixen wyndes two,
> That in contrarie stonden evere mo.
> Allas, what is this wondre maladie?
> For hote of cold, for cold of hote, I dye. (1.414–20)

Troilus has catalogued a daunting series of questions and paradoxes, describing his experience as a new lover through the figure of *contentio*.[11] Here he finds closure in four different, apparently contradictory, ways: he adds a last (though not conclusive) step to his argument; he develops a brief nautical metaphor to describe his relationship to the argument; he cries out a question (returning to the dominant mode of the first two stanzas) that invokes a different metaphor, that of illness; he defines this illness in a confident statement that piles paradox upon paradox. The stanza is thus overtly fragmentary—it incorporates different representations and different modes of discourse. What is not in question in this stanza is the unity of the voice that expresses the sense of contradiction. Contradiction is explicitly thematized; the ceaseless alternation between perspectives and tones is the very subject of the poem. And the relation between contradictory moments is clearly defined. The metaphors of the ship and of illness do not combine to form a single picture, for instance, yet because they are marked off from each other they do not clash.

The second *Canticus Troili* does not so much contain contradictions, in the manner of the first, as imply contradictory contexts. It is overdetermined;[12] it shuttles between different narratives, between different discursive realms. Yet the evocation of contexts is always problematic, depending on interpretive decisions that the reader is forced to make, often with insufficient guidance. And the contradictions the song attempts to negotiate are not contradictions outright: although Troilus himself stands "bitwixen hope and drede" (5.630), his poem is not stalled "bitwixen wyndes two, / That in contrarie stonden evere mo." Rather, the relationships between contexts can shade from direct opposition (is the voyage happy or sad?) to a mild slippage of emphasis (Charybdis is a form of death). This very uncertainty makes the drifting between contexts a treacherous business.

I do not think, then, that the critical consensus is wrong in finding less to remark upon in the second *Canticus Troili* than in the first. This poem carries, indeed, rather little definite content; I shall not argue for a cargo of meaning previously undetected. What is fascinating about this song, though, is its navigation. It sails between a bewildering variety of contexts—not only within the text of the *Troilus*, as I have been arguing, but also in the world of literature and history that the *Troilus* inhabits. In this chapter I shall attempt to show that the second *Canticus Troili* is—like the first, but in a quite different way—adapted from a sonnet of Petrarch's, and that Chaucer most likely knew some version of the entire *Canzoniere*; that Chaucer's use of Petrarchan sonnets in the *Troilus* is part of the continuing medieval examination of the relation between lyrics and books; that the second *Canticus Troili* simultaneously evokes a passage from the *Thebaid* that casts its own light on the *Troilus* and adds another element to Chaucer's representation of literary history; and that the second *Canticus Troili* evokes, and yet rejects, a mode of political discourse that had a particularly topical force in England in the 1380s.

The meaning of this moment in the *Troilus*, however, cannot be referred to any one of these contexts: rather, it has to do with the somewhat stormy region between them. The second *Canticus Troili*, I shall argue, inhabits and defines a liminal space: not the sharp-edged "bitwixen" of the first song, but something more like Victor Turner's "betwixt and between," an area between structures "which is neither this nor that, and yet is both."[13] The ambiguous relation to contexts is reflected in a corresponding critical problem. The song's significance may be referred to a number of different interpretive narratives, and the choice between them is not clear. It is possible to read the song as part of Troilus's psychological life; as part of his brief career as a writer; as part of the story of the Narrator's narration (the voyage of the boat of his "connyng" [2.4]); as part of the web of meanings that make up the *Troilus* as a text; as part of Chaucer's poetic career; part of the story of his life as an Englishman; part of literary history; part of history. My discussion will shift within this range of critical contexts. I believe this is a shiftiness that the second *Canticus Troili* demands; with this text it is impossible to escape the problem of steering.

2. Chaucer and the *Canzoniere*

The *Canticus Troili* in the first book of *Troilus and Criseyde* is a fairly close translation of Petrarch's Sonnet 132, "S'amor non è." There is universal agreement that these three stanzas are the only appearance of Petrarch's *Canzoniere* in English until the sixteenth-century translations of Sir Thomas Wyatt,[14] and near-universal agreement that Chaucer shows no sign of familiarity with any Petrarchan lyric other than Sonnet 132.[15] I believe, however, that the second *Canticus Troili* is itself an adaptation of Petrarch's Sonnet 189, "Passa la nave mia colma d'oblio" (well known in English through Wyatt's version, "My galy charged with forgetfulness"[16]). My argument is based on probabilities. I shall argue, first, that the odds are better than even that Chaucer had seen a collection of Petrarchan lyrics that included both 132 and 189; second, that although this stanza is in no way a simple translation of Sonnet 189, there are elements in Chaucer's stanza that most plausibly derive from Petrarch's sonnet.

The best clue for understanding the circumstances of Chaucer's reading of Petrarch is of course the first *Canticus Troili*. E. H. Wilkins, who undertook to describe in detail the formation of the *Canzoniere* and the early circulation of Petrarch's lyrics, shows that there were three forms of

Sonnet 132 in existence: an early (or "pre-Chigi") text, the text that is found in the Chigi collection (the first version of the *Canzoniere* that Petrarch released), and the text in the final version of the *Canzoniere*. From the evidence of minor but significant variations among the three texts, Wilkins showed that Chaucer was working from either the second or third form of the sonnet, but not the first: that is, the version of 132 that Chaucer had seen was one that appeared in some form of the *Canzoniere*.[17] Wilkins leaves open the question of whether Chaucer had seen the sonnet in a collection or by itself.

> If Chaucer made use of only one of the poems of the *Canzoniere*, that circumstance is explicable either (1) on the supposition that he knew many or all of the poems of the *Canzoniere*, but did not find occasion to make use of any of the others, or (2) on the supposition that *S'amor non è* came to his knowledge as a single poem circulating independently, or as contained in some small collection.[18]

Wilkins does not adjudicate between these two possibilities. Yet his own work suggests that the first is substantially more likely than the second. Wilkins examined every manuscript he could locate that contained Petrarchan lyrics singly or in small collections. Among these, he found eight examples of Sonnet 132, of which seven have the pre-Chigi text (the text Chaucer did not follow); only one has the Chigi form. Wilkins himself states, "Petrarch from time to time, and *for the most part before the release of the Chigi form* [of the *Canzoniere*], released copies of individual poems or of small groups of poems."[19] It appears that the circulation of single Petrarch lyrics (or at least the circulation of 132 by itself) mostly predates the formation of the *Canzoniere*; once the lyrics were collected into the Chigi form, circulation of the whole collection largely replaced circulation of separate poems.

Thus, although it is possible that Chaucer had seen the Chigi or final form of Sonnet 132 by itself, the manuscript evidence that has come down to us suggests that this is unlikely. Wilkins found only one manuscript like the one Chaucer would have to have seen—that is, one copy of the Chigi 132 by itself—while there are at least eight examples of the Chigi form of the *Canzoniere*[20] and many early examples of the final form. Other things being equal, Chaucer's use of either a Chigi or final text of 132 would be sufficient ground for presuming that he had seen some version of the entire *Canzoniere*. Indeed, once Wilkins's findings are taken into account, the only reason for thinking that Chaucer had seen 132 by itself is that he never quotes from any other part of the *Canzoniere*. Yet if we reverse our initial assumption, suppose that Chaucer had read some form of the *Canzoniere*, and listen for Petrarchan echoes—as we listen for, say, Dantean echoes—I believe that there is one to be heard in the second *Canticus Troili*.

Before turning to Sonnet 189, we should examine the possible sources for the second *Canticus Troili* within the *Filostrato*. The song that Troiolo sings at the corresponding moment in Boccaccio's narrative is a lament, extending over five eight-line stanzas, which entirely lacks nautical imagery (5.62–66). William Michael Rossetti made an ingenious suggestion, repeated by modern editors, that the metaphor of a voyage is due to Chaucer's misreading of a phrase in the first stanza of Troiolo's song: "disii porto di morte," which means "I carry desires of death" but which could plausibly be misconstrued as "I desire the harbor of death."[21] It is not necessary to suppose a simple mistranslation, however. Troiolo's lament is dominated by the desire for death, and Chaucer had seen this desire expressed in seafaring terms earlier in the *Filostrato*:

> Ed or foss'io pur venuto al porto
> al qual la mia sventura ora mi mena!
> Questo mi saria grazia e gran conforto,
> perché morendo uscirei d'ogni pena. (1.54)
>
> [And now if I were arrived even at the port
> to which my misfortune now leads me!
> —this would be a grace and a great comfort to me,
> for by dying I would leave every pain]

This is translated in the first book of the *Troilus*: "God wold I were aryved in the port / Of deth, to which my sorwe wol me lede!" (1.526–27). It seems to me entirely possible that Chaucer was struck by the words "porto di morte" in *Filostrato* 5.62 and was reminded, through some mixture of faulty Italian and free association, of the idea of sailing toward death. Yet it must be stressed that the second *Canticus Troili* owes almost nothing to Troiolo's song in the *Filostrato*: even "disii porto di morte," if it is relevant at all, has been altered considerably, since the voyage is now lamented rather than desired.

Howard R. Patch suggested another source within the *Filostrato* for the second *Canticus Troili*. After the exchange with the Greeks has been announced, Troiolo, urging Criseida to steal off with him, addresses her thus:

. . . o chiara stella,
per cui io vado a grazioso porto;
se tu mi lasci, pensa ch'io son morto. (4.143)

[O bright star,
by which I go to a gracious port;
if you forsake me, remember that I shall die.]

Patch comments, "Here we have the whole idea: the star, the port, and death, though with a difference in the allusion intended in 'porto.'"[22] This passage is indeed a very likely source for certain elements in the second *Canticus Troili*: the address to the star,[23] and the poetic conceit labeled (2) in the discussion above, the idea that a lover's voyage can be sabotaged by the loss of his lady's guidance. But there is rather more to the second *Canticus Troili* than the "whole idea" that Patch mentions.

Here is Petrarch's Sonnet 189:

Passa la nave mia colma d'oblio
per aspro mare a mezza notte il verno
enfra Scilla et Caribdi, et al governo
siede 'l signore anzi 'l nimico mio;
à ciascun remo un penser pronto et rio
che la tempesta e 'l fin par ch' abbi a scherno;
la vela rompe un vento umido eterno
di sospir, di speranze et di desio;
pioggia di lagrimar, nebbia di sdegni
bagna et rallenta le già stanche sarte
che son d'error con ignoranzia attorto.
Celansi i duo mei dolci usati segni,
morta fra l'onde è la ragion et l'arte
tal ch' i' 'ncomincio a desperar del porto.[24]

[My ship laden with forgetfulness
passes through a harsh sea, at midnight, in winter,
between Scylla and Charybdis, and at the tiller
sits my lord, rather my enemy;
each oar is manned by a ready, cruel thought
that seems to scorn the tempest and the end;
the sail is broken by a wet changeless wind
of sighs, hopes, and desires;

> a rain of weeping, a mist of disdain
> wet and loosen the already weary ropes,
> made of error twisted up with ignorance.
> My two usual sweet stars are hidden;
> dead among the waves are reason and skill;
> so that I begin to despair of the port.]

The essential logic of this sonnet is the same as that of the passage from the *Filostrato* quoted by Patch: this text too advances the idea that a successful voyage depends on the guidance of the beloved. Again, the port (mentioned in the last line) is desirable. Yet the second *Canticus Troili*, as a whole, is much closer to this sonnet than to Boccaccio's metaphor. In the *Filostrato* the voyage is still a happy one ("io vado a grazioso porto"), while here the dreaded event has come about: the speaker has lost all the light of his lady's eyes, described as stars ("Celansi i duo mei dolci usati segni").[25] In Troiolo's speech the loss of Criseida means, simply, death; here the ship sails on, "evere derk in torment . . ." The passage from the *Filostrato* barely evokes a nautical scene; there is no concrete detail, and the ship is not evoked as an object (Troiolo says, "*io* vado"). Here, as in the second *Canticus Troili*, the speaker is a sailor on an objectified ship ("la nave mia"; "My ship and me"). The situation is presented vividly and in some detail: it is a night voyage ("a mezza notte"; "nyght by nyght"); there is wind. Most tellingly, both Petrarch and Chaucer specifically name, as a threat to the voyage, Charybdis.

Another concrete detail in the second *Canticus Troili* has been obscured, I believe, by a mistaken gloss. In the line "Toward my deth with wynd in steere I saille," the phrase *in steere* is usually glossed, "astern, at my back."[26] The authority for this reading is the Oxford English Dictionary (s.v. "steer," sb. 2, 2d). Yet the OED cites only one example of this use of "in steer"—this very line—and one example of "on steer."[27] It is not necessary to read "in steere" as a rare idiom. "Steere" may have either or both of its two most common meanings here: "1. The action of directing or governing; guidance, control, rule, government" (for which the OED cites an example of "in stere," c. 1250); "2. A rudder, helm." When Chaucer translated Petrarch's Sonnet 132 in the first *Canticus Troili*, "senza governo" became "Al sterelees." "Stere" is indeed the best translation for "governo," since the two have roughly the same semantic range, from the concrete "rudder" to the abstract "control." Here I believe "in steere" translates "al governo," and that it means "at the rudder, in control."[28] Chaucer has conflated two elements of Sonnet 189, the wind that rips the sails and the enemy/lord who sits "al governo"; Troilus's boat is not only driven but also steered by the wind.

In literary form, as in metaphorical content, the second *Canticus Troili* is closer to Petrarch's sonnet than to Boccaccio's metaphor. Troiolo uses the image of a sea-voyage in passing, as part of a speech to Criseyde; it has a rhetorical purpose, certainly, but in the fiction of the *Filostrato* it is not "literature." The second *Canticus Troili* is not a dramatic speech but, like Petrarch's sonnet, a lyric poem. Both lyrics develop a nautical metaphor from the first line to the last. Sonnet 189 is a self-contained work, yet in the context of the *Canzoniere* it recalls earlier lyrics that have used nautical imagery, including Sonnet 132.[29] Similarly, the second *Canticus Troili* is a self-contained lyric that recalls another lyric, a lyric with the same manuscript rubric, and, if only briefly, the same nautical metaphor—Chaucer's translation of Sonnet 132 in the first *Canticus Troili*.

There is one more link between the second *Canticus Troili* and Petrarch's sonnet that seems less tangible than those I have named, but even less likely to be coincidental. Sonnet 189 clearly anticipates, in its own way, the double logic of Troilus's song, the slippage between two representations of the lover's plight. The first eleven lines describe an absolutely hopeless voyage; the ship's destination is not stated, but since the ship is steered by the lover's lord and enemy it is not likely to be pleasant. Every element of the scene—ocean, time of day and of year, weather, crew—is hostile to the sailor. Once this is established, what is the force of the last tercet?

> Celansi i duo mei dolci usati segni,
> morta fra l'onde è la ragion et l'arte
> tal ch' i' 'ncomincio a desperar del porto.

> [My two usual sweet stars are hidden;
> dead among the waves are reason and skill;
> so that I begin to despair of the port.]

If a sworn enemy sits at the helm and the ship is breaking up, it hardly matters that navigation is becoming more difficult; "la ragion et l'arte" will scarcely be missed, since they are either hostile (if they belong to the pilot) or ineffectual (if they belong to the poem's speaker); the last line would seem to be a remarkable understatement. Now, this may not be a problem in Sonnet 189. I think the narrative inconsistency is not troubling because the sonnet is not, essentially, a narrative: rather than presenting a sequence of events it describes a single moment, qualifying this moment in different ways, and the logical priority of the final tercet only gives a feeling of closure, as if the poet has finally arrived at his statement. But it is nonetheless true that Sonnet 189, like the second *Canticus Troili*, begins with a ship that is sailing on a steady course ("Passa . . . enfra Scilla et Caribdi"), sailing in misery, and adds to this abject voyage the threat of shipwreck, consequent upon losing the lady's stellar guidance.

Chaucer has rearranged elements in the sonnet (so that Charybdis is now the primary threat to the voyage, for example) and has altered the text in many other ways—this is far from a direct translation. In the process, I believe that he has created poetic problems that do not exist in his source. I shall have more to say about this; for now it is enough to note that the finality of Petrarch's "Celansi i . . . segni" [the stars are hidden] has shifted toward the formulation in the *Filostrato*, "o chiara stella . . . Se tu mi lasci, pensa . . ." [O bright star . . . If you forsake me, remember . . .], and that this has transformed the rhetorical turn of Sonnet 189 into a puzzling near-contradiction: "O sterre, of which I lost have al the light . . . if that I faille / The gyding of thi bemes bright . . ." Yet the basic pattern for the discursive progress of the second *Canticus Troili* may be found—along with the essential conceit and poetic form—in Sonnet 189.

It is impossible to prove beyond doubt, from the evidence I have assembled, that Chaucer ever read Petrarch's Sonnet 189. Yet I hope I have shown that the long-accepted alternative—that he developed the second *Canticus Troili* from certain hints he found in the *Filostrato*—involves some startling coincidences. Moreover, the strong similarities between the second *Canticus Troili* and Sonnet 189 only work to confirm a supposition that might have been drawn from the evidence of the first *Canticus Troili*: that Chaucer read some version of Petrarch's lyric collection. For if Chaucer knew two poems from the *Canzoniere*, it becomes unlikely that he did not see a manuscript of the entire work in some form. Again, it cannot be stated with certainty that Chaucer read other lyrics in the collection, or that he knew the book of lyrics had a single author (rather than being a scribal compilation), or that he knew the author's name.[30] Yet if he resorted to the same collection twice for exactly the same purpose, to find a song for Troilus, the repetition suggests that he was aware of the *Canzoniere* as a single literary work. I believe that the *Canzoniere* is one of those master-texts—along with the *Filostrato*, the *Thebaid*, the *Consolation of Philosophy*, and a handful of others—that lie behind *Troilus and Criseyde*.

3. The Lyrical Book

Chaucer draws from the *Canzoniere* twice, then, at two formally similar moments in the *Troilus*. Why are the two Petrarchan sonnets handled so differently? The first *Canticus Troili*—though it skips a line in its source, adds a metaphor, expands fourteen lines into twenty-one, occasionally misconstrues[31]—is clearly a "translation" in the modern sense. Its project is to follow its exemplar as closely as possible. The method of the second *Canticus Troili* is sharply different. Most of Sonnet 189 is simply missing from its English counterpart; what is carried over is rearranged; and the Petrarchan text is combined with elements from other sources (including, as we have already seen, the *Filostrato*). If the first *Canticus Troili* is a translation, the second can only be called a very free adaptation.[32] Why does Chaucer change his method? To answer this, we must reexamine the literary status of the first *Canticus Troili*.

The translation of Sonnet 132—the *fact* of translation—has not seemed problematic to critics. It may be somewhat irregular for a medieval author to be reading a Renaissance author, but once this is accepted, there is nothing unusual about Chaucer's response to his reading: it seems only natural that he should translate directly. The early history of Petrarch in England—the history that begins again with Thomas Wyatt—is a history of direct translation. It could be argued that this attitude towards Petrarch's *rime*, the idea that they are most appropriately translated whole, is in fact a reflection of the logic of the *Canzoniere*: English adapters and literary historians are simply replicating Petrarch's own fetishization of his lyric texts.[33] In any case, Chaucer seems to be the first in the series; the first *Canticus Troili* can be taken as a "pointer to future Petrarchan imitations."[34] Yet the second *Canticus Troili* shows that Chaucer could imagine other approaches to Petrarch. The appearance of Sonnet 132 in the first *Canticus Troili*, the form of its appearance, is in fact a polemical gesture that looks not only forward in literary history but also backward.

To describe the polemical force of the first *Canticus Troili*, it is necessary to resume the story of the medieval "lyrical book." As we have seen, a number of late medieval vernacular writers sought to develop lyric poetry into book-length structures, so as to bestow upon the vernacular lyric a measure of the *auctoritas* that had previously been reserved for the Latin *liber*. In the *Vita Nuova*, Dante frames his own sonnets and *canzoni* in a prose narrative. Although the formal affiliations of the *libello* are multiple and complex, one especially important model is the glossed Book of Psalms; prose is to verse as gloss to text, and we have further seen that Dante draws an analogy between the formal pair "prose/verse" and the human pair "Dante/Beatrice." The textual hierarchy secures *auctoritas* for the work by positing a quasi-divine extratextual source from whom authority can flow. In the *Filostrato*, Boccaccio proposes a self-authenticating vernacular *auctoritas* by collapsing the textual hierarchy of the *Vita Nuova*: he fuses lyric and narrative in a stanzaic narrative, and this specular assimilation of formal modes is matched by a mutual identification among the three main male characters in the text, Troiolo, Pandaro, and the fictional narrator Filostrato.

Chaucer pulls apart the narcissistic structure of the *Filostrato* and establishes hierarchical difference in the very constitution of his text. Pandarus is now a generation removed from the young lovers—he is not Criseyde's cousin but her uncle—and he is more clearly excluded from the amorous dance (he hops always behind [2.1107]) than was Pandaro. The Chaucerian narrator is even further removed from the experience of love: he is entirely shut out from it, because of his "unliklynesse" (1.16). The three male figures, then, offer more than grammatical variation: the discrepancy between their perspectives adds considerably to the complexity of love's treatment in the romance.

The *Troilus* is, like the *Filostrato*, a long stanzaic poem. But the stanzas of the *Filostrato* are by turns lyric and narrative, and the two modes are presented as equivalent; the *Troilus* uses its stanzaic form to juxtapose an array of contrasting poetic modes, lyric and narrative but also descriptive and philosophical and digressive.[35] Chaucer complicates the simplifying equations of the *Filostrato* in other ways as well. Within the *Filostrato*, lyric utterance is associated almost exclusively with Troiolo; Chaucer's Troilus is a conscious lyric poet, but then so are Oenone (1.652–65) and the Trojan "mayde" (2.880) who composed the song Antigone sings in Criseyde's garden (2.827–75).[36] In his poetic singularity, Troiolo mirrors Filostrato, who makes no specific reference to previous texts but rather seems to find his story in his own memory, through an act of introspection.[37] Chaucer's narrator names "Lollius" as his Latin source, and repeatedly cites other writers by name.[38] For Filostrato, *Filostrato* is the only book in sight, while Chaucer's narrator understands the *Troilus* to be one book among many. The *Filostrato* is a unique book in another sense as well: its constituent sections are labeled "Parts," as if to insist that only the entire poem constitutes a whole,[39] while the *Troilus* is a book made of five "Books." What Chaucer introduces is the possibility of a difference in "level" between different textual moments.

To see how these two contrasting strategies manifest themselves in practice, we might briefly consider the episode where Troilus first writes to Criseyde. In the *Filostrato*, as we have seen, Pandaro offers Troiolo rather simple advice based on his own easy identification with his friend: "s'io fossi in te, intera scriverei / ad essa di mia man la pena mia" (2.91) [if I were in your place, I would write to her in my hand about my entire suffering]—and Troiolo does indeed write about his anguish, for eleven stanzas (2.96–106). The letter is quoted directly in the text. The effect of such a long quotation is to make us forget, as it were, the quotation marks: we are no longer reading an account of the letter Troiolo wrote, we are simply reading the letter. Yet there is no feeling of collage at this point in the poem, since the letter perfectly matches—in language, in tone—its surroundings. In *Troilus and Criseyde*, Pandarus devotes three stanzas to sententious rhetorical advice (2.1023–43), and the letter itself is not quoted but described, in a delicately nuanced passage of indirect discourse (2.1065–85). There is an unmistakeable difference between quoting Troilus ("My right lady! My heart's life!" and so on) and recounting what Troilus did:

> First he gan hire his righte lady calle,
> His hertes lif, his lust, his sorwes leche,
> His blisse, and ek thise other termes alle
> That in swich cas thise loveres all seche . . . (2.1065–68)

The effect of the scene depends in part on the variation of perspective between the lover who is sincerity itself, the friend who is a master of rhetoric, and the narrator who is sympathetically aware of Troilus's feelings yet also aware of the conventionality of his language. And this diversity of perspectives is attended by a multiplication of discursive modes: Troilus writes an amorous epistle (though we do not read it), Pandarus quotes the *Ars Poetica*, and the narrator gives a narrative account of a lyrical moment. The *Filostrato* claims a transparent presentation of the lyric—lyric within narrative and lyric as narrative. By contrast the *Troilus* is a complex of mediations.

As the founding moment for textual hierarchy, the moment that decisively constitutes different "levels" of text, I would propose the first *Canticus Troili*. The song is, of course, an interpolation between two stanzas of the *Filostrato*. Yet Chaucer was certainly capable of weaving Petrarch's sonnet seamlessly into his adaptation of Boccaccio—in content, it does not differ radically from later speeches of Troilus—and he chooses not to do this. He takes pains to draw a frame around the Petrarchan text. To begin with, these three stanzas are not speech but song: this is signalled by the rubric and the triple use of the significant word "song" (1.389, 393, 397). Moreover, the *Canticus Troili* arises not from unmediated expression but from careful literary work:

> . . . he thoughte
> What for to speke, and what to holden inne;
> And what to arten hire to love he soughte,
> And on a song anon-right to bygynne,
> And gan loude on his sorwe for to wynne;
> For with good hope he gan fully assente
> Criseyde for to love, and nought repente. (1.386–92)

Troilus chooses his words carefully, and considers their rhetorical effect—he wishes to "arten" Criseyde to love, and he seems to have her in mind as an audience for the song. Most strikingly, the last two lines of this stanza establish a discrepancy between the song's content and the singer's emotional state. The song is said to express anguish (he "gan loude on his sorwe for to wynne"), and it does in fact express a confusing mixture of pleasure and pain—yet at the moment of composition Troilus is committing himself wholeheartedly and hopefully to love. This is not hypocrisy: Troilus is evidently "concerned not with a confession, but with a song."[40] The *Canticus Troili* is a carefully wrought literary invention even within the fiction of the *Troilus*.

Chaucer's narrator goes on to mark off another sort of frame: this song is not only a different sort of utterance from the narration and dialogue that surround it, it derives from a different source.

> And of his song naught only the sentence,
> As writ myn auctour called Lollius,
> But pleinly, save our tonges difference,
> I dar wel seyn, in al, that Troilus
> Seyde in his song, loo, every word right thus
> As I shal seyn . . . (1.393–98)

The claim is paradoxical. The narrator reminds us that he is drawing the events in Troy from a written source—he has waited till now to name the author of this source, "Lollius"—and yet he asserts that he is going beyond his written source to provide a direct transcription (or rather a faithful translation) of Troilus's song.[41] The paradox seems to continue in the confusion between speech and writing (made emphatic by *rime riche*) at the end of the stanza:

> . . . and whoso list it here,
> Loo, next this vers he may it fynden here. (1.398–9)

The assertion of direct experience, of the unmediated voice, closely qualified by the reminder of textuality—the "writtenness" of the voice—is typical of the *Troilus*.[42] But whatever we are to think of the source of Troilus's song, there is a source and it is not Lollius.

The first *Canticus Troili* is thus framed, marked off as different, in the fictional narrative and in the story of the fictional narrator's narration. It is finally also framed in the story of Chaucer's relation to his actual sources—he departs here from the *Filostrato* to translate a sonnet by Petrarch. Some readers will feel that this last fact is not properly part of the meaning of the *Troilus*, since it was inaccessible to Chaucer's own readers.[43] It is true that the status of this "meaning" is problematic, but I think it cannot simply be exiled to footnotes. The negative view—that since Chaucer's audience did not know Petrarch, Chaucer's use of Petrarch is not in itself a part of the signifying matter of the text—is reassuringly clear but seems inadequate on at least two counts. First, it is impossible to be certain that Chaucer was the only Englishman to have read Petrarch in the 1380s. It may well be that courtly society, or a handful of Chaucer's friends, had read Petrarch's work, or had heard Sonnet 132, or simply knew that Chaucer was translating Petrarch. Second, "Chaucer's audience," although it sounds concrete, is an abstraction that conceals a multiplicity. Works of literature have many audiences, whether their authors intend for them to or not. (Clearly authors often do intend this, writing for different publics and different sorts of posterity, but the relation of the author's intention to the problem is another problem.) Some readers of the *Troilus* have read only the *Troilus*; some have a dim memory of Boethius as well; some keep the *Filostrato* and Sonnet 132 next to their edition of Chaucer. For some readers, then, the attribution to Petrarch is part of the meaning of the first *Canticus Troili*.[44] In this case, the fact of Chaucer's use of the *Canzoniere* only confirms what is evident in other ways: that the lyric is framed as a complete text drawn from an unexpected new source.

Why does Chaucer reject the seamless fusion of the *Filostrato* in favor of a clearly defined framing structure? Again (as at the end of the last chapter) I would refer to C. S. Lewis's argument that Chaucer "medievalizes" Boccaccio's poem.[45] According to Lewis, the *Filostrato* already looks toward the Italian Renaissance, and Chaucer goes to some trouble to correct, by a medieval standard, what is most modern in his source. Indeed, the *Troilus* returns to the practice of the text against which the *Filostrato* takes its stand, though Chaucer himself seems not to have read this work: the first *Canticus Troili* and its frame together make a sort of ad-hoc *Vita Nuova*. Lyric and narrative refer to each other, but from a certain ontological distance: each text has its own mode of existence. As in the *Vita Nuova*, there is an implied hierarchy. Eugene Vance, discussing the "lyrical cores" of the *Troilus*, argues that lyric moments actually generate an interpretive narrative: "Narrative mediates or translates into the dimensions of time and space the more universal 'truth' of lyric."[46] But this statement by itself applies equally well to the *Filostrato*; it does not take account of the structural position of the lyric. There are lyrical *cores* in the *Troilus* precisely because of the action of framing: the lyric is assigned a privileged textual space.

If the *Troilus* corrects the *Filostrato* here, it corrects another innovative lyrical book as well: Petrarch's *Canzoniere*, which eliminates the central hierarchy of the *Vita Nuova* by dispersing narrative into lyric fragments. Chaucer takes one leaf from this uncentered text and treats it, paradoxically, as a center. The first *Canticus Troili*, for all that it expresses confusion and dismay, is a moment of order and comfort. The security of the frame even enters the language of the song: when Troilus says that he is "withinne a boot . . . Amydde the see, bitwixen wyndes two" (1.416–17), the series of prepositions (not to be found in the Petrarchan original) generates a sense of concentric enclosure that goes a long way toward allaying the fear of being "possed to and fro" (1.415).

The faithfulness of translation in the first *Canticus Troili* is a significant part of this constitutive gesture: the privilege of the lyric moment is partly defined by the care with which Troilus chooses his words, the care with which the narrator claims to transcribe these words, the care with which Chaucer translates the words of Sonnet 132. Although Chaucer's treatment of Petrarch will come to seem natural, in the context of the *Troilus* it represents a commitment to an ideologically charged form.

Troilus and Criseyde is a work, however, that challenges commitments, stretching them till they break. I do not believe that Chaucer "medievalizes" his source simply to reaffirm his own version of the orthodox. The *Troilus* establishes the possibility of hierarchy, of stable literary structures, only to question this possibility from all sides. Critics have discussed the "lyrical cores" or "lyric inserts" in the poem as if the poem itself were a synchronic structure with a single formal method from beginning to end.[47] In fact the *Troilus* is partly a narrative of form: discursive modes and levels of text are distinguished as elements in a changing literary economy, and framing is an action that can be performed, or not—will be undone, or not—in time. Source study has described, and continues to describe, the "patchwork and embroidery of inserted and expanded passages of varying sizes [with which] Chaucer has overlaid the existing structure of his main narrative source."[48] But Chaucer's stitching is not invisible mending. The differential deployment of sources is not merely a fact about the text, available to scholars—it is part of the meaning of the poem, and in some form it is available to every reader. The play of textual mediation in Troilus's first letter-writing scene, for example, does not depend on knowledge of the *Filostrato*, although it is enriched (I think) by this knowledge.

The claim of the first *Canticus Troili* to establish a stable textual frame is challenged almost immediately. The frame is already complicated at the end of the song, when Troilus simply turns and speaks to the God of Love, as if he has been speaking and not singing all along. (Early readers who liked the song had difficulty deciding where it ended.[49]) Indeed, the establishment of a clear frame may have been undermined in advance—when the narrator treats the historical context of his story as an internal digression, for example (1.141–47). As Vance has argued, lyric discourse in the *Troilus* involves a denial of what is historically inevitable.[50] Yet the gesture of establishment, however foredoomed, is of signal importance for the *Troilus* as a whole. A complex drama of framing extends throughout the poem. A full account of this drama would have to focus on the central attempt to construct a frame—spatial, temporal, textual—for the consummation scene in Book 3.[51] Here I must move abruptly forward, from the founding instance of the lyrical frame in Book 1 to the moment in Book 5 that most clearly answers it: the second *Canticus Troili*.

The second *Canticus Troili* is marked off just as clearly as the first: "[Troilus] gan synge as ye may heere. . . . *Canticus Troili* . . . This song whan he thus songen hadde . . ." (5.637, rubric, 645). But here the frame fails utterly. Troilus, as poet, no longer has the aesthetic distance from his experience that he showed in Book 1. Then, there was a significant discrepancy between his mood and the content of his song; now, he sings to unburden himself:

> . . . hym likede in his songes shewe
> Th'enchesoun of his wo, as he best myghte;
> And made a song of wordes but a fewe,
> Somwhat his woful herte for to lighte. (5.631–34)

The lack of detachment on the part of the singer is paralleled by a distracting failure to differentiate clearly between the text and its context. In the song, Troilus addresses a metaphoric lost star in the metaphoric dark night of his soul; in the very next stanza, he will address a literal "brighte moone" (5.648) on a rather well-lit night. In the allegory of the ship, the wind is a powerful, hostile force; five stanzas later, Troilus stands on the walls of Troy and feels the "wynd" from the Greek camp bearing, as he imagines, Criseyde's sighs (5.673–79). In both cases the relation between song and story is not outright contradiction (since one is metaphoric, the other literal), nor is it collaboration—there is an uneasy slippage. Most important, perhaps, the distinction between lyric and narrative is hopelessly compromised. The second *Canticus Troili* begins as pure lyric—the expression, like the first *Canticus Troili*, of a timeless state of mind. As we have seen, however, Troilus is incapable of maintaining the same rhetorical stance for more than four lines; he remembers his current situation in the narrative and changes his tune mid-stanza, so that a similarly uneasy slippage enters the confines of the song. The shift is punctuated by the banal intrusion of an undisguised plot element: "the tenthe nyght."

Chaucer enacts the same failure of framing in his treatment of Petrarch's Sonnet 189. In treating Sonnet 132 he drew a clear line (as his fictional narrator claimed) between sources; here there is no such line, and elements from Sonnet 189 fuse with similar elements from the *Filostrato* in a way that damages the logic of the song. But even those elements that are drawn from Sonnet 189 are altered—through a confusion, again, of lyric and narrative. Sonnet 189 contains a number of temporal paradoxes. As we have noted, what ought to be the first sign of danger at sea—the loss of the lady's guiding stars—appears in the text only after an elaborate account of the doomed voyage onward. Moreover, the sonnet describes a particular time, a winter midnight, yet the wind of sighs, hopes, and desires is eternal, and this eternal wind is somehow eternally ripping the sail. These paradoxes are well-crafted, though: clearly the sonnet describes a sort of eternal present ("*Passa* la nave mia . . ."), in which it is eternally midnight in winter and the sail is eternally tearing. The moment is not timeless, but time is loosed from its linear progress and is the agent of endless torment; this is what Thomas M. Greene calls the "iterative present tense" of the *Canzoniere*.[52] Now consider this phrase from the second *Canticus Troili*: "evere derk in torment, nyght by nyght." In the translation from "a mezza notte" to "nyght by nyght," the linear time of Troilus's predicament has entered the lyric; yet "eterno" has been preserved in "evere derk." The result—as so often in the second *Canticus Troili*—is almost, but not quite, an absurdity. Either the voyage is simply "evere derk," and the nocturnal setting makes no difference, or else the voyage is somehow conducted during a series of dark, starless nights (raising the question of where the ship goes during the day). "Eternal night" is a familiar idea; "eternal darkness, night by night" is not entirely logical yet not clearly paradoxical.

The second *Canticus Troili* fails, then, through a collapse of its framing structure. Discursive realms that are meant to be distinct—and that *are* distinct in the case of the first *Canticus Troili*—here lack clear boundaries; there is difference, but no distance, between Troilus's emotional life and his textual production, between the song and its context in Book 5, between Sonnet 189 and the *Filostrato*, between lyric and narrative as such. The result, however, is not a specular fusion, as in Boccaccio's text. There *is* difference between these discursive realms, and the problematic logic of the song raises the very question of explanatory contexts, so that the second *Canticus Troili*—rather than occupying a safe middle ground of synthesis or paradox—drifts ambiguously. This poem strikes one as a failure because it seems not to be in control of its own interpretive destiny. With the collapse of the frame, the lyric has lost its privilege.

The *Troilus*, then, improves upon its proto-Renaissance source by constructing a typically medieval edifice, only to see this edifice crumble. Yet this account of a fall is itself typically medieval—a Boethian warning on the frailty of human achievement. Troilus falls "out of joie" and then falls on the battlefield; Pandarus loses control of his plot; the narrator, facing an ending that he can hardly bear to write, falters in his narration.[53] The collapse of the lyric frame clearly belongs to the general trend of the poem. It is hard to know exactly which narrative this particular event belongs to. The Chaucerian narrator—so eager to construct an explicit frame around the first *Canticus Troili*—is quietly businesslike here; is he part of the drama in his very reticence? Troilus himself can be blamed for the weakness of the second *Canticus Troili* as poetry; but can he have anything to do with its faulty rendering of Petrarch? The idea is not as absurd as it may sound: the first *Canticus Troili* was attributed to Troilus himself, so perhaps in some metaphorical way the *Canzoniere* itself is part of Troilus's psyche, the very inscription of the courtly lover's discourse, and he composes well only when he translates well. As a last alternative, perhaps the formal breakdown that contaminates the second *Canticus Troili* is a *de casibus* tragedy on the level of pure literary form: as if "the lyric" itself has fallen off the wheel. Yet it may not be necessary to locate the event so precisely; the collapse of the structure speaks for itself.

This Boethian reading of the situation, though plausible, is not the only possible reading. From the viewpoint of Troilus, or of Troy, the collapse of a structure does indeed speak for itself; but there are other viewpoints in Book 5. The narrator may falter, but he finishes his story. And though his discourse becomes fragmentary in the last eighteen stanzas, and his view of the work he has just finished changes alarmingly, and even his persona begins to lose its clear definition (as more and more we seem to hear the self-conscious poet behind the well-intentioned pedant)—though nothing seems stable in this ending until the final prayer to the Trinity, one thing that is never questioned is the status of the *Troilus* as a finished work of literature. The poem itself is not said to fail. It may not be a very important success; it may finally contain nothing but "thise wrecched worldes appetites" and "the forme of olde clerkis speche" (5.1851, 1854). But it is sent out into the world as completed: "Go, litel bok, go, litel myn tragedye" (5.1786). It is sent out in many directions at once. It will be read, or heard, by "every lady bright of hewe" (5.1772) and by "yonge, fresshe folkes, he or she" (5.1835); it is to be "subgit . . . to alle poesye," kissing the steps of the epic poets (5.1790–92); it is to receive the benign correction of Gower and Strode (5.1856–59) and it must endure the peril of linguistic change and scribal error (5.1793–96). The work, then, must make its own way in the world of Fortune, without the guidance of the poet who bids it farewell. But though it may be "litel," in value and in strength, the work is a book.[54]

The second *Canticus Troili* is an image for this book: its very failure, as it drifts uncertainly between interpretive contexts, is an image for the success of the *Troilus*, a work that finally bases its claim to stature on instability—a work that, rather than finding a new and better constitution for the relations between lyric and narrative, makes the dismantling of the lyrical book a (lyrical) book. The literary method of the second *Canticus Troili* resembles that of the work as a whole. Although, as is well known, medieval ideas of translation were different from ours, in the Chaucerian canon there is a clear functional distinction between close translations (the *Boece* or *The Romaunt of the Rose*) and free translations or adaptations (*The Knight's Tale* or *Troilus and Criseyde*). For the first *Canticus Troili*, Chaucer translates closely from Petrarch. For the second, he writes something much nearer in method to the *Troilus* itself: a work with a single source, yet with a multitude of sources (we shall shortly add to the list) and finally with no clear source. The ship of the first song enjoys a paradoxical harbor mid-ocean, sheltered by two contrary winds; the ship of the second song is cut loose from its Petrarchan moorings and drifts free. This is indeed a failure, seen from the perspective of anyone within the world of the *Troilus* intent on finding a lasting home. But from the perspective of the writer who sends the *Troilus* out into the world, or the reader who encounters the *Troilus* in the world and is curious to see how it generates its meanings, the indefinite circulation of the second *Canticus Troili* is exemplary.

4. Sailing to Thebes

I have discussed the "collapse of the lyric frame" as if it were simply an entropic dissolution, the loss of distinction between the only available structure and its textual setting. The second *Canticus Troili*, however, breaks its strict faith with Petrarch's Sonnet 189 partly in order to make other connections with other powerful texts. Now, except for the *Filostrato* and the *Consolation of Philosophy*, no literary work is more important for the *Troilus* than the *Thebaid*. Chaucer draws on Statius's epic for Theban history and classical lore; moreover the *Thebaid* seems to appear as a text within the fiction of the *Troilus*.[55] When Pandarus finds Criseyde with her ladies at the beginning of Book 2, the women are reading some version of the Theban story, and Pandarus refers to the *Thebaid* in particular: "herof ben ther maked bookes twelve" (2.108). Again, Cassandra interprets Troilus's dream in Book 5 by telling him "a fewe of olde stories" (5.1459), and includes in her story-telling a lengthy synopsis of the *Thebaid* (5.1485–1510).[56] The *Thebaid* may be said, then, to lie behind the entire *Troilus*, an alternative to the *Filostrato* both as a source of information and as a literary model. I believe that the second *Canticus Troili* deliberately evokes one passage in this eminently available context.

At the beginning of the third book of the *Thebaid*, Eteocles spends a sleepless night in Thebes. He has dispatched a party of fifty soldiers to ambush Tydeus, who has come representing Polynices in a futile attempt to secure peace and is now on his way back to Argos; we know that Tydeus has slaughtered his assailants, but Eteocles merely knows that the party is late in returning. Eteocles's tormented anxiety is described in an epic simile.

velut ille
fluctibus Ioniis Calabrae datus arbiter alno—
nec rudis undarum, portus sed linquere amicos
purior Olenii frustra gradus impulit astri—,
cum fragor hiberni subitus Iovis, omnia mundi
claustra tonant multusque polos inclinat Orion,
ipse quidem malit terras pugnatque reverti,
fert ingens a puppe notus, tunc arte relicta
ingemit et caecas sequitur iam nescius undas:
talis Agenoreus ductor caeloque morantem
Luciferum et seros maerentibus increpat ortus. (3.22–32)[57]

[like the
appointed helmsmen of a Calabrian bark upon Ionian waters
(nor does he lack sea-craft, but the Olenian star rising clearer
than its wont has beguiled him to leave a friendly haven)
when a sudden uproar fills the wintry sky, and all heaven's
confines thunder, and Orion in full might brings low the poles—
he himself indeed prefers the land, and struggles to return,
but a strong south wind astern bears him on; then, abandoning his
skill,
he groans, and heedless now follows the blind waters:
such is the Agenorean chieftain, and he upbraids Lucifer,
yet lingering in the heavens, and the sun, so slow to rise on the
distressed.]

The simile, from "velut" to "talis," presents a self-contained nautical scene rather similar to that of the second *Canticus Troili*. An unusually bright star has lured a sailor away from his safe harbor, and now its light is gone. Unable to navigate, the sailor despairs; yet the voyage is not over. A strong wind bears the ship on ("fert ingens a puppe notus")—it is a wind astern and also, apparently, a wind in control of the ship, since the sailor himself no longer works the rudder. The voyage is in the most extreme peril; yet the scene ends not with a shipwreck but with the static condition of peril, as the sailor groans and follows the blind waters.

Chaucer knew many classical passages describing sea-voyages, but none as close to the second *Canticus Troili* as this. Still, the general resemblance between the two passages would not seem to justify a claim of intertextual allusion: there are no verbal echoes (except conceivably "a puppe notus" for "wynd in steere"), and Chaucer found the same sort of voyage in Petrarch's Sonnet 189, after all. If we consider, however, along with nautical content, the narrative context of the Statian simile, it begins to seem strikingly apposite. The simile of the endangered ship is introduced into the narrative of the *Thebaid* precisely to express the emotional plight of a major character. Just before he sings his second song, Troilus is said to stand "bitwixen hope and drede" (5.630); so Eteocles is "tormented by various gusts of passion" ("vario . . . turbidus aestu / angitur," 3.18–19) and vacillates between two dominant feelings, shame and regret (3.22). Troilus chooses the metaphor of a ship to describe, as well as he can, his own emotional tempest; the ship of Eteocles is an invention of the narrator's, yet the simile is associated with self-expression, since the groaning of the sailor reflects Eteocles's own exclamations to himself (3.6–18). The simile leads into a description of Eteocles "upbraiding" the morning star and the sun (3.31–32), as Troilus, in the stanza after the second *Canticus Troili*, tells his sorrow to the moon.

The clearest connection between this passage from the *Thebaid* and the second *Canticus Troili* is also the strangest. The narrative context of the Statian simile is a nightmarish revision of Troilus's situation in his own story. To paraphrase my earlier synopsis: Eteocles waits in Thebes, the city whose fall to the Argive host foreshadows the fall of Troy to the Greeks. He has sent a trusted party outside the walls of the city to engage in certain dealings with a representative of the enemy, Tydeus; this party is to return to Thebes quickly. Eteocles waits in vain, however, for Tydeus has occupied this party in quite another way, so that there can be no question of return. In his anxiety he cries out, "unde morae?" (3.7) [why this tarrying?]. *Talis Troilus* . . .. The analogy is startling, but Troilus has sent Criseyde out of Troy with "the sone of Tideus" (5.88 and passim), and what is meant to be a brief strategic mission will become, through the prowess of Diomede, a permanent absence. Both Troilus and Eteocles consider public murder of the enemy's delegate; both choose a deceptive ruse instead, and both at least partly repent the decision.[58] Both give vent to their confused feelings (feelings best compared to those of an imperiled mariner) at a time when the outcome of the strategic mission is not yet settled, but has begun to look bad.

Is the *Thebaid*, then, a source for the second *Canticus Troili*? In the normal sense of the word, clearly not. There is nothing in the text of the song, and nothing in its setting in Book 5, that can be said to derive from the Statian simile. We can hardly ask, as we would ask about a source, "how, and why, has this text been altered?"—since the differences between the two passages could be catalogued indefinitely. Rather, the *Troilus* has conjoined two sources—the simile of Sonnet 189 and the plot of *Filostrato*—in such a way that the conjunction itself evokes a moment in the *Thebaid*. The second *Canticus Troili* is not a translation from Statius in any sense, but in its setting it constitutes an allusion—oblique and strange, but clear—to a work whose importance for the *Troilus* is well-established.[59]

If Statius is to be understood primarily as a historian,[60] so that Chaucer is here alluding not so much to a particular epic poem as to the story of Thebes, the general import of the allusion seems clear. To begin with, Troy is like Thebes. This is implied in some way by every Theban reference in the text; the story of Thebes comments ironically on the events in Troy, since the Trojan characters know the story, yet fail to understand it as a typological warning. For Criseyde and Pandarus, the "romaunce . . . of Thebes" (2.100) can be set aside; for Troilus, Cassandra's history lesson is an irrelevant *exemplum* in support of false prophecy (he offers Alceste as an equally bookish counter-*exemplum* [5.1527–33]). The allusion thus foretells, like Cassandra, the fall of Troy—and of Troilus in particular, since Troilus is implicitly compared to the ruler of Thebes. This too belongs to a general pattern: Troilus elsewhere compares himself to Oedipus (4.300) and uses the language of Statius's Oedipus;[61] he prays that Cupid will be kinder to him than Juno was to Thebes (5.599–602).

The second *Canticus Troili*, then, contributes to the general effect of the Theban subtext in the *Troilus*. More specifically, there may be a dire warning here that Troilus's anxious wait will turn out no better than Eteocles's. It is hard to know, though, just how far the analogy between the two passages is meant to extend. The insomnia of the king in his Theban palace is a compelling image for the desolation that Troilus feels in Troy. Does the perfidy of Eteocles somehow attach to Troilus? Eteocles has just taken the action that guarantees war, and ultimately the fall of his city; is Troilus also at fault for giving up Criseyde? Does the savage battle of the ambush correspond to a sexual encounter because love is conventionally (and elsewhere in the *Troilus*) a delightful war, or because sexuality at this point in the story has come to seem dishonorable and violent, or because Diomede in particular—he of the large tongue, laying out hook and line for Criseyde (5.804, 777)—is seen as brutally seductive? Do the fifty murderous soldiers prefigure Criseyde's treachery, in their ambush, or her weakness, in their easy defeat? And whose representation of Criseyde is this? Does the strained analogy between one "trusted party" and the other somehow reflect the fact that Criseyde is the chief puzzle for all systems of representation in the *Troilus*?[62]

The allusion encourages a kind of free association, I think, precisely because its scope in the text is so limited. Although Thebes is a dark analogue for Troy throughout Chaucer's poem, and Diomede is indeed the son of Tydeus, there seems to be no pattern of allusion associating Eteocles with Troilus or the botched ambush with Criseyde's faithlessness. Taking a step away from the two metaphoric ships, one becomes aware of the world of difference between the two narratives. The second *Canticus Troili* opens up a peculiar vantage point within the *Thebaid*: surveyed from this point, the Statian context looks deceptively like the *Troilus*. The meaning of this surprising appearance is left to the reader.

Perhaps the precise significance of the Theban allusion is less important than the very fact of its presence in the second *Canticus Troili*. "Thebes" is the bleak destination of both Troilus and Troy; they approach their fate unknowingly. The narrator too seems to read Statius poorly. When he invokes Clio as the muse of the second book (2.8), we are reminded uncomfortably that he has already asked the Fury Tisiphone (1.6) to guide the entire poem. In the *Thebaid*, the epic poet invokes Clio (1.41) and then Oedipus begins the epic action by invoking the wrath of Tisiphone (1.59); the separation of divine powers guiding discourse and story partly defines the detachment of the Statian narrator. The Chaucerian narrator attempts to find a comfortable narrative stance somewhere between this detachment and the narcissistic identification of "Filostrato," but by taking over both invocations, and reversing their order, he starts his own poem on the slide toward Thebes.[63] The voyage of the second *Canticus Troili* can be read as a similar fall: the song drifts from its courtly origin toward the *Thebaid*. The willful, one-eyed quality of the allusion suggests that the song, like Troy and like Troilus, is doomed to repeat the text of Theban history without understanding it.

Thebes is a Charybdis, within the fictional world of the *Troilus*. But the perspective of Troy is not the only perspective, and the evocation of the *Thebaid* in the second *Canticus Troili* underscores this. For if Theban history is a failure that threatens the Trojan characters and the narrator, the *Thebaid* itself is—for the poet of *Troilus and Criseyde*—a successful epic, an authoritative book. When Chaucer bids his tragedy to

> kis the steppes where as thow seest pace
> Virgile, Ovide, Omer, Lucan, and Stace, (5.1791–92)

saving Statius for the end and adapting Statius's tribute to the *Aeneid* ("vestigia semper adora" [*Thebaid* 12.817; ever venerate its footsteps]), it is clear that he is reaching not toward the story of Thebes but toward the epic discourse of the *Thebaid*. The second *Canticus Troili* stands for *Troilus and Criseyde* as a whole when it undertakes a voyage (successful or not) from Petrarchan sonnet to epic simile.

Far from simply collapsing categories, the second *Canticus Troili*, though unresolved in itself, establishes a kind of order in its contextual universe. It strays from its source only to mediate between two texts, one nearly contemporary and the other classical. The mediation is complex: the song not only juxtaposes the *Canzoniere* and the *Thebaid*, but also manages to establish a form of communication between them. The allusion makes contact with each text at the moment when it is most like the other: Sonnet 189 and the simile describing Eteocles are corresponding moments, not only in the scenes they describe, but also in relation to the texts they inhabit. Each passage must be read in the light of earlier and later ship metaphors, and each can be described as a turning point in its series, a threshold moment when a protagonist loses control.[64] Each is a threshold moment in another sense as well. In Petrarch's collection of lyrics, Sonnet 189 is a relatively narrative moment; in Statius's sweeping narrative the simile at the beginning of Book 3 is a lyrical pause. The second *Canticus Troili* may spoil the neat distinction between lyric and narrative that was proposed by the first *Canticus Troili*; in the context of the medieval "lyrical book" it may represent failure. As a loss of control—here formal control—it may match its analogues from Petrarch and Statius. But in this new perspective that includes the *Thebaid*, the Chaucerian passage seems to construct, not within itself but around itself, a well-controlled pattern that delicately balances the lyrical and the narrative.

The space between the world of contemporary courtly literature and the world of the *Thebaid* is a treacherous region: the Trojan characters and the Chaucerian narrator sail unwillingly toward the Theban vortex.[65] But it is also the literary space of the *Troilus* itself, the space for the creation of a book. The chaos of the liminal, in Victor Turner's analysis, is associated with a *rite de passage*; it can be a "fruitful darkness."[66] The *Troilus* may never complete its journey toward the classical epic. The most likely source for the list of poets, "Virgile, Ovide, Omer, Lucan, and Stace," is Boccaccio's *Filocolo*;[67] in a more complex mediation, Chaucer gives Troilus himself an uncertain destination by departing from the *Filostrato* and borrowing a passage from Boccaccio's modern supplement to the *Thebaid*, the *Teseida* (5.1807–27). Certainly the poem does not engage in any simple rite of passage; even Chaucer's attitude toward the possibility of being a *poeta* is complex.[68] But the poem does make a departure, does enter the space of passage.

The liminal region is treacherous and fruitful, and the two qualities depend upon each other. The second *Canticus Troili* is a failure because it is sent—like Eteocles's fifty soldiers, like Criseyde—on an errand it cannot perform. Troilus means to address Criseyde, to unburden his heart, to compose a poem, and in every respect his words go astray. The song departs from its source, the text that is supposed to guide it—whether this is seen as Troilus's intention or Petrarch's sonnet—to engage, ambiguously, other intentions and other texts. It is like Criseyde; it is like the *Troilus*. The faithlessness of its translation is like the faithlessness of the "changed" Criseyde, who forgets her courtly lover for the son of Tydeus. The moral judgment passed on Criseyde may seem unambiguous; indeed the analogy with the *Thebaid* depicts her as quite literally murderous, supporting the uneasy suspicion that she is not only the port and the guiding star but also the fatal destination, Charybdis.[69] But the poet of the *Troilus* had a more complex awareness of the dangers and advantages of less-than-faithful translation.

The gratuitous echo of Eteocles's sleepless night in the second *Canticus Troili* thus has two aspects, corresponding to the double valence of the *Thebaid* as Theban history and as epic poem; from both perspectives the allusion is, as we have seen, ambiguously suggestive. I believe that the reference to Statius makes another connection as well: not so much to a specific text (although one work by John Gower is especially relevant) as to a cultural convention, a floating commonplace. In the light of this commonplace, and the kinds of discourse it evokes, the ambivalent excursus on literary form in the second *Canticus Troili* is a pastoral refuge. For the Statian simile involves a thematic realm that would seem to be entirely foreign to Troilus's song: the realm of the political. At the start of *Thebaid* 3, the problem of Thebes is not yet the tactical problem of warfare, but rather the political problem of right government. And, as a modern commentator notes and as I think Chaucer would have recognized, in the nautical simile "we find the metaphor ship-state."[70]

5. The Ship of State

What is the source of Petrarch's ship in Sonnet 189? There are many sources, obviously. For the comparison of the lover to a storm-tossed ship, there are precedents in Provençal verse.[71] For the elaborate allegorization of the different elements of the nautical scene, there are various patristic ships to choose from, notably the Ship of the Church and the Ship of the Soul.[72] Clearly the sonnet, drawing from many sources, creates its own "réseaux memoriels" [memorial networks], in the phrase of Dominique Diani; as Diani points out, for example, "aspro mare" in the second line recalls Virgil's "maria aspera" (*Aeneid* 6.351).[73] Yet I believe there is one outstanding source for the sonnet as a whole. Petrarch knew a lyric poem that describes, from beginning to end, a ship: a ship on the point of shipwreck yet sailing on, a clearly allegorical ship embodying the desires of the poet. This is Horace's Ode 1.14, "O navis"[74]—the most important source in Western literature for the familiar image of the Ship of State.[75] Some modern critics have wanted to deny the poem's reference to the *res publica*, but there is general agreement that these lines near the end cannot be addressed to a literal ship:[76]

> nuper sollicitum quae mihi taedium,
> nunc desiderium curaque non levis. (17–18)

> [you who were not long ago to me a source of worry and weariness,
> but are now my love and anxious care]

For Petrarch the allegorical nature of Horace's ship could not have been in doubt. He read the poem with the commentary of Pseudacron, which explains that "By allegory this ode designates the civil war, as some say, or the republic as others say," and which glosses the different elements of the scene: "WITHOUT ROPES. To be understood either as 'without administrators' or as 'without payments and money.'"[77] These ropes, whether administrative or financial, seem quite different from Petrarch's "sarte / che son d'error con ignoranzia attorto" (10–11) [ropes, made of error twisted up with ignorance]; and indeed there are no specific verbal resemblances between Sonnet 189 and Ode 1.14. But Horace's poem is the closest model for the formal project of Sonnet 189; it is the point of departure.

Petrarch has taken Horace's lyric on the Ship of State and denatured the allegory, assigning new meanings to the ropes, the storm, the port. What is omitted is of course the State; the patriotic "desiderium" of the ode has become the "vento umido eterno / di sospir, di speranze et di desio" (7–8) [wet, changeless wind of sighs, hopes, and desires] that blows through the *Canzoniere*. The poem's relationship to this source-text typifies a process visible elsewhere in the collection. Petrarch writes about contemporary politics, notably in *Canzone* 53 ("Spirto gentil") and *Canzone* 128 ("Italia mia"); yet, as Attilio Momigliano points out, the political cannot be for Petrarch "a motif in itself"; rather it must be "one of the notes that compose the elegiac texture of his book, one of the themes of his contemplative and melancholy story."[78] These poems describe the speaker's relation to Italy, and Italy's relation to its own desires, in exactly the language that characterizes Petrarch's love of Laura and of fame.[79] Again, when Petrarch refers to classical epic poets and heroes—as in two sonnets that closely precede 189 (Sonnets 186, 187)—he assimilates their national and historical concerns to his own amorous plight. Speaking of Scipio Africanus (the subject of his own epic, *Africa*) and of Laura he writes:

> Quel fiore antico di vertuti et d'arme,
> come sembiante stella ebbe con questo
> novo fior d'onestate et di bellezze! (186.9–11)
>
> [That ancient flower of virtue and arms,
> what a similar star he had with this
> new flower of chastity and beauty!]

Petrarch's treatment of Ode 1.14 contributes to what Thomas M. Greene has called "a *lyricization* of epic materials."[80] The effect is not merely to absorb the epic into the lyrical, the political into the erotic, but also to expand the domain of the erotic lyric. Sonnet 189 is not explicitly about love any more than is Horace's ode. Of course it *is* about love, readers agree; the "signore/nimico" [lord/enemy] must be Amor. But the abstractions of the allegory concern hope and despair in the most general sense; the sonnet contributes to the depiction, throughout the *Canzoniere*, of a pattern of desire that involves the love of Italy along with the love of Laura. Petrarch's navigation is by turns erotic, religious, political, authorial, but it is finally the operation of the subject as such;[81] in this Ship of the Self, the Ship of State is not suppressed but subsumed.

There is no direct evidence that Chaucer knew the Horatian "O navis,"[82] or that he recognized Petrarch's *nave* as a revision of the Ship of State. In the intertextual economy of the second *Canticus Troili*, Sonnet 189 appears to represent the purely lyrical impulse at the source of the song, the impulse that is either contaminated or enriched by exposure to the epic concerns of the *Thebaid*. Yet Chaucer could hardly have missed the sonnet's epic setting, between Scylla and Charybdis; when he plays the sonnet against the *Thebaid*, he is partly undoing the lyricization that Greene describes.[83] I believe that the process continues, although it is hard to say whether this further step falls within Chaucer's reading of Petrarch or even within his intentions as a writer. The Ship of State reappears, as if reemerging from Sonnet 189, to play an intriguing but problematic role in the context of the second *Canticus Troili*.

Chaucer and his medieval readers knew the Ship of State as a commonplace, a familiar figure of which the Statian simile is only one rather atypical instance. It is possible to discern, if not to distinguish sharply, at least three broad traditions for the diffusion of the image. To begin with, the Ship of State is cited *as* a commonplace—as a well-known example of simile, metaphor, or allegory—in a series of rhetorical treatises that begins with Aristotle's *Rhetoric* and includes the influential *Rhetorica ad Herennium*.[84] Dante is thus writing by the book when, in a famous apostrophe ("Ahi serva Italia . . ."), he addresses Italy as "nave sanza nocchiere in gran tempesta" (*Purgatorio* 6.77) [ship without pilot in great tempest]. Yet Dante is here drawing on a second tradition, a tradition of political philosophy that again springs from Aristotle. Charles Singleton glosses this line by referring to a passage in the *Convivio* where Dante argues the excellence of monarchy (4.4.5–7). There Dante attributes to Aristotle's *Politics* the idea that any group of men with a common aim ought to have a single leader; to support this idea he develops an analogy (from Aristotle by way of Aquinas[85]): "Sì come vedemo in una nave . . ." [As we see in a ship . . .]. The single leader of a ship is its rudder; the rudder of the Empire will be the Emperor. In the *Purgatorio*, then, the simile conveys more than the idea of a nation in trouble—it refers specifically to the political situation of the time and to Dante's own views on government. In this tradition the figure of the Ship of State is not an ornamental trope but an instructive analogy. It contains a real insight into the order of things, the insight that is preserved in the derivation (noted by Aquinas) of *gubernare*, "to govern," from *gubernare*, "to steer [a ship]."

To the common rhetorical figure and the philosophical analogy, a third Ship of State can be added—that of topical political allegory. An English poem dated 1377 turns from a general lament on the loss of "He that was vr moste spede" to the description of a ship:

> Sum tyme an Englisch schip we had,
> Nobel hit was, and heih of tour . . .
> Now is that schip, that bar the flour,
> Selden seye and sone foryete. (17–24)[86]

The anonymous poet describes the different parts of the ship; the rudder receives special emphasis:

> Scharpe wawes that schip has sayled,
> And sayed alle sees at auentur;
> ffor wynt ne wederes neuer hit fayled,
> Whil the rothur mihte enduir. (33–36)

After five stanzas devoted to this ship, the riddle is explained:

> The rothur was nouther ok ne elm;
> Hit was Edward the thridde, the noble kniht. (57–58)

The poem is a lament on the death of the king; succeeding stanzas name the other parts of the English Ship of State, which is now in such difficulty ("this gode comunes . . . / I likne hem to the schipes mast" [73–74]; "the wynd that bleugh the schip with Blast, / Hit was gode preyers" [77–78]), before abandoning the figure of the ship for a comparison of the dead king to a fallen tree.

This is writing in an entirely different register from that of the *Thebaid* or the *Convivio*. G. R. Owst compares this poem with an English sermon that also employs the ship allegory to describe the present condition of England, and concludes that—although this particular sermon is of a later date than the poem—the political poet has borrowed from the homiletic tradition. The secular Ship of State is a variant on the preacher's Ship of Faith, or of the Good Man, or of the Church.

> Holy Scripture and the pulpit, we see, were the real first parents of the whole idea as developed alike in poem and in sacred discourse. The political poet, who . . . is often none other than the professional homilist himself, goes naturally to the fountain-head, not of elegant Romantic imagery meet for aristocratic ears, but of the popular imagery employed in the current preaching.[87]

Owst's assertion is supported by the structure of the poem, which suggests a homiletic origin. In describing a literal ship and then glossing each of its parts, the poem imitates the exegetical procedure of the preacher. A twelfth-century sermon, for example, states that "To cross that sea [of the world] we must have a ship, mast, sail, etc. The ship signifies the Faith; the sentences of Holy Scripture are its planks, and the authorities of the Holy

Doctors its rudder."[88] The allegory of the political poet differs strikingly from the homiletic allegories in one way, however: rather than reading the parts of the literal ship as the eternal abstractions of religious truth—or, for that matter, of political philosophy—this allegory reveals a specific and literal meaning at every point. The rudder of England was, until 1377, Edward III.

The tradition of the topical Ship of State—a popular tradition, or at least not erudite—is exemplified in a number of English poems. Owst cites a patriotic celebration of the Ship ("The furst anker, hole & sounde, / he is named the lord beamond," and so on) from 1458,[89] and a passage from the satire *Mum and the Sothsegger*, written between August 1399 and February 1400.[90] This last text is of special interest for the student of reading conventions, because its author "shows no traces of exceptionally wide reading or of university training,"[91] yet his realistic description of the Parliament of Shrewsbury (January 1398) slides easily and without introduction into twelve lines of full-blown ship-allegory, as if such a figure will be familiar to all.[92] A modern note on the passage suggests that "This nautical metaphor is especially natural on the lips of a Bristol man."[93] Without disputing this, I would point out that nature has led the Bristol man to a well-worn topos—one that appears, just as naturally, in a Latin poem on the Council of London in 1382, the year of the ominous earthquake. There the allegory is confined to a single line, in which "navigium" [ship] stands for England.[94] The idea that a ship was a fitting emblem for England—and particularly for England in trouble, as it often seemed to be in the late fourteenth century—was available to writers with a wide range of learning.[95]

The topical Ship of State may seem far removed from the world of *Troilus and Criseyde*. But there are surprising similarities between the second *Canticus Troili* and the most elaborate fourteenth-century English example of the Ship of State: the ship that appears in John Gower's remarkable account of the Peasants' Rising of 1381, Book One of the *Vox Clamantis*.[96] This text—2,150 lines of Latin verse, divided into a Prologue and twenty-one chapters—presents three separate, but linked, allegorical visions. In the first vision, peasants appear as animals. In the second vision (ch. 13–15), London is represented as a new Troy: the leaders of England are Trojan heroes, such as Hector, Calchas, and Troilus (992, 961, 993). In a transitional chapter, the Dreamer enters his own dream "quasi in propria persona" (ch. 16, rubric) [as if in his own person]; he surveys the damage done to his city, and laments its fall. In the third vision (ch. 17–20), the Dreamer sees a ship and enters it, along with the entire nobility of England

(1606). This ship is first identified as the Tower of London and later as the Dreamer's own mind, searching for peace[97]—but clearly it is also, as Eric W. Stockton points out, the Ship of the English State.[98] The ship leaves the shore under favorable conditions (1618) only to run into a terrible storm. (Gower borrows about half of the lines in his description of this storm from Ovid's tempest in the story of Ceyx and Alcyone.[99]) Everyone on board is terrified; the captain himself is paralyzed with fear (1692). And now the ship is threatened by a new danger, a devouring monster that rises from the deep. The monster at first seems like both Scylla and Charybdis,[100] and the Dreamer cannot decide what to call it,[101] but he later he simply calls it Scylla (1768 and passim). The allegorical meaning of this Scylla is never explained, either in text or in rubric; clearly it stands for the mob outside the Tower, or the rebellion as a whole. The helmsman faces the "whirlpool's thirsty mouth" (1843) but cannot even steer his ship;[102] the ship sails on without hope, at the mercy of the wind. But the Dreamer has prayed to a guiding Star, either Christ or the Virgin.[103] As the ship heads for the bottom, a voice from heaven causes Scylla to loose its jaws, so that the ship sails free (1857–96). Gower's voyage ends very differently from Troilus's,[104] but the two descriptions of peril at sea are, I think, strikingly similar.

Does the second *Canticus Troili* refer in some way to the English Ship of State? Surely Chaucer's stanza is not a topical allegory, in any simple sense of the term. Troilus's ship is the ship of the Petrarchan lover, and as it drifts toward Thebes it evokes a *classical* Ship of State and the world of epic history, but there appears to be nothing topical, nothing specifically contemporary, about it. Perhaps, however, we are meant to see a general allusion to the difficulties faced by England, or to the *mode* of writing employed by Gower and other political poets. How do we decide whether the Ship of State is a significant context for the second *Canticus Troili*?

It is possible that Book One of the *Vox Clamantis* was part of Chaucer's own most immediate context when he wrote *Troilus and Criseyde*. Certainly Chaucer knew Gower: he made him his attorney during the trip to Italy in 1378 and he "directed" the *Troilus* to him (5.1856); between 1376 and 1386, according to John H. Fisher, "they appear to have been living close together."[105] The first book of the *Vox Clamantis* was written—after most of the rest of the work—between 1381 and 1386.[106] Modern scholars have tended to date the *Troilus* in the mid-1380s; it may have been completed as late as 1387.[107] Either text may have preceded the other, therefore, but they are nearly contemporaneous. Despite their obvious differences in form, mode, and subject, *Troilus and Criseyde* and Book One of the *Vox Clamantis* are linked by many points of similarity: Gower's pen weeps as he writes (Prologue 37), for example, while Chaucer's verses weep as he writes (1.7).[108] Most strikingly, the almost theatrical anguish of Gower's Dreamer in the sixteenth chapter is repeatedly reminiscent of Troilus's misery after Criseyde has left.[109] But these internal similarities could result from borrowing in either direction, or perhaps both directions at once[110]—or they could arise from the shared cultural context of the two writers. In any case, the accumulation of internal and external evidence about the relationship between the two texts will not in itself establish the existence or non-existence of a Chaucerian allusion to the topical Ship of State. If Chaucer knew *Vox Clamantis* 1 when he wrote *Troilus* 5, he may nonetheless have considered it irrelevant to his work; if Chaucer did not know Gower's text he may nonetheless have meant to refer to the tradition on which Gower also drew.

As a way of deciding whether the topical Ship of State is a significant context for the second *Canticus Troili*, we might try to determine Chaucer's attitude toward topical writing in general. He seems to have avoided it. His poetry has little in common with the rich body of topical complaints and satires produced in the last half of the fourteenth century, the writing that Janet Coleman has called "the literature of social unrest."[111] As John P. McCall and George Rudisill put it, "literary critics have indicated that his writings are all but free of political allusions";[112] Lee Patterson, more sweepingly, states that "Chaucer ruled out much of his contemporary historical world as an object of attention."[113] Yet these critics have called attention to one passage in the *Troilus* that does seem to refer to recent political events. A brief consideration of this most topical passage will suggest what is at stake for Chaucer in the possibility of topical reference as such.

McCall and Rudisill suggested in 1959 that when Chaucer extensively rewrites the Trojan conference at the beginning of Book 4, he is not merely turning Boccaccio's "parlamento" (4.13) [parley] into an English-style "parlement" (4.143), as Rossetti pointed out, but also referring specifically to the Wonderful Parliament of 1386, in which some supporters of Richard II, including Chaucer, lost their sinecures and others their lives.[114] Patterson has recently revived and greatly strengthened this suggestion, by pointing to a set of specific analogies between the historical parliament and Chaucer's.[115] But the allusion seems oddly isolated in the *Troilus*; moreover, it positively conflicts with one of the very few topical references suggested earlier. Carleton Brown argued in 1911 that the following lines, describing the parliamentary clamor for the exchange of Criseyde, contain a reference to the Peasants' Rising:

> The noyse of peple up stirte thanne at ones,
> As breme as blase of straw iset on-fire. (4.183–84)[116]

McCall and Rudisill assume that the Trojan parliament cannot be modeled simultaneously on the English Parliament of 1386 and on the Rising of 1381; they conclude that there is simply no reference to the Rising. Yet it is impossible to read these lines next to Gower's account of the Rising, and his puns on the name of Jack Straw—as Brown did[117]—without feeling certain that Chaucer's contemporaries would have seen a reference to the Peasants' Rising here. If there is indeed a double allusion, what does its doubleness mean?

If the entire episode is a satiric criticism of the English Parliament, a passing reference to the Peasants' Rising is the most damning possible comparison for the politicians at whose hands Chaucer suffered. The point would be that the lords of the Parliament have reduced themselves to the moral and social level of peasants, and rebellious peasants at that. This reading is a little too neat, however. Neither allusion is explicit, and the two possibilities are close enough to create a sort of interference: like the second *Canticus Troili*, the Trojan parliament scene drifts between the interpretive contexts (here, contemporary events) it evokes. Perhaps the ambiguity is part of the point. The mistake of the Trojan parliament is represented as a descent into several kinds of chaos. The noisy people desire "hire confusioun" (4.186), and they engender a semiotic confusion; the mob and the reader of the mob are alike enveloped in "cloude of errour" (4.200).

Beyond this, however, it is possible to discern an attitude that is supported, throughout the Chaucerian canon, almost entirely by negative evidence—the view that contemporary political history is by its very nature a kind of terrifying chaos, and that to write about that history is to involve oneself in its dangers.[118] The reference to the Parliament and/or the Rising is tellingly placed: the most topical passage in the *Troilus* is also the only scene in which the courtly decorum of Troy is disrupted. In its ideal state, Chaucer's poem is a closed world like the closed world of Trojan nobility; even to make mention of current events is to open this world to the disorder outside.[119] This attitude might be called Boethian: the virtuous enemy of Fortune must inevitably totalize history as an unvaried nightmare. There is little to choose between Fortune's gifts and her injuries; even less, of course, to choose between the crises that beset England in the 1380s. At the same time, Chaucer's attitude might be called culturally reactionary. Gower writes a staunchly conservative description of the horrors of popular revolt. But if Chaucer knew the first book of the *Vox Clamantis*, he knew that Gower's Ship of State, despite its Ovidian dress, derives from a convention associated with (in Owst's phrase) "popular imagery."[120] From the perspective of the *Troilus*, to defend high culture by writing topical satire would be to lose half the battle.

If the second *Canticus Troili* refers to the topical Ship of State, the reference is oblique and fleeting: the realm of the political is not contained within the ship but looms as a horizon, or an abyss, briefly glimpsed. The meaning of this reference would be complex indeed. If Chaucer's amorous Charybdis is a response to Gower's political Scylla, it must signal a rejection of Gower's mode of writing; Chaucer has taken the painfully timely Ship of State and stripped it of its contemporary reference, returning it to the sheltered harbor of classical learning and Italian love-poetry. But such a gesture would be inevitably ambiguous: to evoke Gower's text is to evoke by implication its mode and its world of reference. If the second *Canticus Troili* takes a stand against topical allegory, then it verges on topical allegory. I offer this doubled reading in the conditional mood, however, because the underlying question—is there a reference to the topical Ship of State?—has not been settled. *If* Chaucer intended to refer to that tradition, or the *Vox Clamantis* in particular, the reference is an enigmatic gesture, the sort of gesture that makes positive recognition difficult. But it is entirely possible that Chaucer intended no such reference.

In most respects the literary failure of the second *Canticus Troili* reflects contradictions that are successfully resolved in the *Troilus* as a whole. The space between interpretive contexts, in which the song drifts uncertainly, is the very space of Chaucer's poetry. If the lyric fails to distinguish itself—as a great poem, like the first *Canticus Troili*, or even as a *separate* poem within the romance—the collapse of distinction is part of a modulated drama of form, a careful dismantling of hierarchies. The deviation from Sonnet 189 is a model for the deviation from the *Filostrato* that makes the *Troilus* what it is; the drift toward Thebes, fatal for characters and narrator, is inseparable from the poet's aspiration to move beyond courtly romance toward the epic of Thebes. The problem of contemporary history, however, is fated to remain unresolved. This lack of resolution arises in part from Chaucer's complex reaction to the frightening context of history, and it arises in part from something that Chaucer cannot have specifically intended—our own historically determined ignorance. More precise information about the original context of the *Troilus*—about the dating of the *Vox Clamantis*, say, or about contemporary responses to the *Troilus*—might shift our interpretation in one direction or another.[121] There is nothing inherently unknowable about this information; it just happens that we do not know it.

I began this chapter by claiming that the second *Canticus Troili* raises "context" as a problem, yet I have till now discussed particular contexts according to a traditional philological model of allusion and influence: I have tried to show that Chaucer was referring, more or less obliquely, to a set of pre-existing texts that he knew. My proposals involved local uncertainties. In the case of Petrarch, there was no firm proof that Chaucer knew Sonnet 189, and I resorted to probabilities; in the case of Statius, where Chaucer's knowledge was not in doubt, the connections between Troilus's song and the ship simile of *Thebaid* 3 were strange enough to prompt some speculation about the role of free association in the diagnosis of allusion. In both cases, I emphasized the uncertainties, treating them as essential elements in the experience of interpreting the song, yet I argued for clear indebtedness on Chaucer's part. With the topical Ship of State, the difficulty of recognizing Chaucer's contexts becomes the very heart of the matter.

In the face of such uncertainty, one option would be to abandon the notion of context to which I have been clinging and adopt another model of intertextuality in which authorial knowledge and control do not figure. According to such a model, we might say that the *Troilus*'s ship and Gower's Ship of State answer each other no matter what Chaucer or Gower happened to know; that the two texts embody contrasting condensations of culturally determined themes. This option has its attractions: it would allow a fully comparative reading to proceed unhampered by an accidental lack of information. If we rule out considerations of authorial intention, however, we are not thereby escaping the problematics of authorship as defined by the *Troilus*. One of the striking contrasts between Troilus's two songs is the way authorial intention is represented. The first *Canticus Troili* describes a divided subjectivity, but every aspect of its textual frame points to a unified and controlling intention. Troilus knows what he wants to say, and says it; the narrator somehow has access to Troilus's exact words, and presents them; Chaucer has the text of Petrarch in front of him, and translates it. Everything about the first *Canticus Troili* encourages a positivist, intentionalist model of literary transmission. In the second *Canticus Troili*, I have argued, that model is challenged to the point of breakdown. If we give up the idea of authorial control at *this* point we are following the story line set down by our author.

This last paradox suggests that *Troilus and Criseyde* establishes a complex new form of *auctoritas*. Chaucer seems to undermine the lyric authority of Boccaccio's *Filostrato*, in two ways: first, he restores the framing textual hierarchy that Boccaccio eliminates, as if to insist that the lyric voice cannot claim a transcendent authority of its own; second, he dismantles the very hierarchy he has established. When the frame around the song collapses, what remains is not the song standing alone but rather the song at the mercy of new and unreadable controlling forces. This may seem to show a more poignant awareness of the limitations of literary achievement than is available to the love-poet Filostrato. But at the same time it makes possible a powerful version of authorship that moves beyond Filostrato's lyric authority. The indeterminacy of history has a double import within the *Troilus*. On the one hand, it is a threat, a "cloude of errour" or a hostile wind or a Charybdis; on the other hand, it is the dynamic force that allows an escape from the narcissistic circle of the *Filostrato*. History is the space of difference between the Chaucerian narrator and the Chaucerian protagonist, and the space of difference between Chaucer and his readers: the narrator notes the change "in forme of speche" (2.22) that makes Troilus's behavior difficult to understand, and one of the many worries expressed at the end of the entire poem is that "diversite / In Englissh" (5.1793–94) will disrupt the transmission of the text. The variability of the historical world enables the Chaucerian author to stand apart from his work. When Boccaccio's Filostrato dispatches his poem, he directs it only to Filomena: the poem continues to circulate within the narrative of desire it describes, and the fictive writer remains identified with the limits of his writing. Boccaccio's own *Decameron* shows how easy it is to mock Filostrato's version of lyric authority.[122] The Chaucer who sends *Troilus and Criseyde* on its way is aware that he is giving up control over its destiny, and this awareness constitutes him as a site of intention and ironic insight beyond the text. The unchartable sea of the second *Canticus Troili* is the realm in which Chaucer claims his authority.

Afterword. Looking Back

A submerged theme in this book has been the interplay of memory and forgetting. In Chapter 6 I argued that the second *Canticus Troili* is a free adaptation of Petrarch's Sonnet 189, a poem that begins with the striking and difficult image of a ship laden with forgetfulness ("la nave mia colma d'oblio"). If Chaucer knew this image, however, he chose to omit it from his stanza: both memory and forgetfulness are forgotten in Troilus's song, which is oriented toward a moment in the near future ("the tenthe nyght"). Elsewhere in Book 5, it is true, Troilus develops an interest in cataloguing things he remembers (e.g., 5.561–81) and in determining how he himself will be remembered (e.g., 5.309–15). He imagines composing, and even somehow publishing, his own Book of Memory:

> Thanne thoughte he thus: "O blisful lord Cupide,
> Whan I the proces have in my memorie
> How thow me hast wereyed on every syde,
> Men myght a book make of it, like a storie." (5.582–85)

The attempt to clarify and frame subjective experience is apparent also in the second *Canticus Troili*, I think, in the self-consciousness of "wel oughte I to biwaille," a phrase that suggests Troilus is prescribing for himself a rhetorical mode in which to inscribe himself. But the second *Canticus Troili* is "laden with forgetfulness," in a way that Troilus (unlike Petrarch) does not control; the song's wishful and fearful focus on the private present tense of Troilus's own life is one of the reasons for its inadequacy both as a poem and as a personal meditation. My aim in Chapter 6 was, in effect, to remember *for* the text, to begin to recover the sources and contexts that make it possible to gloss the second *Canticus Troili* as an exploration of the very problem of forgetting.

One autumn afternoon in the last stage of the writing of this book, while checking quotations in the Regenstein Library at the University of Chicago, I came across a marginal inscription of extraordinary interest, at least for me. In a somewhat battered copy of the 1927 Root edition of *Troilus and Criseyde*, at the second *Canticus Troili*, someone had written in the right margin, in a neat hand, in pencil:

See Petrarca:
Egerton MS. 2711
#28
Wyatt, Muir
PR 2400
A5M9

The reference, including call number, is to the 1949 *Collected Poems of Sir Thomas Wyatt*, edited by Kenneth Muir, and to one sonnet in that book (identified by its original manuscript location): "My galy charged with forgetfulnes." The writer of the note evidently knew "My galy" to be a translation from Petrarch; perceiving some similarity between the *Troilus* stanza and the Wyatt sonnet, he or she seems to have speculated that Chaucer was adapting the same text as Wyatt.

My discovery in the Regenstein took me back to a different afternoon, an autumn Sunday afternoon some years ago, in an apartment in Ithaca, New York, when the same speculation first occurred to me. Like the anonymous scholiast (as I imagine), I was reading the *Troilus* when I seemed to hear, in the second *Canticus Troili*, an echo of Wyatt's memorable line:

The starres be hid that led me to this pain.

Looking for a diversion, I reached for the *Norton Anthology of English Literature*, which I had acquired as a graduate teaching assistant in the English survey at Cornell. At this point I had better luck than the writer of the marginal note. He or she went to some trouble to pin down the particular Wyatt text, but the Muir edition, located some thirty feet away in the library stacks, fails to identify the particular Petrarch poem that Wyatt translates. He or she had to settle for the small triumph of "See Petrarca." The *Norton* was more helpful; it named Sonnet 189, and from my Durling *Petrarch* I learned that 189 has something the Wyatt translation lacks—the reference to Charybdis. (Wyatt saves some syllables by rendering "enfra Scilla et Caribdi" as "Twene Rock and Rock.") I think of that moment as the first moment in the writing of this book.

When I found the pencil inscription in Chicago, however, my mood was not nostalgic but anxious. I had a thought that must be familiar to every academic: do I need to footnote this? I had presented my source attribution for the second *Canticus Troili* as an original discovery, but now I knew that somebody else had gone most of the way to the same discovery, at some point after 1949 but probably before I entered graduate school. (The handwriting of the note seems to match a user's signature in the back of the volume, dated in the spring of 1956, when, as a two-and-a-half-year-old in Cambridge, Massachusetts, I was on the threshold of my own earliest memories. I omit mention of the name that is signed, to avoid a possibly undeserved imputation of library vandalism.) I tried to imagine the footnote I could write: "See also the Root ed., copy 1, third-floor stacks, Chicago, ad loc."? I consoled myself by reflecting that I had never believed the connection between the Chaucer stanza and Sonnet 189 to be anything but, actually, obvious. Like the even more obvious link between Filostrato and Philostratus, the value of this connection depended on the way it was explored within a critical argument, and my critical argument had, too slowly of course, grown into a whole long book.

Amid these academic anxieties, I had another, more detached thought, one that must be familiar to every nonacademic reader of academic writing. The critical response in the margin began to look pedantic, self-important, and all-but-irrelevant to the work it claimed to illuminate. For the first time, I could see my own "original" insight as though it were someone else's, and could smile at its pretensions. What kind of person would hear Troilus's agonized and faltering lament and respond, "See Petrarca"? An academic person, a person wasting a warm fall afternoon in the fluorescent asepsis of the university library. The second *Canticus Troili* is not a great poem—in itself it is surely inferior both to Petrarch's Sonnet 189 and to Wyatt's "My galy"—but it comes from some kind of construction of a human heart, and its very inarticulateness is unspeakably more moving than the precision of "PR 2400.A5M9." Troilus too tries to find comfort in numbers—"the tenthe nyght"—but his cares are far from academic. The fear he expresses in the last line of the song,

> My ship and me Caribdis wol devoure,

has less in common with the well-channeled anxieties of a graduate student or an assistant professor than with the profound terrors of, say, a two-and-a-half-year-old. At this point I realized that I had succumbed to something I had meant to resist, and implicitly to argue against, in my book: the sentimentalization of Troilus.

No writer has explored the relationship between sentimental identification and bookish authority more imaginatively than Chaucer. To illustrate this claim, I want to cite a brief passage that focuses not on Troilus but on Criseyde. This appears in the long consummation scene in Book 3; she has just forgiven Troilus for his (feigned) suspicion of her fidelity, and, "with blisse of that supprised" (3.1184) Troilus has suddenly taken her into his arms.

> Criseyde, which that felte hire thus itake,
> As writen clerkes in hire bokes olde,
> Right as an aspes leef she gan to quake,
> When she hym felte hire in his armes folde. (3.1198–1201)

In Chapter 6, you may recall, I spoke in passing of "the central attempt to construct a frame—spatial, temporal, textual—for the consummation scene in Book 3." These four lines seem to contribute to that project. In close compass we read about Criseyde, in Troilus's arms, and about a group of clerks writing about Criseyde in old books. It is not hard to hierarchize these elements: the image of Criseyde is clearly central, and the citation of "clerkes" amounts to a kind of footnote or marginal apparatus. Yet the disposition of the poetic text reverses that imagined structure.

The inner experience of Criseyde appears in the two outermost lines, which echo each other and insist upon her feeling ("felte," twice). Moreover, these lines convey the physicality of what she feels, the entanglement of two persons, through their deployment of personal pronouns: in the first line all pronouns refer to Criseyde ("which that," "hire"), while in the fourth line *she* and *he* alternate ("she," "hym," "hire," "his"). The two middle lines contain the sentence's main verb ("she gan to quake"), but notably this verb refers not to feeling but to a kind of outward behavior that manifests feeling. The two middle lines also contain a simile describing Criseyde's quaking in terms of the natural world ("Right as an aspes leef"), and the reference to the clerks and their books.

This intrusion of bookish men *into* the erotic scene is also characteristic of Book 3.[1] For example, just above the lines I have quoted, Troilus's embrace of Criseyde is followed by a different simile, that of a lark caught in the foot of a sparrowhawk. This image seems to describe Criseyde, who has physically been seized, or perhaps Troilus, who has put all in God's hand (3.1185)—seized, as it were, by an idea ("sodeynly avysed," 3.1186). Yet the simile is separated from Troilus and Criseyde by three lines describing the bookish Pandarus going to bed (3.1188–90), and it is immediately followed by a description of the narrator's plight:

> What myghte or may the sely larke seye,
> Whan that the sperhauk hath it in his foot?
> I kan namore; but of thise ilke tweye—
> To whom this tale sucre be or soot—
> Though that I tarie a yer, somtyme I moot,
> After myn auctour, tellen hire gladnesse,
> As wel as I have told hire hevynesse. (3.1191–97)

If the simile looks back at Criseyde and Troilus, it also looks ahead to the narrator; the lark has no choice about what to "seye," and neither does the narrator, who is bound by his commitment to a powerful "auctour." ("I kan namore" elides a verb of speaking and may mean either "I can say no more than this" or "I can say no more than the lark.") The simile's ambiguous application makes a connection between the scene of writing and the scene of sexual encounter: the narrator's textual bondage takes on erotic overtones, and, just as important, the lovers' experience is flavored with the sweetness and bitterness, the delay and fulfillment, experienced by those who read the romance about them.

So, in the four lines quoted earlier, the reference to "clerkes" intrudes into the description of Criseyde's feeling as a reminder of the narrator's position with respect to his matter. Once again the simile serves to blur the boundary between the dusty world of old books and the private world of two lovers. Not only is the simile a textbook *comparatio*, applied to the trembling Criseyde by a poet seeking rhetorical effect; beyond this, the words "leef" and "folde" link the outer and the inner scene. Criseyde is described as a leaf, and she is folded (in Troilus's arms); she is like a page being bound into a book.

Carolyn Dinshaw has brilliantly described the analogy, in Chaucer and in Chaucer criticism, between the figure of woman and the figure of the text in need of interpretation.[2] Here, at the very moment that we are most tempted to identify *with* Criseyde's sensations, we are reminded that she is a text glossed by clerks—and by the narrator, by Pandarus, by Troilus. Troilus has, this once, found a way to control the unstable signification of a text: he folds it shut. Yet the appeal of a text lies less in the promise of ultimate closure than in the delight afforded by its endless and endlessly partial interpretation. Dinshaw points out that both Criseyde and the narrative of *Troilus and Criseyde* offer the "pleasure of the text" that Roland Barthes writes about;[3] in the lines I have cited, the textual alternation of Criseydan sensation with scholarly apparatus provides a perfect example of the "intermittence" that is, for Barthes, "the figure of pleasure in reading."[4] Rather than simply sharing Criseyde's feelings, we glimpse them in our reading, and glimpse as well the erotic potential in the very act of reading.

I have been speaking of Criseyde's "feelings" as though we knew what they were. But the verb "felte" refers only to the physical situation that Criseyde registers in her body: she feels *that* Troilus is embracing her. How does she feel *about* this? Her quaking seems to signal a strong emotion, but no emotion is specified in the text. In Chaucer's body language, quaking can be a sign of rage ("For ire he quook," 5.36) or, more often, a sign of fear ("Quaketh for drede," 4.14).[5] Are we to suppose that Criseyde—"the ferfulleste wight / That myghte be" (2.450–51)—here feels the way a lark feels in the grasp of a hawk? Certainly if she did not quake we would not suspect her of fearing Troilus at this moment. A few stanzas later we are told that Criseyde is now "al quyt from every drede and tene" (3.1226), but this does not settle the issue: it may be that she was afraid in the first moment of Troilus's embrace and then (at some point not clearly defined) ceased to be afraid, but it may also be that she has lost her fear at the very moment of being embraced, and that she quakes for some other reason. In the *Romaunt of the Rose*, the Lover is said to "quake" from unfulfilled erotic desire.[6] And in another Chaucerian translation, quaking is associated both with fear *and* with desire:

> whoso that, qwakynge, dredeth or desireth thyng that nys noght stable of his ryght, that man that so dooth hath cast awey his scheeld, and is remoeved from his place, and enlaceth hym in the cheyne with whiche he mai ben drawen. (*Boece* 1.m4.17–22)

Clearly Criseyde is in the grip of some strong feeling—desire or fear or even, just conceivably, lingering anger over Troilus's possessiveness—but her quaking remains a sign in need of a gloss.[7]

The gloss I have imported from the *Boece* may lead us to another way of reading Criseyde's aspen-leaf-like quaking. Lady Philosophy is making the point that to dread or desire an unstable thing is to become, in oneself, unstable. (Her recommendation is that we "Hope aftir no thyng, ne drede nat," 1.m4.15.) The adjective "qwakynge" has a double force: it intensifies the emotion of dread or desire and criticizes the unsteadiness that inevitably results from such an emotion. The one who quakes is soon "remoeved from his place." I have been speculating about the feeling that causes Criseyde to tremble, but a less sympathetic, more "philosophical" reading might associate her trembling with other manifestations of vacillation and instability. Criseyde—characteristically "Now hoot, now cold" (2.811), characteristically "slydinge of corage" (5.825)—is profoundly associated with the things of Fortune. As she submits to her desire for one of those things, she herself becomes one.

This unsympathetic reading is strengthened by another available gloss. If the reference to "clerkes" prompts us to look for trembling leaves in Chaucer's real sources, we will find them in the *Filostrato*, prominently displayed near the beginning and near the end. Troiolo, in his early misogynist phase, asks

> Che è a porre in donna alcuno amore?
> Ché come al vento si volge la foglia,
> così 'n un dì ben mille volte il core
> di lor si volge. (1.22)
>
> [Why place any love in a woman?
> For as a leaf turns itself with the wind,
> so a thousand times a day their hearts
> turn.]

And the narrator Filostrato finally endorses this sentiment, in his own misogynist diatribe at the end of the poem: he says that a young woman is fickle ("mobile") and

> volubil sempre come foglia al vento. (8.30)
>
> [unsteady always as a leaf in the wind]

Neither of these passages is translated at the corresponding place in the *Troilus*. Rather, I suggest, they are both folded into the very center of Chaucer's poem, and the very center of Criseyde's subjectivity.

In the four-line passage I have quoted from Book 3 of the *Troilus*, Criseyde's subjectivity is made fictively vivid through the sharp contrast between her person—located, seized, quaking—and the indefinite group of old anonymous clerks writing about her. Yet Chaucer shows that the frame that seems to separate personal subjectivity from its social definition and expression is illusory. One of the most poignant things about Criseyde is that she herself seems to understand this. If she is afraid when Troilus embraces her, it is partly because she is quite reasonably concerned for her reputation, on which her security in Troy depends. Criseyde may be quaking precisely *because* she knows her behavior now will cause her to be represented, ultimately, as an unstable, quaking creature. Certainly by the end of the poem she comes to imagine herself, bitterly, as the object of an eroticized verbal transmission:

> Allas, of me, unto the worldes ende,
> Shal neyther ben ywriten nor ysonge
> No good word, for thise bokes wol me shende.
> O, rolled shal I ben on many a tonge! (5.1058–61)[8]

The apparatus of a pervasively misogynist textual tradition, folded into the imagined figure of a woman, becomes the very ground of inner complexity and compelling subjective reality.

Masculine subjectivity is often described as though it had no such internal contradictions. Troilus lacks both Criseyde's instability and her consciousness of the way a textual frame constitutes consciousness. In the lines quoted on the first page of this Afterword, he too imagines becoming the object of a textual tradition, but he supposes that he will determine the content of that tradition through his own memorial introspection. Troilus quakes rather frequently, from fear or from ire, and he is of course profoundly committed to an unstable object of desire. But in himself he is a model of stability, self-presence, and self-knowledge: where Criseyde is "Now hoot, now cold" (2.811), Troilus sings himself into textual focus as simultaneously both: "For hote of cold, for cold of hote, I dye" (1.420). I have associated Troilus's sense of himself with the privileged space of the first *Canticus Troili* (in which this line appears), and I have argued that Chaucer dismantles the frame around the lyric in the course of the poem. But Troilus himself is not dismantled; rather, his utterly stable subjectivity gradually loses its connection to the surrounding world. In Book 5 he cries out

> I ne kan nor may,
> For al this world, withinne myn herte fynde
> To unloven yow a quarter of a day! (5.1696–98)

and for this fidelity—or this failure to find contradiction within—he is rewarded with a totalizing vision, from a detached height, of "This litel spot of erthe" (5.1815).

In his wholeness and his presence to himself, Troilus prefigures the modern subject. He has enough complexity to be interesting, and he gives an impression of deep feeling that can make glossing and source-hunting seem like an impertinence. Criseyde, by contrast, not without some bitterness, accommodates such pursuits. She is a textual figure permeated with the shifting, diffuse verbal apparatus that surrounds her: she is more medieval than Troilus (for example, she understands the medieval principle of exemplarity better than he does), but she could also be described as more postmodern. Troilus is the modern, sovereign, and typically masculine self: he seems to stand apart from his context, not a shifting signifier in the realm of the symbolic but an imaginary vision of unity and fullness.

Post-structuralists and feminists have, of course, revealed this construction of sexual difference as a ruse of logocentric patriarchy: the selfsame nature of the masculine subject is founded upon its difference from, and its rejection of, a feminine Other. We can see this foundational contrast, for example, in the juxtaposition of Criseyde's quaking with Troilus's response, described in the next line:

> But Troilus, al hool of cares colde . . . (3.1202)

A critical reader might suggest that Troilus is *made* whole through his difference from the quaking and permeable Criseyde. My aim in this book, however, has not been merely to reaffirm that the autonomous subject is constituted and not natural; rather, I have tried to go back over the history of masculine subjectivity in some detail, remembering one particular textual sequence that has contributed to the construction of a specifically authorial self.[9] At this late date I want to recall the story.

Dante begins the *Vita Nuova* within the framework of the medieval tradition of commentary, positing Beatrice as a luminous image of wholeness and himself as a changing, internally divided, verbally prolific scribe and glossator. He uses the hierarchy of text and gloss to establish an unprecedented form of *auctoritas* for his little book, but his strategy requires precisely that he *not* identify himself, personally, with that *auctoritas*. Boccaccio makes a radical transformation of Dante's authoritative structure in the *Filostrato*: he imagines an authorial subjectivity that is whole and self-sufficient. He collapses Dante's hierarchy of text and gloss, lyric and narrative, into a single *modus faciendi librum*, and imagines a total identification of unitary book, totemic protagonist, and reflective Author.

At this point in the story, we might say that a new and dynamic subjectivity has emerged from out of the orthodox hierarchies of biblical commentary—having been constructed from the very materials that seem to be left behind. Like Criseyde, Boccaccio's "Filostrato" is shaped within, and thus constituted by, the institutions of medieval textual dissemination: the difference is that Filostrato has forgotten that fact while Criseyde cannot forget. But Chaucer takes the story a step forward, by taking a step back: he "medievalizes" his proto-Renaissance source, providing an implicitly conservative critique of Filostrato's forgetful self-understanding, but at the same time he invents a still more modern, still more lasting form of authorial subjectivity. In the schematic terms I am using here, Chaucer's Troilus is like Boccaccio's Troiolo, and thus like Boccaccio's Pandaro and like Filostrato. But Chaucer posits difference between Troilus and Pandarus and the narrator of the *Troilus* and makes explicit (in a way that Dante and Boccaccio do not) the difference between the text's narrator and the person we must call its "author." This allows him to stage a drama of lyric framing and subjective constitution on the far side of *Filostrato*'s imaginary self-reflection: a drama in which the privileged status of the lyric and of the masculine self is presented as a given at the beginning of the text, but is unveiled by the end as a problematic fiction.

At this late date (I write this sentence on a winter night, past midnight, in the third year of the Bush administration, with a subzero wind outside my tenth-floor window) there is much to be said for learning to see through, and see beyond, the authority of sovereign authors. For this project, Chaucer is both a vital and a frustrating writer to be reading. On the one hand he writes a complex, multifaceted critique of the sort of author Filostrato claims to be; on the other hand, through the very complexity of his vision—the way he embraces at once forgetfulness and memory, at once the fantasy of original authorship and the consciousness that all authority is derived—he creates a version of the author that is more influential and harder to get around than the brave early efforts of Dante and Boccaccio. He writes a book in which it is possible to identify with Troilus or with Criseyde or with the narrator who identifies (in different ways) with both—or to resist identification with those sympathetic figures, writing a learned commentary that is rendered marginal in advance because it is folded, already, into the book.

Notes

Introduction

1. Bonaventure, *Opera Theologica Selecta* vol. 1, 12. Emphasis mine.

2. It is quoted, for example, in Parkes, "The Influence of the Concepts of *Ordinatio* and *Compilatio* on the Development of the Book" 127–28; in Minnis, *Medieval Theory of Authorship* 94; and in Hult, *Self-Fulfilling Prophecies* 61n.

3. I discuss Bonaventure's larger argument briefly in Chapter 1.

4. Dante, *Vita Nuova* 1.1 and passim; Boccaccio, *Filostrato*, Proem 32; Chaucer, *Troilus and Criseyde* 5.1786. (For the editions employed, see the prefatory Note on Texts and Translations.)

5. The tradition effectively begins with Lewis, "What Chaucer Really Did to *Il Filostrato*" (1932) but has thrived especially in the last decade. A list of the most important books must include Boitani, ed., *Chaucer and the Italian Trecento* (1983); several studies by Boitani, such as *Chaucer and Boccaccio* (1977); Havely, *Chaucer's Boccaccio* (1980); Shoaf, *Dante, Chaucer, and the Currency of the Word* (1983); Wetherbee, *Chaucer and the Poets* (1984); Chaucer, *Troilus and Criseyde*, ed. Windeatt (1984); Wood, *The Elements of Chaucer's Troilus* (1984); Wallace, *Chaucer and the Early Writings of Boccaccio* (1985); David Anderson, *Before the Knight's Tale* (1988); Taylor, *Chaucer Reads "The Divine Comedy"* (1989); Fleming, *Classical Imitation and Interpretation in Chaucer's Troilus* (1990). I have profited from all these books, and most recently from Fleming's: although it appeared when my own argument was essentially complete, I have taken encouragement from Fleming's eloquent description of a sophisticated and self-critical philological awareness on Chaucer's part. Certain intertextualists specializing in Italian literature have also been crucial to my own enterprise: here I will mention only Giuseppe Mazzotta and Teodolinda Barolini.

6. Two important philological studies of the medieval idea of authorship are Spitzer, "Note on the Poetic and the Empirical 'I' in Medieval Authors," and Chenu, "Auctor, actor, autor," expanded in *Toward Understanding Saint Thomas* 126–39. The two crucial post-structuralist essays on "the author" are Foucault, "What Is an Author?" and Barthes, "The Death of the Author"; see, more recently, Kamuf, *Signature Pieces*.

7. The best treatment of the explicit theorization of *auctoritas* is Minnis, *Medieval Theory of Authorship*. On the medieval intellectual practices of authorship, see Chenu, *Toward Understanding Saint Thomas*; Allen, *The Ethical Poetic of the Later Middle Ages*; and Carruthers, *The Book of Memory*, especially Chapter 6, "Memory and authority." An excellent introduction to the forms and institutions of medieval

learning is Kenny and Pinborg, "Medieval Philosophical Literature." The collection of medieval texts edited by Minnis and Scott, *Medieval Literary Theory and Criticism*, is indispensable.

8. Critical works that explore the historical problem of medieval and Renaissance *auctoritas* through readings of individual literary texts include Hult, *Self-Fulfilling Prophecies* (especially the lucid and suggestive discussion of "The Medieval Author," 25–64); Quint, *Origin and Originality in Renaissance Literature*; Guillory, *Poetic Authority*; Brownlee, *Poetic Identity in Guillaume de Machaut*; Miller, *Poetic License*; and the essays collected in Brownlee and Stephens, eds., *Discourses of Authority in Medieval and Renaissance Literature*, especially the Introduction and Ascoli, "The Vowels of Authority."

9. Vandelli, "Un autografo della *Teseide*" 47: "un piccolo sfogo che prorompe dal cuore innamorato del poeta." The autograph manuscript is Biblioteca Laurenziana, Cod. Acquisti e Doni 325.

10. Vandelli, "Un autografo della *Teseide*" 47: "come se si trattasse di parole da mettere in mostra il meno possibile e . . . di confidenza segreta."

11. Hollander, "The Validity of Boccaccio's Self-Exegesis in His *Teseida*" 174–75. Another important discussion of the *Teseida*'s glosses (which makes, however, no reference to "che sono io") is Noakes, *Timely Reading* 87–97.

12. Spitzer, "Note on the Poetic and the Empirical 'I'" 416.

13. Spitzer, "Note on the Poetic and the Empirical 'I'" 418: "un monsieur qui raconte et qui dit 'je.'"

14. Spitzer, "Note on the Poetic and the Empirical 'I'" 419.

15. Brownlee, *Poetic Identity in Guillaume de Machaut* 16.

16. Foucault, "What Is an Author?" 115. Further quotations will be identified in the text.

17. Fineman, *Shakespeare's Perjured Eye: The Invention of Poetic Subjectivity in the Sonnets* 1 and 82.

18. See the critical summary of these Renaissance constructions in Lee Patterson, "On the Margin: Postmodernism, Ironic History, and Medieval Studies" 95–99.

19. This tradition would include Lewis, *The Allegory of Love*, which describes a "great change in our sentiments" (8) in the love poetry of the later Middle Ages that produced a modern "erotic tradition" with which we are so familiar "that we mistake it for something natural and universal and therefore do not inquire into its origins" (3); Morris, *The Discovery of the Individual 1050–1200*; Hanning, *The Individual in the Twelfth-Century Romance*. More recently, David Aers, in *Community, Gender, and Individual Identity*, and Lee Patterson, in *Chaucer and the Subject of History*, have offered sophisticated and circumspect accounts of the construction of new forms of individuality and subjectivity in the later Middle Ages.

20. Oppenheimer, *The Birth of the Modern Mind: Self, Consciousness, and the Invention of the Sonnet* 3.

21. Guillaume de Lorris and Jeun de Meun, *Le Roman de la Rose*, ed. Félix Lecoy.

22. Barthes, *Fragments d'un discours amoureux* 13; further quotations will be identified in the text. Translations are from *A Lover's Discourse*, trans. Howard.

23. I refer to Barthes, "From Work to Text": "The author is reputed to be the

father and the owner of his work . . . The Text, on the other hand, is read without the Father's inscription" (61). On the author as father, see Jack Stillinger, *Multiple Authorship and the Myth of Solitary Genius*.

24. See Barthes, "The Death of the Author."

25. *Teseida*, ed. Limentani, 891 n. 16: "la punta di maggior civetteria nel fantasioso edificio dell'autobiografia del B."

26. See David Anderson, *Before the Knight's Tale* 52–54.

27. The poet and the glossator write for different *audiences*, as Vandelli acutely noted (69–70). The poem is addressed to Fiammetta alone, and the poet says that he has written a poem full of "storia," "favola," and "chiuso parlare" [history, fable, figurative or allegorical speech], which most ladies dislike because of their poor understanding, but which Fiammetta will both understand and appreciate ("A Fiammetta," 247). The glossator ends his long gloss on the house of Mars at 7.30 by saying that he is "scrivendo questo ad instanzia di donne" [writing this at the instance of women]; he is providing explanations that Fiammetta would not need.

28. In addition, Emilia's singing is mentioned (with forms of "cantare," "canto," or "canzone") at 3.11, 3.26, 3.29, 3.39, and 3.40.

29. Hamburger, *The Logic of Literature*; see Chapter 4, "The Lyrical Genre," and especially the section headed "The Constitution of the Lyric I" (272–92). On the denaturing of deictics within the lyric, see Culler, *Structuralist Poetics* 164–70. Karla Taylor discusses the problem of deictic reference in medieval literature in *Chaucer Reads "The Divine Comedy."*

30. Roland Greene, *Post-Petrarchism* 9. Greene lucidly discusses the conflict between Hamburger's model and an older, and still widespread, "fictionalist" view of the lyric I.

31. Zumthor, *Essai de poétique médiévale* 189: "mode de dire entièrement et exclusivement référé à un *je* qui, pour n'avoir souvent d'autre existence que grammaticale, n'en fixe pas moins le plan et les modalités du discours." See also Zumthor, "Le *je* de la chanson et le moi du poète," *Langue, texte, énigme* 181–96; Dragonetti, *La technique poétique des trouvères dans la chanson courtoise*, Conclusion, "Essai d'interprétation de la poétique du grand chant courtois" (539–80); Vance, "Love's Concordance."

32. Zumthor, *Essai de poétique médiévale* 189: "hors de toute narration."

33. I shall treat these critical discussions much more fully below, of course; as a token documentation of my claim here I would mention, for the *Vita Nuova*, Harrison, *The Body of Beatrice*; for the *Filostrato*, Natali, "Progetti narrativi e tradizione lirica in Boccaccio"; for *Troilus and Criseyde*, Wimsatt, "The French Lyric Element in *Troilus and Criseyde*."

34. See, for example, Zumthor, *Essai de poétique médiévale* ch. 7, "Chant et récit," and *passim*; Zumthor, "De la chanson au récit: *La Châtelaine de Vergi*," *Langue, texte, énigme* 219–36; Bloch, *Etymologies and Genealogies* ch. 3, "Literature and Lineage"; Colby-Hall, "Frustration and Fulfillment"; Huot, *From Song to Book*. Francies Regina Psaki's 1989 Cornell University dissertation treats "medieval lyric-narrative hybrids" in many languages.

35. For a survey, see Gybbon-Monypenny, "Guillaume de Machaut's Erotic 'Autobiography.'"

36. See Hult, *Self-Fulfilling Prophecies* ch. 3, "Lyric and Romance."

37. See Poe, *From Poetry to Prose in Old Provençal.*

38. See Bossy, "Cyclical Composition in Guiraut Riquier's Book of Poems." On manuscript *chansonniers* in general, see Huot, *From Song to Book.*

39. Virgil's "arma virumque cano" is echoed in his self-description in *Inferno*: "Poeta fui, e cantai di quel giusto / figliuol d'Anchise . . ." (1.73–74) [I was a poet, and I sang of that just son of Anchises]. In his later Dante commentary, Boccaccio explains that "cantai" is used figuratively: "Usa Virgilio questo vocabolo in luogo di 'composi'" [Virgil uses this word in place of 'I composed'], *Esposizioni sopra la Comedia di Dante*, ed. Padoan, 1(1).113, p. 43. Boccaccio himself uses *cantare* in this sense repeatedly in the *Teseida*, e.g. at 3.1.

40. Isidore, *Etymologiae* 10.2: "Auctor ab augendo dictus. Auctorem autem femino genere dici non posse."

41. Aers, *Community, Gender, and Individual Identity* ch. 3, "Masculine identity in the courtly community: The self loving in *Troilus and Criseyde*"; here 121.

42. For a brilliant recent exploration of the sexual implications of lyric-narrative relations, see Sedgwick, "A Poem Is Being Written." There are interesting links between this experimental essay, which mixes verse and prose, and the *Vita Nuova*: both begin with the vision of a nine-year-old girl, for example.

43. Jacobus, "The Law of/and Gender: Genre Theory and *The Prelude*" 57. The fundamental theoretical statement on the mutual articulation of gender and genre is Derrida, "The Law of Genre."

44. There is a growing body of feminist interpretation of medieval literature; see for example (despite a disavowal of "feminism") Delany, *Writing Woman*; Fisher and Halley, *Seeking the Woman in Late Medieval and Renaissance Writings*; Dinshaw, *Chaucer's Sexual Poetics*. I shall discuss Dinshaw's argument very briefly in my Afterword; her cross-reading of textual and sexual politics is a crucial precedent for what I attempt in this book.

45. See for example Fried, "Andromeda Unbound: Gender and Genre in Millay's Sonnets"—a brilliant essay of wider relevance than its title may suggest.

46. The other escape from worldly time in the *Teseida* is Arcite's post mortem ascent to the eighth sphere, from which he looks down upon the entire world (11.1–3). It is worth remarking that this passage and the lyric scene of Book Three are approximately balanced in the work: one occurs just after the first two books of the poem, and the other at the beginning of the final two.

47. Kirkham, "'Chiuso parlare' in Boccaccio's *Teseida*." I take this opportunity to note that the textual location of the "che sono io" gloss accords well with Kirkham's numerological interpretation of the *Teseida*. Kirkham stresses the symbolic importance of the numbers 3 (associated with Venus), 5 (associated with Mars), and 7 (associated with Diana, as well as the mystic marriage of Venus and Mars). The verse that prompts the "che sono io" gloss is a textual locus of extraordinary power, a moment of narrative stasis in which all the poem's divine planets are lined up: its number is 3.35.7.

48. On these "matters," see Anderson, *Before the Knight's Tale*.

49. See the Limentani ed., 891, nn. 18–19. Both the *Teseida* and the *Filostrato* were begun in Naples between 1335 and 1341, although it is likely that the *Teseida*

commentary was completed after Boccaccio's removal to Florence in 1341. If Branca's ordering of the two works is correct, and the *Teseida* follows the *Filostrato*, then the *Teseida* passage is an echo and encapsulation of the earlier work; this would be an early instance of the autocitation that continues throughout Boccaccio's career. Branca's dating has been widely accepted, but others have argued that the *Teseida* is the earlier work, for example Muscetta, *Giovanni Boccaccio* 98 and Natali, "Progetti" 389. In this case we could understand the *Filostrato* as a deliberate expansion of an earlier brief passage. It is also quite possible, of course, that the two poems' periods of composition (or planning) overlapped. I take no position on the relative dating of the two poems, but I think it is quite clear that Boccaccio (at some date) came to think of them as companion pieces.

50. De Man, *Allegories of Reading* 3–5.

51. In Middle English criticism, see for example Coleman, *Medieval Readers and Writers, 1350–1400* (1981); Knight, *Geoffrey Chaucer* (1986); Aers, *Community, Gender, and Individual Identity* (1988); Strohm, *Social Chaucer* (1989); Knapp, *Chaucer and the Social Contest* (1990); Patterson, ed., *Literary Practice and Social Change in Britain, 1380–1530* (1990). The historicist critic who has written most searchingly about the *problem* of history in medieval English literature is Patterson, in his articles and in *Negotiating the Past* (1987), and *Chaucer and the Subject of History* (1991).

Chapter 1

1. De Hamel, *Glossed Books of the Bible and the Origins of the Paris Booktrade* 4–9. See also Lobrichon, "Une nouveauté: les gloses de la Bible." The groundbreaking work on the *Glossa Ordinaria* is of course that of Beryl Smalley: see *The Study of the Bible in the Middle Ages* 46–66. I follow De Hamel (rather than Smalley) in using "Glossa Ordinaria" and "the Gloss" to refer to the glossed Bible no matter which "glosatura" it contains. There is no reliable modern edition of the Gloss. The early printed editions of the *Glossa Ordinaria* which I have seen include only Anselm's Psalm commentary; the Psalter commentary of Peter Lombard appears in *PL* 191.

2. For an excellent brief discussion of the *Glossa Ordinaria* page format in the context of the medieval theory and practice of memory, see Carruthers, *The Book of Memory* 214–18.

3. De Hamel, *Glossed Books* 25–26.

4. Parkes, "The Influence of the Concepts of *Ordinatio* and *Compilatio* on the Development of the Book," Plate IX. For other examples, see De Hamel, *Glossed Books*, Plate 10; Carruthers, *Book of Memory*, Plate 5.

5. Parkes, "The Influence of the Concepts of *Ordinatio* and *Compilatio*" 116.

6. De Hamel, *Glossed Books* 14.

7. Parkes, "The Influence of the Concepts of *Ordinatio* and *Compilatio*" 117, quoting Hugh of St. Victor from *PL* 176.185. Translation mine.

8. Parkes, "The Influence of the Concepts of *Ordinatio* and *Compilatio*" 117.

9. *Convivio* 1.5.6: "conviene questo comento, che è fatto invece di servo a le 'nfrascritte canzoni, esser subietto a quelle in ciascuna sua condizione ed essere conoscente del bisogno del suo signore e a lui obediente" [it is fitting that this

commentary, which is made in the place of a servant to the *canzoni* written below, be subject to them in all its aspects, and be aware of the needs of its lord and obedient to him]. Dante specifically rejects the idea that the commentary might act "a suo senno e a suo volere" [according to its own judgment and its own will]—in that case, the commentary would be a friend rather than a servant to the text, a condition which Dante describes as "disordinazione" [disorder] (1.5.5–6).

10. On medieval "hierarchical thinking," and some of the differences between hierarchies, see Mazzeo, *Medieval Cultural Tradition in Dante's Comedy* ch. 1, "The Medieval Concept of Hierarchy."

11. Augustine, *Confessions*, ed. Skutella and Solignac. Citations will be identified by book, chapter, and paragraph number in the text.

12. See the discussion of time in 11.10–28, which culminates in the image of the speaking of a *canticum*: the psalm is a totality before and after it is recited, but in the recital it becomes a sequence of words passing from expectation to memory (11.28.38).

13. Solignac regards this as an inconsistency, attributable to the fact that the *Confessions* is a free meditation rather than a logical exposition of ideas (*Confessions*, ed. Skutella and Solignac, 632).

14. See also Solignac's note in Augustine, *Confessions*, ed. Skutella and Solignac, 622–29; Solignac stresses both the flexibility of Augustine's free meditation and the overall coherence of his interpretation.

15. Dionysius the Pseudo-Areopagite, *The Ecclesiastical Hierarchy* 1.5, in *The Complete Works*, trans. Luibheid, 199. The other statements in this paragraph can be documented in 5.1 (233–39). I have been guided by Roques, *L'univers dionysien*; see 68–69, 174–75. See also Mazzeo, *Medieval Cultural Tradition* ch. 1. For the medieval Latin translations by John Scotus Erigena and John the Saracene, see Chevallier, ed., *Dionysiaca*.

16. For a concise statement of Pseudo-Dionysius's Christian Neoplatonism, see Roques, *L'univers dionysien* 315–18. Augustine describes his own reading of Neoplatonic texts in *Confessions* 7.9–21; for the Neoplatonism of the *Confessions*, see the Introduction (especially 100–112) and notes of the Skutella and Solignac edition.

17. *Ecclesiastical Hierarchy* 5.7 (*Complete Works* 242).

18. *Ecclesiastical Hierarchy* 1.4 (*Complete Works* 198).

19. Roques, *L'univers dionysien* 210.

20. Parkes, "The Influence of the Concepts of *Ordinatio* and *Compilatio*" 116n.

21. In the Preface to his Psalms commentary, Peter Lombard comes close to saying that David is the *auctor* of the Psalms: he writes that "David autem solius Spiritus sancti instinctu sine omni exteriori adminiculo, suam edidit propheticam" (*PL* 191.55) [David uttered his prophecy with the prompting of the Holy Spirit alone and without any external aid], and he rejects the view that the Psalter had several "scriptores, vel auctores" (*PL* 191.59) [writers, or authors] in favor of the view that David alone composed them. He does not, however, apply the term "auctor" to David. On the authorship of the Psalms and Peter's treatment of this question, see Minnis, *Medieval Theory of Authorship* 43–48; on the later establishment of the idea of human *auctores* for Scripture, see 75–84. Peter Lombard's Preface is translated in Minnis and Scott, eds., *Medieval Literary Theory and Criticism* 105–112; I have

occasionally drawn from this translation. In quoting from Peter Lombard, I omit the (originally marginal) identification of his sources which can be found in Migne; it should be understood that Peter is usually quoting, but my concern here is with what his book says.

22. Bonaventure, *Opera Theologica Selecta* vol. 1, 10.

23. Dante, *Monarchia*, ed. Bruno Nardi, 3.3.9–16. Quotations will be identified parenthetically in the text. Obviously I do not mean to be presenting Dante's entire understanding of *auctoritas* in this paragraph—rather to show that the idea of a gradual descent of *auctoritas* from God to modern humanity was available to him.

24. For a purely visual representation of a complex hierarchy of inspiration and understanding, see the mid-fourteenth-century painting of the Apotheosis of St. Thomas Aquinas in the Church of S. Caterina in Pisa, attributed to a follower of Francesco Traini, reproduced as Plate 84 in Antal, *Florentine Painting and Its Social Background*. In Antal's succinct description (258–59), "The rays, signifying inspiration, ultimately emanate from the crowning feature of the composition, Christ floating in his mandorla. Certain rays lead straight down to the figure of St. Thomas immediately below, who is surrounded by a glory of his own and holds the *Summa contra Gentiles* and others of his works open in his hands. Other rays reach him indirectly by way of St. Paul (Epistles), Moses (Tables of the Law), and the four Evangelists (Gospels), who encircle St. Thomas. These, then, are the paths of Theology, of Divine Inspiration. Other rays lead to Thomas from the heathen philosophers Aristotle and Plato, who are standing on a much lower level and are not touched by any divine ray of light, and from their open books (*Ethics* and *Timaeus* respectively). These rays, which do not, like the others, lead to the crown of St. Thomas' head, but to a lower spot nearer his ear, are the paths of philosophical knowledge. . . . Many rays symbolising instruction lead from the works of Thomas to the world below, represented by the numerous friars (especially Dominicans) and faithful laymen standing on either side of the lower zone."

25. The analogy I am suggesting is related, of course, to the general medieval topos of the Book of the World. On this topos see Curtius, *European Literature and the Latin Middle Ages* ch. 16, "The Book as Symbol," especially 319–26; for two recent discussions, with very different emphases, see Gellrich, *The Idea of the Book in the Middle Ages*, and Demaray, *Dante and the Book of the Cosmos*. My own discussion concerns, however, the form of a single page; the page is literally part of a book, but my point is that it is configured as a model of a much larger Book.

26. De Hamel, *Glossed Books* ch. 4, "The So-Called 'Pontigny' School of Illumination."

27. De Hamel, *Glossed Books* 33; for the last example cited, see Plate 11.

28. De Hamel, *Glossed Books* 25.

29. As it happens, this particular page does describe a hierarchy of God, Church, and humanity, in the comment on 46:4, "subjecit populos nobis; et gentes sub pedibus nostris" [He hath subdued the people under us; and the nations under our feet]. I quote from the text of Migne: "*Subjecit populos nobis*. . . . Loquitur in persona Ecclesiae. Quasi dicat: Et ideo etiam plaudite, quia subjecit populos nobis, id est universali Ecclesiae" (*PL* 191.455) [*He hath subdued the people under us*. . . . He speaks in the person of the Church. As if he said: And therefore applaud indeed,

since he subjects the people to us, that is to the universal Church]. The faithful are placed beneath the Church so that they may be led upward. The commentator adds that "pedes" may be understood as "praedicatores . . . quibus populi subjecti sunt" [preachers, to whom the people are subject].

30. Lobrichon, "Une nouveauté" 111: "appartient au ciel de l'abstraction, apparemment sans date ni lieu."

31. In the rest of this paragraph, and the first sentence of the next, I follow De Hamel, *Glossed Books* ch. 2, "The Layout of the Pages."

32. De Hamel, *Glossed Books* 20.

33. Lobrichon, "Une nouveauté" 98: "Le zèle sacré des copistes juifs de la Torah ne semble pas s'être relâché au point d'introduire des gloses de main d'homme dans l'espace réservé à la Bible." Lobrichon suggests that Western scribes may have been following the method used for classical texts such as Virgil and Ovid.

34. De Ghellinck, "'Pagina' et 'Sacra pagina.'"

35. Similarly Lobrichon, "Une nouveauté" 97: "Une ambition pointe ici, à peine masquée, qui porte les maîtres du XIIe siècle peu à peu au rang d'autorités. Se fait jour ici la conscience d'un nouveau magistère, qui vaut bien celui des docteurs de l'âge héroïque" [An ambition springs here, scarcely masked, which carries the masters of the twelfth century little by little to the rank of authorities. What forces its way through, here, is the consciousness of a new magisterial authority, which matches that of the doctors of the heroic age]. A twelfth-century formulation that captures the manuscript page's mixture of ambition and self-abasement is Bernard of Chartres's oft-quoted statement that "we are as dwarfs perched upon the shoulders of giants"; see Miller, *Poetic License* 9–20.

36. See especially Chenu, "Auctor, actor, autor," and Ascoli, "The Vowels of Authority."

37. On the glossing of Justinian, see Hermann Kantorowicz, "Note on the Development of the Gloss to the Justinian and the Canon Law," in Smalley, *Study of the Bible* 52–55.

38. Smalley, *Study of the Bible* 64; similarly Lobrichon, "Une nouveauté" 110. The development which I sketch out in the next two paragraphs is a secondary theme in Smalley, passim; she does not emphasize it, because her topic throughout is the way the Bible itself was studied, but it is clearly discernible in her richly detailed history. Especially interesting is the reaction of Roger Bacon against the trend: he objects to those who give commentators the authority which ought to be reserved for Scripture (Smalley 175), just as he objects to the substitution of the *Sentences* for the Bible as the main object of study at the University of Paris (Chenu, *Toward Understanding Saint Thomas* 266n.).

39. Smalley, *Study of the Bible* 66–82; Chenu, *Toward Understanding Saint Thomas* 85–88.

40. Chenu, *Toward Understanding Saint Thomas* 264–66.

41. Bonaventure, *Opera Theologica Selecta* vol. 1, 12; Bonaventure's entire discussion of *auctoritas* is translated in Minnis and Scott, eds., *Medieval Literary Theory and Criticism* 228–30.

42. I describe the form of this commentary somewhat more fully in Chapter 2.

43. So Chenu, *Toward Understanding Saint Thomas* 272.

44. Chenu, *Toward Understanding Saint Thomas* 299.

45. Chenu, *Toward Understanding Saint Thomas* 300.

46. Boutière and Schutz, eds., *Biographies des troubadours*. For a good secondary account, see Poe, *From Poetry to Prose in Old Provençal*.

47. Bird, "The Canzone d'Amore of Cavalcanti According to the Commentary of Dino del Garbo." For another discussion, see Shaw, *Guido Cavalcanti's Theory of Love* 149–63.

48. On *divisio textus* as the form of the *Convivio*, see below, Chapter 2.

49. Ascoli, "The Vowels of Authority."

50. For a good brief treatment of the medieval thinking on what we call "lyric," see Edwards, *Ratio and Invention*, Interchapter 1, "Medieval Lyric."

51. A commonplace; for its expression in the commentary of Peter Lombard, see *PL* 191.55: "Dicitur quoque Psalterium, quod nomen accepit a quodam musico instrumento, quod Hebraice nablum, Graece psalterium . . . Latine organum dicitur, quod est decachordum et a superiori reddit sonum per manuum tactum. Ab illo autem instrumento ad litteram ideo nominatur liber iste, quia ad vocem illius instrumenti David decantabat psalmos ante arcam in tabernaculo Domini" [It is also called the Psalter, taking its name from a certain musical instrument called *nablus* in Hebrew, *psalterium* in Greek, *organum* in Latin, which has ten strings and gives forth a sound when touched by the hand from above. This book is named from that instrument, in the literal sense, because David sang forth psalms to the sound of that instrument before the ark in the tabernacle of the Lord].

52. See Introduction, 12 and n. 34.

53. As we shall see in the next chapter, one of the first duties of the commentator is to specify this historical context.

54. *In Psalmos Davidis Expositio* 148. The Psalms' distinctive mode does not place a limitation on what they can express: "quidquid in aliis libris praedictis modis dicitur, hic ponitur per modum laudis et orationis" [whatever is said in other books in the aforesaid modes, is posited here in the mode of praise and prayer]. The prologue to Thomas Aquinas's commentary (from which I quote here) is discussed in Minnis, *Medieval Theory of Authorship* 86–90.

55. "De ordine quoque psalmorum, qui a serie historiae discordant quaeri solet, quare scilicet non sunt eo ordine dispositi quo compositi" (*PL* 191.59) [Concerning the order of psalms that are out of line with the sequence of history, it is customary to ask why they are not disposed in the order in which they were composed]. The Psalms were arranged by Esdras, inspired by the Holy Spirit (*PL* 191.60).

56. "[David] alludat diversis historiis, tamen ex eis nil didicit, sed in eis quod per Spiritum sanctum ante cognoverat, figurari intellexit" (*PL* 191.58–59) [David alludes to diverse histories, but he did not learn anything from them, but understood that that which he already knew from the Holy Spirit was figured in them].

57. "Materia itaque hujus libri est totus Christus, scilicet sponsus et sponsa" (*PL* 191.59) [The subject-matter of this book is the whole Christ, that is the bridegroom and the bride]; "in hoc libro consummatio est totius theologicae paginae; hic enim describuntur praemia bonorum, supplicia malorum, rudimenta incipientium, progressus proficientium, perfectio pervenientium, vita activorum, speculatio

contemplativorum" (*PL* 191.57) [in this book is the sum of the whole field of theology; for here are described the rewards of the good, the punishments of the wicked, the first steps of beginners, the progress of those who advance, the perfection of those who arrive, the life of the active, the speculation of the contemplative].

58. Barolini, *Dante's Poets* 275–79.

59. As De Robertis notes in his edition of the *Vita Nuova*, this phrase echoes several scriptural passages, including Ps. 50:16–17; I shall discuss it further in Chapter 3.

60. *Trattatello in laude di Dante*, ed. Ricci, 480 (prima redazione, 174); cited in Minnis, *Medieval Theory of Authorship* 215.

61. I shall return to this subject briefly at the end of Chapter 4.

62. Pseudo-Thomas Aquinas, *Commentum super Librum Boetii de Consolatu Philosophico* 4: "Boetius utitur in hoc libro tam prosa quam metro . . . Sicut enim potio curativa quae amara est, delectabilius sumitur, si fuerit aliqua dulcedine permixta, sic rationes philosophiae in prosa traditae libentius a Boetio suscipiantur si fuerint jucunditate metri dulcoratae. Et ideo Boetius nunc utitur metro, nunc prosa; quia alternatis uti delectabilius est."

63. Similarly Gybbon-Monypenny, "Guillaume de Machaut's Erotic 'Autobiography'" 139: "the essence of the *prosimetrum* is that prose and verse alternate in a continuous flow of narrative or discussion and the verse cannot stand on its own as independent poetry."

Chapter 2

1. *Vita Nuova*, ed. De Robertis, 13.

2. Boccaccio writes, in his life of Dante, "Egli primieramente, duranti ancora le lagrime della morte della sua Beatrice, quasi nel ventesimosesto anno compose in uno volumetto, il quale egli intitolò *Vita nova*, certe operette, sì come sonetti e canzoni, in diversi tempi davanti in rima fatte da lui, maravigliosamente belle; di sopra da ciascuna partitamente e ordinatamente scrivendo le cagioni che a quelle fare l'avea[n] mosso, e di dietro ponendo le divisioni delle precedenti opere" (*Trattatello in laude di Dante*, ed. Ricci, 481 [prima redazione, 175]) [He first, still during his tears for the death of his Beatrice, in about his twenty-sixth year, arranged in a little volume, which he entitled *Vita Nuova*, certain little works, such as sonnets and *canzoni*, made in verse by him at diverse times in the past, marvelously beautiful; writing above each one, separately and in order, the reasons which had moved him to write them, and placing afterward the divisions of the preceding works]. Again in the next paragraph Boccaccio refers to the volume as "questa compilazione" [this compilation]. (We shall see that Boccaccio provides a more complex comment in his manuscript copy.) Early manuscripts almost always group the *Vita Nuova* with miscellaneous lyrics by Dante and others; see the register of manuscripts in Barbi's 1932 edition, xix–lxxxviii.

3. So Vallone, *La prosa della "Vita Nuova"* 1.

4. The movement "from lyric to narrative temporality" (93) is a declared topic of the second half of *The Body of Beatrice*; Harrison's evaluation of the two

modes is concisely suggested by two chapter titles, "Beyond the Lyric" (ch. 6) and "The Narrative Breakthrough" (ch. 7). Further quotations from this text will be identified parenthetically. It should go without saying that I am here presenting only one aspect of Harrison's complex argument, which should be consulted. Another important recent critique of Singleton's *Essay* is Menocal, *Writing in Dante's Cult of Truth* ch. 1, "Synchronicity: Death and the *Vita nuova*," especially 13–18.

5. Durling and Martinez, *Time and the Crystal* ch. 1, "Early Experiments: *Vita nuova* 19." Although this reading is clearly much more than a revival of Singleton, Singleton is mentioned with approval on 55 and 64.

6. For Isidore of Seville, indefinite extendibility is part of the meaning of "prosa": "Alii prosam aiunt dictam ab eo, quod sit profusa, vel ab eo, quod spatiosius proruat et excurrat, nullo sibi termino praefinito" (*Etymologiae*, 1.38.1) [Others say prose is so called because it is poured out, or because it rushes forth and runs out more expansively, with no limit fixed for it in advance].

7. Zumthor, *Langue, texte, énigme* 186: "La narrativité de la chanson est ainsi purement virtuelle."

8. On the *ars* of versification as an atemporal constraint on speech, prescribing its own order, see Augustine, *Confessions* 3.7.14: "cantabam carmina et non mihi licebat ponere pedem quemlibet ubilibet, sed in alio atque alio metro aliter atque aliter et in uno aliquo versu non omnibus locis eundem pedem; et ars ipsa, qua canebam, non habebat aliud alibi, sed omnia simul" [I sang songs, and I was not at liberty to place each foot wherever I wanted, but in one meter in one place and in another meter elsewhere; and in any single verse not the same foot in all places; and this very art, by which I sang, did not have different things in different places but had all things at once].

9. The two important exceptions are both very recent: Harrison, *The Body of Beatrice* ch. 1, "Dante's Dream," and Menocal, *Writing in Dante's Cult of Truth* 38–50. These accounts are quite different from mine, but usefully complementary.

10. Nolan, "The *Vita Nuova*: Dante's Book of Revelation" 59.

11. For some interpretive purposes, it would be necessary to maintain a terminological distinction between the various Dantes of the *Vita Nuova*: the protagonist(s) of the lyrics, the speaker(s) of the lyrics, the protagonist of the autobiographical prose, the implied author of the *libello*, the real historical author, and perhaps others. I use the name "Dante" for each of these persons, in part because Dante himself insists on the continuity between his various roles. In the dream of Chapter 3, for example, Dante's utter passivity makes it difficult to distinguish between the man who sees Amore enter his room and the man who dreams that he sees it.

12. Singleton, *Essay* 22.

13. Again, the notable exception is Harrison, who stresses the complex differences within the work and argues against efforts to explain (away) its difficulty.

14. All critics agree that "proemio" must refer to the first chapter, which reads: "In quella parte del libro de la mia memoria dinanzi a la quale poco si potrebbe leggere, si trova una rubrica la quale dice: *Incipit vita nova*. Sotto la quale rubrica io trovo scritte le parole le quali è mio intendimento d'assemplare in questo libello; e se

non tutte, almeno la loro sentenzia" [In that part of the book of my memory before which little could be read, there is a rubric which says: *Incipit vita nova*. Under which rubric I find written the words which it is my intention to assemble in this little book; and if not all of them, at least their meaning].

15. An abbreviated survey. J. E. Shaw, who devotes an essay to the question, provides what is still, I think, the most plausible solution. In the proem, Dante stated that he was transcribing from his own memory, and his statement at 28.2 "means that he had no memory of the circumstances of the death of Beatrice, and that, owing to the suddenness and shocking character of the event, he had no memory of his own feelings on becoming aware of it" (*Essays on the Vita Nuova* 151). Singleton dismisses this explanation as ploddingly literal-minded and at the same time illogical: Dante *must* remember Beatrice's death, since the other two reasons he offers presuppose that he could write about it if he chose to (*Essay* 31–32). I am not convinced that this demolishes Shaw's reading: perhaps Dante knows enough about the event to write about it, but derives his knowledge from hearsay rather than from his own memory. This may seem over-complex; in any case, Shaw's solution has not found wide acceptance. Singleton's own view is that if Dante wrote about Beatrice's death he would be writing "here and now" rather than merely transcribing as he has promised (*Essay* 32). Since Singleton does not explain why Beatrice's death should differ, in this respect, from all the other events in the book, his account remains confusingly incomplete. De Robertis mentions and rejects other possible readings and offers his own: "In realtà la morte di Beatrice non tocca la *Vita Nuova* in altro senso: che nulla è veramente accaduto, che il rinnovamento è interamente compiuto" [In reality the death of Beatrice does not touch the *Vita Nuova* in another sense: that nothing has truly happened, that the renewal is entirely accomplished] (*Vita Nuova*, note ad. loc.; more fully in *Il libro della "Vita Nuova"* 160–61). He does not say how a reader will know this from rereading the proem, and it hardly seems fair to say that Beatrice's death "non tocca la *Vita Nuova*."

16. All translations from the *Divine Comedy* are those of Singleton.

17. Freccero, "Medusa: The Letter and the Spirit"; quoted phrase from 119.

18. A similar moment in the purgatorial Valley of Princes suggests even more explicitly that the allegorical veil of the poem may vary in thickness: "Aguzza qui, lettor, ben li occhi al vero, / ché 'l velo è ora ben tanto sottile, / certo che 'l trapassar dentro è leggero" (*Purgatorio* 8.19–21) [Reader, here sharpen well your eyes to the truth, for the veil is now indeed so thin that certainly to pass within is easy].

19. Rajna, "Lo schema della *Vita Nuova*."

20. Rajna, "Per le 'divisioni' della *Vita Nuova*."

21. Rajna, "Per le 'divisioni'" 114: "Volgiamo ora un momento lo sguardo allo schema tutto intero della *Vita Nuova*. I due suoi elementi costitutivi provengono da origini addirittura opposte. L'uno viene dalla giulleria, dalle corti, dai tripudii: l'altro dal mondo dei dotti, dalle fredde sale delle scuole, dalla vita severa. Ma tutto nella mente di Dante si concilia, tutto produce armonia."

22. Picone, "Strutture poetiche e strutture prosastiche nella *Vita Nuova*" (I quote from the title).

23. D'Andrea, "La struttura della *Vita Nuova*" 25: "l'interferenza di due prospettive."

24. Harrison, *The Body of Beatrice* ix.

25. Vallone, "Apparizione e disdegno di Beatrice" 35: "opera nata tutta insieme."

26. *Vita Nuova*, ed. De Robertis, 5: "convocazione e concentrazione di modelli."

27. The connection between the *Vita Nuova* and the *vidas* and *razos*, though it is sometimes questioned, has been reasserted many times, e.g. by Zumthor, *Langue, texte, énigme* 177–78.

28. See, more recently, D'Andrea, "La struttura della *Vita Nuova*: le divisioni delle rime."

29. Dante's formal debt to Boethius is already generally supposed by the time of Rajna, though he argues against it ("Lo schema," 161). It has been asserted often since then.

30. D'Andrea, "La struttura della *Vita Nuova*" 41–47.

31. A commonplace, but see for example *Vita Nuova*, ed. De Robertis, 13.

32. Mazzaro, *The Figure of Dante* 28 and 62.

33. Singleton, *Essay* ch. 2, "The Book of Memory."

34. Mazzaro, *The Figure of Dante* 27–50; Courcelle, *Les confessions de saint Augustin dans la tradition littéraire* 330.

35. Three traditions "particularly useful to Dante" named by Nolan, "The *Vita Nuova*: Dante's Book of Revelation" 51. On the importance of Guido Cavalcanti's poetry for the *Vita Nuova*, see Mazzotta, "The Light of Venus," especially 153–55; Harrison, *The Body of Beatrice* ch. 4, "The Ghost of Guido Cavalcanti."

36. De Robertis, *Il libro della "Vita Nuova"*: for Cicero, see 21–24; Brunetto, 208–31; Andreas, 44–53; Psalms, 102–7. On Andreas see also Picone, "Modelli e struttura nella *Vita Nuova*" 51. On the Psalms see also Scott, "Dante's 'Sweet New Style' and the *Vita Nuova*."

37. Moleta, "The *Vita Nuova* as a Lyric Narrative."

38. Bossy, "Cyclical Composition in Guiraut Riquier's Book of Poems" especially 287–91; see also Bertolucci, "Libri e canzonieri d'autore nel Medioevo."

39. A. Marigo, *Mistica e scienza nella Vita Nuova di Dante* (1914), cited in Mazzaro, *The Figure of Dante* 76; Singleton, *Essay* 105–9.

40. Branca, "Poetica del rinnovamento e tradizione agiografica nella *Vita Nuova*."

41. Picone, "Rito e *narratio* nella *Vita Nuova*"; Mazzaro, *The Figure of Dante* 104–11.

42. Mazzaro, *The Figure of Dante* 51–70.

43. *Desires*: Amore assigns Dante's heart to a (feigned) "novo piacere" [new pleasure] at 9.11; Dante receives "uno spiritel novo d'amore" [a new little spirit of love] for the Donna Gentile at 38.10, and "intelligenza nova" [new intelligence] about his love for Beatrice at 41.10. *Mental and physical states*: Dante presents a ludicrous "figura nova" [strange or new figure] to a group of ladies at 14.11; this is described as a "nuova trasfigurazione" [new transfiguration] at 15.1. His nightmare is a "nova fantasia" [new fantasy] at 23.18. He experiences a "nuova condizione" [new condition] at 24.2 and again at 38.1. *Poetic project*: he takes up "matera nuova" [new matter] at 17.1 and 17.2, and again at 30.1. The rubric "Incipit vita nova" (1.1) [Here begins the New Life] may belong to more than one of these categories.

44. Again, her appearance as she smiles is a "novo miracolo" [new miracle] at

21.4. This note and the last, and the paragraph they depend on, contain all uses of "nuovo" in the *Vita Nuova* listed in the E. S. Sheldon *Concordanza*.

45. The modern theoretical opposition between metonymy and metaphor is relevant here. Roman Jakobson and others associate metonymy with prose narrative and metaphor with lyric poetry. (See Jakobson, "Two Aspects of Language.") In Chapter 3, Dante slides metonymically between his various roles as dream protagonist, dreamer, waking protagonist, and autobiographer, while Beatrice has two distinct roles, her dream representation functioning as a metaphoric translation of her real identity.

46. D'Andrea, "La struttura della *Vita Nuova*" 26–30; "si può dire che la *Vita Nuova* continua ad esser letta come se le divisioni non esistessero" (30).

47. D'Andrea tells the story succinctly (26–28); a complete description of the manuscripts and their filiation is available in Barbi's 1932 edition.

48. Singleton errs when he states that Boccaccio "simply omitted" the divisions (*Essay* 46). Critics occasionally repeat this error.

49. In this quotation and the next I cite Boccaccio's text as it appears (aptly, in a footnote) in the Barbi edition of the *Vita Nuova*, xv–xvi. Barbi also includes a facsimile of the manuscript page containing the note, after cccix. The only critical discussion of Boccaccio's note known to me is that of Susan Noakes, in *Timely Reading* 80–87; my translation is only lightly modified from hers (83).

50. Similarly Boccaccio's account of the *Vita Nuova* in his life of Dante privileges the lyrics; see n. 2 above.

51. The rest of Boccaccio's note is worth quoting. "La seconda ragione è che, secondo che io ho già più volte udito ragionare a persone degne di fede, avendo Dante nella sua giovanezza composto questo libello, e poi essendo col tempo nella scienza e nelle operazioni cresciuto, si vergognava avere fatto questo, parendogli opera troppo puerile; e tra l'altre cose di che si dolea d'averlo fatto, si ramaricava d'avere inchiuse le divisioni nel testo, forse per quella medesima ragione che muove me; là onde io non potendolo negli altri emendare, in questo che scritto ho, n'ho voluto sodisfare l'appetito de l'autore." [The second reason is that, according to what I have several times heard recounted by persons worthy of credit, Dante, having written this little book in his youth, and then having with time grown in knowledge and practical experience, became ashamed of having done this, for it seemed to him too childish a work; and, among the other things he lamented having done, he regretted having included the divisions in the text, perhaps for the same reason that motivates me; whereas I, not being able to remedy the other things, in this copy that I have written I have wished to satisfy the desire of the author.] (Again I adapt the translation of Noakes.) The status of the *later* intentions of an author is a vexed question in the theory of editing even now. This "second reason" conveys, more clearly than the first, the basic attitude of disdain that has characterized later treatments of the *divisioni*. On the other hand, one might argue that this line of reasoning establishes the *divisioni* as the truly characteristic element of the *Vita Nuova*: Dante regretted the whole work, and what he *most* regretted was the inclusion of the *divisioni* in the text. I think the *divisioni* probably play a larger part in the reading experience of most readers—a distinctive and perhaps annoying element in the total flavor of the work—than is reflected in the criticism.

52. *Vita Nuova*, ed. De Robertis, 13.

53. I have suggested that the *Vita Nuova* constructs an analogy between its two main characters and its two primary kinds of writing. Here I would add an optional, marginal feature to my internal model for the form of the work. As a mediating force of uncertain textual status, the *divisioni* correspond to Amore. Amore is the mediator who brings together Dante and Beatrice and holds them together in various mediated relationships, and he appears, enigmatically, both as a divinity and as a figure of speech, vanishing after being revealed as "uno accidente in sustanzia" (25.1) [an accident in a substance] in Chapter 25.

54. D'Andrea makes a somewhat similar claim, arguing that one function of the *divisioni* is to work against the transparent expressiveness of the poems and bring them into the enigmatic continuity of the *libello*; thus their inexpressiveness is deliberate and useful. "Le divisioni, con il loro linguaggio scolastico, *scientifico*, con la loro aria di precisione, con la sottigliezza e la simmetria delle loro distinzioni, con la loro stessa pretesa ḍi chiarezza . . . riescono ad alimentare l'allusività, le volute ambiguità, gli studiati silenzi del libello" ("La struttura della *Vita Nuova*" 54) [The divisions, with their scholastic, *scientific* language, with their air of precision, with the subtlety and symmetry of their distinctions, with their very claim of clarity . . . succeed in feeding the allusiveness, the willed ambiguity, the studied silences of the *libello*]. A related argument appears in a brief but provocative 1957 article by Elias L. Rivers, "Dante at Dividing Sonnets." In the *Vita Nuova*, Dante "forged a new poem . . . To this end, [the lyrics'] autonomous individuality had to be violated; by division and abstraction they were, partially at least, assimilated into the larger whole" (293). The *divisioni* are able to accomplish this because they are "anti-poetic, not, as Professor Singleton has shown, with respect to the *Vita Nuova* as a whole, but with respect to the single, the supposedly individual poems" (293).

55. Rajna, "Per le 'divisioni'" 114: "dal mondo dei dotti, dalle fredde sale delle scuole, dalla vita severa."

56. Vossler, quoted in MacLennan, "Autocomentario en Dante y comentarismo latino" 82: "l'amaro *baculus* del maestro di scuola."

57. Rajna, "Per le 'divisioni'" 113: "esempio cospicuo."

58. Singleton, *Essay* 134.

59. D'Andrea, "La struttura della *Vita Nuova*" 34: "seguono lo schema comune ai commenti scolastici del XIII secolo." For D'Andrea's discussion of the Albertus Magnus *Sentences* commentary, see 34–37; for the Pseudo-Thomas Aquinas *Consolation* commentary, 42–47. In the course of his review of other critics, D'Andrea convincingly dismisses (31–38) a claim made by De Robertis that Brunetto Latini's *Rettorica* is an especially important model for Dante's divisions.

60. Singleton, *Essay* 134. I have restored a sentence that Singleton omits. Singleton cites the Quaracchi edition of the *Opera Omnia*; the same text appears in Bonaventure, *Opera Theologica Selecta*, vol. 2, 8.

61. I have silently altered Migne's punctuation to clarify the structure of the *divisio*.

62. The four books together make up one work, of course, but the *divisio* of the work is somewhat ambiguous. Bonaventure notes that Peter separates the books in two different ways (1–3 and 4, or 1 and 2–4; *Opera Theologica Selecta* vol. 1, 19),

and in his own proem he associates the four books with the four meanings of a scriptural verse (vol. 1, 3–5). Within each of the four books the structure of divisions is univocal and explicit.

63. Bonaventure, *Opera Theologica Selecta* vol. 2, 506.

64. Bonaventure, *Opera Theologica Selecta* vol. 2, 8.

65. Occasionally, a thirteenth-century commentary will distinguish between *divisio textus* and *expositio textus*. For example, in the *Sentences* commentary of Albertus Magnus, the first "Divisio textus" is preceded by an "Expositio textus," which elucidates certain difficult phrases (14). Later in this volume, however, an "Expositio" appears only when no division is necessary, and the "Divisiones" stand alone. The expository function of the *divisio textus* is made clear by a phrase that sometimes ends the "Divisio": "Per hanc divisionem patet sententia" [Through this division the meaning is evident] (116; similarly at, e.g., 103, 136).

66. Pseudo-Thomas Aquinas, *Commentum super Librum Boetii* 4.

67. See above, 42.

68. About half of the poems resist subdivision. These are shorter poems, which the commentator describes as containing one or more metaphors or *exempla* in support of the larger argument; the commentator provides for these a running comment rather than a systematic division. The other poems are treated as passages *of* argument.

69. Harry V. Jaffa describes "Thomas' method of dividing up the text of the *Ethics*" in terms that apply equally well to many other thirteenth-century commentaries: "These divisions might be compared to a modern analytical table of contents, yet their significance is much greater. . . . The outline that Thomas follows in the course of his interpretation is an integral part of that interpretation; or, stated somewhat differently, it is the form of the commentary, and is in itself an exemplification of the principles underlying the commentary as a whole" (*Thomism and Aristotelianism* 35).

70. There is, of course, prefatory discussion of the *Liber psalmorum* as a whole. "Consistit autem liber iste in centum et quinquaginta psalmis, non praeter altioris significantiae rationem" (*PL* 191.56) [This book consists of one hundred and fifty psalms, not without a reason of higher significance]. The number of Psalms, 150, is a composite allegory, containing either an eighty and a seventy or else three fifties. For Peter, though, these are not structural divisions of the Book of Psalms. The division of the Psalter into five books, approved by Jerome, is rejected (*PL* 191.58). Rather the Psalter is a single object, like the musical instrument also called *psalterium* (*PL* 191.55); in the first stage of division it has one hundred and fifty parts. In the commentary, the number of a Psalm is sometimes interpreted allegorically: e.g., on Psalm 50, "est iste psalmus quartus in ordine poenitentialium, et in ordine psalmorum, quinquagesimus est, pro modo jubilei, quia hic est psalmus remissionis" (*PL* 191.484) [this Psalm is fourth in the order of the penitential psalms, and fiftieth in the order of the Psalms, in the manner of jubilee, since this is a Psalm of remission]—but there is no reminder that Psalm 50 marks the end of the first third of the book.

71. So, in Peter Lombard's discussion of Psalm 3, at verse 5: "*Ego dormivi*. . . . Hic est secunda pars hujus psalmi, ubi ostenditur finis rei, id est passionis" (*PL* 191.79 [*I have slept*. . . . Here is the second part of this Psalm, where is set forth the

end of the matter, that is of the Passion]. There is no other reference, in the running commentary, to the *partes*.

72. D'Andrea, "La struttura della *Vita Nuova*" 39–40. The four digressions concern Beatrice's *saluto* (*Vita Nuova* 11), the propriety of addressing one's own poem (12.17), the figure of Amore (25), and the number nine (29).

73. They would not, though, be called *soliloquia*, since *soliloquia* are inspired directly by the Holy Spirit without the mediation of dreams or visions (*PL* 191.58). The possible exception here is "Donne ch'avete intelletto d'amore," the first line of which comes to Dante mysteriously and without mediation (19.2).

74. Scott, "Dante's 'Sweet New Style' and the *Vita Nuova*" 102; reference and translation added.

75. De Robertis, *Il Libro della "Vita Nuova"* 102–7; "il tema della lode beatificante" (104).

76. Part of the familiar distich on the fourfold sense of Scripture; see Minnis, *Medieval Theory of Authorship* 34.

77. See de Lubac, *Exégèse médiévale*, Part 1, vol. 2, ch. 7: "Le fondement de l'histoire."

78. I treat this latter subject very generally toward the end of Chapter 1; it deserves much more detailed consideration.

79. Writing of the "obtuse" Jews, Paul writes, "usque in hodiernum enim diem, id ipsum velamen in lectione veteris testamenti manet non revelatum quoniam in Christo evacuatur" (2 Cor. 3:14) [For, until this present day, the selfsame veil, in the reading of the old testament, remaineth not taken away (because in Christ it is made void)].

80. Here—as he discards the David story—Peter may seem to differ from later Psalm commentators, closer to Dante's own time. As Beryl Smalley and A. J. Minnis have shown, biblical commentators in the thirteenth and fourteenth centuries manifest an increasing interest in establishing and exploring the particulars of the "historical" or "literal" sense of the Old Testament; the commentary of Peter Lombard is typically twelfth-century in the haste with which it moves beyond the historical narrative. Still, the structure of signification does not essentially change: the Psalm refers in the first instance to the life of David, and the events in David's life refer to Christian truth. What is new in the thirteenth and fourteenth centuries, as Minnis demonstrates, is an Aristotelian model of multiple causes that allows the human author of Scripture to be understood as an "efficient cause"; this idea, combined with the typological understanding of Old Testament history as both concretely true and figurally significant, encouraged commentators to dwell on the literal. See Smalley, *The Study of the Bible in the Middle Ages*, esp. 281–355; Minnis, *Medieval Theory of Authorship* 73–112.

81. Singleton, *Essay* 52; further quotations will be identified in the text.

82. Singleton, *Essay* 20–24 and passim.

83. In this respect, then, Singleton resembles a thirteenth- or fourteenth-century commentator more than he resembles Peter Lombard; see n. 80.

84. Again, "We are always led back to the fact that the little world of the *Vita Nuova* (without the prose it would not be a little world) is open at the top. There, at the top, God's light enters" (101).

85. Harrison, *The Body of Beatrice* 4–13.

86. Patterson, *Negotiating the Past* 34.

87. Singleton, *Essay* 46: "to the contemplative eye of man in the Middle Ages the world revealed an order and a harmony which it was not possible that it should not have, having the Creator that it had; . . . the world might even be seen as a book written by God, because like that other book of God, the Bible, the creation was addressed to man. In either case, man is the reader. The Book of the World is written for him."

Chapter 3

1. The first sustained sustained treatment of the *meaning* of division in the *Vita Nuova*, to my knowledge, is the 1990 essay by Durling and Martinez (*Time and the Crystal* ch. 1, "Early Experiments"). I mentioned this essay briefly at the beginning of the previous chapter and shall return to it somewhat more fully below. My own findings overlap in important ways with those of Durling and Martinez, as I shall make clear, but it is worth noting that we arrived at our findings independently; my discussion of the *Vita Nuova* was drafted before the Durling-Martinez book appeared.

2. According to the Sheldon concordance, forms of "divisione" and "dividere" appear 47 times in the *Vita Nuova*; in every case but two (31.13, 38.5), the reference is to the *divisioni* of the poems. Another key term from the *divisioni* appears nearly as often outside them: "parte." (Of 105 occurrences in the text, 42 by my count fall outside the *divisioni*.) "Parte" is of course a common word in any case, but its frequency in the *Vita Nuova* supports a general correspondence between the parts of Dante's poems and the parts of his lived world: the places he inhabits (e.g. 3.1), the sections of his Book of Memory (1.1), and his own physical and mental regions (e.g., 2.6). The aim of this section is to establish and explore this correspondence more systematically.

3. Macrobius, *I Saturnali*, ed. and trans. Marinone, 1.15.17, p. 226.

4. On "division" as a Neoplatonist term, see Durling and Martinez, *Time and the Crystal* 54.

5. In describing the seamless coat, Peter echoes John 19.23: "Erat autem tunica inconsutilis, desuper contexta per totum" [Now the coat was without seam, woven from the top throughout].

6. Minnis, *Medieval Theory of Authorship* 122–23. Sometimes "modus probativus et improbativus" replaces "modus collectivus."

7. Minnis, *Medieval Theory of Authorship* 122. The Latin text is quoted in Parkes, "The Influence of the Concepts of *Ordinatio* and *Compilatio*" 119: "talis modus debet esse in humanis scientiis, quia apprehensio veritatis secundum humanam rationem explicatur per divisiones, definitiones, et ratiocinationes."

8. Gilby, *Barbara Celarent: A Description of Scholastic Dialectic* ch. 20, "Division."

9. *Summa Theologiae* Pt. 1 Q. 85 Art. 5. The two complementary processes are more often called "compositio" and "resolutio"; Thomas uses "divisio" as a synonym for "resolutio," as in the passage cited, but John Scotus Erigena and Albert

the Great had used "divisio" as a synonym for "compositio." Even within this theological tradition, "divisio" is an omnipresent but slippery term. See Régis, "Analyse et synthèse dans l'oeuvre de saint Thomas."

10. Green, "Hugo of St. Victor: *De Tribus Maximis Circumstantiis Gestorum*" 489–90: "dividendo et distinguendo imprimis librum per psalmos deinde psalmum per versus, tantam prolixitatem ad tantum compendium et brevitatem redegi"; "memoria . . . semper gaudet et brevitate in spatio et paucitate in numero." Translation adapted from Mary Carruthers, *The Book of Memory*, Appendix A, 263. I am grateful to Mary Carruthers for calling this text to my attention and sharing with me her translation when it was still unpublished.

11. Rouse and Rouse, "*Statim invenire*: Schools, Preachers, and New Attitudes to the Page."

12. There are two important recent discussions of this: Allen, *The Ethical Poetic of the Later Middle Ages* ch. 3, "Poetic disposition and the forma tractatus," and Minnis, *Medieval Theory of Authorship* 145–59.

13. Quoted in Minnis, *Medieval Theory of Authorship* 149.

14. This paraphrase combines elements of the two chapters in which "modus legendi in dividendo constat" appears: Hugh of St. Victor, *Didascalicon*, ed. Buttimer, 3.9 and 6.12. Jerome Taylor translates "legendi" in these chapters with the phrase "expounding a text," and it should be remembered that "legere" could have this strong force; but it also means "read" in the broader sense. In *Vita Nuova* criticism, D'Andrea ("La struttura della *Vita Nuova*" 31) cites Hugh's phrase and notes that it has been cited by other critics discussing the *divisioni*.

15. Minnis, *Medieval Theory of Authorship* 149. Emphasis mine. Minnis adds that "in this case the development, and indeed the sophistication, of the descriptive vocabulary lagged far behind that of the techniques to which it referred."

16. Paré, Brunet, and Tremblay, *La renaissance du XIIe siècle* 119: "Le procédé essentiel de l'enseignement, comme d'ailleurs de l'étude personnelle, est la *divisio*. 'Modus legendi in dividendo constat.' Il est assez difficile de voir ce qu'entend Hugue de Saint-Victor par cette investigation (dividendo investigat), dont le premier acte semble l'analyse morcelée du texte dans son agencement grammatical et logique (partitio), mais qui se développe en une recherche spéculative débordant l'exégèse textuelle. *Dividere*, c'est l'oeuvre propre de l'esprit humain, de la 'raison,' qui descend de l'universel au particulier . . ."

17. Allen, *Ethical Poetic* 138.

18. In the *Rhetorica ad Herennium* once attributed to Cicero, the sections of a speech are *exordium*, *narratio*, *divisio*, *confirmatio*, *confutatio*, *conclusio*. "Divisio est per quam aperimus quid conveniat, quid in controversia sit, et per quam exponimus quibus de rebus simus acturi" (1.3.4) [The division is that through which we open up what is agreed upon and what is contested, and through which we explain what matters we intend to take up].

19. Charland, *Artes Praedicandi* 150–63; for *divisio intra* and *extra*, see 162.

20. Robert of Basevorn, *Forma Praedicandi* ch. 19–20, 33, 39. The Latin text appears in Charland, *Artes Praedicandi* 231–323; an English translation (trans. Leopold Krul) in Murphy, ed., *Three Medieval Rhetorical Arts* 109–215. "Dividere" becomes synonymous with "dilatare" in the fifteenth-century *De divisione thematis* of Simon

Alcok—a "tractatus de modo dividendi thema, pro materia sermonis dilatanda" [treatise on the mode of dividing themes, for expanding the materials of a speech] (Boynton, "Simon Alcok on Expanding the Sermon"; quoted phrase from 206).

21. For a medieval division of division, in Raoul de Longchamp's commentary on the *Anticlaudianus* of Alanus de Insulis, see Allen, *Ethical Poetic* 127–28. This passage, like Allen's chapter, deals only with the positive, logical kinds of division—as Durling and Martinez, for their part, deal only with Neoplatonic division.

22. A similar claim has been made by Durling and Martinez in their analysis of one chapter of the *Vita Nuova*; once again, I postpone a discussion of their important reading.

23. De Robertis mentions (*Vita Nuova*, note ad loc.) that some readers have taken "quella" to mean Death, but he convincingly dismisses this reading.

24. Similarly, Dante says "io temo forte non lo cor si schianti" (36.4) [I fear greatly that my heart may split] when his eyes are torn between gazing on the Donna Gentile and weeping for Beatrice.

25. See Chapter 2, n. 43.

26. See Roland Greene's eloquent discussion of this passage, *Post-Petrarchism* 39–41.

27. *Confessions* 11.15.20.

28. On the Neoplatonic "metaphysics of light" in the *Convivio* and *Paradiso*, see Mazzeo, *Medieval Cultural Tradition in Dante's Comedy* ch. 2, "The Light-Metaphysics Tradition," and ch. 3, "Light Metaphysics in the Works of Dante."

29. Singleton, *Essay* 44.

30. Singleton, *Essay* 79, 80; see Singleton ch. 4.

31. The unfinished *canzone* of Chapter 27, which breaks off after one stanza with the news of Beatrice's death, is also undivided; here Dante does not comment on the omission.

32. Only two other Psalms are undivided, 116 and 150. In both cases Peter applies the term "atomus," and glosses it as "sine divisione." Psalm 116 is said to be "quasi punctus psalmorum" (*PL* 191.1032–33) [like a point for the Psalms]. Psalm 150 is indivisible because it urges the praise of God, who "congregavit sanctos, et deposita fragilitate suae imagini restituit, et jam conformes gloriae suae in beatitudine locavit, ubi est omnis abundantia" (*PL* 191.1291) [gathered his saints together, and restored the dead through the frailty of his image, and placed those faithful to his glory in beatitude, where all abundance is].

33. Isidore of Seville, *Etymologiae* 1.30.1.

34. Gianfranco Contini writes that even now this sonnet "Passa per il tipo di componimento linguisticamente limpido, che non richiede spiegazioni, che potrebbe 'essere stato scritto ieri'" [Serves as the type of the linguistically transparent composition, which does not require explication, which could have been "written yesterday"] ("Esercizio d'interpretazione sopra un sonetto di Dante" 161). See also the discussion of the sonnet in Mazzotta, "The Language of Poetry" 11: "any distinction between things and essences collapses in Beatrice, who could be called the point of fusion of signifier and signified."

35. De Robertis, *Il libro della "Vita Nuova"* 130: "Un nuovo oggetto di poesia: la donna; un nuovo genere di poesia: la lode; un nuovo modo di proporre queste

ragioni: le ascoltanti chiamate ad allargare la portata del suo discorso, a collaborare al trionfo di questa poesia." Similarly Singleton, who names Dante's first subject "The effects of love on the poet" and his second subject "In praise of his lady" (*Essay* 87).

36. See O'Donnell, *Cassiodorus* 150–52; Hahner, *Cassiodors Psalmenkommentar* 65–95. O'Donnell notes that Cassiodorus attributes the technique to Augustine, in his comment on Psalm 106, but that Augustine only wrote one *divisio psalmi*; Cassiodorus transforms the method of this one passage into a regular procedure.

37. Cassiodorus, *Expositio Psalmorum*, ed. Adriaen, Preface, chap. 14, p. 17. Translations are adapted from *Explanation of the Psalms*, trans. Walsh.

38. Cassiodorus, *Expositio Psalmorum* 28.

39. A single example of each. For a "varietas loquentium" [variety of speakers], see Psalm 17, where the speakers are "propheta," "Ecclesia," "vox Domini Salvatoris," and again "Ecclesia" (Cassiodorus, *Expositio Psalmorum* 151) [the Prophet, the Church, the voice of the Savior, the Church]; for a change of addressee see the *divisio* to Psalm 3, quoted below; for a change in mode of speaking, see Psalm 6: "Quatuor modis in hoc psalmo vir confitens et religiosus exorat" (72) [In this Psalm the man of piety who confesses his sins prays in four ways]; for a "mutatio rerum" [change of topics] see the *divisio* of the first Psalm.

40. Rahner, *Cassiodors Psalmenkommentar* 65–70. Rahner cites Cicero's *De Inventione* 1.31.

41. O'Donnell, *Cassiodorus* 243–44; Cassiodorus, *Explanation of the Psalms*, trans. Walsh, vol. 1, 19–20.

42. For this dating, see Minnis, *Medieval Theory of Authorship* 41 and 105.

43. For example, here is an excerpt from the *divisio* to Psalm 50 as it appears in Cassiodorus and Honorius. The Psalm has five parts. Cassiodorus (*Expositio Psalmorum* 454): "Prima est satisfactio perfectissimae humilitatis. Secunda confidentia misericordiae Domini, quam fideles semper habere proficuum est" [First is the satisfaction of most perfect humility. Second, trust in the Lord's mercy, which it is always profitable for the faithful to have]. Honorius (*PL* 172.284): "Primum est: *Miserere mei, Deus*, in quo poenitentis satisfactio. Secundum est: *Asperges me hyssopo*, in quo misericordiae confidentia" [First is *Have mercy on me, O God*, in which the satisfaction of penitence (is expressed). Second is *Thou shalt sprinkle me with hyssop*, in which the confidence of mercy]. Honorius improves the parallelism of the five "membra" as he abridges.

44. Cassiodorus, *Expositio Psalmorum* 35.

45. *Glossa Ordinaria*.

46. Cassiodorus, *Expositio Psalmorum* 51.

47. Cassiodorus, *Expositio Psalmorum* 17.

48. These dates from Minnis, *Medieval Theory of Authorship* 11 and 86.

49. Hugh of St. Cher, *Biblia latina*.

50. Thomas Aquinas, *In Psalmos Davidis Expositio* 156.

51. Panofsky, *Gothic Architecture and Scholasticism* 31; further quotations will be identified in the text. Other general accounts of Scholasticism include Baldwin, *The Scholastic Culture of the Middle Ages* (especially good on social-historical background), and Piltz, *The World of Medieval Learning*.

52. For a critique of Panofsky's argument, see Gellrich, *The Idea of the Book* 69–74; Gellrich argues that Gothic architecture and Scholasticism should not be connected directly to each other (as Panofsky connects them) but rather to a more general pattern of medieval "mythologizing thought" (74). In my own view this is a question of emphasis.

53. Panofsky, *Gothic Architecture and Scholasticism* 48.

54. De Robertis, quoted in *Dante's Lyric Poetry*, ed. Foster and Boyde, vol. 2, 95.

55. Durling and Martinez, *Time and the Crystal* ch. 1, "Early Experiments"; here 58. Durling and Martinez refer to earlier work by Leo Spitzer and by Bruno Sandkühler.

56. Durling and Martinez, *Time and the Crystal* 63.

57. As we shall see below, however, in the *Convivio* Dante does implicitly rank the eyes above the mouth (3.8).

58. Furthermore, Dante ends the entire *divisione* with the general comment that further division would be possible; he fears, though, that he may already have revealed too much to too many: "a più aprire lo intendimento di questa canzone, si converrebbe usare di più minute divisioni; ma tuttavia chi non è di tanto ingegno che per queste che sono fatte la possa intendere, a me non dispiace se la mi lascia stare, ché certo io temo d'avere a troppi comunicato lo suo intendimento pur per queste divisioni che fatte sono, s'elli avvenisse che molti le potessero audire" (19.22) [in order to open further the meaning of this *canzone* one would have to use further minute divisions; but in any case, whoever has not sufficient wit that he can understand it by these that have been made, it will not displease me if he let it stand, for certainly I fear that I have communicated its meaning to too many by these divisions, if it should happen that many could hear and heed them].

59. De Robertis (*Libro* 276), notes that the *divisione* here "non trova fondamento . . . nel testo poetico" [does not have a basis in the poetic text].

60. The word "bocca" appears twice in Dante's lyrics, both times in connection with pain: "dolgasi la bocca / de li uomini" [let the mouth of men wail] ("Tre donne intorno al cor" 66–67, *Dante's Lyric Poetry* vol. 1, 178); "L'angoscia . . . spira / fuor de la bocca" [My anguish breathes out from my mouth] ("Amor, da me convien pur ch'io mi doglia" 28–29, *Dante's Lyric Poetry* vol. 1, 206).

61. *Inferno*, ed. and trans. Singleton, 5.133–36: "Quando leggemmo il disïato riso / esser basciato da cotanto amante, / questi, che mai da me non fia diviso, / la bocca mi basciò tutto tremante" [When we read how the longed-for smile was kissed by so great a lover, this one, who never shall be parted from me, kissed my mouth all trembling]. Singleton notes that "bocca" answers "disiato riso" as a "corresponding but impressively stark" term. Natalino Sapegno writes (*La Divina Commedia*, note ad loc.), "al *disiato riso* di Ginevra (perifrasi squisitamente poetica), si contrappone, con realismo tutto nuovo di linguaggio, la *bocca* di Francesca" [to the *desired smile* of Guinevere (exquisitely poetic periphrasis) is contrasted, with an entirely new realism of language, the *mouth* of Francesca].

62. *Vita Nuova*, ed. De Robertis, 116. See also Scott, "Dante's 'Sweet New Style' and the *Vita Nuova*."

63. *Summa Theologiae* Pt. 1 Q. 85 Art. 5.

64. In an extremely helpful personal communication responding to an earlier version of this chapter, Ronald Martinez suggests that, "Neoplatonically speaking, one might argue that the *divisio* must, at its extreme point, touch on 'defiling' matter at some point, must at least be tangent with the possibility of a 'vizioso pensier.'"

65. Contini, in his discussion of *pare* as the poem's key word, describes this well. "A Dante, qui, non interessa punto un visibile, ma, ch'è tutt'altra cosa, una visibilità" ("Esercizio d'interpretazione" 168) [To Dante, here, what is interesting is not at all a visible thing, but something entirely different, a visibility].

66. *Dante's Lyric Poetry* vol. 2, 132.

67. Mazzotta, "The Language of Poetry" 9.

68. So Singleton, *Essay* 87.

69. Dante's eyes are mentioned at 31.8, 32.5, 34.10, 35.5, 36.4, 36.5, 37.6, 39.8. The "occhi" at 38.10 belong to the Donna Gentile.

70. Only one poem before "Venite a intender" has an ostensible speaker other than Dante: the second sonnet of Chapter 22, which is written in the persona of certain *donne* who address Dante, but with no attempt at deception.

71. Once again, Harrison is the notable exception (*The Body of Beatrice* 110–17).

72. See, for example, De Robertis, *Libro* 271–79.

73. Singleton, *Essay* 104–5.

74. See n. 58. The comment at 41.9 reads, in full, "Potrebbesi più sottilmente ancora dividere, e più sottilmente fare intendere; ma puotesi passare con questa divisa, e però non m'intrametto di più dividerlo" [It could be divided even more subtly, and explained more subtly; but it can pass with this division, and therefore I will not take the trouble to divide it further].

75. The fifth part comments on Dante's relationship to the experience he describes: "Ne la quinta dico che, avvegna che io non possa intendere là ove lo pensero mi trae, cioè a la sua mirabile qualitade, almeno intendo questo, cioè che tutto è lo cotale pensare de la mia donna, però ch'io sento lo suo nome spesso nel mio pensero: e nel fine di questa quinta parte dico 'donne mie care,' a dare ad intendere che sono donne coloro a cui io parlo" (41.7) [In the fifth I say that, although I cannot understand what my thought takes me to, that is to her miraculous quality, at least I understand this, that this thought is entirely of my lady, since I hear her name often in my thought: and at the end of this fifth part I say "my dear ladies," to make it understood that those to whom I speak are ladies]. The last phrase of the sonnet, describing its rhetorical situation, would be considered a distinct part in a "rhetorical" division, but it is not considered a distinct part here.

76. Minnis, *Medieval Theory of Authorship* 16.

77. In his discussion of "cleansing the bread," Dante mentions three specific "macule" in his discourse: that he speaks of himself (1.2); that his expositions are too profound (1.3–4); that he writes in the vernacular (1.5–13). At least two of these "stains"—the first and third—inhere in the *Vita Nuova*, where they occasion no apology. All three inhere in the *Convivio*, of course: Dante's aim is to cleanse them by excusing them. I am arguing for a more decisive elimination of certain other, unspecified "macule."

78. For a fuller and more nuanced statement of this, see Shapiro, "On the Role of Rhetoric in the *Convivio*."

79. As Foster and Boyde state (*Dante's Lyric Poetry* vol. 2, Appendix, 360): "in the *Convivio* where . . . philosophy triumphs, this triumph entails no *condemnation* of Beatrice; she is simply set aside, is politely—indeed reverently—relegated to a sphere (the heavenly one) other than that of D's present interests (*Con.* II.ii.1; viii.7). And here again her relation, in the *Convivio*, to the individual Dante—separated from him, but not renounced—has a certain likeness to the relation, in that work, between theology (and the heavenly 'beatitudine' of which it speaks) and philosophy (and the earthly temporal 'beatitudine'—of which it speaks and to which, especially as moral philosophy, it can and should lead)."

80. The quoted phrase comes from a discussion of the prefatory part of a *canzone*; in the *canzone*'s central part, "si tratta quello che dire s'intende, cioè la loda di questa gentile" (3.1.13) [is treated what is intended to be spoken of, namely the praise of this gentle one]. It should be noted, though, that the analysis of the proem takes a paradoxical turn. Dante recognizes that the assertion of ineffability is a *topos*, and the admission of linguistic inadequacy becomes a sign of rhetorical skill: "la lingua mia non è di tanta facundia che dire potesse ciò che nel pensiero mio se ne ragiona; per che è da vedere che, a rispetto de la veritade, poco fia quello che dirà. E ciò risulta in grande loda di costei, se bene si guarda, ne la quale principalmente s'intende; e quella orazione si può dir bene che vegna da la fabrica del rettorico, ne la quale ciascuna parte pone mano a lo principale intento" (3.4.3) [my tongue lacks the eloquence to be able to express what is spoken of her in my thought; consequently it will be apparent that what I shall say concerning the truth will be quite little. And this, upon close examination, brings great praise to her, which is my principal purpose; and that speech in which every part contributes to the principal purpose can properly be said to come from the workshop of the rhetorician]. I have emphasized the subordination of Rhetoric within the *Convivio*; since this subordination allows Rhetoric a well-defined relationship to Philosophy, the limitation of power amounts to a kind of empowerment as well. On this see Shapiro, "On the Role of Rhetoric"; Ascoli, "The Vowels of Authority"; Mazzotta, "The Light of Venus."

81. Singleton, *Essay* 42: "Quite a large part of the *Vita Nuova* is reasonable. At least, almost everything outside of the poems is reasoned."

82. "[D]icemo noi 'philos' quasi amore, e 'sophos' quasi sapiente. Per che vedere si può che questi due vocabuli fanno questo nome di 'filosofo,' che tanto vale a dire quanto 'amatore di sapienza'" (3.11.5) [we say *philos* for love, and *sophos* for wise man. From which it can be seen that these two words make up this name of "philosopher," meaning "lover of wisdom"].

83. Mazzotta, "The Language of Poetry" 3; see also Harrison, *The Body of Beatrice*.

Chapter 4

1. Wallace, *Chaucer and the Early Writings of Boccaccio* 91. Similarly Muscetta, *Giovanni Boccaccio* 96: "I due livelli narrativo e lirico del *Roman du Chastelain* sono dal Boccaccio unificati nell'ottava" [The two levels of the *Roman du Chastelain*,

narrative and lyric, are unified by Boccaccio in the octave]. See his complete discussion of the *Filostrato*, 79–98.

2. Burrow, *Ricardian Poetry* 53; similarly Natali, in the articles cited below. An important early discussion of Boccaccio's overriding "liricità," which treats the *Filocolo*, the *Ameto*, and the *Decameron* but not the *Filostrato*, is Battaglia's 1935 essay "Schemi lirici nell'arte del Boccaccio."

3. Windeatt, "Classical and Medieval Elements in Chaucer's *Troilus*" 125; similarly Serafini-Sauli, *Giovanni Boccaccio* 35.

4. The notable exception to this generalization is the argument presented by Giulia Natali in "Progetti narrativi e tradizione lirica in Boccaccio" and (somewhat less fully, but with other new material) in "A Lyrical Version: Boccaccio's *Filostrato*." I will briefly discuss this argument below.

5. See Derrida, "The Law of Genre."

6. Smarr, *Boccaccio and Fiammetta* 21–33.

7. See Branca's notes at 1.29, 1.39, 1.56, 3.93, 4.28, 4.35, 4.96, 4.100, 4.156, 5.60, 7.23, 7.24, 8.4. Some of these echoes are general—the *Vita Nuova* is cited as one typical stilnovistic source—and some are quite specific. Smarr omits them in her list of the Dantean allusions noted by Branca (237–38).

8. Boccaccio concludes his account of the dream with a direct verbal quotation, noted by Branca: "questo ruppe il sonno deboletto" (7.24) [this broke his feeble sleep]; "lo mio deboletto sonno . . . si ruppe" (*Vita Nuova* 3.7) [my feeble sleep was broken].

9. Smarr, *Boccaccio and Fiammetta* 31.

10. See Gybbon-Monypenny, "Guillaume de Machaut's Erotic 'Autobiography'"; Poe, *From Poetry to Prose in Old Provençal*.

11. Muscetta, *Giovanni Boccaccio* 94. Muscetta explains: "Innestare brani lirici in un contesto narrativo, anzi, attribuire i più impegnativi al protagonista, che è presentato come eroe e poeta insieme, era la caratteristica originale del *Roman du Chastelain de Couci*" [To graft lyric passages into a narrative context, indeed, to attribute the most compelling to the protagonist, who is presented as hero and poet at once, was the original characteristic of the *Roman du Chastelain de Couci*].

12. See the works cited in the Introduction, n. 34.

13. Natali, "Progetti" 382: "Il quadro letterario nel quale s'inscrivono le prime prove narrative del giovane Boccaccio—parlo di *Filostrato*, *Filocolo* e *Teseida*—è senza dubbio egemonizzato dall'esperienza lirica che ha ormai raggiunto altissimi livelli di perfezionamento e di codificazione." The phrase "gerarchia letteraria" [literary hierarchy] appears at 393.

14. Natali, "Progetti" 382: "esigenze della fantasia."

15. *Le Roman du Castelain de Couci et de la Dame de Fayel*, ed. Delbouille.

16. Natali, "Progetti."

17. Among the numerous *Vita Nuova* echoes noted by Branca in the Proem to *Filostrato*, especially relevant is the passage in which Dante turns to verse to assuage his grief over Beatrice's death (*Vita Nuova* 31.1; *Filostrato*, ed. Branca, p. 848, n. 24). I would also mention—though there is no sharp verbal parallel—Dante's earlier decision to address a sonnet to Beatrice in the hope of regaining her favor: "mi ritornai ne la camera de la lagrime; ne la quale, piangendo e vergognandomi, fra me

stesso dicea: 'Se questa donna sapesse la mia condizione, io non credo che così gabbasse la mia persona, anzi credo che molta pietade le ne verrebbe.' E in questo pianto stando, propuosi di dire parole, ne le quali, parlando a lei, significasse la cagione del mio trasfiguramento . . ." (*Vita Nuova* 14.9–10) [I returned to the room of tears; in which, weeping and ashamed, I said to myself: "If this lady knew my condition, I do not believe she would mock my appearance, rather I believe great pity would come to her." And amidst this weeping I decided to speak words, in which, addressing her, I might signify the cause of my transfiguration . . .]. This is close to Filostrato's strategy, and to the non-strategy of Troiolo's which Pandaro mocks: "cre' tu per pianto forse riaverla?" (4.49) [do you think, perhaps, by weeping to regain her?].

18. The relative dating of the two poems is not firmly established; see Introduction, n. 49. For my purposes here, it is enough to note that each poem is a formal breakthrough; each explores the possibilities of the octave stanza as if for the first time. Rather than playing on the relationship between lyric and narrative, the *Teseida*, I would argue, takes advantage of the pictorial possibilities inherent in the text's spatial division into stanzas; in this respect it is the more influential of the two for the Renaissance tradition of stanzaic narrative.

19. See Branca's introduction, 7–10.

20. Dionisotti, "Appunti su antichi testi"; for the octave stanza in *trouvère* poetry, Roncaglia, "Per la storia dell'ottava rima," and Picone, "Boccaccio e la codificazione dell'ottava."

21. Balduino, ed., *Cantari del trecento* 19–21, 257–59; Franceschetti, "Rassegna di studi sui cantari" 570–74—cited, with approval, in Wallace, *Chaucer and the Early Writings of Boccaccio* 194 n. 108.

22. In the *Roman du Chastelain de Couci*, the lyric interpolations disrupt the couplet frame in another way as well: in most cases, the inset song is introduced by what ought to be the *first* line of a couplet—but this line receives no octosyllabic partner, being echoed instead by one of the song's rhyme-sounds. In effect, the entire *chanson* completes the couplet.

23. Roncaglia, "Per la storia dell'ottava rima" 11.

24. Burrow, *Ricardian Poetry* 53. In one case, there is a frame that disavows framing. The important hymn to Venus in Part 3 is introduced thus: "poi . . . cominciava . . . / dolcemente a cantare in cotal guisa, / qual qui sanz'alcun mezzo si divisa" (3.73) [then joyfully he began to sing in such a manner as is here set forth without any change]. "Sanz'alcun mezzo" might mean "without change," "without mediation," or "without delay": what is being claimed is an *immediate* presentation of the song. But this is a relatively elaborate introduction; more typically, the aubade at 3.44 is introduced, "Poi cominciò in verso lei dicendo . . ." [Then he began saying to her . . .].

25. Dante, *On Eloquence in the Vernacular* 50; "equalium stantiarum sine responsorio ad unam sententiam tragica coniugatio" (*De Vulgari Eloquentia*, ed. Mengaldo, 2.8.8).

26. Curtius, *European Literature and the Latin Middle Ages* 128–30.

27. This *canzone* ("Li occhi dolenti," *Vita Nuova* 31) would seem to have special importance in the *Filostrato*. As Branca notes, the Proem recalls Dante's

prose introduction of it (*Filostrato*, ed. Branca, p. 848, n. 24), and the body of the *Filostrato* alludes to the body of the *canzone* at 4.28 and 4.35. Another clear allusion appears in Troiolo's lament at 7.60: "Gli occhi dolenti, dopo il tuo partire, / di lagrimar non ristetter giammai" [The eyes sorrowing after your departure never ceased weeping]; compare the beginning of the *canzone* at *Vita Nuova* 31.8, "Li occhi dolenti per pietà del core / hanno di lagrimar sofferta pena" [The eyes sorrowing out of pity for the heart have endured great suffering from weeping]. Since I am arguing that the entire *Filostrato* can be read as a single *canzone*, I might add that it can be read as a revision of "Li occhi dolenti" in particular. The possibility of an analogy (or ironic contrast) between Beatrice's death and Filomena's departure is strengthened by another allusion not mentioned by Branca: Filostrato's description of Filomena as "la donna gentil della mia mente" (9.5) [the noble lady of my mind] takes Dante's description of Beatrice as "la gloriosa donna de la mia mente" (*Vita Nuova* 2.1) [the glorious lady of my mind] and substitutes the *Vita Nuova*'s "donna gentile" for Beatrice.

28. Pandaro has just urged a similar directness between Troiolo and himself: "fa tu ch'io / aperto veggia il tuo alto disio" (2.90) [let me see openly your noble desire]. The transparent expression of feeling in a letter or a conversation is analogous to the "ponding" of lyric verse on the surface of the narrative poem.

29. The writer of the Proem identifies himself as "Filostrato" in the rubric to the Proem: "Filostrato alla sua più ch'altra piacevole Filomena salute" [Filostrato salutes his Filomena who is more pleasing than any other woman]. "Filostrato" is an epithet for Troiolo in the overall rubric, and the title of the work both in that rubric and in the rubrics to all nine of the separate Parts.

30. I have discussed a related problem in the *Decameron*, in "The Language of Gardens: Boccaccio's *Valle delle Donne*."

31. Benoît de Sainte-Maure, *Le Roman de Troie*, ed. Constans.

32. Muscetta, *Giovanni Boccaccio* 94.

33. Freccero, "The Fig Tree and the Laurel: Petrarch's Poetics."

34. It is not clear whether Boccaccio had encountered Petrarch's *Canzoniere* when he wrote the *Filostrato*. Branca's 1335 dating of the *Filostrato* would make such an encounter impossible, but Natali supports a dating of 1339 or 1340 by drawing attention to some intriguing similarities between the Proem and a Petrarchan *canzone* ("Progetti" 387–89).

35. C. S. Lewis, cited in *Petrarch's Lyric Poems*, ed. and trans. Durling, 9–10. See also Warkentin, "The Form of Dante's 'Libello' and its Challenge to Petrarch."

36. As Freccero states, the poetic persona dwells "in what the verses leave unsaid, in the blank spaces separating these lyric 'fragments,' as they were called, from each other. . . . Because it is a composite of lyric instants, the portrait [of the poet as 'eternally weeping lover'] has no temporality . . . For the same reason, it is immune from the ravages of time, a mood given a fictive *durée* by the temporality of the reader, or a score to be performed by generations of readers from the Renaissance to the Romantics. It remained for centuries the model of poetic self-creation even for poets who, in matters of form, thought of themselves as anti-Petrarchan" ("The Fig Tree and the Laurel" 34). On the authorial proper name, see Foucault, "What Is an Author?" 121–24.

37. I should note, however, a possible trace of Boccaccio's own name in the text of the *Filostrato.* Filostrato's phrase in the Proem, "il vostro nome di grazia pieno" (16) [your name, which is full of grace], is a clue that Filomena's true name is Giovanna (see Branca's introduction, 4), which could imply yet another specular relationship, between Giovanna and Giovanni. I take it that such a reference would be oblique and playful.

38. For a brilliant account of the *Canzoniere*'s treatment of lyric and narrative—and thus its rendering of temporality—see Barolini, "The Making of a Lyric Sequence."

39. Furthermore, the tale Filostrato tells on his own day (*Decameron* 4.9) is a version of the "coeur mangé" story; it thus recalls Troiolo's dream (7.23–24) and two texts that may lie behind that dream, Dante's dream in *Vita Nuova* 3 and the main plot of the *Roman du Chastelain de Couci.* Filostrato is one of two story-tellers to sing a *canzone* on the day of his own reign; his song laments the faithlessness of his beloved, and it is the only one of the ten *canzoni* in the *Decameron* to include an envoi in which the singer addresses his song. Finally, I think it is striking that, in the festivities after Filostrato accepts the crown, Dioneo and Fiammetta sing a song "di messer Guiglielmo e della Dama del Vergiù" (3 concl. 8)—that is, a *cantare* based on the French poem *La Châtelaine de Vergi,* another important experiment in the grafting of *trouvère* lyric into couplet narrative (see Zumthor, "De la chanson au récit: *La Châtelaine de Vergi,*" in *Langue, texte, énigme* 219–36). *Decameron* quotations are from the Branca edition; translations from the McWilliam translation.

40. "[N]on d'altra materia domane mi piace che si ragioni se non di quello che a' miei fatti è più conforme, cioè di *coloro li cui amori ebbero infelice fine*" (3 concl. 6) [I . . . decree that the subject of our discussions for the morrow should be none other than the one which applies most closely to myself, namely, *those whose love ended unhappily*]. For mockery from the other storytellers see, e.g., Lauretta's comment at 4.3.3 and Filostrato's general response at 5.4.3.

41. Hollander, *Boccaccio's Two Venuses* 93. See Hollander's discussion of the *Filostrato* in particular, 49–53. Smarr's account (*Boccaccio and Fiammetta* 14–33) is more nuanced and more tolerant of ambiguity, but comes to a similar conclusion. Discussing Dantean allusions in the *Caccia di Diana* and *Filostrato,* she writes: "The result can be interpreted either as a conscious rebellion against Dante's kind of love, or else as an ironic comment on Boccaccio's poet-lover. In the *Caccia* we cannot perhaps be entirely sure which is meant, but the *Filostrato* seems to me to point toward the latter interpretation" (32).

42. On the older biographical criticism see Smarr, *Boccaccio and Fiammetta* 3–4.

43. If Filostrato is not fully Christian, in Hollander's terms, he is certainly not pagan; he cites Jeremiah by name (Proem 13).

Chapter 5

1. Wallace, *Chaucer and the Early Writings of Boccaccio* 104.
2. Howard, *Chaucer* 198.

3. Williams, "Marianne Moore" 315–16.

4. The literature on ekphrasis is vast; works I have found especially helpful are Dubois, *History, Rhetorical Description and the Epic: From Homer to Spenser*; Meltzer, *Salome and the Dance of Writing*; Mitchell, "On Poems On Pictures: Ekphrasis and the Other." On text and image, an even larger subject, see for example Mitchell, *Iconology*, and Mitchell, ed., *The Language of Images*.

5. McGregor, *The Shades of Aeneas* ch. 2, "*Filostrato*: 'De' Troian L'Amor Fallace.'" The occlusion of Trojan material in the *Filostrato* does not, of course, weaken McGregor's argument: a moral commentary can be all the more pointed for being implicit. I do not, however, share McGregor's view that the concept of "false love" is the single key to both the public story of Troy and the private story of Troiolo.

6. McGregor himself makes a related observation, in a separate study that catalogues descriptions of the pagan world in the *Filostrato*, the *Filocolo*, and the *Teseida* (McGregor, *The Image of Antiquity*). Repeatedly McGregor notes that the *Filostrato* is poor in concrete descriptions: for example, "temples are rare in *Filostrato*, as is every other detail of setting" (27). McGregor attributes this quality to Boccaccio's own limitation as a writer; he suggests that Boccaccio's "ability grows and develops in the roughly seven years that separate the *Filostrato* from *Teseida*" (167). I question this account of Boccaccio's early career: I am reluctant to set a limit on Boccaccio's ability at any age, and I would point out that there is little external evidence that the *Filostrato* precedes the *Teseida*, let alone by "roughly seven years." (McGregor admits early in his book that the *Filostrato* "is as complex and as fully realized as any of Boccaccio's early works, and it may well belong to a date other than that to which it is usually assigned" [15]. On the dating of *Filostrato* and *Teseida*, see Introduction, n. 49.) Still, McGregor may be right that the poet of the *Filostrato* was simply not capable of writing vividly about an ancient setting. This would not invalidate my own view that the omissions of the *Filostrato* should be read as deliberate choices. Artists often transform their own limitations of technique into motivated formal features.

7. In the poem's invocation, Troiolo is mentioned twice as a person with a sorrowful life (1.3, 1.6); in the body of the narrative, "Troiolo" first appears as the first word of a new stanza: "Troiolo giva, come soglion fare / i giovinetti" (1.20) [Troiolo went about, as young men are accustomed to]. Priam is first mentioned at 4.4.

8. On the *Teseida* and epic, see David Anderson, *Before the Knight's Tale*; Winthrop Wetherbee, "Epic and Romance in the *Teseida*."

9. McGregor, *The Shades of Aeneas* 84.

10. *Teseida* 12.84; see the Limentani ed., "Introduzione," 231.

11. Given the *Filostrato*'s continual reference to the *Vita Nuova*, I would suggest that Filostrato's initial position is a satiric reduction of the revelation Dante achieves in *Vita Nuova* 18. Dante, in a sort of impromptu court of love, explains to a group of ladies that the goal of his love is now no longer Beatrice's *salute*, because that has been denied him, but rather his own self-sustaining words of praise. When Filostrato goes on to change his own focus *from* solipsistic thought *to* external vision, he is both mocking and reversing Dante's conversion.

12. "[Q]uello che io per la vostra presenza doveva conoscere, molto meglio, non conoscendolo, per lo suo contrario prestamente mi si fece conoscere, cioè per la privazione di quella" (Proem 8) [what I ought to have known much better through your presence, but did not recognize, was immediately made known to me through its contrary, that is, through deprivation of it].

13. Bennett, *Chaucer's Book of Fame* 14.

14. *Purgatorio* 12.61–63; *Erec et Enide*, ed. Carroll, 5289–5307; *Intelligenza*, in Petronio, ed., *Poemetti del duecento*, stanzas 240–86; Chaucer, *House of Fame* 151–467; Shakespeare, *Rape of Lucrece* 1366–1568.

15. Richard of Fournival, *Bestiaire d'amour*, cited in Solterer, "Letter writing and picture reading: medieval textuality and the *Bestiaire d'Amour*" 131.

16. The various writers known as Philostratus, and their works, are discussed in Graham Anderson, *Philostratus*. The epigram on Telephus is 16.110, in *Greek Anthology*, ed. Paton, vol. 5. In stressing the Trojan and ekphrastic writings attributed to Philostratus, I do not mean to deny the possible relevance of other works: for example, as a Christian writing about a pagan hero, Boccaccio would have been interested to hear about the *Life of Apollonius of Tyana*, a sort of pagan saint's life, and the title of *Lives of the Sophists* might serve as a tendentious subtitle for the *Filostrato*. These connections do seem to me more tenuous, however, than the obvious sharing of Trojan subject matter.

17. Philostratus, *Imagines*, ed. Fairbanks, 9.

18. On the popularity of the *Imagines* in Byzantium between the thirteenth and sixteenth centuries, see *Die Bilder*, ed. Kalinka and Schönberger, 63–64.

19. On the Greek translators, see Roberto Weiss, "The Translators from the Greek of the Angevin Court of Naples." More generally, on the presence of Greek culture in Naples, see Weiss, "The Greek Culture of Southern Italy in the Later Middle Ages"; Branca, *Boccaccio: The Man and His Works* 33–34; Setton, "The Byzantine Background to the Italian Renaissance"; Berschin, *Greek Letters and the Latin Middle Ages* 263–64.

20. So Padoan, "Mondo aristocratico e mondo comunale nell'ideologia e nell'arte di Giovanni Boccaccio" 6–7.

21. Hutton, *The Greek Anthology in Italy* 81–85.

22. *Boccaccio on Poetry* 113–15 (*Genealogy* 15.6). Leontius Pilatus later translated Homer into Latin, and in Florence tried to teach Boccaccio Greek (*Boccaccio on Poetry* 120; *Genealogy* 15.7).

23. Salutati, *Epistolario* vol. 3, 547–50. The letter is dated September 25, 1401. Salutati quotes from the *Heroicus*, but refers to Philostratus's book as *De deorum imaginibus et heroum*; as Salutati's editor Novati observes, this title evidently conflates the *Heroicus* and the *Imagines* into a single work.

24. I know of only one previous speculation on a possible connection between Boccaccio's Filostrato and the Greek writer, and that merely an open question about the *Decameron* storyteller: in their introduction to the *Imagines*, Kalinka and Schönberger write, "Man möchte auch gerne wissen, wohern schon Boccaccio den Namen Filostrato in seinem Decamerone hatte" (Philostratus, *Bilder* 65) [One would also like to know where Boccaccio obtained the name "Filostrato" in his *Decameron*].

25. If Boccaccio had heard of Philostratus but thought of him as an inaccessible Greek writer, then his gesture in attaching the name to his book is rather like Chaucer's gesture in attributing his version of the Troilus story to a certain "Lollius." Chaucer seems to have derived the name from an epistle of Horace's, and he presents Lollius (both in *Troilus* and in *House of Fame* 1468) as an ancient writer on Troy. On Lollius see, most recently, Fleming, *Classical Imitation and Interpretation* 179–200.

26. Salutati obtained his Philostratus book from Iacopo Angeli (see Salutati, *Epistolario* vol. 3, 522–23). Angeli had been in Constantinople in 1395–96, and he either brought the book back with him or received it from a correspondent soon after; see Weiss, "Iacopo Angeli da Scarperia" 258–62.

27. Scholars have mostly been content to repeat Boccaccio's own faulty etymology for "Filostrato" as though it explained the name. But an etymology does not preclude other kinds of reference: the *accessus ad auctores* often gloss the names of real writers through etymology, as in Boccaccio's own discussion of the name "Dante," which he derives from the verb "to give" (*Esposizioni sopra la Comedia di Dante*, ed. Padoan, Accessus 37). One other source for "Filostrato" has been proposed. Aldo S. Bernardo suggests that Boccaccio may have taken the name from a lost comedy of Petrarch's; although this work is usually referred to as *Philologia*, it appears as *Philostratus* in Boccaccio's life of Petrarch and *Philologia Philostrati* in a 1343 letter of Petrarch's (*Petrarch, Laura, and the Triumphs* 172). This may well be the source of Boccaccio's "Filostrato," but Bernardo presents the possibility only as a speculation. (And it is conceivable, of course, that Petrarch himself intended an allusion to the Greek writer.) I am far from insisting on a direct connection between Boccaccio's Filostrato and the ancient Philostratus; I leave it to my reader to decide whether the homonymy of the two writers on Troy is a mere coincidence.

28. For the *Aeneid*, text and (modified) translations are from the Loeb Library edition of Fairclough.

29. Boitani, "Antiquity and Beyond"; on the story as reflected in ancient art, see 9–10.

30. R. D. Williams, "The Pictures in Dido's Temple" 149.

31. Patterson, "'Rapt With Pleasaunce': Vision and Narration in the Epic" 458.

32. Patterson offers a more fully dialectic treatment of the *Aeneid* in a later essay, "Virgil and the Historical Consciousness of the Twelfth Century: The *Roman d'Eneas* and *Erec et Enide*" (*Negotiating the Past* ch. 5). Although this later essay is not specifically concerned with visual images, Patterson also comments (as I do immediately below) on the belt of Pallas as an "occasion . . . for Aeneas' violence" (164). Despite our different emphases and (mostly) different examples, I take Patterson's profound meditation on "historical consciousness" in Virgil, *Eneas*, and Chretien de Troyes as an important model for the sort of intertextual reading I am attempting in this chapter.

33. On this passage see Conte, *The Rhetoric of Imitation* ch. 6, "The Baldric of Pallas: Cultural Models and Literary Rhetoric."

34. Barthes, *Camera Lucida* 25–27.

35. Meltzer, *Salome and the Dance of Writing* 52.

36. Meltzer, *Salome and the Dance of Writing* 102.

37. Boitani, "Antiquity and Beyond" 5.

38. Philostratus, *Imagines* 7.

39. On this subject see Patterson, *Chaucer and the Subject of History* 114–26.

40. Guido delle Colonne, *Historia Destructionis Troiae*, trans. Meek, 9–10; Griffin ed. 11: "ab hiis malis per Troye casum tanta bona processerunt ut ipsa Troya deleta insurexerit, causa per quam Romana urbs, que caput est urbium, per Troyanos exules facta extitit vel promota."

41. On the Palladium see Fleming, *Classical Imitation and Interpretation* 124–36.

42. The *Filostrato* is linked to Virgil's picture of Troilus in another way as well. Bernhard König argues that Aeneas's first encounter with Dido, in the temple of Juno, is the basis for the topos of the "meeting in the temple," a topos revived in Troiolo's first encounter with Criseida, as well as in *Vita Nuova* 5, the Introduction to the First Day of the *Decameron*, and Petrarch's fictive autobiography. See König, *Die Begegnung im Tempel*, and McGregor's summary and discussion in *The Image of Antiquity* 9–12.

43. Albert de Stade, *Troilus*, ed. Merzdorf; cited in Boitani, "Antiquity and Beyond" 4.

44. Benson, *The History of Troy in Middle English Literature* 4–5. Salutati, for example, in the letter discussed above, asserts that Guido drew his facts directly from Dares and Dictys (*Epistolario* vol. 3, 546).

45. Line references for *Eneas* are to the Salverda de Grave edition; translations adapted from the Yunck translation.

46. On the celebration of lineal descent in twelfth-century French literature, see Bloch, *Etymologies and Genealogies*, and Patterson, *Negotiating the Past* 170–83.

47. Bloch, *Etymologies and Genealogies* 76.

48. On blazonry in the *romans antiques*, see Brault, *Early Blazon*; Adam-Even, "Les usages héraldiques au milieu du XIIe siècle d'après le *Roman de Troie* de Benoît de Sainte-Maure et la littérature contemporaine."

49. Guido delle Colonne, *Historia Destructionis Troiae*, trans. Meek, 170; Griffin ed., 177: "quandam auream statuam, similitudinem Hectoris describentem, habentem ensem nudum in manu, cuius aspectus et facies erat ex ea parte in qua Grecorum exercitus in eorum tentoriis morabatur, qui cum eius ense Grecis minas inprimere videbatur."

50. Guido delle Colonne, *Historia Destructionis Troiae*, trans. Meek, 170–71; Griffin ed., 177–78: "quodam artificioso foramine constituto"; "primo derivabatur ad frontis ambitum per partes intrinsecas, deinde ad oculos et nares."

51. On the double theme of Benoît's poem, analyzed in the context of medieval historiography, see again Patterson, *Chaucer and the Subject of History* 114–26.

52. See Vickers, "'The Blazon of Sweet Beauty's Best': Shakespeare's *Lucrece*."

53. Guido delle Colonne, *Historia Destructionis Troiae*, trans. Meek, 176–77; Griffin ed., 184: "Nunquid color vividus suarum maxillarum, qui rosarum rubedine coloraverat genas suas, propter sui doloris angustias a sui vigoris vivida claritate fuerat exhaustus, aut nativus eius color roseus labiorum ablatus, vel forte lacrime fluviales ab eius oculis decurrentes splendorem suorum offuscaverant oculorum.

Sane sic revera videbatur intuentibus ut eius defluentes lacrime per maxillas instar illud proprie viderentur habere veluti siquis tabulam recentis eboris, in suo lacteo candore nitentem, ex guttis aque lucide et preclare desuper irroraret; sic eius aurea et flava cesaries in multis dispersa capillis auri similitudinem presentabat ut quasi non viderentur capilli esse sed coniuncta pocius auri fila."

54. Guido delle Colonne, *Historia Destructionis Troiae*, trans. Meek, 82; Griffin ed., 83: "Et quia Frigius Dares voluit in hoc loco quorundam Grecorum et Troyanorum colores et formas describere, qui, etsi non omnium, saltem describere voluit famosiorum. Asseruit enim in codice sui operis, Greca lingua composito, omnes illos suis oculis inspexisse. Nam sepius inter treugas factas inter exercitus ipse se ad Grecorum tentoria conferebat, uniuscuiusque maioris formam inspiciens et contemplans ut ipsorum in suo opere sciret describere qualitates. Dixit enim primo Helenam speciositate nimia refulsisse . . ."

55. Guido delle Colonne, *Historia Destructionis Troiae*, trans. Meek, 84–85; Griffin ed., 86: "Troylus vero, licet fuerit corpore magnus, magis fuit tamen corde magnanimus, animosus multum sed multam habuit in sua animositate temperiem, dilectus plurimum a puellis, cum ipse aliqualem servando modestiam delectaretur in illis. In viribus vero et strennuitate bellandi vel fuit alius Hector vel secundus ab ipso. In toto eciam regno Troye iuvenis nullus fuit tantis viribus nec tanta audacia gloriosus."

56. Mitchell, "On Poems On Pictures."

57. Joseph of Exeter, *The Iliad of Dares Phrygius*, trans. Roberts, 40; *Yliados*, in *Werke und Briefe*, ed. Gompf, 4.35–42 (p. 139): "utinam . . . vultus . . . peremptos / Suscitet eloquii virtus, oculisque sepulti / Pectoribus vivant scripto precone tiranni! / Sic olim positos populis mirantibus offert / Elinguis pictura viros, sic culta profatur / Carta duces, oculis hec blandior, auribus illa."

58. This is the Bodmer manuscript of Guido's *Historia Destructionis Troiae*, amply described and discussed in Buchthal, *Historia Troiana*.

59. Guido delle Colonne, *Historia Destructionis Troiae*, trans. Meek, 83: "deceiving in promises"; Griffin ed., 84: "in promissis fallax." Diomede has by far the least attractive personality in the catalogue of portraits: besides being deceitful, he is quick to do injury, annoying to the servants, and licentious.

60. Schapiro, *Words and Pictures* ch. 4, "Frontal and Profile as Symbolic Forms"; quotation from 38–39.

61. Camille, "Seeing and Reading" 27–28 and n. 11.

62. Buchthal, *Historia Troiana* 45.

63. G. De Blasiis, "Immagini di uomini famosi in una sala di Castelnuovo attribuite a Giotto." The sonnets are printed again in Gilbert, "Boccaccio Looking at Actual Frescoes," Appendix, 238–39. Gilbert discusses the Giotto paintings at some length (230–38).

64. Creighton Gilbert writes, "Giotto was Boccaccio's favorite painter; Boccaccio's admiration was certainly generated in Naples, where he spent his teens and twenties at the court and which is the only place where he may (very probably) have had contact with the then distinguished artist. So we can be sure he was acquainted with that decoration of a royal hall" ("Boccaccio Looking at Actual Frescoes" 231). Gilbert argues that Boccaccio refers to the Giotto paintings in the Conclusion to the

Decameron; he does not discuss the possible influence of those paintings on the works that Boccaccio wrote while living in Naples. I had arrived at my own view of the importance of the *Sala* before encountering Gilbert's fascinating article; I take it as a partial independent confirmation.

65. De Castris, *Arte di corte nella Napoli angioina* 313: "con la sua duplice volontà di espansione dell'egemonia politica angioina sulla penisola e di creazione d'una corte dotta e 'moderna' che di questa egemonia fosse lo specchio e la guistificazione."

66. Buchthal, "Hector's Tomb."

67. Panofsky, *Tomb Sculpture* 73. On the tomb of Charles of Calabria, see 86.

68. Buchthal, "Hector's Tomb" 184.

69. Similarly McGregor, *The Shades of Aeneas* 15–16.

70. Lewis, "What Chaucer Really Did to *Il Filostrato*."

71. "Troye" and "joye" appear as rhyme-words thirty times in the poem. On three occasions, they occupy the B position of the ABABBCC stanza, and thus require a third rhyme; in each case, this is associated with the breaking of a relationship. In the poem's first stanza, the third rhyme is the narrator's "er that I parte fro ye"; in Book 4, Criseyde rhymes "Troye/joye" with the verb "anoye" (4.1304), while convincing Troilus that she should depart from Troy; in Book 5, Diomede decides to "acoye" Criseyde's heart (5.782), and thus initiates the triangle that tears apart the couple.

72. Vance, *Mervelous Signals* 278.

73. Guido delle Colonne, *Historia Destructionis Troiae*, trans. Meek, 43; Griffin ed., 44: "illa nobilissima et mirabilis magna Troya."

74. The three main characters, for example, are rhymed significantly. "Troilus" and "Pandarus" are frequently paired. "Troilus," however, rhymes even more often with "thus," the adverb of simple affirmation. Pandarus, who is guided by two-faced Janus (2.77), has a name that rhymes in two directions; as "Pandarus" he mirrors his friend (or, less often, "thus" or "us"), while as "Pandare" he is almost always answered by "care" or "fare." "Criseyde" rhymes most frequently with "seyde" (35 out of 53 appearances), but also with a range of past-tense verbs: "deyde" (notably in Criseyde's first and last rhyme, 1.55–56 and 5.1833–34), "leyde," "pleyde," "preyde"—as if Criseyde's true counterpart were not so much speech or death as the morpheme indicating pastness, *-ede*. Vance discusses Chaucer's rhyming technique and lists some other habitual rhymes in *Mervelous Signals* 278.

75. "Troia" appears as a rhyme-word eleven times in the *Filostrato*; in nine cases it is rhymed with "noia" (1.13, 2.3, 4.3, 4.38, 4.133, 4.142, 6.4, 6.23, 7.68). On three occasions, "Troia" and "noia" take a third rhyme: "moia" [die] at 2.3, and "gioia" at 4.133 and 6.4. Only twice does "Troia" appear as a rhyme-word and *not* rhyme with "noia": both times the rhyme is "gioia," at 4.8 and 5.37. When "gioia" appears as a rhyme for "Troia," it is never an unmixed joy: in both the "Troia/noia/gioia" stanzas, Criseida is speaking about her departure from Troy, and Troy's double rhyme may be a sign of her ambivalence; of the two "Troia/gioia" pairs, the first appears when Calchas is demanding that the Greeks obtain Criseida for him, and the second when Troiolo describes the absent Criseida as "cagion di tormento e di gioia" [cause of torment and of joy].

76. On this see McCall, "The Trojan Scene in Chaucer's *Troilus*."
77. Lewis, "What Chaucer Really Did" 19.
78. *Troilus and Criseyde*, ed. Windeatt, 7.
79. *Troilus and Criseyde*, ed. Windeatt, 4.

Chapter 6

1. On the rubrics see the textual notes in Windeatt's edition.

2. It is possible that Root and Robinson were themselves partly motivated by a recognition of these connections when they reserved "Canticus Troili" ("Cantus Troili" in Root) for the first and last songs. The manuscripts give somewhat better support for the rubrication adopted by Barney and Windeatt. I want to underline the arbitrariness of my own designation for "O sterre": since I will be concerned solely with the first and last songs, "third *Canticus Troili*" seemed ungainly; "the last *Canticus Troili*" seemed portentous.

3. The first stanza (1.400–406) appears alone in a fifteenth-century religious treatise, the *Disce Mori*, and one other manuscript; another collection of lyrics preserves the first *Canticus Troili* and the two stanzas which follow it (Troilus's speech to the God of Love) as a single poem. See the list of manuscript extracts in Brown and Robbins, *Index of Middle English Verse* 530; on the Chaucerian quotation in the *Disce Mori* see Patterson, "Ambiguity and Interpretation: A Fifteenth-Century Reading of *Troilus and Criseyde*," in *Negotiating the Past* 115–53.

4. Spurgeon, *Five Hundred Years of Chaucer Criticism and Allusion* vol. 1, 350–52.

5. Patterson, *Negotiating the Past* 145.

6. Thomson, "The 'Canticus Troili'" 313. Similarly, Boitani, *Chaucer and the Italian Trecento*, "Introduction" 5: "[Chaucer's use of Petrarch's Sonnet 132] is an isolated problem, which does not recur in Chaucer's works. Interesting and fascinating as a singular accident in the history of literature, it could be seen as a simple case of missed opportunity for Chaucer as well as for fourteenth-century English literature."

7. This approach is best represented in the work of E. T. Donaldson, notably "The Ending of *Troilus*."

8. Curtius writes that "Nautical metaphors originally belong to [i.e. refer to] poetry" (*European Literature and the Latin Middle Ages* 129; see the entire excursus on "Nautical Metaphors," 128–30). The "ship of poetry" will not appear again in this essay; I will be arguing, however, that the second *Canticus Troili* is about literature in a complex way.

9. A reader commenting on an early draft of this chapter made a marginal annotation next to the Chaucerian stanza: "Note the logical contradiction" (with arrows to the first and fifth lines); then, as a comment on this comment, "Well maybe not." I suspect that many readers of the stanza have enacted the same interpretive drama.

10. Some representative examples: Troilus says that he will bewail Criseyde if he loses her (4.272); everyone ought to bewail the death of Troilus (5.1556). There is no instance in Chaucer of a feared event being bewailed.

11. Payne, *The Key of Remembrance* 202.

12. On "over-determination" as the intersection of "various chains of meaning," see Laplanche and Pontalis, *The Language of Psycho-Analysis*, s.v. "Over-Determination." Although my argument is not explicitly psychoanalytic, I believe that dream interpretation is the nearest model for the sort of interpretation I will be pursuing in this chapter.

13. Turner, *The Forest of Symbols* ch. 4, "Betwixt and Between: The Liminal Period in *Rites de Passage*." In Turner's analysis, the liminal period is defined by culture and occupies an area between well-defined structures, yet it is paradoxically outside of all cultural structures. Turner describes a "coincidence of opposite processes and notions in a single representation [which] characterizes the peculiar unity of the liminal: that which is neither this nor that, and yet is both" (99).

14. This is a commonplace, but see for example Mann, "La prima fortuna del Petrarca in Inghilterra" 280. For an illuminating discussion of Wyatt's translations from Petrarch, with an overview of earlier criticism, see Dasenbrock, *Imitating the Italians* ch. 1, "Understanding Renaissance Imitation: The Example of Wyatt."

15. The one avowed dissenter from this consensus known to me is John Fleming, in his recent *Classical Imitation and Interpretation*. Fleming suggests "that in the *Troilus* Chaucer is fully conscious of the fictive erotic biography of the *Canzoniere* no less than he is aware of that of the *Roman de la Rose*" (120–21). He bases his suggestion upon "the detailed thematic justice of the [first] 'Canticus Troili' within the *Troilus*" (121), noting that the next poem after Sonnet 132 begins with a line that might describe Troilus's own wounding by the God of Love: "Amor m'à posto come segno a strale" [Love has set me up like a target for arrow]. Since Love's archery is a conventional motif, Fleming's claim may not convince a philological skeptic. I myself am convinced, and I share Fleming's general willingness to impute wide learning and deep sophistication to Chaucer, but in the next few pages I attempt to present the sort of evidence that might convince a skeptic.

16. Wyatt, *Collected Poems*, ed. Muir, 22–23.

17. Wilkins, *The Making of the "Canzoniere" and Other Petrarchan Studies* ch. 19, "Cantus Troili." Wilkins's ground-breaking work on the history of Petrarch's collection (see especially ch. 9, "The Making of the *Canzoniere*") has not, to my knowledge, been challenged in a way that would affect my argument. His hypothesis that the *Canzoniere* existed in one or more pre-Chigi forms has been questioned by Durling (*Petrarch's Lyric Poems* 646) and by Barolini ("The Making of a Lyric Sequence" 18), but Wilkins does not draw on this hypothesis in his discussion of the first *Canticus Troili*.

18. Wilkins, *The Making of the "Canzoniere"* 308.

19. Wilkins, *The Making of the "Canzoniere"* 253; emphasis added.

20. Wilkins, *The Making of the "Canzoniere"* 199–203. Interestingly, in the Chigi form of the *Canzoniere*, Sonnet 189 had a place of special importance—it was clearly marked as the last lyric in the first of the book's two main parts.

21. Rossetti, *Chaucer's Troylus and Cryseyde Compared with Boccaccio's Filostrato* ad loc.

22. Patch, "Two Notes on Chaucer's *Troilus*" 11–12.

23. Troiolo has addressed Criseida as a star more recently, as well: "O luce bella, o stella mattutina" (5.44) [O beautiful light, O morning star].

24. Both text and translation (with one modification) are from *Petrarch's Lyric Poems*, ed. and trans. Durling.

25. The "dolci segni" are always glossed as Laura's eyes; compare *Canzoniere* 73.46–51.

26. So Root, Robinson, Barney, and Windeatt.

27. The Middle English Dictionary also gives "in stere" as an idiom for "astern," but does not offer any new citations.

28. This view is partially supported by two *auctoritates*: Skeat (*The Complete Works of Geoffrey Chaucer*, Glossary, vol. 6) glosses "in steere" as "upon my rudder"; Donaldson (*Chaucer's Poetry*, note ad loc.) glosses "steere" as "control."

29. Diani discusses the especially close connections between Sonnets 132 and 189 in particular, in "Pétrarque: *Canzoniere* 132" 157.

30. Patricia Thomson poses, and leaves unanswered, several "unanswerable questions on points of fact." "Did Chaucer encounter all Petrarch's *Rime*, or only Sonnet 132, circulating independently? Did he deliberately choose it from the mass of the sonnets to Laura, or did it simply cross his path by chance? . . . Did he think that Boccaccio was the author, not only of *Il Filostrato* . . . but also of the sonnet? Or, on the other hand, did he suppose Petrarch to have written both?" (Thomson, "The 'Canticus Troili'" 313). I believe that it is reasonable to assume more awareness of the Italian literary scene than these questions imply. Chaucer visited Italy twice at a time when Boccaccio and Petrarch were celebrated literary figures; inevitably, more information circulated in the fourteenth century than has come down to us. Recent scholarship has tended to be less conservative about Chaucer's familiarity with contemporary Italian culture; see especially Wallace, "'Whan She Translated Was': A Chaucerian Critique of the Petrarchan Academy."

31. For a close reading of the relationship between the first *Canticus Troili* and Sonnet 132, which incorporates the findings of Wilkins, see Thomson, "The 'Canticus Troili.'"

32. For a typology of four modes of literary imitation, see Thomas M. Greene, *The Light in Troy* 37–48. In Greene's terms, the first *Canticus Troili* is a "reproductive or sacramental" imitation, while the second would appear to be either a "heuristic" or a "dialectical" imitation.

33. Several critics have discussed this fetishization or idolatry; see especially Freccero, "The Fig Tree and the Laurel."

34. Thomson, "The 'Canticus Troili'" 316.

35. Obviously this list could be extended. For example, one might speak of a "proemial" mode in the *Troilus*: each Book except the last begins with a proem (rubricated as a "prohemium" in Books 2–4), totaling twenty-six stanzas, in which the narrator reflects upon the story as a whole and his own complex relationship to it. In the *Filostrato*, the first and third Parts begin with authorial invocations, totaling eight stanzas, but since these invocations address Filostrato's Filomena they contribute to the lyric effect of the whole.

36. James I. Wimsatt writes that "whereas Troilo presents three-quarters of the lyrics in Boccaccio's poem, with the narrator and Criseida making small contributions and Pandaro none, Troilus is the speaker in only two-fifths of the lyrics in Chaucer's work, with the narrator, Criseyde, and Pandarus all participating importantly" ("The French Lyric Element in *Troilus and Criseyde*" 20). It should be noted,

however, that Wimsatt employs a broader definition of "lyric" than I am employing here. I distinguished above between different non-narrative modes, to make the point that Chaucer employs more of these modes than Boccaccio does, but Wimsatt (with equal validity) applies the term "lyric" to any stanza that halts the action; the one-stanza portrait of Diomede, for example, appears on his list of "Developed Lyric Passages" (31).

37. "Meco . . . cominciai a rivolgere l'antiche storie" (Proem 27) [I began to turn over in my mind the old stories]. The only reference to a written source for Filostrato's poem is the phrase "antiche lettere" in the next sentence, but there is no sign that he consults these "lettere" as he writes; he seems to know them already.

38. On the relative "bookishness" of the *Troilus*, see Taylor, *Chaucer Reads "The Divine Comedy,"* especially 53–55.

39. I made this point in Chapter 5, and suggested that the singularity of the whole *Filostrato* is reinforced by its avoidance of framed images: the poem itself is the most striking visible object evoked by Filostrato. In contrast, *Troilus and Criseyde* is verbally historiated with pictures of Troy.

40. Robert Guiette, discussing "the poets of *langue d'Oïl,*" cited and translated in Nichols, "A Poetics of Historicism?" 82.

41. Critics sometimes read the stanza as announcing that Lollius *is* the source of Troilus's song; for a defense of this reading, see Taylor, *Chaucer Reads "The Divine Comedy"* 242 n. 59. I do not find this view plausible. The stanza's explicit statement is that Lollius has written the "sentence" of the song and that the Chaucerian narrator is going to provide not merely the sentence but everything Troilus said. It is of course possible that Lollius, in addition to writing the "sentence," *also* wrote every word of the song, but Chaucer does not say so: the phrase "As writ myn auctour called Lollius" clearly attaches to "the sentence" and not to "his song" or "every word." The most natural reading of the text, I believe—along with other critics such as Dinshaw (*Chaucer's Sexual Poetics* 42–43) and Fleming (*Classical Imitation and Interpretation* 182–83)—is that Lollius has been the source so far ("myn auctour" seems to imply a long-term relationship) but that Lollius provides "only the sentence" of the *Canticus Troili*, so that the actual text must come from another source. Although I assume this reading in the discussion that follows, I do not think my argument depends upon it: in any case it is clear that the Lollius stanza claims some kind of special and all-but-unmediated transmission for the first *Canticus Troili*.

42. The *Troilus* presents itself as both an oral performance and an act of writing from its very first stanza: ". . . er that I parte fro ye . . . Thise woful vers, that wepen as I write." In the *rime riche* of "here" and "here" (1.398–99) the verb *hear* implies oral delivery and the adverb *here* implies a written text. On this subject, and for another discussion of the frame around the first *Canticus Troili*, see H. Marshall Leicester, Jr., "Oure Tonges *Différance*: Textuality and Deconstruction in Chaucer."

43. John Norton-Smith expresses a related view: "A thorough knowledge of Boccaccio's poem is very useful, always fascinating, invariably rewarding, but it was never any part of Chaucer's creative intention that we should repetitiously experience his poem in a comparative mood" (*Geoffrey Chaucer* 161). Norton-Smith himself goes on to provide a fine comparative analysis of the poem.

44. An unqualified affirmative answer to the question posed by this paragraph—yes, Chaucer's relation to his sources is a deliberate and controlled aspect of the meaning of his text—seems to me to raise problems of its own. In its extreme form, this view requires that we treat this "Chaucer" as a fictional character who is manipulated by whatever Chaucer we take to have actually written the poem, and I am not sure the text can sustain this many authors from beginning to end. It seems more likely that different figures of authorship are created, as "reading effects," at different moments in the text. In my view, Chaucer's actual use of his sources raises a problem of "status" which cannot be resolved; this body of meaning shifts uncertainly between our narrative about the text and the text's narrative about itself.

45. Lewis, "What Chaucer Really Did to *Il Filostrato*."

46. Vance, "Mervelous Signals: Poetics, Sign Theory, and Politics in Chaucer's Troilus" 310. This article is now revised as chapter 9 of Vance's *Mervelous Signals: Poetics and Sign Theory in the Middle Ages*—without, however, the quoted sentence.

47. Vance, "Mervelous Signals" 303–11 ("lyrical cores" at 304); Payne, *Key of Remembrance* 184–87, 201–9 ("lyric inserts" at 201). See also Wimsatt's important article, "The French Lyric Element." W. A. Davenport, in *Chaucer: Complaint and Narrative*, offers a more dynamic account of the changing role of lyric complaint within the *Troilus* (ch. 6) and throughout Chaucer's career; Davenport's central concern, however, is not with lyric as a form but with complaint as a mode (6–9).

48. Windeatt, "The Text of the *Troilus*" 1.

49. Separate manuscript copies of the first *Canticus Troili* extend to one stanza or five, but not three; see n. 3. Among modern critics, Payne, without explanation, extends the first *Canticus Troili* to five stanzas (*The Key of Remembrance* 185). The manuscripts do not mark the song's ending with a rubric, but the next line after the third stanza announces the beginning of a new utterance, which is spoken rather than sung: "And to the God of Love thus seyde he . . ." (1.421).

50. The first *Canticus Troili* (the only lyric which Vance discusses specifically) "is the first lyrical 'core' of the *Troilus*, and Chaucer's gesture of lifting Troilus's song from Petrarch's *Canzoniere* ought not to be dismissed as a mere 'lyrical ornament,' nor even as the graceful tribute of a young English poet to a revered continental master, but as a more wily attempt to challenge the consecrated conventions of the medieval erotic lyric with the logic of narrative, a harsh logic that would succeed in linking the latent violence of the 'tragic style' to full-blown historical events that are its consequence" (Vance, "Mervelous Signals" 317). Since I argue for an eventual collapse of the lyric frame, I cannot entirely disagree with this account: but I think it is necessary to stress the efficacy of the initial frame, the degree to which it does temporarily exclude the narrative.

51. On "nested spaces" in the *Troilus*, see Holley, *Chaucer's Measuring Eye* 74–93.

52. Thomas M. Greene, *The Light in Troy* 120. Other critics have discussed the paradoxical temporality of the *Canzoniere*: see for example Waller, *Petrarch's Poetics and Literary History*; Barolini, "The Making of a Lyric Sequence"; and Roland Greene, *Post-Petrarchism* ch. 1, "Founding Fiction: The Temporality of Petrarch's *Canzoniere*." Roland Greene describes the characteristic experience of the Petrarchan lover as "[p]rocess without progress, time's relentless passing without percep-

tible advancement in the fortunes or attitudes of the lover" (55), a description that applies well to Sonnet 189.

53. Donaldson, "The Ending of *Troilus*."

54. In saying this I part company with the view of Vance, who argues that the *Troilus* finally judges courtly literature, and indeed all literature and all language that is not Christian prayer, from an austere Boethian—or perhaps Robertsonian—perspective. See "Mervelous Signals" and, more explicitly, "Chaucer, Spenser, and the Ideology of Translation." Vance sees more variety in the text than does D. W. Robertson (for whom the poem is anti-courtly at every point; see *A Preface to Chaucer* 472–502), yet he argues for a univocal ruling ideology. *Translatio*—metaphor, and figurative language generally, but also the inevitable faithlessness of what we call translation—is inevitably a fall for Vance's Chaucer; Troy, Troilus, and the *Troilus* are doomed by poetic discourse. "Chaucer shows us how metaphors, jokes, rhetorical persuasion and lies vitiate the institution of language and destroy, thereby, the capacity of those who speak it to act responsibly" ("Chaucer, Spenser" 230); at the end of the poem, "Chaucer . . . felt compelled to renounce the poetic heritage of the *auctores* in the *Troilus* in favor of contemplation, philosophy and prayer" ("Chaucer, Spenser" 238). It is certainly true that the final stanza of the *Troilus* is a prayer; it is hard, though, to see any renunciation of "Virgile, Ovide, Omer, Lucan, and Stace" (5.1792). Vance contrasts Chaucer with Spenser, who "endows the idea of translation with a sense of creativity which makes it akin to his own artistic performance" ("Chaucer, Spenser" 238); in the discussion that follows I argue for just such a sense of creative translation in Chaucer.

55. Wise, *The Influence of Statius upon Chaucer*; Clogan, "Chaucer and the Medieval Statius"; Clogan, "Chaucer's Use of the *Thebaid*"; Clogan, "Chaucer and the *Thebaid* Scholia"; David Anderson, "Theban History in Chaucer's *Troilus*." For sophisticated critical treatments of Chaucer's deployment of Statius and other poets ancient and medieval, see Wetherbee, *Chaucer and the Poets*, and Fleming, *Classical Imitation and Interpretation*. See also Lee Patterson's brilliant discussion of "Thebanness" throughout *Chaucer and the Subject of History*, especially 75–78 (for a succinct definition) and ch. 2 (on Thebanness in *Troilus*).

56. The deliberate reference to the *Thebaid* is underscored, in almost every manuscript of the *Troilus*, by the interpolation of a twelve-line Latin argument of the *Thebaid* into Cassandra's synopsis; see the Barney edition, footnote to 5.1498. Windeatt takes the logical step of printing the Latin argument as part of the text of the *Troilus*.

57. Text and (modified) translation are from the Loeb Library edition of Mozley.

58. When Diomede comes for Criseyde, Troilus asks himself: "Why nyl I brynge al Troie upon a roore? / Why nyl I slen this Diomede also?" (5.45–46). He later exclaims, "I not, allas, whi lete ich hire to go" (5.226). Eteocles, during his sleepless night, "sese culpat super omnia, qui non / orantem in mediis legatum coetibus ense / perculerit foedasque palam satiaverit iras" (3.19–21) [above all blames himself, that he struck not the envoy with his sword as he spoke in mid assembly, nor openly sated to the full his savage wrath].

59. In its "strangeness," and in its assimilation of Trojan eros to Theban

violence, this allusion fits a general pattern described by Wetherbee. Wetherbee describes Chaucer's "use of Theban material throughout most of the *Troilus*" as "a mode of allusion that is ironic, always on the edge of parody, and highly conscious of incongruity. There is something inescapably comic about the preoccupation of Chaucer's Trojans with love; it is hard at times to remember that this folly and the code that legitimizes it are Chaucer's equivalent for the Theban madness . . . The combination of innocence and pride, true and false idealism in [Trojan] chivalry is as different from the madness of the house of Oedipus as Pandarus from Capaneus, but we must finally take its contradictions and its potentially subversive influence equally seriously" (*Chaucer and the Poets* 120).

60. This is the claim of David Anderson, "Theban History."

61. See the Riverside note to 4.279.

62. Fleming arrives at a similarly strained but telling analogy for Criseyde when he discusses another Statian allusion in the *Troilus*. In the earlier scene (4.1366–1414) in which Criseyde tells Troilus how she will convince Calchas to let her return to Troy, she echoes a line from *Thebaid* 3, from a scene somewhat later than the scene I have quoted above (*Troilus* 4.1408; *Thebaid* 3.661). Fleming argues that "For this textual moment Criseyde is being cast as Statius' Capaneus; and for all the difference between Statius and Chaucer, the two scenes reveal extensive parallels" (*Classical Imitation and Interpretation* 85; for the whole discussion see 83–87).

63. See Wetherbee, *Chaucer and the Poets* 31–36.

64. Of the simile at the beginning of *Thebaid* 3, David Vessey writes: "Fully to appreciate the simile, it is necessary to compare it with two earlier ones. . . . Polynices [at 1.370 ff] had wandered through the storm like a *navita* and the threat of his brother's treachery was likened to hidden reefs; in book 2 [105–8], Eteocles is compared to the *magister* of a vessel who ignores the warning given by black clouds of a storm to come; by the time of the simile in book 3, the storm has broken and Eteocles has lost control of events" (Vessey, *Statius and the Thebaid* 110). For a complete list of nautical metaphors in the *Thebaid*, see Legras, *Étude sur la Thébaide de Stace* 297. The nautical metaphors of the *Canzoniere* have been discussed by several critics. Among them, Waller argues that the various nautical metaphors in the *Canzoniere* constitute a "reverse voyage" that reflects the fragmentary temporality of the work (*Petrarch's Poetics and Literary History* 80–83); Diani's analysis of 132 includes a fascinating discussion of Petrarchan navigation generally ("Pétrarque: *Canzoniere* 132" 157–65). In a discussion of the Chigi form of the *Canzoniere*, Bernardo's comment on 189 is close to Vessey's comment on the Statian simile: "In No. 189, which closed Part I of this Chigi form, the bubble bursts. The poet can no longer control his passion. He pictures himself as a ship tossed around by a storm" (*Petrarch, Laura, and the Triumphs* 33). In the final form of the *Canzoniere*, of course, Part I (the so-called "In Vita" section) continues for seventy-four more poems, not all of which are despairing. In any context, though, Sonnet 189 would seem to represent, however statically, a turning point in an emotional narrative: "i' 'ncomincio a desperar del porto" [I begin to despair of the port].

65. Since "contemporary courtly literature" includes the *Filostrato*, and the *Filostrato* includes the story of Troiolo's downfall, it may seem perverse to call this downfall a journey away from contemporary courtly literature toward the *Thebaid*.

But Chaucer, in a series of additions to his primary source, consistently identifies the threat to Troilus and to Troy with Theban history; it seems to me that this creates a differential structure in which Troilus's decline is associated with a movement from the purely Boccaccian text to a text that is somewhere between Boccaccio and Statius—and this is a movement in the direction of Statius.

66. Turner, *Forest of Symbols* 110.

67. See the Riverside note to 5.1786.

68. See, again, Wetherbee, *Chaucer and the Poets*. Chaucer's choice of the *Thebaid* as the epic poem *par excellence* may suggest his ambivalence about the stature of the classical poet. With the *Aeneid*, for example, there is no contradiction between story and discourse; the founding of Rome is like the writing of the great Roman epic. The *Thebaid*, in contrast, carries contradiction in itself.

69. In its only other appearance in the Chaucerian canon, Charybdis is used as an image for love. In the *Romaunt of the Rose*, Reason describes love as "A swete perell in to droun; / An hevy birthen, lyght to bere; / A wikked wawe, awey to were. / It is Karibdous perilous, / Disagreable and gracious" (4710–14). In the second *Canticus Troili*, Criseyde has the power to save Troilus, and therefore the power to doom him; the oxymoronic attributes of Reason's love are divided between the gracious star and the disagreeable Charybdis, but both are finally aspects of Criseyde or of Troilus's love for her. The misogynist implications of the image of the devouring vortex need hardly be stressed.

70. Snijder, *Thebaid: A Commentary on Book III* 57.

71. Jeanroy cites three examples of nautical metaphors in Provençal verse; these are far closer in form to the three-line metaphor of Sonnet 132 than to the extended allegory of 189 (*La Poésie lyrique des troubadours* vol. 2, 125 and 126n; cited in Thomson, "Canticus Troili" 325n).

72. See Rahner, *Greek Myths and Christian Mystery* 341–86.

73. Diani, "Pétrarque: Canzoniere 132" 157.

74. Text and (modified) translation are quoted from the Loeb Library edition of Bennett. For Petrarch's familiarity with the entire Horatian canon, see de Nolhac, *Petrarque et l'humanisme* vol. 1, 180–85. According to de Nolhac, Petrarch cites Horace "sans cesse" (181), more than any other Latin poet except Virgil. Petrarch's verse letter to Horace (*Familiares* 24.10) is a virtual cento of quotations from the Horatian canon, including Ode 1.14 (*Petrarch's Letters to Classical Authors*, trans. Cosenza, 125–35).

75. The Ship of State in classical Greek and Roman literature is discussed in Kahlmayer, *Seesturm und Schiffsbruch als Bild*. Other articles deal with the post-medieval as well as the classical era: Schäfer, "Das Staatsschiff. Zur Präzision eines Topos"; Beller, "Staatsschiff und Schiff des Lebens als Gleichnisse der barocken Geschichtsdichtung." Little has been written about the medieval Ship of State (but see Owst, discussed below). The image is generally described as a classical commonplace that was not fully revived until the Renaissance: Beller, for example, writes that it became a poetic commonplace specifically through numerous translations and citations of the Horatian ode, which was not well-known in the Middle Ages.

76. See for example Fraenkel, *Horace* 154.

77. Keller, ed., *Pseudacronis Scholia in Horatium Vetustiora* vol. 1, 64–65: "Per allegoriam ode ista bellum civile designat, ut quidam volunt, alii rempublicam"; "SINE FUNIBUS. Aut sine administratoribus intellegendum aut sine expensis et pecunia."

78. Momigliano, "L'elegia politica del Petrarca" 19: "un motivo a sé"; "una delle note che compongono il tessuto elegiaco del suo libro, uno dei temi della sua storia di contemplativo e di malinconico."

79. Discussing the second of these two *canzoni*, Durling writes, "The appearance of 125–29 as a group (in violation of chronological order and geographical logic) is an enactment of relative psychological integration around the image of Laura; it is also an important formal node, a poetic integration, of the book. That 'Italia mia,' Petrarch's most important patriotic poem, is part of this group, is not accidental: surrounded by the great love *canzoni*, with which it has many structural and poetic similarities, it is meant to be related to the critical psychological insights of these poems" (*Petrarch's Lyric Poems* 24). Durling here stresses integration and insight over the fragmentation and blindness discussed elsewhere in his introduction; it should be noted that the lords of Italy are, like the Petrarchan lover in some of his moods, lost in "Vano error" (128.23).

80. Thomas M. Greene, *The Light in Troy* 115; Greene's emphasis.

81. See Mazzotta, "The *Canzoniere* and the Language of the Self."

82. On Chaucer's reading of Horace, see Hoffman, "The Influence of the Classics on Chaucer" 193–94, and Fleming, *Classical Imitation and Interpretation*, especially 179–200.

83. Vance, writing of Chaucer's treatment of Sonnet 132, says, "Petrarch's song itself may perhaps have been seen by Chaucer as an artful but dangerous reduction of a heroic narrative world, since it too resonates with classical metaphors which call to mind the wanderings of other amorous heroes—Odysseus, for example, or the less temperate Aeneas" ("Mervelous Signals" 317). This would seem to be even more true of 189.

84. Schäfer ("Staatsschiff" 260) cites Aristotle, *Rhetoric* 1406.b.35 (simile); [Cicero], *Rhetorica ad Herennium* 4.44.57 (simile); Demetrius, *De Elocutione* 78 (metaphor); Quintilian, *Institutio Oratoria* 8.6.44 (allegory, using the example of Horace's Ode 1.14).

85. In their edition of the *Convivio* Busnelli and Vandelli (note to 4.4.5) cite Thomas Aquinas's commentary on Aristotle's *Politics*, book 3 *lectio* 3, and *De regim. princ.*, book 1 ch. 2 and especially ch. 14.

86. No. 39 in Robbins, ed., *Historical Poems of the XIVth and XVth Centuries* 102–6.

87. Owst, *Literature and Pulpit in Medieval England* 76. The homiletic Ship is discussed on 66–76.

88. Owst, *Literature and Pulpit* 68, translating from Hauréau, *Notices et extraits* vol. 3, 38. The Latin text reads: "Ad transeundum illud mare necessaria est nobis navis, malus, velum, et cet. Navis significat fidem cujus tabulae sacrae Scripturae sententiae sunt, clavum vero auctoritates sanctorum doctorum sunt." Given the larger argument of this book, it is worth underlining this metaphorization of "auctoritates": the total image here corresponds to the page of commentary dis-

cussed in Chapter 1, with the scriptural text occupying the substantial center (as the planks of the ship) and the *auctoritates*, or writings of the Fathers, placed (as a rudder) at the edge but assigned a powerful guiding role.

89. No. 78 in Robbins, *Historical Poems* 191–93. Angus Fletcher prints this poem and discusses it briefly in *Allegory: The Theory of a Symbolic Mode* 77–81. It is mentioned (along with *Mum and the Sothsegger*) in Owst, *Literature and Pulpit* 76.

90. Day and Steele, eds., *Mum and the Sothsegger* 25, 4.71–82. Owst referes to this text by the title that Skeat assigned it, *Richard the Redeles*.

91. Day and Steele, eds., *Mum and the Sothsegger* xxiv.

92. Day and Steele, eds., *Mum and the Sothsegger* 4.71–82.

93. Day and Steele, eds., *Mum and the Sothsegger* 106, n. to 4.71–82.

94. Wright, ed., *Political Poems and Songs Relating to English History* vol. 1, 253: "Heu! quanta desolatio Angliae praestatur, / Cujus regnum quodlibet hinc inde minatur, / Et hujus navigium pene conquassatur" (1–3) [Alas, what desolation is given to England, whose kingdom of whatever sort is pushed from all sides, and its ship is practically shaken apart]. The poem is in fact macaronic: the fifth line of each six-line stanza begins with an English refrain, "With an O and an I," before reverting to Latin.

95. Before turning to an extended passage from Gower, I would add one more brief example, also from Gower—from "In Praise of Peace," dated soon after 1399. Gower is arguing that when the head of the Church fails to maintain civil peace, secular kings must step in: "These kynges oughten of here rightwisnesse / Here oghne cause among hemself redresse: / Thogh Petres schip as now hath lost his stiere, / It lith in hem that barge forto stiere" (*The Complete Works of John Gower*, ed. Macaulay, vol. 3, 488).

96. *The Complete Works of John Gower*, ed. Macaulay, vol. 4. English translations are adapted from *The Major Latin Works of John Gower*, trans. Stockton.

97. See the rubric to Chapter 20, which in itself seems reminiscent of Petrarch's Sonnet 132 or the first *Canticus Troili*: "Hic loquitur adhuc de navi visa in sompnis, id est de mente sua adhuc turbata, ut si ipse mentaliter sompniando, quasi per navem variis ventis sine gubernaculo agitatam, omnes partes mundi pro pace mentis scrutanda investigasset" [Here he speaks of the ship he still saw in his sleep—that is, of his confused mind, as if he himself, while dreaming in his thoughts, had, as if by a ship driven rudderless by various winds, sought out all parts of the world in order to discover peace of mind]. For the identification with the Tower of London, see the rubric to Chapter 17 and lines 1743–66.

98. *Major Latin Works of Gower*, trans. Stockton, 16.

99. Stockton provides a table of the borrowings (367–68).

100. "Frater erat Cille, furiens magis ipse Caribdi, / Et velut os Herebi, que voret ipse petit" (1723–24) [It was brother to Scylla, raging more than Charybdis; and, like the jaws of hell, it sought things to devour].

101. "Visa michi Cilla fuit et tunc visa Caribdis, / Devoret ut navem spirat utrumque latus" (1741–42) [First it seemed like Scylla to me, and then Charybdis, as it was eager to devour the ship from both sides].

102. "Iamque gubernator, tollens ad sidera palmas, / Exposcit votis inmemor artis opem: / Vincitur ars vento, neque iam moderator habenis / Utitur, immo vaga

per freta navis arat" (1727–30) [And the helmsman, raising his hands towards the heavens, implores aid with his prayers, forgetting his art: his skill is conquered by the wind, and the steersman no longer handles the helm; instead, the ship plows aimlessly across the sea].

103 "Tu michi, stella maris, sis previa, quo ferar undis; / Sit tibi cura mei, te duce tutus ero" (1615–16) [Go Thou before me, O Star of the Sea, wherever I may be borne by the waves; take charge of me, I shall be safe with Thee as my guide]. In the line which seems to introduce the prayer, the Dreamer says he is praying to Christ (1614), but "stella maris" usually applies to Mary, and later the Dreamer gives thanks to "Stella Maria maris" (2083).

104. It is not clear that Gower's voyage ends happily: when the ship strikes land, it finds an island "more oppressive than Scylla" (1952)—namely the former "Island of Brut" (1963), now a wasteland. Perhaps on the verge of another vision, the Dreamer wakes up.

105. Fisher, *John Gower* 207.

106. Fisher, *John Gower* 102. The version of *Vox Clamantis* containing Book One was completed by "about 1386" (108); Book One may well predate 1386, but it was obviously begun after the Rising of 1381.

107. A summary of scholarly views on the dating of the *Troilus* appears in Barney's Riverside edition, 1020. The apparent *terminus ad quem* is March 1388, when Thomas Usk, who refers to "the boke of Troilus," was executed; Barney favors a "date of composition 1382–85," but he notes that "new evidence could easily controvert" this dating. Patterson argues that Chaucer was still working on the poem through 1387 (*Chaucer and the Subject of History* 156n.).

108. Again, both poems are written in a mournful style to accord with a mournful subject (*Vox Clamantis* Prologue 33–34; *Troilus* 1.12–14).

109. Troilus dreams that he has fallen among all his enemies, and wakes with a start to the reality of his loss (5.246–61); the Dreamer has literally fallen among his enemies (see especially 1413–14), and within the vision he is tormented by dreams that mimic his misfortunes, dreams from which he awakes to his real suffering (1425–26). Troilus stands in front of Criseyde's empty house (5.526–53); the Dreamer gazes at the abandoned buildings of his native land (1430). This list of shared motifs could be extended.

110. This last suggestion has been made in a general way by Chauncey Wood: "we might envision Chaucer and Gower working on *Troilus* and *Vox Clamantis* in the turbulent years from 1375 to 1385—influencing each other, perhaps, and being influenced by the course of history" (*The Elements of Chaucer's Troilus* 32). Wood—uniquely, to my knowledge—offers a suggestive discussion of possible links between the two poems (especially 31–37, 59–62); his emphases are very different from mine. On the literary relations of Chaucer and Gower, see also Fisher, *John Gower* ch. 5, and Whitman, "*Troilus and Criseyde* and Chaucer's Dedication to Gower."

111. See Coleman, *Medieval Readers and Writers* ch. 3.

112. McCall and Rudisill, "The Parliament of 1386 and Chaucer's Trojan Parliament" 281.

113. Patterson, *Chaucer and the Subject of History* 25.

114. McCall and Rudisill, "The Parliament of 1386 and Chaucer's Trojan Parliament."

115. Patterson, *Chaucer and the Subject of History* 156–61; Patterson elsewhere describes the passage as "a royalist commentary" on the Parliament (51).

116. Brown, "Another Contemporary Allusion in Chaucer's *Troilus*."

117. Brown notes that Gower punned at least twice on the name of Jack Straw (*Vox Clamantis*, 1.651–52, 655–56). He lists other possible Chaucerian allusions to the Rising of 1381, notably the explicit comparison of the fox-hunters in *The Nun's Priest's Tale* to "Jakke Straw and his meynee" slaughtering the Flemish merchants (VII.3393–97).

118. The most thorough discussion of this issue is Patterson's, *Chaucer and the Subject of History* ch. 2. Patterson explores a range of different kinds of historical and historiographic reference in *Troilus and Criseyde*, but concludes that "the poem's deepest message is not about the failure of any particular historical moment but about the failure of history, and of historical understanding, per se" (163).

119. The *Troilus*'s only other reference to the political realities of England might seem to be an exception to my generalization—the compliment paid to Queen Anne in an early description of Criseyde: "Right as oure firste lettre is now an A, / In beaute first so stood she, makeles" (1.171–72; see the Riverside note). But there is at least a disturbing undercurrent here. The adverb "now" reminds us of the contrast between the lasting order of the alphabet and the passing of kings and queens; moreover, a comparison with Criseyde may be a compliment in Book 1 but it is hardly a stable compliment.

120. Owst, *Literature and Pulpit in Medieval England* 76.

121. For example, Patterson shows that Chaucer was "deeply, and unhappily, involved in the factionalized political world of the mid-1380s," and immediately adds: "Nor should we too quickly assume that the writing of *Troilus and Criseyde* was not itself an act that carried with it important, and even dangerous, political consequences" (*Chaucer and the Subject of History* 161). It is easy to imagine documentary evidence that would make this appealing speculation more plausible or less plausible.

122. See my discussion at the end of Chapter 4.

Afterword

1. Besides the example I discuss in the rest of this paragraph, I might mention the narrator's response to the sexual consummation: he exclaims "O blisful nyght" (3.1317), but goes on to reflect for two stanzas about his own limitations as a writer, noting that he has followed his "auctour" as well as he could, but that he may have "in eched" some words, "for the beste," and that in any case those who know about love should feel free to correct his language, adding or deleting as they see fit (3.1324–37). At the center of the sexual experience is a blank to be filled in by the reader.

2. Dinshaw, *Chaucer's Sexual Poetics*, especially ch. 1, "Reading Like a Man: The Critics, the Narrator, Troilus, and Pandarus."

3. Dinshaw, *Chaucer's Sexual Poetics* 41.

4. Dinshaw, *Chaucer's Sexual Poetics* 41. Dinshaw quotes Barthes's description of "intermittence": "The intermittence of skin flashing between two articles of clothing (trousers and sweater), between two edges (the open-necked shirt, the glove and the sleeve); it is this flash itself which seduces, or rather: the staging of an appearance-as-disappearance" (Barthes, *The Pleasure of the Text* 10).

5. The comparison with the aspen leaf does not indicate one emotion more than the other: a fearful Hypermnestra "quok as doth the lef of aspe grene" (*Legend of Good Women* 2648), but the Summoner "lyk an aspen leef . . . quook for ire" (*Summoner's Prologue* III. 1667).

6. "For certeynly, in every membre / I quake, whanne I me remembre / Of the botoun . . ." (*Romaunt* 4109–11). Similarly in the speech of the God of Love to the Lover (from which I quoted in my Introduction): "And eke thy blod shal al toquake" (2527).

7. The *Troilus* offers one other instance of quaking for which the emotional content is unspecified: after Diomede asserts that he is as eager to serve Criseyde as any Trojan, "in his speche a litel wight he quok" (5.926). Once again, the quaking may bespeak some mixture of shyness, desire, and anger (at the Trojans)—but because the quaking voice belongs to Diomede we are more likely to take it as a carefully chosen effect designed to give the *impression* of strong feeling and utter sincerity.

8. These lines appear in Criseyde's last speech in the poem. (She will later write Troilus a letter.) The speech ends, "But al shal passe; and thus take I my leve" (5.1085). Criseyde is not literally going anywhere at this point—she is in the Greek camp with Diomede—so why this exit line? She seems to be conscious that she is leaving the poem. And if she is conscious of that, she may also be aware of an ambiguity in the line. "Thus" can mean "with these words," but it can also mean "therefore": all earthly, mutable things shall pass, and I am one of those things, so I must pass as well.

9. I might drastically schematize the difference between a critical project like Dinshaw's and my own project in this book by referring to the formula that characterizes "state philosophy" according to Deleuze and Guattari: x = x = not y. (I quote from Brian Massumi's foreword to his translation of Deleuze and Guattari, *A Thousand Plateaus*, xii.) Where Dinshaw explores the negation that governs the representation of women, x = not y, my own topic has been the history of the masculine x = x.

Bibliography

Adam-Even, Paul. "Les usages héraldiques au milieu du XIIe siècle d'après le *Roman de Troie* de Benoît de Sainte-Maure et la littérature contemporaine." *Archivum Heraldicum* 77 (1963) 18–29.

Aers, David. *Community, Gender, and Individual Identity: English Writing 1360–1430*. London: Routledge, 1988.

Albert de Stade. *Troilus*. Ed. T. Merzdorf. Bibliotheca Scriptorum Graecorum et Romanorum Teubneriana. Leipzig: Teubner, 1875.

Albertus Magnus. *Commentarii in Primum Librum Sententiarum*. Dist. I–XXV. *Opera Omnia*. Vol. 25. Ed. A. Borgnet. Paris: Vivès, 1893.

Allen, Judson B. *The Ethical Poetic of the Later Middle Ages: A Decorum of Convenient Distinction*. Toronto: University of Toronto Press, 1982.

Anderson, David. *Before the Knight's Tale: Imitation of Classical Epic in Boccaccio's* Teseida. Philadelphia: University of Pennsylvania Press, 1988.

———. "Theban History in Chaucer's *Troilus*." *Studies in the Age of Chaucer* 4 (1982) 109–33.

Anderson, Graham. *Philostratus: Biography and Belles Lettres in the Third Century A.D.* London: Croom Helm, 1986.

Antal, Frederick. *Florentine Painting and Its Social Background*. Cambridge, Mass.: Harvard University Press, 1986.

Ascoli, Albert Russell. "The Vowels of Authority (Dante's *Convivio* IV.vi.3–4)." Brownlee and Stephens, *Discourses of Authority*. 23–46.

Augustine. *Confessions*. Ed. M. Skutella and A. Solignac, trans. E. Tréhorel and G. Bouissou. *Oeuvres de Saint Augustin*. Vol. 13–14. Paris: Desclée de Brouwer, 1962.

Balduino, Armando, ed. *Cantari del trecento*. Milan: Marzorati, 1970.

Baldwin, John W. *The Scholastic Culture of the Middle Ages, 1000–1300*. Lexington, Mass.: D. C. Heath, 1971.

Barolini, Teodolinda. *Dante's Poets: Textuality and Truth in the Comedy*. Princeton, N. J.: Princeton University Press, 1984.

———. "The Making of a Lyric Sequence: Time and Narrative in Petrarch's *Rerum vulgarium fragmenta*." *Modern Language Notes* 104 (1989) 1–38.

Barthes, Roland. *Camera Lucida: Reflections on Photography*. Trans. Richard Howard. New York: Hill and Wang, 1981.

———. "The Death of the Author." *The Rustle of Language*. Trans. Richard Howard. New York: Hill and Wang, 1986. 49–55.

———. *Fragments d'un discours amoureux*. Paris: Éditions du Seuil, 1977.

———. "From Work to Text." *The Rustle of Language*. Trans. Richard Howard. New York: Hill and Wang, 1986. 56–64.

———. *A Lover's Discourse: Fragments*. Trans. Richard Howard. New York: Farrar, Straus and Giroux, 1978.

———. *The Pleasure of the Text*. Trans. Richard Miller. New York: Hill and Wang, 1975.

Battaglia, Salvatore. "Schemi lirici nell'arte del Boccaccio." *La Coscienza letteraria del medioevo*. Naples: Liguori, 1965. 625–44.

(Pseudo-)Bede. *De Psalmorum Libro Exegesis*. *PL* 93.477–1098.

Beller, Manfred. "Staatsschiff und Schiff des Lebens als Gleichnisse der barocken Geschichtsdichtung." *Arcadia* 15 (1980) 1–13.

Bennett, J. A. W. *Chaucer's Book of Fame: An Exposition of "The House of Fame."* Oxford: Clarendon Press, 1968.

Benoît de Sainte-Maure. *Le Roman de Troie*. Ed. Léopold Constans. 6 vols. Paris: Firmin-Didot, 1904–12.

Benson, C. David. *The History of Troy in Middle English Literature: Guido delle Colonne's Historia Destructionis Troiae in Medieval England*. Woodbridge, Suffolk: D. S. Brewer, 1980.

Bernardo, Aldo S. *Petrarch, Laura, and the Triumphs*. Albany: State University of New York Press, 1974.

Berschin, Walter. *Greek Letters and the Latin Middle Ages: From Jerome to Nicholas of Cusa*. Trans. Jerold C. Frakes. Rev. ed. Washington: Catholic University of America Press, 1988.

Bertolucci, Valeria. "Libri e canzonieri d'autore nel Medioevo: prospettive di ricerca." *Morfologie del testo medievale*. Studi Linguistici e Semiologici 28. Bologna: Mulino, 1989. 125–46.

[Bible.] *The Holy Bible: Douay-Rheims Version*. New York: Benziger Brothers, 1941.

Biblia Sacra Iuxta Vulgatam Versionem. 2 vols. Stuttgart: Württembergische Bibelanstalt, 1969.

Bird, Otto. "The Canzone d'Amore of Cavalcanti According to the Commentary of Dino del Garbo: Text and Commentary." *Mediaeval Studies* 2 (1940) 150–203.

Bloch, R. Howard. *Etymologies and Genealogies: A Literary Anthropology of the French Middle Ages*. Chicago: University of Chicago Press, 1983.

Boccaccio, Giovanni. *Boccaccio on Poetry: Being the Preface and the Fourteenth and Fifteenth Books of Boccaccio's Genealogia Deorum Gentilium*. Trans. Charles G. Osgood. 2nd ed. Library of Liberal Arts. Indianapolis, Ind.: Bobbs-Merrill, 1956.

———. *Decameron*. Ed. Vittore Branca. *Tutte le opere*. Vol. 4. 1976.

———. *The Decameron*. Trans. G. H. McWilliam. Middlesex: Penguin, 1972.

———. *Esposizioni sopra la Comedia di Dante*. Ed. Giorgio Padoan. *Tutte le opere*. Vol. 6. 1965.

———. *Filostrato*. Ed. Vittore Branca. *Tutte le opere*. Vol. 2. 1–228. 1964.

———. *Il Filostrato*. Ed. Vincenzo Pernicone, trans. Robert P. apRoberts and Anna Bruni Seldis. Garland Library of Medieval Literature. New York: Garland, 1986.

———. *Teseida delle nozze d'Emilia*. Ed. Alberto Limentani. *Tutte le opere*. Vol. 2. 229–664. 1964.

———. *Trattatello in laude di Dante*. Ed. Pier Giorgio Ricci. *Tutte le opere*. Vol. 3. 423–538. 1974.

———. *Tutte le opere di Giovanni Boccaccio*. Ed. Vittore Branca. 12 vols. Verona: Mondadori, 1964–.

Boitani, Piero. "Antiquity and Beyond: The Death of Troilus." Boitani, *The European Tragedy of Troilus*. 1–19.

———. *Chaucer and Boccaccio*. Medium Aevum Monographs n.s. 8. Oxford: Society for the Study of Medieval Languages and Literature, 1977.

———, ed. *Chaucer and the Italian Trecento*. Cambridge: Cambridge University Press, 1983.

———, ed. *The European Tragedy of Troilus*. Oxford: Clarendon Press, 1989.

Bonaventure. *Opera Theologica Selecta*. Ed. L. M. Bello. 5 vols. Florence: Quaracchi, 1934–64.

Bossy, Michel-André. "Cyclical Composition in Guiraut Riquier's Book of Poems." *Speculum* 66 (1991) 277–93.

Boutière, J., and A.-H. Schutz, eds. *Biographies des troubadours*. Paris: A. G. Nizet, 1964.

Boynton, Mary Fuertes. "Simon Alcok on Expanding the Sermon." *Harvard Theological Review* 34 (1941) 201–16.

Branca, Vittore. *Boccaccio: The Man and His Works*. Trans. Richard Monges. New York: New York University Press, 1976.

———. "Poetica del rinnovamento e tradizione agiografica nella *Vita Nuova*." *Studi in onore di Italo Siciliano*. Florence: Olschki, 1967. 123–48.

Brault, Gerard J. *Early Blazon: Heraldic Terminology in the Twelfth and Thirteenth Centuries with Special Reference to Arthurian Literature*. Oxford: Clarendon Press, 1972.

Brown, Carleton. "Another Contemporary Allusion in Chaucer's *Troilus*." *Modern Language Notes* 26 (1911) 208–11.

Brown, Carleton, and Rossell Hope Robbins. *The Index of Middle English Verse*. New York: Columbia University Press, 1943.

Brownlee, Kevin. *Poetic Identity in Guillaume de Machaut*. Madison: University of Wisconsin Press, 1984.

Brownlee, Kevin, and Walter Stephens, eds. *Discourses of Authority in Medieval and Renaissance Literature*. Hanover, N. H.: University Press of New England, 1989.

Bruno the Carthusian. *Expositio in Psalmos*. *PL* 152.637–1420.

Buchthal, Hugo. "Hector's Tomb." *Art of the Mediterranean World, A.D. 100 to 1400*. Washington, D.C.: Decatur House, 1983. 178–87.

———. *Historia Troiana: Studies in the History of Mediaeval Secular Illustration*. London: Warburg Institute, 1971.

Burrow, J. A. *Ricardian Poetry: Chaucer, Gower, Langland and the Gawain Poet*. London: Routledge and Kegan Paul, 1971.

Camille, Michael. "Seeing and Reading: Some Visual Implications of Medieval Literacy and Illiteracy." *Art History* 8 (1985) 26–49.

Carruthers, Mary J. *The Book of Memory: A Study of Memory in Medieval Culture*. Cambridge: Cambridge University Press, 1990.

Cassiodorus. *Explanation of the Psalms*. Trans. P. G. Walsh. 3 vols. Ancient Christian Writers. Vol. 51–53. New York: Paulist Press, 1990.

———. *Expositio Psalmorum*. Ed. M. Adriaen. 2 vols. Corpus Christianorum Series Latina. Vol. 97–98. Turnhout, Belgium: Brepols, 1958.

Charland, Th.-M. *Artes Praedicandi: contribution à l'histoire de la rhétorique au moyen âge*. Paris: J. Vrin, 1936.

Chaucer, Geoffrey. *Chaucer's Poetry*. 2nd ed. Ed. E. T. Donaldson. Glenview, Ill.: Scott, Foresman, 1958.

———. *Chaucer's Troylus and Cryseyde Compared with Boccaccio's Filostrato*. Ed. William Michael Rossetti. 1873; rpt. New York: Johnson Reprint Corporation, 1967.

———. *The Complete Works of Geoffrey Chaucer*. Ed. Walter W. Skeat. 7 vols. Oxford: Clarendon Press, 1894–97.

———. *The Riverside Chaucer*. 3rd ed. Ed. Larry D. Benson. Boston: Houghton Mifflin, 1987.

———. *Troilus and Criseyde*. Ed. Robert Kilburn Root. Princeton, N. J.: Princeton University Press, 1926.

———. *Troilus and Criseyde*. Ed. B. A. Windeatt. London: Longman, 1984.

———. *Troilus and Criseyde*. Ed. Stephen A. Barney. *The Riverside Chaucer*. 471–585.

———. *The Works of Geoffrey Chaucer*. 2nd ed. Ed. F. N. Robinson. Boston: Houghton Mifflin, 1957.

Chenu, M.-D. "Auctor, actor, autor." *Bulletin du Cange* 3 (1927) 81–86.

———. *Toward Understanding Saint Thomas*. Trans. A.-M. Landry and D. Hughes. Translation of *Introduction à l'étude de Saint Thomas d'Aquin*, 1950. Chicago: Henry Regnery, 1964.

Chevallier, Philippe, ed. *Dionysiaca*. 2 vols. Paris: Desclée de Brouwer, 1937 and 1950.

Chretien de Troyes. *Erec et Enide*. Ed. and trans. Carleton W. Carroll. Garland Library of Medieval Literature. New York: Garland, 1987.

[Cicero.] *Rhetorica ad Herennium*. Ed. and trans. Harry Caplan. Loeb Classical Library. Cambridge: Harvard University Press, 1954.

Clogan, Paul M. "Chaucer and the Medieval Statius." Ph.D. dissertation, University of Illinois, 1961.

———. "Chaucer and the *Thebaid* Scholia." *Studies in Philology* 61 (1964) 599–615.

———. "Chaucer's Use of the *Thebaid*." *English Miscellany* 18 (1967) 9–31.

Colby-Hall, Alice M. "Frustration and Fulfillment: The Double Ending of the *Bel Inconnu*." *Yale French Studies* 67 (1984) 120–34.

Coleman, Janet. *Medieval Readers and Writers, 1350–1400*. New York: Columbia University Press, 1981.

Conte, Gian Biagio. *The Rhetoric of Imitation: Genre and Poetic Memory in Virgil and Other Latin Poets*. Ithaca, N. Y.: Cornell University Press, 1986.

Contini, Gianfranco. "Esercizio d'interpretazione sopra un sonetto di Dante." *Varianti e altra linguistica; una raccolta di saggi (1938–1968)*. Turin: Giulio Einaudi, 1970. 161–68.

Courcelle, Pierre. *Les Confessions de Saint Augustin dans la tradition littéraire*. Paris: Études Augustiniennes, 1963.

Culler, Jonathan. *Structuralist Poetics: Structuralism, Linguistics, and the Study of Literature*. Ithaca, N. Y.: Cornell University Press, 1975.

Curtius, Ernst Robert. *European Literature and the Latin Middle Ages*. Trans. Willard R. Trask. Princeton, N. J.: Princeton University Press, 1953.

D'Andrea, Antonio. "La struttura della *Vita Nuova*: le divisioni delle rime." *Il nome della storia: Studi e ricerche di storia e letteratura*. Naples: Liguori, 1982. 25–58.

Dante Alighieri. *Il Convivio*. Ed. G. Busnelli and G. Vandelli. 2 vols. Florence: Felice Le Monnier, 1954.
———. *Il Convivio*. Ed. Maria Simonelli. Bologna: Riccardo Pàtron, 1966.
———. *Dante's Il Convivio (The Banquet)*. Trans. Richard H. Lansing. Garland Library of Medieval Literature. New York: Garland, 1990.
———. *Dante's Lyric Poetry*. Ed. and trans. K. Foster and P. Boyde. 2 vols. Oxford: Clarendon Press, 1967.
———. *Dante's Vita Nuova: A Translation and an Essay*. Trans. Mark Musa. Bloomington: Indiana University Press, 1973.
———. *De Vulgari Eloquentia*. Ed. Pier Vincenzo Mengaldo. *Opere minori*. Vol. 2. Milan: Riccardo Ricciardi, 1979. 1–237.
———. *La Divina Commedia*. Ed. Natalino Sapegno. Rev. ed. Florence: Nuova Italia, 1985.
———. *The Divine Comedy*. Ed. and trans. Charles S. Singleton. 3 vols. Princeton, N. J.: Princeton University Press, 1970–1975.
———. *Monarchia*. Ed. Bruno Nardi. *Opere minori*. Vol. 2. Milan: Riccardo Ricciardi, 1979. 239–503.
———. *On Eloquence in the Vernacular. Literary Criticism of Dante Alighieri*. Ed. and trans. Robert S. Haller. Lincoln: University of Nebraska Press, 1973. 3–60.
———. *Vita Nuova*. Ed. Michele Barbi. Florence: R. Bemporad e Figlio, 1932.
———. *Vita Nuova*. Ed. Domenico De Robertis. Milan: Riccardo Ricciardi, 1980.
Dasenbrock, Reed Way. *Imitating the Italians: Wyatt, Spenser, Synge, Pound, Joyce*. Baltimore: Johns Hopkins University Press, 1991.
Davenport, W. A. *Chaucer: Complaint and Narrative*. Cambridge: D. S. Brewer, 1988.
Day, Mabel, and Robert Steele, eds. *Mum and the Sothsegger*. Early English Text Society. London: Oxford University Press, 1936.
De Blasiis, G. "Immagini di uomini famosi in una sala di Castelnuovo attribuite a Giotto." *Napoli Nobilissima* 9 (1900) 65–67.
de Castris, Pierluigi Leone. *Arte di corte nella Napoli angioina*. Florence: Cantini, 1986.
de Ghellinck, Joseph. "'Pagina' et 'Sacra pagina': Histoire d'un mot et transformation de l'objet primitivement désigné." *Mélanges Auguste Pelzer*. Louvain: Bibliothèque de l'Université, 1947. 23–59.
De Hamel, C. F. R. *Glossed Books of the Bible and the Origins of the Paris Booktrade*. Woodbridge, Suffolk: D. S. Brewer, 1984.
de Lubac, Henri. *Exégèse médiévale: Les quatre sens de l'écriture*. 4 vols. Paris: Aubier, 1959–64.
de Man, Paul. *Allegories of Reading: Figural Language in Rousseau, Nietzsche, Rilke, and Proust*. New Haven, Conn.: Yale University Press, 1979.
de Nolhac, Pierre. *Pétrarque et l'humanisme*. Nouvelle édition. 2 vols. Paris: Honoré Champion, 1965.
De Robertis, Domenico. *Il libro della "Vita Nuova"*. 2nd ed. Florence: G. C. Sansoni, 1970.
Delany, Sheila. *Writing Woman*. New York: Schocken, 1983.
Deleuze, Gille, and Félix Guattari. *A Thousand Plateaus: Capitalism and Schizophrenia*. Trans. Brian Massumi. Minneapolis: University of Minnesota Press, 1987.

Demaray, John G. *Dante and the Book of the Cosmos*. Philadelphia: American Philosophical Society, 1987.

Derrida, Jacques. "The Law of Genre." Trans. Avital Ronell. *Critical Inquiry* 7 (1980) 55–81.

Diani, Dominique. "Pétrarque: *Canzoniere* 132." *Révue des études italiennes* n.s. 18 (1972) 111–67.

Dinshaw, Carolyn. *Chaucer's Sexual Poetics*. Madison: University of Wisconsin Press, 1989.

Dionisotti, C. "Appunti su antichi testi." *Italia medioevale e umanistica* 7 (1964) 77–131.

Dionysius, Pseudo-. *The Complete Works*. Trans. Colm Luibheid and Paul Rorem. New York: Paulist Press, 1987.

Donaldson, E. Talbot. "The Ending of *Troilus*." *Speaking of Chaucer*. New York: W. W. Norton, 1970. 84–101.

Dragonetti, Roger. *La technique poétique des trouvères dans la chanson courtoise: Contribution à l'étude de la rhétorique médiévale*. Bruges: De Tempel, 1960.

Dubois, Page. *History, Rhetorical Description and the Epic: From Homer to Spenser*. Cambridge: D. S. Brewer, 1982.

Durling, Robert M., and Ronald L. Martinez. *Time and the Crystal: Studies in Dante's Rime Petrose*. Berkeley: University of California Press, 1990.

Edwards, Robert R. *Ratio and Invention: A Study of Medieval Lyric and Narrative*. Nashville, Tenn.: Vanderbilt University Press, 1989.

Eneas, roman du XIIe siècle. Ed. J.-J. Salverda de Grave. 2 vols. Classiques Français du Moyen Âge. Paris: Édouard Champion, 1925–29.

Eneas, A Twelfth-Century French Romance. Trans. John A. Yunck. New York: Columbia University Press, 1974.

Fineman, Joel. *Shakespeare's Perjured Eye: The Invention of Poetic Subjectivity in the Sonnets*. Berkeley: University of California Press, 1986.

Fisher, John H. *John Gower: Moral Philosopher and Friend of Chaucer*. New York: New York University Press, 1964.

Fisher, Sheila, and Janet E. Halley, eds. *Seeking the Woman in Late Medieval and Renaissance Writings: Essays in Feminist Contextual Criticism*. Knoxville: University of Tennessee Press, 1989.

Fleming, John V. *Classical Imitation and Interpretation in Chaucer's Troilus*. Lincoln: University of Nebraska Press, 1990.

Fletcher, Angus. *Allegory: The Theory of a Symbolic Mode*. Ithaca, N. Y.: Cornell University Press, 1964.

Foucault, Michel. "What Is an Author?" *Language, Counter-Memory, Practice*. Ed. Donald F. Bouchard, trans. Donald F. Bouchard and Sherry Simon. Ithaca, N. Y.: Cornell University Press, 1977. 113–38

Fraenkel, Eduard. *Horace*. Oxford: Clarendon Press, 1957.

Franceschetti, Antonio. "Rassegna di studi sui cantari." *Lettere Italiane* 25 (1973) 556–74.

Freccero, John. "Medusa: The Letter and the Spirit." *Dante: The Poetics of Conversion*. Ed. Rachel Jacoff. Cambridge, Mass.: Harvard University Press, 1986. 119–35.

———. "The Fig Tree and the Laurel: Petrarch's Poetics." *Diacritics* 5 (1975) 34–40.

Fried, Debra. "Andromeda Unbound: Gender and Genre in Millay's Sonnets." *Twentieth Century Literature* 32 (1986) 1–22.

Gellrich, Jesse M. *The Idea of the Book in the Middle Ages: Language Theory, Mythology, and Fiction*. Ithaca, N.Y.: Cornell University Press, 1985.

Gilbert, Creighton. "Boccaccio Looking at Actual Frescoes." Gabriel P. Weisberg and Laurinda S. Dixon, eds. *The Documented Image: Visions in Art History*. Syracuse, N. Y.: Syracuse University Press, 1987. 225–41.

Gilby, Thomas. *Barbara Celarent: A Description of Scholastic Dialectic*. London: Longmans Green, 1949.

[*Glossa Ordinaria.*] *Biblia latina, cum glossa ordinaria Walafridi Strabonis aliorumque et interlineari Anselmi Laudunensis, et cum postillis ac moralitatibus Nicolai de Lyra et expositionibus Guillelmi Britonis in omnes prologos S. Hieronymi et additionibus Pauli Burgensis replicisque atthiae Doering*. Basel: Johann Froben and Johana Petri, 1498.

Gower, John. *The Complete Works of John Gower*. Ed. G. C. Macaulay. 4 vols. Oxford: Clarendon Press, 1899–1902.

———. *The Major Latin Works of John Gower*. Trans. Eric W. Stockton. Seattle: University of Washington Press, 1962.

The Greek Anthology. Ed. and trans. W. R. Paton. 5 vols. Loeb Classical Library. Cambridge, Mass.: Harvard University Press, 1915–18.

Green, William M. "Hugo of St. Victor: *De Tribus Maximis Circumstantiis Gestorum*." *Speculum* 18 (1943) 484–93.

Greene, Roland. *Post-Petrarchism: Origins and Innovations of the Western Lyric Sequence*. Princeton, N. J.: Princeton University Press, 1991.

Greene, Thomas M. *The Light in Troy: Imitation and Discovery in Renaissance Poetry*. New Haven, Conn.: Yale University Press, 1982.

Guillaume de Lorris and Jean de Meun. *Le Roman de la Rose*. Ed. Félix Lecoy. Classiques Français du Moyen Âge. 3 vols. Paris: Champion, 1973–75.

Guido delle Colonne. *Historia Destructionis Troiae*. Ed. Nathaniel Edward Griffin. Cambridge, Mass.: The Mediaeval Academy of America, 1936.

———. *Historia Destructionis Troiae*. Trans. Mary Elizabeth Meek. Bloomington: Indiana University Press, 1974.

Guillory, John. *Poetic Authority: Spenser, Milton, and Literary History*. New York: Columbia University Press, 1983.

Gybbon-Monypenny, G. B. "Guillaume de Machaut's Erotic 'Autobiography': Precedents for the Form of the *Voir-Dit*." W. Rothwell et al., eds. *Studies in Medieval Literature and Languages in Memory of Frederick Whitehead*. Manchester: Manchester University Press, 1973. 133–52.

Hahner, Ursula. *Cassiodors Psalmenkommentar: Sprachliche Untersuchungen*. Münchener Beiträge zur Mediävistik und Renaissance-Forschung, 13. Munich: Arbeo-Gesellschaft, 1973.

Hamburger, Käte. *The Logic of Literature*. 2nd ed. Trans. Marilynn J. Rose. Bloomington: Indiana University Press, 1973.

Hanning, Robert W. *The Individual in the Twelfth-Century Romance*. New Haven, Conn.: Yale University Press, 1977.

Harrison, Robert Pogue. *The Body of Beatrice*. Baltimore: Johns Hopkins University Press, 1988.

Havely, N. R. *Chaucer's Boccaccio: Sources of Troilus and of the Knight's and Franklin's Tales*. Cambridge: D. S. Brewer, 1980.

Hoffman, Richard L. "The Influence of the Classics on Chaucer." Beryl Rowland, ed. *Companion to Chaucer Studies*. Revised Edition. New York: Oxford University Press, 1979. 185–201.

Hollander, Robert. *Boccaccio's Two Venuses*. New York: Columbia University Press, 1977.

———. "Dante's Use of the Fiftieth Psalm (A Note on *Purg*. XXX, 84)." *Studies in Dante*. Ravenna: Longo Editore, 1980. 107–113. Reprinted from *Dante Studies* 91 (1973) 145–50.

———. "The Validity of Boccaccio's Self-Exegesis in His *Teseida*." *Medievalia et Humanistica*, n.s. 8 (1977) 163–83.

Holley, Linda Tarte. *Chaucer's Measuring Eye*. Houston: Rice University Press, 1990.

Honorius of Autun. *Selectorum Psalmorum Expositio*. *PL* 172.269–312.

Horace. *The Odes and Epodes*. Ed. and trans. C. E. Bennett. Loeb Classical Library. Cambridge, Mass.: Harvard University Press, 1914.

Howard, Donald R. *Chaucer: His Life, His Works, His World*. New York: Fawcett Columbine, 1987.

Hugh of St. Cher. *Biblia latina cum postillis Hugonis de s. Charo*. Basel: Johann Amerbach for Anton Koberger, 1498–1504.

Hugh of St. Victor. *De Sacramentis Christianae Fidei*. *PL* 176.173–618.

———. *Didascalicon*. Ed. C. H. Buttimer. Washington, D.C.: Catholic University Press, 1939.

———. *The Didascalicon of Hugh of St. Victor*. Trans. Jerome Taylor. New York: Columbia University Press, 1961.

Hult, David F. *Self-Fulfilling Prophecies: Readership and Authority in the First Roman de la Rose*. Cambridge: Cambridge University Press, 1986.

Huot, Sylvia. *From Song to Book: The Poetics of Writing in Old French Lyric and Lyrical Narrative Poetry*. Ithaca, N. Y.: Cornell University Press, 1987.

Hutton, James. *The Greek Anthology in Italy to the Year 1800*. Cornell Studies in English, 23. Ithaca, N. Y.: Cornell University Press, 1935.

Isidore of Seville. *Etymologiarum sive originum libri XX*. Ed. W. M. Lindsay. 2 vols. Oxford: Clarendon Press, 1911.

Jacobus, Mary. "The Law of/and Gender: Genre Theory and *The Prelude*." *Diacritics* 14.4 (Winter 1984) 47–57.

Jaffa, Harry V. *Thomism and Aristotelianism: A Study of the Commentary by Thomas Aquinas on the Nicomachean Ethics*. Chicago: University of Chicago Press, 1952.

Jakobson, Roman. "Two Aspects of Language and Two Types of Aphasic Disturbances." *Selected Writings*, vol. 2. The Hague: Mouton, 1971. 239–59.

Jeanroy, Alfred. *La Poésie lyrique des troubadours*. 2 vols. Toulouse: Édouard Privat, 1934.

Joseph of Exeter. *The Iliad of Dares Phrygius*. Trans. Gildas Roberts. Capetown: Balkema, 1970.

[Joseph of Exeter.] Joseph Iscanus. *Werke und Briefe*. Ed. Ludwig Gompf. Leiden: E. J. Brill, 1970.

Kahlmayer, J. *Seesturm und Schiffsbruch als Bild*. Hildesheim, Germany: Gebr. Fikuart, 1934.

Kamuf, Peggy. *Signature Pieces: On the Institution of Authorship*. Ithaca, N. Y.: Cornell University Press, 1988.

Keller, Otto. *Pseudacronis Scholia in Horatium Vetustiora*. 2 vols. Leipzig: B. G. Teubner, 1902–4.

Kenny, Anthony, and Jan Pinborg. "Medieval Philosophical Literature." Norman Kretzmann, Anthony Kenny, and Jan Pinborg, eds. *The Cambridge History of Later Medieval Philosophy: From the Rediscovery of Aristotle to the Disintegration of Scholasticism, 1100–1600*. Cambridge: Cambridge University Press, 1982. 11–42.

Kirkham, Victoria. "'Chiuso parlare' in Boccaccio's *Teseida*." Aldo S. Bernardo and Anthony L. Pellegrini, eds. *Dante, Petrarch, Boccaccio: Studies in the Italian Trecento in Honor of Charles S. Singleton*. Binghamton, N. Y.: Medieval and Renaissance Texts and Studies, 1983. 305–51.

Knapp, Peggy. *Chaucer and the Social Contest*. New York: Routledge, 1990.

Knight, Stephen. *Geoffrey Chaucer*. Oxford: Blackwell, 1986.

König, Bernhard. *Die Begegnung im Tempel: Abwandlungen eines literarischen Motivs in den Werken Boccaccios*. Hamburg: De Gruyter, 1960.

Laplanche, J., and J.-B. Pontalis. *The Language of Psycho-Analysis*. Trans. Donald Nicholson-Smith. New York: Norton, 1973.

Legras, Léon. *Étude sur la Thébaide de Stace*. Paris: Société Nouvelle de Librairie et d'Édition, 1905.

Leicester, H. Marshall, Jr. "Oure Tonges *Différance*: Textuality and Deconstruction in Chaucer." Laurie A. Finke and Martin B. Shichtman, eds. *Medieval Texts and Contemporary Readers*. Ithaca, N. Y.: Cornell University Press, 1987. 15–26.

Lessing, Gotthold Ephraim. *Laocoön: An Essay on the Limits of Painting and Poetry*. Trans. Edward Allen McCormick. Library of Liberal Arts. Indianapolis: Bobbs-Merrill, 1962.

Lewis, C. S. *The Allegory of Love: A Study in Medieval Tradition*. 1936; rpt. New York: Oxford University Press, 1958.

———. "What Chaucer Really Did to *Il Filostrato*." Richard J. Schoeck and Jerome Taylor, eds. *Chaucer Criticism, Volume II: Troilus and Criseyde and the Minor Poems*. Notre Dame, Ind.: University of Notre Dame Press, 1961. 16–33. Reprinted from *Essays and Studies* 17 (1932) 56–75.

Lobrichon, Guy. "Une nouveauté: les gloses de la Bible." Pierre Riché and Guy Lobrichon, eds. *Le Moyen Âge et la Bible*. Paris: Beauchesne, 1984. 95–114.

MacLennan, L. Jenaro. "Autocomentario en Dante y comentarismo latino." *Vox Romanica* 19 (1960) 82–123.

Macrobius. *I Saturnali*. Ed. and trans. Nino Marinone. Turin: Unione Tipografico Editrice Torinese, 1967.

Mann, Nicholas. "La prima fortuna del Petrarca in Inghilterra." Giuseppe Billanovich and Giuseppe Frasso, eds. *Il Petrarca ad Arquà: Atti del Convegno di Studi nel VI Centenario (1370–1374)*. *Studi sul Petrarca* 2. Padua: Antenore, 1975. 271–89.

Mazzaro, Jerome. *The Figure of Dante: An Essay on the Vita Nuova*. Princeton, N. J.: Princeton University Press, 1981.

Mazzeo, Joseph Anthony. *Medieval Cultural Tradition in Dante's Comedy*. Ithaca, N. Y.: Cornell University Press, 1960.

Mazzotta, Giuseppe. "The *Canzoniere* and the Language of the Self." *Studies in Philology* 75 (1978) 271–96.

———. "The Language of Poetry in the *Vita Nuova*." *Rivista di studi italiani* 1 (1983) 3–14.

———. "The Light of Venus and the Poetry of Dante." Arthur Groos, ed. *Magister Regis: Studies in Honor of Robert Earl Kaske*. New York: Fordham University Press, 1986. 147–69.

McCall, John P. "The Trojan Scene in Chaucer's *Troilus*." *ELH* 29 (1962) 263–75.

McCall, John P., and George Rudisill, Jr. "The Parliament of 1386 and Chaucer's Trojan Parliament." *Journal of English and Germanic Philology* 58 (1959) 276–88.

McGregor, James H. *The Image of Antiquity in Boccaccio's Filocolo, Filostrato and Teseida*. New York: Peter Lang, 1991.

———. *The Shades of Aeneas: The Imitation of Vergil and the History of Paganism in Boccaccio's Filostrato, Filocolo, and Teseida*. Athens: University of Georgia Press, 1991.

Meltzer, Françoise. *Salome and the Dance of Writing: Portraits of Mimesis in Literature*. Chicago: University of Chicago Press, 1987.

Menocal, María Rosa. *Writing in Dante's Cult of Truth: From Borges to Boccaccio*. Durham, N. C.: Duke University Press, 1991.

Miller, Jacqueline T. *Poetic License: Authority and Authorship in Medieval and Renaissance Contexts*. New York: Oxford University Press, 1986.

Minnis, A. J. *Medieval Theory of Authorship: Scholastic Literary Attitudes in the Later Middle Ages*. 2nd ed. Philadelphia: University of Pennsylvania Press, 1988.

Minnis, A. J., and A. B. Scott, eds. *Medieval Literary Theory and Criticism, c. 1100–c. 1375: The Commentary-Tradition*. Oxford: Clarendon Press, 1988.

Mitchell, W. J. T. *Iconology: Image, Text, Ideology*. Chicago: University of Chicago Press, 1986.

———. "On Poems On Pictures: Ekphrasis and the Other." Forthcoming.

———, ed. *The Language of Images*. Chicago: University of Chicago Press, 1980.

Moleta, Vincent. "The *Vita Nuova* as a Lyric Narrative," *Forum Italicum* 12 (1978) 369–90.

Momigliano, Attilio. "L'elegia politica del Petrarca." *Introduzione ai poeti*. Rome: Tumminelli, 1946. 7–19.

Moore, Marianne. *The Complete Poems of Marianne Moore*. New York: Macmillan, 1967.

Morris, Colin. *The Discovery of the Individual 1050–1200*. New York: Harper and Row, 1973.

Murphy, James J., ed. *Three Medieval Rhetorical Arts*. Berkeley: University of California Press, 1971.

Muscatine, Charles. *Poetry and Crisis in the Age of Chaucer*. Notre Dame, Ind.: University of Notre Dame Press, 1972.

Muscetta, Carlo. *Giovanni Boccaccio*. Bari: Laterza, 1972.

Natali, Giulia. "A Lyrical Version: Boccaccio's *Filostrato*." Boitani, *The European Tragedy of Troilus*. 49–73.

———. "Progetti narrativi e tradizione lirica in Boccaccio." *Rassegna della letteratura italiana* 90 (1986) 382–96.

Nichols, Stephen G., Jr. "A Poetics of Historicism? Recent Trends in Medieval Literary Study." *Medievalia et Humanistica*, n.s. 8 (1977) 77–101.

Noakes, Susan. *Timely Reading: Between Exegesis and Interpretation*. Ithaca, N. Y.: Cornell University Press, 1988.

Nolan, Barbara. "The *Vita Nuova*: Dante's Book of Revelation." *Dante Studies* 88 (1970) 51–77.

Norton-Smith, John. *Geoffrey Chaucer*. London: Routledge and Kegan Paul, 1974.

O'Donnell, James J. *Cassiodorus*. Berkeley: University of California Press, 1979.

Oppenheimer, Paul. *The Birth of the Modern Mind: Self, Consciousness, and the Invention of the Sonnet*. New York: Oxford University Press, 1989.

Owst, G. R. *Literature and Pulpit in Medieval England*. 2nd ed. Oxford: Basil Blackwell, 1961.

Padoan, Giorgio. "Mondo aristocratico e mondo comunale nell'ideologia e nell'arte di Giovanni Boccaccio." *Il Boccaccio, le Muse, il Parnaso, e l'Arno*. Florence: Leo S. Olschki, 1978. 1–91.

Panofsky, Erwin. *Gothic Architecture and Scholasticism*. New York: New American Library, 1951.

———. *Tomb Sculpture*. Ed. H. W. Janson. New York: Harry N. Abrams, 1964.

Paré, G., A. Brunet, and P. Tremblay, *La renaissance du XIIe siècle: les écoles et l'enseignement*. Paris: J. Vrin, 1933.

Parkes, M. B. "The Influence of the Concepts of *Ordinatio* and *Compilatio* on the Development of the Book." J. J. G. Alexander and M. T. Gibson, eds. *Medieval Learning and Literature: Essays Presented to Richard William Hunt*. Oxford: Clarendon Press, 1976. 115–41.

Patch, Howard R. "Two Notes on Chaucer's *Troilus*." *Modern Language Notes* 70 (1955) 8–12.

Patterson, Lee. *Chaucer and the Subject of History*. Madison: University of Wisconsin Press, 1991.

———. *Negotiating the Past: The Historical Understanding of Medieval Literature*. Madison: University of Wisconsin Press, 1987.

———. "On the Margin: Postmodernism, Ironic History, and Medieval Studies." *Speculum* 65 (1990) 87–108.

———. "'Rapt With Pleasaunce': Vision and Narration in the Epic." *ELH* 48 (1981) 455–75.

———, ed. *Literary Practice and Social Change in Britain, 1380–1530*. Berkeley: University of California Press, 1990.

Payne, Robert O. *The Key of Remembrance: A Study of Chaucer's Poetics*. New Haven, Conn.: Yale University Press, 1963.

Peter Lombard. *In Psalmos Davidicos Commentarii*. *PL* 191.9–1302.

Petrarca, Francesco. *Petrarch's Letters to Classical Authors*. Trans. Mario Emilio Cosenza. Chicago: University of Chicago Press, 1910.

———. *Petrarch's Lyric Poems: The Rime Sparse and Other Lyrics*. Ed. and trans. Robert M. Durling. Cambridge, Mass.: Harvard University Press, 1976.

Petronio, Giuseppe, ed. *Poemetti del duecento*. Turin: Unione Tipografico, 1951.

Philostratus. *Die Bilder*. Ed. and trans. Ernst Kalinka and Otto Schönberger. Munich: Ernst Heimeran, 1968.

———. *Imagines*. Ed. and trans. Arthur Fairbanks. Loeb Classical Library. Cambridge, Mass.: Harvard University Press, 1931.

Picone, Michelangelo. "Boccaccio e la codificazione dell'ottava." Marga Cottino-Jones and Edward F. Tuttle, eds. *Boccaccio: Secoli di vita*. Ravenna: Longo Editore, 1977. 53–65.

———. "Modelli e struttura nella *Vita nuova*." *Studi e problemi di critica testuale* 15 (1977) 50–61.

———. "Rito e *narratio* nella *Vita Nuova*." *Dal Medioevo al Petrarca: Miscellanea di studi in onore di Vittore Branca*. Florence: L. S. Olschki, 1983. 141–57.

———. "Strutture poetiche e strutture prosastiche nella *Vita Nuova*." *Modern Language Notes* 92 (1977) 117–29.

Piltz, Anders. *The World of Medieval Learning*. Trans. David Jones. Translation of *Medeltidens lärda värld*, 1978. Totowa, N. J.: Barnes and Noble, 1981.

Poe, Elizabeth Wilson. *From Poetry to Prose in Old Provençal: The Emergence of the Vidas, the Razos, and the Razos de Trobar*. Birmingham, Ala.: Summa Publications, 1984.

Psaki, Francies Regina. "The Medieval Lyric-Narrative Hybrid: Formal Play and Narratorial Subjectivity." Ph.D. dissertation, Cornell University, 1989.

Quint, David. *Origin and Originality in Renaissance Literature: Versions of the Source*. New Haven, Conn.: Yale University Press, 1983.

Rahner, Hugo. *Greek Myths and Christian Mystery*. Trans. Brian Battershaw. New York: Biblo and Tannen, 1963.

Rajna, Pio. "Per le 'divisioni' della *Vita Nuova*." *Strenna dantesca* 1 (1902) 111–14.

———. "Lo schema della *Vita Nuova*." *Biblioteca delle scuole italiane* 2 (1890) 161–64.

Régis, Louis-M. "Analyse et synthèse dans l'oeuvre de saint Thomas." *Studia Mediaevalia in Honorem Admodum Reverendi Patris Raymundi Josephi Martin*. Bruges: De Tempel, 1948. 303–30.

Rivers, Elias L. "Dante at Dividing Sonnets." *Symposium* 11 (1957) 290–95.

Robertson, D. W. *A Preface to Chaucer: Studies in Medieval Perspectives*. Princeton, N. J.: Princeton University Press, 1962.

Robbins, Rossell Hope, ed. *Historical Poems of the XIVth and XVth Centuries*. New York: Columbia University Press, 1959.

Le Roman du Castelain de Couci et de la Dame de Fayel. Ed. Maurice Delbouille. Paris: Société des Anciens Textes Français, 1936.

Roncaglia, Aurelio. "Per la storia dell'ottava rima." *Cultura neolatina* 25 (1965) 5–14.

Roques, René. *L'univers dionysien: Structure hiérarchique du monde selon le Pseudo-Denys*. 1954; rpt. Paris: Éditions du Cerf, 1983.

Rouse, Richard H., and Mary A. Rouse. "*Statim invenire*: Schools, Preachers, and New Attitudes to the Page." Robert L. Benson and Giles Constable, eds. *Renaissance and Renewal in the Twelfth Century*. Cambridge, Mass.: Harvard University Press, 1982. 201–25.

Salutati, Coluccio. *Epistolario*. Ed. Francesco Novati. 4 vols. Rome: Forzani, 1891–1905.

Schäfer, Eckart. "Das Staatsschiff. Zur Präzision eines Topos." Peter Jehn, ed. *Toposforschung: Eine Dokumentation*. Frankfurt am Main: Athenäum, 1972. 259–92.

Schapiro, Meyer. *Words and Pictures: On the Literal and the Symbolic in the Illustration of a Text*. The Hague: Mouton, 1973.

Scott, J. A. "Dante's 'Sweet New Style' and the *Vita Nuova*." *Italica* 42 (1965) 98–107.

Sedgwick, Eve Kosofsky. "A Poem Is Being Written." *Representations* 17 (Winter 1987) 110–43.

Serafini-Sauli, Judith Powers. *Giovanni Boccaccio*. Boston: Twayne, 1982.

Setton, Kenneth M. "The Byzantine Background to the Italian Renaissance." *Proceedings of the American Philosophical Society* 100 (1956) 1–76.

Shakespeare, William. *The Complete Works*. Ed. Stanley Wells and Gary Taylor. Oxford: Clarendon Press, 1986.

Shapiro, Marianne. "On the Role of Rhetoric in the *Convivio*." *Romance Philology* 40 (1986) 38–64.

Shaw, James Eustace. *Essays on the Vita Nuova*. Princeton, N. J.: Princeton University Press, 1929.

———. *Guido Cavalcanti's Theory of Love: The Canzone d'amore, and other related problems*. Toronto: University of Toronto Press, 1949.

Sheldon, E. S. *Concordanza delle opere italiane in prosa e del Canzoniere di Dante Alighieri*. Oxford: Oxford University Press, 1905.

Shoaf, R. A. *Dante, Chaucer, and the Currency of the Word: Money, Images, and Reference in Late Medieval Poetry*. Norman, Okla.: Pilgrim Books, 1983.

Singleton, Charles S. *An Essay on the Vita Nuova*. Cambridge, Mass.: Harvard University Press, 1949.

Smalley, Beryl. *The Study of the Bible in the Middle Ages*. Notre Dame, Ind.: University of Notre Dame Press, 1964.

Smarr, Janet Levarie. *Boccaccio and Fiammetta: The Narrator as Lover*. Urbana: University of Illinois Press, 1986.

Snijder, H. *Thebaid: A Commentary on Book III*. Amsterdam: M. Hakkert, 1968.

Solterer, Helen. "Letter writing and picture reading: medieval textuality and the *Bestiaire d'Amour*." *Word and Image* 5 (1989) 131–47.

Spitzer, Leo. "Note on the Poetic and the Empirical 'I' in Medieval Authors." *Traditio* 4 (1946) 414–22.

Spurgeon, Caroline F. E. *Five Hundred Years of Chaucer Criticism and Allusion (1357–1900)*. 3 vols. Cambridge: Cambridge University Press, 1925.

Statius. [*Works.*] Ed. and trans. J. H. Mozley. 2 vols. Loeb Classical Library. Cambridge, Mass.: Harvard University Press, 1928.

Stillinger, Jack. *Multiple Authorship and the Myth of Solitary Genius*. New York: Oxford University Press, 1991.

Stillinger, Thomas C. "The Language of Gardens: Boccaccio's *Valle delle Donne*." *Traditio* 39 (1983) 301–21.

Strohm, Paul. *Social Chaucer*. Cambridge, Mass.: Harvard University Press, 1989.

Taylor, Karla. *Chaucer Reads "The Divine Comedy."* Stanford, Calif.: Stanford University Press, 1989.

(Pseudo-)Thomas Aquinas. *Commentum super Librum Boetii de Consolatu Philosophico*. Thomas Aquinas. *Opera Omnia*. Vol. 24. 1869; rpt. New York: Musurgia, 1950. 1–147.
Thomas Aquinas. *In Decem Libros Ethicorum Aristotelis ad Nicomachum Expositio*. Ed. A. M. Pirotta. Turin: Marietti, 1934.
———. *In Psalmos Davidis Expositio*. *Opera Omnia*. Vol. 14. 1863; rpt. New York: Musurgia, 1949. 148–253.
———. *Summa Theologiae*. Ed. P. Caramello. Rome: Marietti, 1950.
Thomson, Patricia. "The 'Canticus Troili': Chaucer and Petrarch." *Comparative Literature* 11 (1959) 313–28.
Turner, Victor. *The Forest of Symbols: Aspects of Ndembu Ritual*. Ithaca, N. Y.: Cornell University Press, 1967.
Vallone, Aldo. "Apparizione e disdegno di Beatrice (*Vita Nuova*, I–X)." *Nuove letture dantesche* 8 (1976) 35–51.
———. *La prosa della "Vita Nuova."* Florence: Felice le Monnier, 1963.
Vance, Eugene. "Chaucer, Spenser, and the Ideology of Translation." *Canadian Review of Comparative Literature* 8 (1981) 217–38.
———. "Love's Concordance: The Poetics of Desire and the Joy of the Text." *Diacritics* 5 (1975) 40–52.
———. *Mervelous Signals: Poetics and Sign Theory in the Middle Ages*. Lincoln: University of Nebraska Press, 1986.
———. "Mervelous Signals: Poetics, Sign Theory, and Politics in Chaucer's *Troilus*." *New Literary History* 10 (1979) 293–337.
Vandelli, Giuseppe. "Un autografo della *Teseide*." *Studi di filologia italiana* 2 (1929) 5–76.
Vessey, David. *Statius and the Thebaid*. Cambridge: Cambridge University Press, 1973.
Vickers, Nancy. "'The Blazon of Sweet Beauty's Best': Shakespeare's *Lucrece*." Patricia Parker and Geoffrey Hartman, eds. *Shakespeare and the Question of Theory*. New York: Methuen, 1985. 95–115.
Virgil. [*Works*.] Ed. and trans. H. Rushton Fairclough. Revised ed. 2 vols. Loeb Classical Library. Cambridge, Mass.: Harvard University Press, 1934.
Wallace, David. *Chaucer and the Early Writings of Boccaccio*. Woodbridge, Suffolk: D. S. Brewer, 1985.
———. "'Whan She Translated Was': A Chaucerian Critique of the Petrarchan Academy." Patterson, *Literary Practice and Social Change*. 156–215.
Waller, Marguerite. *Petrarch's Poetics and Literary History*. Amherst: University of Massachusetts Press, 1980.
Warkentin, Germaine. "The Form of Dante's 'Libello' and its Challenge to Petrarch." *Quaderni d'italianistica* 2 (1981) 160–70.
Weiss, Roberto. "The Greek Culture of South Italy in the Later Middle Ages." *Medieval and Humanist Greek*. 13–43.
———. "Iacopo Angeli da Scarperia (c. 1360–1410–11)." *Medieval and Humanist Greek*. 255–77.
———. *Medieval and Humanist Greek*. Padua: Antenore, 1977.
———. "The Translators from the Greek of the Angevin Court of Naples." *Medieval and Humanist Greek*. 108–33.

Wetherbee, Winthrop. *Chaucer and the Poets: An Essay on Troilus and Criseyde*. Ithaca, N. Y.: Cornell University Press, 1984.

———. "Epic and Romance in the *Teseida*." Forthcoming.

Whitman, Frank H. "*Troilus and Criseyde* and Chaucer's Dedication to Gower." *Tennessee Studies in Literature* 18 (1973) 1–11.

Wilkins, Ernest Hatch. *The Making of the "Canzoniere" and Other Petrarchan Studies*. Rome: Edizioni di Storia e Letteratura, 1951.

Williams, R. D. "The Pictures in Dido's Temple (*Aeneid* I.450–93)." *Classical Quarterly* n.s. 10 (1960) 145–51.

Williams, William Carlos. "Marianne Moore." *Imaginations*. Ed. Webster Schott. New York: New Directions, 1970. 308–18.

Wimsatt, James I. "The French Lyric Element in *Troilus and Criseyde*." *Yearbook of English Studies* 15 (1985) 18–32.

Windeatt, Barry. "Classical and Medieval Elements in Chaucer's *Troilus*." Boitani, *The European Tragedy of Troilus*. 111–31.

———. "The Text of the *Troilus*." Mary Salu, ed. *Essays on Troilus and Criseyde*. Cambridge: D. S. Brewer, 1979. 1–22.

Wise, Boyd Ashby. *The Influence of Statius upon Chaucer*. 1911; rpt. New York: Phaeton Press, 1967.

Wood, Chauncey. *The Elements of Chaucer's Troilus*. Durham, N. C.: Duke University Press, 1984.

Wright, Thomas, ed. *Political Poems and Songs Relating to English History*. 2 vols. London: Longman, Green, Longman, and Roberts, 1859–61.

Wyatt, Thomas. *Collected Poems of Sir Thomas Wyatt*. Ed. Kenneth Muir. London: Routledge and Kegan Paul, 1949.

Zumthor, Paul. *Essai de poétique médiévale*. Paris: Éditions du Seuil, 1972.

———. *Langue, texte, énigme*. Paris: Éditions du Seuil, 1975.

Index

University of Pennsylvania Press
MIDDLE AGES SERIES
Edward Peters, General Editor

F. R. P. Akehurst, trans. *The* Coutumes de Beauvaisis *of Philippe de Beaumanoir.* 1992
Peter Allen. *The Art of Love: Amatory Fiction from Ovid to the* Romance of the Rose. 1992
David Anderson. *Before the Knight's Tale: Imitation of Classical Epic in Boccaccio's* Teseida. 1988
Benjamin Arnold. *Count and Bishop in Medieval Germany: A Study of Regional Power, 1100–1350.* 1991
Mark C. Bartusis. *The Late Byzantine Army: Arms and Society, 1204–1453.* 1992
J. M. W. Bean. *From Lord to Patron: Lordship in Late Medieval England.* 1990
Uta-Renate Blumenthal. *The Investiture Controversy: Church and Monarchy from the Ninth to the Twelfth Century.* 1988
Daniel Bornstein, trans. *Dino Compagni's* Chronicle *of Florence.* 1986
Betsy Bowden. *Chaucer Aloud: The Varieties of Textual Interpretation.* 1987
James William Brodman. *Ransoming Captives in Crusader Spain: The Order of Merced on the Christian-Islamic Frontier.* 1986
Kevin Brownlee and Sylvia Huot, eds. *Rethinking the* Romance of the Rose*: Text, Image, Reception.* 1992
Otto Brunner (Howard Kaminsky and James Van Horn Melton, eds. and trans.). Land *and Lordship: Structures of Governance in Medieval Austria.* 1992
Robert I. Burns, S.J., ed. *Emperor of Culture: Alfonso X the Learned of Castile and His Thirteenth-Century Renaissance.* 1990
David Burr. *Olivi and Franciscan Poverty: The Origins of the* Usus Pauper *Controversy.* 1989
Thomas Cable. *The English Alliterative Tradition.* 1991
Anthony K. Cassell and Victoria Kirkham, eds. and trans. *Diana's Hunt/Caccia di Diana: Boccaccio's First Fiction.* 1991
Brigitte Cazelles. *The Lady as Saint: A Collection of French Hagiographic Romances of the Thirteenth Century.* 1991
Anne L. Clark. *Elisabeth of Schönau: A Twelfth-Century Visionary.* 1992
Willene B. Clark and Meradith T. McMunn, eds. *Beasts and Birds of the Middle Ages: The Bestiary and Its Legacy.* 1989
Richard C. Dales. *The Scientific Achievement of the Middle Ages.* 1973
Charles T. Davis. *Dante's Italy and Other Essays.* 1984
Katherine Fischer Drew, trans. *The Burgundian Code.* 1972
Katherine Fischer Drew, trans. *The Laws of the Salian Franks.* 1991
Katherine Fischer Drew, trans. *The Lombard Laws.* 1973

Nancy Edwards. *The Archaeology of Early Medieval Ireland.* 1990

Margaret J. Ehrhart. *The Judgment of the Trojan Prince Paris in Medieval Literature.* 1987

Richard K. Emmerson and Ronald B. Herzman. *The Apocalyptic Imagination in Medieval Literature.* 1992

Felipe Fernández-Armesto. *Before Columbus: Exploration and Colonization from the Mediterranean to the Atlantic, 1229–1492.* 1987

Robert D. Fulk. *A History of Old English Meter.* 1992

Patrick J. Geary. *Aristocracy in Provence: The Rhône Basin at the Dawn of the Carolingian Age.* 1985

Peter Heath. *Allegory and Philosophy in Avicenna (Ibn Sînâ), with a Translation of the Book of the Prophet Muḥammad's Ascent to Heaven.* 1992

J. N. Hillgarth, ed. *Christianity and Paganism, 350–750: The Conversion of Western Europe.* 1986

Richard C. Hoffmann. *Land, Liberties, and Lordship in a Late Medieval Countryside: Agrarian Structures and Change in the Duchy of Wroclaw.* 1990

Robert Hollander. *Boccaccio's Last Fiction: Il Corbaccio.* 1988

Edward B. Irving, Jr. *Rereading* Beowulf. 1989

C. Stephen Jaeger. *The Origins of Courtliness: Civilizing Trends and the Formation of Courtly Ideals, 939–1210.* 1985

William Chester Jordan. *The French Monarchy and the Jews: From Philip Augustus to the Last Capetians.* 1989

William Chester Jordan. *From Servitude to Freedom: Manumission in the Sénonais in the Thirteenth Century.* 1986

Ellen E. Kittell. *From* Ad Hoc *to Routine: A Case Study in Medieval Bureaucracy.* 1991

Alan C. Kors and Edward Peters, eds. *Witchcraft in Europe, 1100–1700: A Documentary History.* 1972

Barbara M. Kreutz. *Before the Normans: Southern Italy in the Ninth and Tenth Centuries.* 1992

E. Ann Matter. *The Voice of My Beloved: The Song of Songs in Western Medieval Christianity.* 1990

María Rosa Menocal. *The Arabic Role in Medieval Literary History.* 1987

A. J. Minnis. *Medieval Theory of Authorship.* 1988

Lawrence Nees. *A Tainted Mantle: Hercules and the Classical Tradition at the Carolingian Court.* 1991

Lynn H. Nelson, trans. *The Chronicle of San Juan de la Peña: A Fourteenth-Century Official History of the Crown of Aragon.* 1991

Charlotte A. Newman. *The Anglo-Norman Nobility in the Reign of Henry I: The Second Generation.* 1988

Joseph F. O'Callaghan. *The Cortes of Castile-León, 1188–1350.* 1989

William D. Paden, ed. *The Voice of the Trobairitz: Perspectives on the Women Troubadours.* 1989

Edward Peters. *The Magician, the Witch, and the Law.* 1982

Edward Peters, ed. *Christian Society and the Crusades, 1198–1229: Sources in Translation, including* The Capture of Damietta *by Oliver of Paderborn.* 1971

Edward Peters, ed. *The First Crusade:* The Chronicle of Fulcher of Chartres *and Other Source Materials*. 1971

Edward Peters, ed. *Heresy and Authority in Medieval Europe*. 1980

James M. Powell. *Albertanus of Brescia: The Pursuit of Happiness in the Early Thirteenth Century*. 1992

James M. Powell. *Anatomy of a Crusade, 1213–1221*. 1986

Michael Resler, trans. Erec *by Hartmann von Aue*. 1987

Pierre Riché (Michael Idomir Allen, trans.). *The Carolingians: A Family Who Forged Europe*. 1993

Pierre Riché (Jo Ann McNamara, trans.). *Daily Life in the World of Charlemagne*. 1978

Jonathan Riley-Smith. *The First Crusade and the Idea of Crusading*. 1986

Joel T. Rosenthal. *Patriarchy and Families of Privilege in Fifteenth-Century England*. 1991

Steven D. Sargent, ed. and trans. *On the Threshold of Exact Science: Selected Writings of Anneliese Maier on Late Medieval Natural Philosophy*. 1982

Sarah Stanbury. *Seeing the* Gawain-*Poet: Description and the Act of Perception*. 1992

Thomas C. Stillinger. *The Song of Troilus: Lyric Authority in the Medieval Book*. 1992

Susan Mosher Stuard. *A State of Deference: Ragusa/Dubrovnik in the Medieval Centuries*. 1992

Susan Mosher Stuard, ed. *Women in Medieval History and Historiography*. 1987

Susan Mosher Stuard, ed. *Women in Medieval Society*. 1976

Jonathan Sumption. *The Hundred Years War: Trial by Battle*. 1992

Ronald E. Surtz. *The Guitar of God: Gender, Power, and Authority in the Visionary World of Mother Juana de la Cruz (1481–1534)*. 1990

Patricia Terry, trans. *Poems of the Elder Edda*. 1990

Frank Tobin. *Meister Eckhart: Thought and Language*. 1986

Ralph V. Turner. *Men Raised from the Dust: Administrative Service and Upward Mobility in Angevin England*. 1988

Harry Turtledove, trans. *The* Chronicle *of Theophanes: An English Translation of* Anni Mundi *6095–6305 (A.D. 602–813)*. 1982

Mary F. Wack. *Lovesickness in the Middle Ages: The* Viaticum *and Its Commentaries*. 1990

Benedicta Ward. *Miracles and the Medieval Mind: Theory, Record, and Event, 1000–1215*. 1982

Suzanne Fonay Wemple. *Women in Frankish Society: Marriage and the Cloister, 500–900*. 1981

This book has been set in Linotron Galliard. Galliard was designed for Mergenthaler in 1978 by Matthew Carter. Galliard retains many of the features of a sixteenth-century typeface cut by Robert Granjon but has some modifications that give it a more contemporary look.

Printed on acid-free paper.